The book compares and contrasts the African American and Oromo movements in the global context. It shows how life chances changed for the two peoples as the modern world system developed and became more complex. This global system racialized exploitative structures in African American and Oromo societies and facilitated the national struggles of these two peoples. This work demonstrates the dynamic interplay between social structures and human agencies. African Americans in the United States of America and Oromos in the Ethiopian Empire developed their respective liberation movements in opposition to racial/ethnonational oppression, cultural and colonial domination, exploitation, and underdevelopment. The book also explores the structural limit of nationalism and the potential of revolutionary nationalism in promoting self-determination and a genuine multicultural democracy.

Fighting Against the Injustice of the State and Globalization

Comparing the African American and Oromo Movements

Asafa Jalata

palgrave

FIGHTING AGAINST THE INJUSTICE OF THE STATE AND GLOBALIZATION
© Asafa Jalata, 2001

First published 2001 by PALGRAVE™
175 Fifth Avenue, New York, N.Y. 10010 and
Houndmills, Basingstoke, Hampshire RG21 6XS.
Companies and representatives throughout the world

PALGRAVE is the new global publishing imprint of St. Martin's Press LLC Scholarly and Reference Division and Palgrave Publishers Ltd (formerly Macmillan Press Ltd).

ISBN 0–312–23972–6 hardback

Library of Congress Cataloging-in-Publication Data
Jalata, Asafa, 1954–
Fighting against the injustice of the state and globalization : comparing the African American and Oromo movements / Asafa Jalata.
      p.   cm.
   Includes bibliographical references and index.
   ISBN 0–312–23972–6
   1. Oromo (African people)—Government relations.   2. Ethiopia—Ethnic relations.
3. African Americans—Government relations.   4. United States—Race relations.   5.
Racism.   6. Pluralism (Social sciences)   I. Title.

DT390.G2 J35   2001
305.8'00963—dc21

                                                                        2001021866

A catalogue record for this book is available from the British Library.

Design by Letra Libre, Inc.

First edition: December 2001
10 9 8 7 6 5 4 3 2 1

To Zeituna, Beka, and Kulani

Contents

Preface

Fighting against the Injustice of the State and Globalization: Comparing the African American and Oromo Movements grew out of my personal life experiences as an Oromo/African/Black and my scholarly interests as a critical social scientist. I was born and raised in Oromia (Ethiopia). Since my people, the Oromo, have been the colonial subjects of Ethiopia for a little more than a century, I personally know the bitterness of being treated as a second-class citizen. I remember the cultural humiliation I went through when I was receiving colonial education. My refusal to accept second-class citizenship in the Ethiopian empire and my determination to oppose Ethiopian settler colonialism encouraged me to participate in the Oromo national movement. When the Ethiopian government targeted Oromo nationalists for assassination or imprisonment, I was forced to seek political asylum. As a result, I ended up in the United States as a political refugee in the early 1980s.

After living in the United States and observing the conditions of African Americans, I developed a keen interest in exploring the parallel patterns of racial oppression and exploitation, the racialization/ethnicization of state power, and the way the subjugated ethnonations respond to colonial institutions to change their subaltern positions in the modern capitalist world system. The idea of writing this comparative book came to maturation through my experience of teaching various courses, such as Race and Ethnicity, African and African American Studies, the Modern World System, and the Sociology of Development, at the University of Tennessee. I experimented with my theoretical ideas on my undergraduate and graduate students, who were eager to learn and to comment on the experiences of African Americans and Oromos in the global context. Some of my former graduate students are professors today, and we still maintain our intellectual relationship and dialogue.

Further, this book reflects my accumulated research experience and scholarship in the fields of sociology, political economy, and African and African American studies. I have been researching and writing on the struggles of Oromos and African Americans for some time. My personal and intellectual experiences have enabled me to write this comparative and challenging book, which goes beyond the limitation of current scholarship. By challenging the paradigm of intellectual elites and their knowledge of domination, this book develops an alternative knowledge of liberation.

I have benefited from the suggestions, comments, and critiques of several colleagues in writing this book. My colleagues and friends Bonnie K. Holcomb, Bill Robinson, Faye Harrison, Jon Shefner, Sisai Ibssa, and Baissa Lemmu read drafts of the book and provided important feedback that assisted me in refining my arguments and ideas. I have also greatly benefited from my discussion with my colleague Sherry Cable on theories of social movements. My intellectual discourse with scholars from various backgrounds, including the fields of anthropology, sociology, political economy, and political science, has increased the interdisciplinary content of the book.

I also thank the staff of Palgrave, Global Publishing at St. Martin's Press, including senior editor Karen Wolny, Ella Pearce, Kristine Larson Vesley, Matthew Ritter, and Meg Weaver for working diligently to publish this book. I also appreciate the typing assistance I received from Beka Jalata, Sandy Coward, Betty Lou Widener, and Anne Galloway. Zeituna deserves special appriciation for paying for the preparation of the index.

The encouragement and support that my wife, Zeituna Kalil, provided me is always appreciated. Beka and Kulani, our son and daughter, deserve special appreciation for not complaining too much when I was spending long hours on this project.

Asafa Jalata
Knoxville
May 2001

CHAPTER I

Introduction

The main purpose of this book is to examine, compare, and contrast the African American and Oromo[1] movements by locating them in the global context and by showing how life chances changed for these two peoples and their descendants as the modern world system became more complex and developed. Since the same global system that created racialized and exploitative structures in African American and Oromo societies also facilitated the struggles of these two peoples, this book demonstrates the dynamic interplay between social structures and human agencies in the system. African Americans in the United States and Oromos in the Ethiopian empire developed their respective freedom movements in opposition to racial/ethnonational oppression, cultural domination, exploitation, colonial domination, and underdevelopment. Although the focal point of this book is comparing and contrasting the African American and Oromo movements, related topics explored include the limits of nationalism, and the potential for revolutionary nationalism in promoting revolutionary multicultural democracy.

These two ethnonational minority groups are similar in numerical size, but different in political strength. The size of African American and Oromo populations are almost the same: about 30 million each. But African Americans constitute only 13 percent of the U.S. population of 270 million; Oromos are estimated between 40 percent and 60 percent of the Ethiopian population of 60 million. Because of the Ethiopian colonial politics, disagreement arises over the actual size of the Oromo population. While African Americans are one of the ethnonational minority groups in the United States in number as well as in political and economic power, the Oromos are the largest ethnonation in number, and yet have little political and economic power in Ethiopia. Since the African American case is widely known and often considered a paradigmatic case of racial/ethnonational oppression, the Black movement is well recognized. In contrast, the Oromo collective grievances and national struggle have been denied legitimacy both regionally and internationally.

African Americans were forced to enter into the global capitalist system via racial slavery in the seventeenth century. Oromos were forced into that same system during the last decades of the nineteenth century after this system had gained strength and intensity through colonialism and slavery. In 1619, twenty Africans (seventeen men and three women) were brought by a vessel to a place the newly arrived English settlers called Jamestown, Virginia. These Africans became "indentured servants who had bound themselves to work for masters for a specified length of time in return for paying the cost of their transportation across the Atlantic. Indentured servitude had come early in response to a great need for labor."[2] Considering that this kind of labor recruitment system was expensive, the settlers found a way to reduce the status of Africans who were there and arriving in the colonies to slaves. According to Benjamin Quarles, "By 1700 indentured servitude was no longer the preferred labor base in the plantation colonies. It had been superseded by slavery, brought about by the rising cost of free labor, which had become scarcer, especially after England tightened up on the kidnapping that had been a common practice in her seaport towns."[3] Although indentured servitude was at the beginning practiced on Africans and poor Europeans, the latter were never enslaved. Africans were commodities and "the average cost of a healthy male was $60 in merchandise; a woman could be bought for $15 or less."[4] Slavery was mentioned in Virginia laws in 1662, and it was legalized in Maryland, North Carolina, South Carolina, New York, and New Jersey in 1706.

Since the founding of the thirteen colonies, African Americans have built the United States without enjoying the fruit of their labor. "Except for the Indian [Native American], the Negro is America's oldest ethnic minority. Except for the settlers at Jamestown, the Negro's roots in the original thirteen colonies sink deeper than any other group from across the Atlantic."[5] These Africans resisted slavery by expressing their dissatisfaction through telling stories and singing songs, suicide, killing their masters, poisoning the children of their masters, fleeing, and establishing maroon settlements, which in North America were unsustainable.[6] It was estimated that by 1860 there were 4 million African slaves and 27 million Europeans in the United States.[7] The American capitalist system response to the presence of African Americans was to invent a racial caste system (slavery and later racial segregation) and to maintain it through its institutions to prevent the advancement of African Americans as individuals and an ethnonational group for the benefit of White elites and society. After surviving under racial slavery and American apartheid for more than three centuries in the United States, African Americans effectively consolidated their struggles for social justice, self-determination, freedom, and democracy in the first half of the twentieth century.

In contrast, Oromos strengthened their national liberation struggle in the early 1960s after suffering under settler colonialism for less than a century.[8] Ethiopian settler colonialism was practiced through five institutions: slavery, the nafxanya-gabbar system (semislavery), garrison cities, an Oromo collaborative class, and the colonial landholding system. During their colonial expansion, Abyssinians who later called themselves Ethiopians enslaved some Oromos, Sidamas, Afars, Somalis, Walayitas, Hadiyas, and others; some of these slaves were exported as commodities while others became domestic slaves who preformed duties such as carrying firewood, fetching water, grinding grain, cooking, cleaning, babysitting, and bearing and giving birth to young slaves without any payment except basic food, clothing, and shelter. When Oromos and other colonized peoples failed to pay taxes, their children were enslaved. The number of the Oromo people, according to some estimates, was reduced from ten to five million by slavery, war-induced famine, and destructive wars during the last decades of the nineteenth century.[9] The nafxanya-gabbar system enabled Ethiopian soldiers, clergymen, and colonial administrators and their Oromo collaborators to exact labor and agricultural products from the Oromo farmers. These farmers were divided among these colonial settlers and forced to provide food, tribute, and tax revenues both in cash and in kind. The colonialists built their garrison cities in different parts of Oromia and linked themselves to the Oromo population through an Oromo collaborative class to control the population and extract economic resources. The Oromo intermediaries were given one-fourth of the expropriated Oromo lands, while three-fourths of the lands became the property of the Ethiopian colonial settlers. As a result, the majority of Oromos became landless tenants, sharecroppers, and poor.

What the American racialized capitalist system did to African Americans, Ethiopian settler colonialism and global imperialism did to Oromos by introducing an entire population to previously unknown slavery, semislavery, tenancy, sharecropping, and poverty. The struggles of these two peoples to escape these conditions should best be regarded as an integral part of anticolonial forces that emerged to challenge racial/ethnonational stratification in different parts of the modern world. However, these two movements have not received adequate attention. As African American nationalism developed to resist racial segregation and oppression, colonialism and racist democracy, Oromo nationalism developed to overthrow Ethiopian settler colonialism and its set of oppressive institutions in Oromia. Both African Americans and Oromos have been struggling against the racist policies of the United States and Ethiopia, respectively. Indirectly, Oromos also struggle against U.S.-led global imperialism that sustains Ethiopian colonialism.

The nature and role of the state in the capitalist world system have changed because of the challenges from globalizing structures and actors, such as transnational elites, multinational corporations, technological transformation, the revolution in international communication and information, and forces of ethnonational diversity and multiculturalism. In this context, studying competing nationalisms in the state is necessary. The state was invented as the capitalist world system evolved. With the further intensification of globalization and the movements of the oppressed ethnonational groups, the character of the state and its role will be further changed. Hence, the kind of comparative study presented here will increase our understanding of nationalism and the forces that struggle to change the nature and the role of the state in the global context.

I come to this project with distinctive autobiographical and intellectual insights, rooted in my forced exile from Ethiopian colonial domination, my participation in the Oromo struggle, and my work as a critical Oromo/African scholar in the United States. As an Oromo who was born and raised in Oromia,[10] and who has lived in the United States since 1981, I have been fascinated by the similarities of world system - imposed oppression and exploitation experienced by these two distinct peoples and the parallels and similarities of the national struggles of these two ethnonations. As an Oromo scholar who is seriously interested in Oromo and Ethiopian studies and the Oromo national plight, I am familiar with the factors that affect the Oromo struggle. While researching and teaching in the United States in the areas of the political economy of the modern world system, race and ethnicity, the sociology of development, and multicultural studies, I began to develop a keen appreciation for the literature and the history of the African American experience that influenced me to further study the African American struggle and to compare it with that of the Oromo. My reason for writing this comparative book is to show how the modern world system operates, how African Americans and Oromos respond to it, how their struggles to achieve a level of self-determination have been effective, and how to make these players in the global system aware of each other so that they might share the insights that I have discovered through experience, research, and teaching.

I also decided to write this book on the assumption that it is in the two peoples' interest to critically understand their respective stakes in the struggle against U.S. imperialism and global racism and for revolutionary multicultural democracy; lack of such an understanding has caused Blacks in the diaspora and some Africans to see "Ethiopia" as a symbol of Black freedom when Africa was under European direct colonial occupation. This uncritical position emerged from lack of understanding that the Ethiopian empire was created by the alliance of Ethiopian colonialism and European imperialism during the "scramble" for Africa by enslaving and colonizing Oromos, Sidamas, Somalis, Walayitas, and other ethnonations in the Horn Africa. Ethiopia, which participated in commodifying some Africans and establishing settler colonialism in Oromia and other regions, would not deserve to be the symbol of Black freedom, but the symbol of racial/ethnonational oppression and exploitation. As it is in the interest of African Americans to identify all forms of racism, and it is in the interests of all oppressed groups to challenge and change the racialized global capitalist structures, Oromos have a stake in learning about American Blacks so that they can find effective ways of fighting against the American imperialism and global racism that support and justify the Ethiopian colonial state.

At present, when some African American elites with other progressive forces struggle to positively change U.S. foreign policy toward Africa,[11] it is necessary that these forces of social change understand how the racism of Ethiopia is intertwined with Western racism to maintain racial/ethnonational stratification. Since the Oromo movement challenges the alliance of Ethiopian, or *Habasha,* and Western racism and imperialism, it is one of the African progressive forces that needs to be recognized to bring positive social change in Africa. Hence, there is a need for dominated groups like African Americans and Oromos to know about each other's movements so that they can develop a common frame of reference that can help them to struggle for revolutionary multicultural democracy on regional and global levels by challenging the racialized global capitalist structures. As African Americans need to develop a critical understanding of "Ethiopia" by abandoning a Black North American perspective that claims everyone in Ethiopia is Black and the same, Oromos need to recognize the global nature of their oppression by comparing and contrasting their struggle with that of Black Americans and that of others. This book attempts to open a way for such a critical and global understanding. This introductory chapter deals with theoretical and methodological issues by developing an analytical framework that draws from theories on the world system and globalization, nationalism, revolutions, and social movements. Furthermore, this chapter frames the African American and Oromo nationalisms in the context of the capitalist world system.

Methodological and Theoretical Approaches

Writing this book has been a difficult and complex task encountering several theoretical and methodological challenges. Few scholars use a comparative perspective to address the dialectical interplay of social structures and human agencies in the capitalist world system as a way of demonstrating long-term and large-scale global social transformation. These significant issues are largely absent in studies of nationalism, globalization, and social movements as we shall see. Global studies focus primarily on wide structural changes in the capitalist world system and pay less attention to the role of a human agency. In order to overcome these limitations, this work combines a structural approach to global social change with a social constructionist model of human agency and nationalism. The book demonstrates that the African American and Oromo movements are an integral part of the global projects that have been attempting to humanize and democratize the world by establishing a single standard for humanity. Through examining the dynamic interplay of social structures and human agencies that facilitated the development of these two movements in the global and comparative contexts, this work employs interdisciplinary, multidimensional, historical, and comparative methods, and critical approaches. As Theda Skocpol has noted: "Findings about social revolutions need to be theoretically integrated with findings in closely related kinds of studies. Further scholarship, both causal and interpretive, must be done to clarify the place of ideas, culture and ideologies in the origins and course of social revolutions."[12]

Using comparative causal analysis, this book explains the movements of these two peoples as cultural, social, and political projects that have aimed at transforming the oppressive and exploitative relationships between the colonizing structures of the United States and Ethiopia and the colonized African American and Oromo societies respectively. Exploring how such an approach is useful in this kind of study, Skocpol asserts, "convincing narratives of historical processes—at least narratives of those continuities and changes that are relevant to macroscopic social science—cannot be devised at all without the use of systematic comparative analyses to sort out causal hypotheses and discover new causal analogies. Without tough-minded, analytical comparisons—necessarily cutting through the webs of history for the duration of a given investigation— we can never get straight which structures matter, or which processes count."[13] The comparative problem of this book also requires critical social history that looks at societal issues from the bottom up, specifically critical discourse and the particular world system approach that deal with long-term and world-scale social changes.

Nationalism and the Nation-State:
Born in the Era of Global Capitalism

Nationalism in this era is best understood by exploring its dialectical connection with the nation-state and global capitalism. Global capitalism brought large-scale and long-term structural changes beginning in the sixteenth century. Mercantilism successfully developed into capitalism in Western Europe through the expropriation of the European actual producers and the resources of the indigenous Americas, international trade, and enslavement of some Africans.[14] The development of capitalism, the accumulation and concentration of capital or economic resources through the separation of the actual producers from their means of production, led to racialization/ethnicization and socialization of labor. Exploring the nature of European feudal society and how it was dissolved through the process of original accumulation of capital, Karl Marx observed, "The expropriation of the agricultural producer, of the peasant, from the soil, is the basis of the whole process. The history of expropriation, in different countries, assumes different aspects, and runs through its various phases in different orders of succession, and different periods."[15]

Colonial expansion played a significant role in the processes of capital accumulation and its concentration and the emergence of the Industrial Revolution.[16] Marx contended that further socialization of labor through expropriation of the means of production and colonialism resulted in "the entanglement of all peoples in the net of the world-market, and with this, the international character of the capitalist regime."[17] These factors involved war, genocide or ethnocide, cultural destruction, the intensification of social stratification, and racial slavery, justified by the ideologies of racism, progress, civilization, and modernity.[18] Like the majority of the world populations, African Americans and Oromos were entangled in an already-racialized global capitalist system in the seventeenth and nineteenth centuries, respectively, via slavery and colonialism.

The new political structure that initially emerged with capitalism in Western Europe was the absolutist state. This state was required to balance the actions of the competing social forces such as monarchies, the aristocracy, feudal lords, the nascent capitalist class, the peasantry, and the emerging working class.[19] The absolutist state created a centralized political umbrella under which it managed and controlled these competing social forces. "The centralized monarchies . . . represented a decisive rupture," Perry Anderson notes, "with the pyramidal, parcellized sovereignty of the mediaeval social formations, with their estates and liege-systems."[20] This state created a centralized and concentrated "national" power by destroying a village-level parcellized power. The processes of state- and nation-building had transferred the allegiance of people from a lineage or clan, village or city-state, to a "nation" through developing state nationalism. With the emergence of capitalism, bureaucracy, taxation, trade, and diplomacy were organized at the "national" level.[21]

The development of capitalism also facilitated competition among the emerging European states. John Breuilly suggests that political absolutism developed to overcome various "threats to unity from within and sovereignty from without."[22] Despite the fact that the monarchies struggled to create strong, centralized, and absolutist states, the continued power of aristocracy, the growing power of the merchant class, and the emerging interstate system forced them to need the assistance of either the aristocracy or the merchant class to increase their power.[23] In these processes, "nation-states" and the interstate system emerged with the development of capitalism. The failure of any state to dominate other states in Western Europe made possible the development of an interstate system.[24]

The concepts of nation, nationalism, and the citizen were invented with the emergence of the nation-state in the capitalist world system. Originally state nationalism emerged through restructuring the absolutist state into the nation-state. The capitalist class developed bourgeois democracy and state nationalism with the development of the nation-state in Western countries. The development of state nationalism and bourgeois democracy in France and in other Western countries demonstrated the victory of the capitalist class over the remnants of the feudal class, the peasantry, and the working class.[25] The cases of Great Britain and France make these points clear. "Just as in England the puritans, with their zeal for a new material-spiritual life, left an indelible stamp on the course of English nationalism," Snyder writes, "so in France did the Jacobins, with their call for individualism and democracy, leave an imprint on French nationalism."[26] The absolutist state evolved into the nation-state in England in 1689 and in France in 1789.

Since the absolutist state used arbitrary power against the people it ruled, its subjects struggled to establish the rule of law and democracy. This contributed to the development of the nation-state. With the elimination of absolutism and the emergence of the capitalists as the new dominant class, the popular democracy that the working class, the peasantry, and other revolutionary forces struggled for was suppressed and bourgeois democracy was established. According to Louis Snyder, "The French Revolution asserted nationalism as a revolutionary force among a people who had enjoyed little political freedom. The French version of nationalism was to take on a missionary coloration in its travel through Europe."[27] The French nation-state emerged as a world model; it radically broke away from the old regime and took all necessary steps to build the new state.[28] The French people initiated the French Revolution in 1789 to change their political status from subjects of the monarch to citizens of the French nation, and to transfer sovereignty from the French monarchy to the French nation. As a result, the French people or nation theoretically became the source of all sovereignty and introduced to the world the principles of national self-determination and popular sovereignty.[29] The Constituent Assembly that came to power as the result of the French Revolution declared that "The source of all sovereignty resides essentially in the nation."[30]

Since then the struggle for democracy, national self-determination, and popular sovereignty have become recognized as the important political principles in the modern world system. Practically, however, the European capitalist class and the nation-state intensified the process of class, racial/ethnonational, and gender oppression and colonial expansion. Class oppression, racial/ethnonational stratification, and colonialism led to the emergence of the two types of what the world system theorists call anti-systemic movements: social movements and national movements. "The social movement defined the oppression as that of employers over wage earners, the bourgeoisie over the proletariat. . . . The national movement, on the other hand, defined the oppression as that of one ethnonational group over another."[31] State nationalism and bourgeois democracy conceal the contradictions that exist among the citizens of the nation-state. The concept of common citizenship[32] glosses over the real existing contradictions between the ideological claim of equality of citizens and the vast material differences that are structured into socioeconomic conditions of distinct social forces within the nation-state. As we will see, the cases of African Americans in the United States and Oromos in the Ethiopian empire demonstrate clearly these contradictions.

African Americans and Oromos were in effect denied a basic aspect of their humanity when they were forced to enter into the global capitalist system via slavery and colonialism. Some African warlords, as slavers and colonizers, fully participated as agents of European imperialism in enslaving and colonizing these two peoples. Europeans and their African collaborators were involved in enslaving the ancestors of African Americans and in colonizing and enslaving Oromos: "With a human cargo to dispose of, the native chief was ready to negotiate with the trader. Generally the latter began by offering presents to the king—hats and bunches of beads."[33] Some African chiefs, warlords, and kings captured, enslaved, and exchanged some Africans for European goods with White slave merchants.[34] Similarly, Abyssinian or Ethiopian warlords and England, France, and Italy collaborated in creating the Ethiopian empire and colonizing and enslaving Oromos and other peoples.[35] The capitalist world system through colonial expansion brought the collaborative classes under its control directly or indirectly.[36] Just as African Americans were enslaved and shipped to America by the joined forces of African and European slave hunters and merchants, Oromos were enslaved and colonized by the combined forces of Ethiopians (Amharas-Tigrayans)[37] and European colonialists.

Several scholars have persuasively developed the idea that the capitalist colonial powers used their superior military force and collaborators to colonize directly or indirectly precapitalist societies to exploit their labor power and economic resources through genocide or ethnocide, looting, enslavement, piracy, and annexation; this was the way the original accumulation of capital occurred on a world scale.[38] There have been two global historical waves in the modern world system: The first wave was characterized by mercantilism; war; slavery; conquest and colonization; genocide or ethnocide; intensification of racial/ethnonational, class, and gender stratification; and continued subjugation of peoples by European capitalist powers and their collaborators. This period extended approximately from the seventeenth to the mid-twentieth century. The transformation of mercantilism into industrial capitalism and the expansion of the Industrial Revolution in the eighteenth and nineteenth centuries in Western Europe increased the demand for raw materials, free or cheap labor (mainly slaves), markets, and the intensification of global colonial expansion.[39]

The same global processes that resulted in the colonial beginnings of the United States in the seventeenth century and the emergence of the Ethiopian empire during the second half of the nineteenth century brought about the subjugation of the African American and Oromo peoples in two different corners of the world. Capitalism brought large-scale and long-term structural changes first in Western Europe and then to the whole world. The processes of expropriation, slavery, and colonialism resulted in hierarchical organization of world populations through the creation of an elaborate discourse of racism to maintain the system. It is essential to provide a pragmatic definition of racism in this discussion. As the meaning of *race* is complex, so is that of *racism*.[40] Racism is a discourse and a practice in which a racial/ethnonational project is politically, culturally, and "scientifically" constructed by global and regional elites in the capitalist world system to naturalize and justify racial/ethnonational inequality in which those at the top of the hierarchy oppress and exploit those below them by claiming biological and/or cultural superiority. "*A racial project is simultaneously an interpretation, representation or explanation of racial dynamics,*" Howard Winant notes, "*and an effort to organize and distribute resources along particular racial lines.*"[41] Simply put, racism is an expression of institutionalized patterns of colonizing structural power and social control. It is manifested in individual and cultural practices. Race and racism are socially and culturally constructed to maintain the identities of the dominant population groups and their power and privileges through policy formulation and implementation.[42] By inventing nonexistent "races,"[43] the racist ideology institutionalizes "the hierarchies involved in the worldwide division of labour."[44] Race and racism are sociopolitical constructs since all human groups are biologically and genetically more alike than different.[45] Robert Staples asserts that "it is useful to view race as a political and cultural identity rather than to apply any genetic definitions. Race is a political identity because it defines the way in which an individual or [a group] is to be treated by the political state and the conditions of one's oppression."[46] Race and racism as politicocultural constructs define the relationship between the dominant and subordinated racial/ethnonational groups and legitimate the imposition of dominant values.[47]

To justify racial slavery and colonialism, the ideologies of racism and cultural universalism[48] were developed in scientific clothing and matured during the last decades of the nineteenth and the beginning of twentieth centuries. In this process, class and gender oppression and exploitation were intensified, and naturalized too. The crisis of the capitalist world system during the first half of twentieth century, the intensification of competition among the European colonial powers, and the maturation of the White racist ideology resulted in the First and the Second World Wars. These crises marked the decline of the first global historical wave and the emergence of the second historical wave. The second historical wave emerged as a turning point after the First World War as social movements and national liberation movements or revolutions. Immannuel Wallerstein notes that the Second World War "marked the opening skirmishes of worldwide struggles of movements of national liberation against Europe's world political hegemony, which had been based on the latter's temporary technological advantages and deep-rooted racism."[49] The second global historical wave was characterized mainly by territorial nationalism and ethnonationalism that opposed direct colonial domination.[50] Global historical evidence demonstrates that nationalism has been the leading political ideology in guiding the political and cultural actions of a territorially or culturally defined human group that sees its common destiny as a people or a "nation." The struggles for democracy, national self-determination, and popular sovereignty emerged in opposition to political absolutism and colonialism on the global level. This understanding is necessary to clearly comprehend the principles for which the struggles of African Americans and Oromos developed. The inability of the nation-state to solve the contradictions among competing nationalisms within its geopolitical boundaries facilitated the proliferation of nationalisms.

The nation-state mainly serves the interests of the dominant classes and racial/ethnonational groups whose members occupy key positions in the structures of the state machinery and political economy. For those ethnonations that do not have access to state power and major institutions within a given country or an empire, states have become instruments of oppression, exploitation, cultural destruction, and continued subjugation. As we will see in the following three chapters, the U.S. government until the 1960s and the Ethiopian government until the present have played these destructive roles against African Americans and Oromos respectively.[51] Although the racial caste system was legally dismantled in the United States in the 1960s, the Black majority is still in poverty because of the past historical and structural discrimination and current institutional racism. With regard to the Oromo, as demonstrated in chapter III, the United States as the hegemonic power has played a key role in maintaining Ethiopian settler colonialism and the subordination of the Oromo between the 1950s and the 1970s and from 1991 to present. The Union of Socialist Soviet Republics also played a key role in maintaining the Ethiopian empire during the 1970s and 1980s by allying with the Ethiopian military government. Today, the ideological or biological grandchildren of the Ethiopian warlords have become "pimps" for the West and attempt to destroy the Oromo and their national movement.[52]

Anchored on social stratification and connected to others through the imperial interstate system, the nation-state has become the basic unit of modern political organization. However, with the intensification of globalization and proliferation of ethnonationalisms,[53] the future of the nation-state is not yet clear. Global capitalism has constantly introduced new technology, communication systems, organizational techniques, and economies of scale that have been based on industrialization, exchange, and a global division of labor. This division of labor has been racialized or ethnicized. As the dominant ethnonational groups have used the creation of racial national categories to exploit colonized ethnonational groups, the subjugated ethnonations have used reform or/and revolutionary nationalism to challenge this racism and oppressor nationalism. Capitalism introduced globalism, racism, and nationalism.[54] It facilitated the centralization of political power and the development of a political vision that Anthony Smith calls "the national idea," saying, "No other vision has set its stamp so thoroughly on the map of the world, and on our sense of identity. We are identified first and foremost with our 'nation.' Our lives are regulated, for the most part, by the national state in which we are born."[55] But Smith does not take into account the racial/ethnonational, class, and gender stratification and oppressions that exist and determine our reality within the so-called nation-state. Of course, class and gender contradictions also exist within oppressed ethnonations. Since the ideology of the nation-state has been historically constructed upon racism or ethnocentrism, classism, and sexism, our membership in certain racial/ethnonational, gender, and class categories within the nation-state determines our social position in a given country or an empire.

State nationalism has had a negative effect upon ethnocultural diversity via the imposition of the culture of the dominant ethnonation on other peoples within the nation-state, while ironically even recognizing cultural diversity within the interstate system.[56] Gurutz Bereciartu remarks that the question of the subjugated population or "the national question is a historical one that has not been resolved satisfactorily since the first formation of nation-states in Europe."[57] Some state elites used structural and cultural assimilation effectively; for instance, the English settlers created a White-dominated society in the United States by structurally and culturally assimulating different European ethnonational groups using the ideology of whiteness and apartheid democracy.[58] The English settlers dominated the thirteen American colonies by permitting other Europeans access to Anglo institutions such as the economy, government, religion, education, media, and marriage. Since the assimilation included structural and cultural elements, it was successful. Other European groups were consequently anglicized and almost became the replica of the English settlers under the guise of "Americanization." But for nonwhites, particularly African Americans, structural assimilation was not possible because they were denied access to these major anglicized institutions. But they were de-Africanized and forced to learn the English language, culture, and religion while being denied structural assimilation. Using cultural and structural assimilation in creating White society, the Anglo-American ruling class also created and perpetuated the racial caste system by denying structural assimilation to nonwhite Americans.[59]

When the practice of destroying ethnocultural diversity through forced assimilation to create a "national" culture has become the goal of state nationalism, the subjugated peoples who have been denied structural assimilation and whose history and culture were condemned to death by state nationalism and racism have sought cultural diversity. Some ethnonational movements have sought national independence or autonomy, but others have sought as their goal, along with cultural diversity, structural assimilation in order to achieve access to, and equality within, the social institutions of the economy and the polity. Both African Americans and Oromos initially sought structural assimilation and cultural diversity in their respective struggles. When the goals of structural assimilation and cultural diversity failed, Oromos started to struggle for national independence. It is the flaw of the politics of some scholars to emphasize cultural difference and ignore and even dismiss the structural issues, including the prospect of structural assimilation as an emancipatory possibility.

State elites and some scholars have misunderstood and mispredicted "the assertive renaissance of nationalism" and declared the inevitability of the assimilation and dissolution of the colonized populations.[60] Theoretically, nationalism, as a cultural and political vision, aims at abolishing dictatorial or colonial regimes by establishing national self-determination, popular sovereignty, citizenship and democratic rights, and the rule of law for people that see its common destiny.[61] Despite the fact that national movements have failed to promote popular or representative democracy and to eliminate social stratification, nationalism has remained the strongest ideology that contributes to large-scale and long-term social changes. As the French Revolution shaped the nature of the nation-state and as the emergence of various national movements spawned many nation-states, the failure of various nation-states to transform themselves into multicultural democratic states has facilitated the emergence of oppressed nationalism in the modern world system.[62] Nationalism can be divided into oppressor and oppressed nationalism. While oppressor nationalism maintains racial/ethnonational hierarchy, oppressed nationalism seeks self-determination for dominated ethnonational groups. Oppressed nationalism is a form of opposition politics that serves as an ideology of resistance against a racialized or an ethnicized state within either a country or an empire.[63]

The present work has set out to demonstrate that the processes of colonialism and racialization/ethnicization of the global division of labor have denied or limited the access of African Americans and Oromos to cultural, political, and economic resources within the US and Ethiopian states. Exploring the features of racial/ethnonational and gender stratification, Wallerstein has observed that "capitalism developed an ideological framework of oppressive humiliation which had never previously existed, and which today we call . . . racism."[64] The European colonial powers and their collaborators created stratified multiracial or multiethnic societies in which they practiced racial dictatorship, known as "Herrenvolk" democracies, in countries such as the United States, South Africa, Brazil, and Australia. Gloria Marshall argues that "scientific and lay concepts of race have served to support the economic and political privileges of ruling groups who regard themselves as superior by virtue of phylogenetic heritage rather than because of the accidents of cultural history."[65] Some academic and other elites invented and theorized the issues of race and ethnicity presenting them as natural phenomena.[66] As a result, race was seen as a biological phenomenon that determined a hierarchy that could not be changed.[67]

This discourse was promoted as "scientific," although it ignored historical facts. Rather than explaining the problem of discrepancies among "races" as a problem of the last five hundred years associated with global capitalism, some Euro-American scholars and their collaborators in peripheral areas of the world have attempted to present this problem as a naturally given social process. Noting that several precapitalist empires, such as the Egyptian, Roman, and Muslim empires, brought together various peoples who had different cultures and physical characteristics without developing the ideology of racism,[68] Winant comments, "The five-hundred years of domination of the globe by Europe and its inheritors is the historical context in which racial concepts of difference have attained their present status as fundamental components of human identity and inequality."[69] Pseudoscientific discourses were produced, for instance, in American and Ethiopian studies, which promoted and maintained the privileges of Euro-Americans and their collaborators. Such studies used themes such as civilization, progress, and cultural universalism to justify racial/ethnonational stratification and thus negate the history, culture, and humanity of the colonized peoples of the world. The African American and Oromo peoples provide case studies in this latter category.

Negative views of subjugated people prevented knowledge elites within the colonial system from perceiving the needs, aspirations, and humanity of those people. Some social scientists took it upon themselves to promote the interests of the colonizing "races" or ethnonational groups at the cost of the colonized peoples. Thomas W. Heaney remarks that "with the writing of history, knowledge became power, or rather an expression of power and a tool for maintaining it. History, and later, science, were frequently used not merely to understand, but to legitimize historically shaped political relationships and institutions."[70] Colonialism, migration, and large-scale social changes had caused the disruption of cultures both in the center and the colonized areas of the world. A racist cultural movement emerged in the center to counter any structural assimilation that would undermine the cultural stability of the core countries by promoting ethnonational amalgamation.[71]

Some Euro-American "scientific" elites created the "savagery" of nonwhites and the "civility" of some White groups at the beginning and later all White groups and their collaborators, such as Ethiopians, by defining human history according to the cultural-racial categories of "backwardness," "barbarism," and "civilization" to naturalize and essentialize the phenotypic differences among human groups. By 1850 the Enlightenment views of the universal sameness and equality of humanity were criticized and ridiculed.[72] That is why Robert Young says that "modern racism was an academic creation."[73] The concept "race" entered into European languages in the fifteenth century to identify people; it gained its "scientific" and popular context in the eighteenth and nineteenth centuries.[74] Using geography and overt physical characteristics, some biologists and anthropologists divided human groups into Black/Africa, White/Europe, Yellow/Asia, Red/original America arbitrarily without studying their genotypes. Referring to Cavalli-Sforza's book, *The History and Geography of Human Genes,* and exposing the fallacy of racial classification based on geography and phenotypes, Sribala Subramanian argues, "Once the genes for surface traits such as coloration and stature are discounted, the human 'races' are remarkably alike under the skin. The variation among individuals is so enormous that the whole concept of race becomes meaningless at the genetic level."[75]

With European colonial domination of the world, whiteness was seen as a marker of civilization. Race was theorized and scientificized to justify slavery, colonial domination, and continued subjugation of colonized peoples. Young remarks that "no one bothered too much about the differences between races until it was to the West's economic advantage to profit from slavery or to defend it against the abolitionists."[76] European capitalists who became racists had their own goals and reasons for using racial classification and rationalization. It was in their interest to dominate nonwhites and maximize profit by maintaining a cheap labor force and reducing the cost of production.[77] Through large-scale and long-term social changes and colonial expansion, the continental and national identities of "Europeanness," "Asianness," "Africanness," "Englishness," "Frenchness," "Americanness," and other identities were invented.[78] Taking the identity of "otherness" that was bestowed on them through racism, ethnocentrism, prejudice, and stereotypes, the colonized and enslaved peoples ultimately began to mobilize themselves via the ideology of oppressed nationalism to fight culturally, intellectually, and militarily against Euro-American colonialists and their collaborators. The discourse of oppressed nationalism focuses on the cultural and social histories of the subjugated populations, challenges the dominant top–down paradigm to a historiography, and transforms these populations into subjects rather than objects of history.[79]

The Concept Of Oppressed Nationalism

When the dominant racial/ethnonational groups have justified and rationalized their privileged position by racist and ethnocratic discourse,[80] the oppressed ethnonational groups—among them Oromos and African Americans—that have been denied cultural and economic development and access to state power have developed in response a collective national consciousness to challenge the position of the colonizing structures[81] and to restore some elements of their lost cultural, political, and economic rights. According to Amilcar Cabral, "The return to the source is of no historical significance unless it brings not only real involvement in the struggle for independence but also complete and absolute identification with the hopes of the masses of people, who contest not only the foreign culture but also foreign domination as a whole."[82]

The return to the source involves ethnoclass consciousness and political activism necessary to envision the overthrow of oppressive cultural and economic conditions and of decadent ideological systems. Bereciartu explains how "the national formation of underdeveloped areas" is created within a nation–state, and how "under the pretext of a shared country, there exist in reality persons genuinely without a country."[83] National or ethnonational movements have gained legitimacy because they base their struggles on the grievances of "a collective memory" to regain their economic, political, and cultural rights by rejecting subordination.[84] The movements of the dominated social groups "establish the possibilities for imaginative insights by providing a new vantage point for analysis of existing social conditions and for imagining new human potentials."[85] The colonized peoples struggle against states that have suppressed cultural diversity and at the same time denied structural assimilation in the names of common citizenship and cultural universalism. "National liberation movements challenge," Charles McKelvey contends, "in the realm of politics as well as in the realm of ideas, European domination"[86] and other forms of colonialism.

Oppressed nationalism emerged in the industrialized and less industrialized parts of the world among subjugated peoples who within countries or empires did not have equal access or were totally denied access to state power, cultural or economic resources. It emerged as a formidable ideological and cultural force against the racial/ethnonational stratification of the modern world system.[87] According to L. Adele Jinadu, "The social, political and economic inequalities between ethnic groups, created consciously by state policies, provide part of the explanation for the rise and appeal of ethno-regional movements in contexts as diverse as Western Europe, North America, Asia and Africa."[88] The social sciences have faltered to explain systematically the struggles of the subjugated peoples. Classical Marxism wrongly predicted the dissolution of ethnocultural diversity and nationalism and their replacement by the collective consciousness of class. Likewise, modernization theory wrongly assumed that socioeconomic development would make ethnocultural diversity and nationalism obsolete.[89]

Classical Marxists assumed that capitalism would universalize culture, politics, and language, and divide the world into capitalist and working classes. These theorists also assumed that the course of capitalist development would naturally or automatically produce revolutionary social forces that would dismantle class and ethnonational hierarchies and establish egalitarianism, social justice, socialist economy, and democracy. Classical Marxists in effect accepted modernization theory's premise that assimilation and cultural universalism were inevitable. It is now evident that interests of working classes of different ethnonations do not necessarily coincide due to various factors, such as the scarcity of economic resources, uneven development, and racialization/ethnicization of a labor force.[90] But some radical scholars, including some Marxists, still assume that there is not any fundamental contradiction between the working class of the dominant and dominated racial/ethnonation groups. They believe, therefore, that socialist or social revolutions can eliminate the problems of class and racial/ethnonational stratification. There is substantial evidence, however, as we will see in this work, that although the working classes tend to collaborate against their capitalist oppressors and their collaborators, the working classes of the dominating ethnonational groups embrace racism, ethnocentrism, and sexism and ally with their respective ethnonational elites and the state against the people whom they see as different within and outside of their countries.

Since many socialist–oriented revolutions have emerged and have failed to solve racial/ethnonational problems, it is necessary that the assumptions about proletariat internationalism be rejected or reformulated. As McKelvey expounds, "The claim of a revolutionary class that its goals promote the communal interest has some validity at first, for the revolutionary class does promote the communal interest in the sense that it promotes a further development of the productive forces. However, once the particular interests of the revolutionary class as a dominant class have taken stage, the dominating class begins to promote its particular interests at the expense of the particular interests of the non–ruling classes" and groups.[91] Modernization theorists also believed that the subjugated ethnonational groups would disappear with the transition of "backward" peoples to "modernity" and from "barbarism" to "civilization." They argued that modernization would eliminate social problems by providing opportunities for all groups. John Markakis exposes the weakness of this school by contending that modernization "assumes that development generally has a positive effect upon all population groups and social classes. This assumption is called into question by the concept of uneven development. . . . From this perspective, development is seen as a discontinuous and uneven process which differentiates between regions and economic sectors, depriving some for the benefit of others, and also discriminates among population groups and social classes, conferring power and privilege on some at the expense of others."[92]

Assimilationist theorists assumed that racial/ethnonational identities are premodern phenomena that would disappear with industrialization. Hugh Tinker argues, "The liberal is an heir to the Darwinian philosophy; he believes that a process of evolution is at work, whereby lower forms give way to higher forms. He does not deal in hundreds of thousands of years, but in decades: Yet he still does insist on a time-scale for change: 'it will work, given time . . . given time' is his favourite advice."[93] There have been Marxists who endorsed the Darwinian philosophy of evolving from "lower forms to higher forms." Modernization theorists still believe that social positions are mainly determined by meritocracy, such as education, learned skills, and personal qualities; they fail to address the major contradictions between the colonizing and colonized structures that are located in political economy and cultural arenas. Exposing the fallacy of modernization theory in the United States, Benjamin Schwartz comments that "the history we hold up as a light to nations is a sanctimonious tissue of myth and self-infatuation. We get the world wrong because we get ourselves wrong. Taken without illusion, our history gives us no right to preach—but it should prepare us to understand the brutal realities of nation-building, at home and abroad."[94]

Global experience demonstrates that cultural assimilation has very limited success; wherever these processes have occurred, as in the United States, many vexing problems of racism and discrimination remain unsolved. The failure to solve the national question (or the problem of racial/ethnonational hierarchy) already has led to the disintegration of the USSR, Yugoslavia, and Czechoslovakia. The ethnonational struggles in Canada, the United States, Great Britain, France, and Spain demonstrate that the national question is not resolved in the industrialized West. "A dispassionate appraisal of the contemporary nation-state suggests that, without a serious attempt to address these issues," Ashok Kaul warns, "the society faces the prospect of escalating levels of factional conflict with the 'real' catalyst being socioeconomic inequalities concealed by religious, cultural and ethno-nationalist modes of discourse."[95] Liberal and Marxist historiography has not explained adequately the phenomenon of nationalism and has failed to develop a comprehensive and critical theory of nationalism. Tom Narin points out that "The theory of nationalism represents Marxism's great historical failure."[96] Marxist scholars, including Marx himself, do not have a consistent position on nationalism. Whenever they have thought that nationalism promotes socialism, they have supported it, and whenever they have thought that it did not promote socialism, they have opposed it.[97]

Since the understanding of some Marxists has been limited by their political objectives to the so-called proletariat internationalism and universalism, they have failed to deal with the issues of the national question and multicultural democracy. Today in the modern world system there is no proletariat internationalism, but there is bourgeois internationalism. Fascism, racism, and discrimination prevent the working classes within dominant ethnonational groups from supporting the struggle of the subjugated people. Since some Marxist and liberal scholars "do converge in their negative evaluation of nationalism as anti-democratic, antiprogressive, and ultimately a fundamental threat to interstate relation,"[98] they are blinded to the struggles of the colonized ethnonations for human liberation, social justice, and multicultural democracy. Realizing the significance of these struggles, Crawford Young explains that "the world enters a period of exceptional fluidity—of the sort which historically has usually come about through the dislocation of a major war. Nation and state, as we have known them, are interrogated by history and alternative visions of the future. In this process, the politics of cultural pluralism will influence the outcomes in many important ways. In turn, the prospective impact of cultural pluralism beckons us to continue our quest for a more complete understanding of its inner workings."[99] This work aspires to be part of this quest.

Serious scholars need to challenge the abstract assumption of modernization theorists and some Marxists that attempt to maintain the status quo and fail to explain the contemporary social reality. We need to "abandon fictions like 'Marxists as such are not nationalists,' or 'nationalism is the pathology of modern developmental history,' and, instead, do our slow best to learn the real, and imagined, experience of the past."[100] Revolutionary practices in the former USSR and Yugoslavia, China, former Czechoslovakia, and other socialist-oriented countries demonstrate that "Marxists" have been nationalists, and they used Marxism and state nationalism in combination to advance the process of modernization and nation-building rather than promoting socialist democracy. Benedict Anderson notes that "nationalism has proved an uncomfortable anomaly for Marxist theory and, precisely for that has been largely elided, rather than confronted."[101] Understanding the dilemma of some Marxists and modernization theorists, Edward Said suggests:

> Modern thought and experiences have taught us to be sensitive to what is involved in representation, in studying the Other, in racial thinking, in unthinking and uncritical acceptance of authority and authoritative ideas, in the sociopolitical role of intellectuals, in the great value of skeptical critical consciousness. Perhaps if we remember that the study of human experience usually has an ethical, to say nothing of a political, consequence in

either the best or worst sense, we will not be indifferent to what we do as scholars. And what better norm for the scholar than human freedom and knowledge? Perhaps too we should remember that the study of man [and woman] in society is based on concrete human history and experience, not on donnish abstractions, or on obscure laws or arbitrary stems. The problem then is to make the study fit and in some way be shaped by the experience, which would be illuminated and perhaps changed by the study.[102]

As Said suggests, scholars need to study and understand the experiences of subjugated peoples to find appropriate solutions for their problems. From the perspective of subjugated peoples, oppressed nationalism involves politics and knowledge that can be seen as an integral part of the struggle for identity and human dignity as well as for economic, cultural, and human rights. Following Eric Wolf and exposing the arrogance of some liberal and Marxist scholars who consider subjugated peoples as the peoples without history, Bereciartu explains that the "'peoples without history,' who had seemingly been condemned to oblivion, not only have 'returned to history' now seem on the brink of becoming coparticipants and protagonists, along with 'historical peoples,' in the creation of future society."[103] The idea that nationalism is invented from above[104] or imagined[105] does not capture the whole character of oppressed nationalism since it helps to reclaim, recover, or restore lost cultural, economic, and human rights of the subjugated people.

Without understanding critically how an oppressive and exploitative social system and colonial education creates a nationalist leadership, some scholars see nationalism as a phenomenon invented from above.[106] Eric Hobsbawm asserts that nation and nationalism are "constructed essentially from above, but . . . cannot be understood unless analyzed from below, that is in terms of the assumptions, hopes, needs, longings and interests of ordinary people, which are not necessarily national and still less nationalist."[107] Of course, oppressive socioeconomic conditions do not necessarily produce nationalism; nationalism cannot be invented from above by elites without the existence of oppressive and exploitative conditions. "Social, economic, and political change act indirectly upon incidence and forms of conflict by changing the mobilization potential of various social formations," Anthony Oberschall notes, "by changing the social milieu and ecological locus of capabilities of authorities."[108] National consciousness emerges from certain structural changes and social conditions that facilitate the development of a human agency that attempts to change oppressive structure by mobilizing cultural, ideological, and material resources that are essential for creating a national movement.

The cases of the African American and Oromo movements clearly demonstrate this reality. "*Collective ethnic renewal* involves the reconstruction of an ethnic community," Joane Nagel notes, "by current or new community members who build or rebuild institutions, culture, history, and tradition."[109] Intellectual and professional groups develop political and ideological strategies depending on their political maturity, available political opportunities, indigenous institutions, and the level of their commitment for the liberation of their people. Breuilly notes that the development of "capitalism has created new social groups with new objectives and ways of seeking those objectives which nationalism might help serve."[110] Benedict Anderson believes that nationalism creates an imagined community, although he is not restricted by this idea; he recognizes that "nation-ness, as well as nationalism, are cultural artefacts of a particular kind. To understand them properly we need to consider carefully how they have come into historical being, in what ways their meanings have changed over time, and why, today, they command such profound emotional legitimacy."[111] National movements such as those of African Americans and Oromos emerged from within undemocratic political structures, providing cultural degradation, humiliation, and denial of human rights. Some elements of the educated class can only transform the resistance of the subjugated people into national movements by refashioning it as cultural and political movements. If there are no material and subjective factors for these developments, these intellectuals cannot invent national movements. Therefore, it is essential to explore the dynamic linkage among the structures of racial/ethnonational domination and the origin of conflict, political mobilization, organization, and collective political action when we study national movements.[112]

The emergence of national movements and the critical scientific discourse associated with them challenged the biological theories of race and developmental and evolutionary theories. With the decline of European colonial domination and the flourishing of revolutionary nationalism together with critical scientific discourse, these older theories lost scientific credibility, although they survived as popular ideologies. Gradually, racial/ethnonational stratification came to be seen as social inequality and injustice by critical scholars.[113] One important aspect of oppressed nationalism is the struggle for social scientific knowledge to demystify the racist and ethnocratic discourse of the colonizing structure. To a certain degree critical nationalist discourse exposes and challenges racist distortion of history. Colonialists look at history from the top down and thus erase the historical and cultural experiences of the subject peoples. They praise their own cultural and historical achievements, including the experiences that have been based on the violation of human rights, and deplore the experiences of the dominated populations. Such distorted knowledge has been challenged by emancipatory knowledge. As McKelvey says, "knowledge of objective reality can be attained only when humanity has become unified in a single 'unitary cultural system.' . . . The struggle for truth is therefore interrelated with the struggle for social change and social justice: 'There exists therefore a struggle for objectivity (to free oneself from partial and fallacious ideologies) and this struggle is the same as the struggle for the cultural unification of the human race.'"[114]

The colonial knowledge elites and states have developed policies that denied or limited the accessability of subjugated peoples to education and positions of authority and knowledge-making in universities, business, and government. Oppressed nationalism and emancipatory knowledge attempt to promote social scientific knowledge that is socially and historically conditioned and not eternal.[115] However, such knowledge and its ideology must be reexamined critically. As D. J. Haraway comments, "That of the subjugated are not exempt from critical reexamination, decoding, deconstruction, and interpretation. . . . The standpoints of the subjugated are not 'innocent' positions. On the contrary, they are preferred because in principle they are least likely to allow denial of the critical and interpretative core of all knowledge."[116] Critical social scientific knowledge and nationalism are linked to the cultural and historical experiences of the subjugated population. The comparative study of the African American and Oromo movements reflects this critical social scientific knowledge that is open to re-examination. Since these movements have been promoting the principles of self-determination or multicultural democracy, it is necessary to explore the relationship between oppressed nationalism, cultural rights, and human dignity.

Oppressed nationalism emerges in the process of social transformation when a particular group draws upon certain aspects of its shared historical past in order to respond to pressures felt within the modern world system.[117] There are both objective and subjective factors that need to be considered in studying and understanding nationalism. These factors involve cultural, social, economic, and psychological elements. Nationalism cannot be reduced to any one of these elements. Cabral rejects simplistic forms of economic determinism and asserts that "Culture, whatever its ideological or idealist characteristics of its expression, is . . . an essential element of the history of a people. . . . Like history, or because it is history, culture has its material base at the level of the productive forces and the mode of production. Culture plunges its roots into the humus of the material reality of the environment in which it develops, and it reflects the organic nature of society.[118]

To emphasize either the objective or the subjective factors reduces the complexity of nationalism and distorts our critical understanding of this subject. Therefore, it is necessary to look at the dynamic interplay of the material and the subjective forces when we study nationalism. Cultural resources, such as language and cultural and historical knowledge, can be transformed into material forces through human agencies. It is this process that is not yet well understood. There are scholars who focus on the subjective or objective factors in defining and understanding nationalism. Despite the fact that some analysts consider language, religion, and culture as objective or material as well as subjective factors,[119] there are scholars, such as Connor, who assert that the linguistic, religious, and cultural factors are not determining factors in defining and understanding nationalism.[120] Walker Connor sees a nation as people who believe that they have a common ancestry. He thinks that subjective factors such as "the self-identification of people with a group—its past, its present, and, what is most important, its destiny" are prime requisites in defining ethnonation and nationalism.[121] Although some social scientists emphasize material or objective factors at the cost of subjective ones, the latter "are recorded and immortalized in the arts, languages, sciences and laws of the community which, though subject to a slower development, leave their imprint on the perceptions of subsequent generations and shape the structures and atmosphere of the community through the distinctive traditions they deposit."[122]

The dominant social classes and nations use cultural resources to promote their interests. According to Markakis, "Cultural elements themselves may have a material dimension if, as often the case, they mediate access to power and privilege. Language, the basic cultural attribute of nationalism, often plays this role in multiethnic states with a single official language. Groups whose languages are ignored by the state may find themselves at a distinct disadvantage in competing for access to education and state office. . . . Similarly, religion may be endowed with a material dimension."[123] When we study anticolonial nationalism, we must explore how colonized populations were cut off from their historical and cultural roots and civilizations—degraded and dehumanized by being reduced from autonomy to dependence by losing access to their previously empowering cultural and economic resources, and rendered powerless by colonial rule or racial/ethnonational domination. However, unless they commit genocide, colonial powers cannot eradicate the cultures of the colonized populations; one of the major reasons that oppressed nationalism emerges is the resilience of the cultures of the dominated populations. Because of this, national liberation is seen as an act of cultural struggle.[124] Returning to their historical and cultural roots and developing political programs, some elements of the educated elite contribute to the development of nationalism as "a vision of the future which restores to [men and women their] basic patterns of living and being, which was once [their] undisputed birthright. It is not a mechanical linking of the tradition into the modern."[125]

Even Smith,[126] who impressively contributes to studies of nationalism by exploring how cultural, historical, social, ideological, and political factors facilitate the emergence of oppressed nationalism, fails to see the interplay of the material and subjective forces. He does not explain how political economy and racial/ethnonational stratification are interwoven and result in irreconcilable contradiction between the colonizing structures and the colonized ones. There are scholars who give less importance to the complex issues that Smith seriously addresses, and who only deal with one or more factors. For instance, John Breuilly sees nationalism as a form of opposition politics that seeks to gain access to state power.[127] He identifies three functions of nationalism as coordination, mobilization, and legitimation of a national movement. Nationalism coordinates diverse political and class interests, and mobilizes new groups to join the movement by providing it with a unity of purpose and value in articulating its political objectives. He also notes that the movement needs ideological legitimation to be acceptable to its sympathizers and outsiders to get political, moral, and material support. But Breuilly considers culture and other factors as secondary issues in studying and understanding nationalism. Breuilly says that focusing "upon culture, ideology, identity, class, or modernization is to neglect the fundamental point that nationalism is, above and beyond all else, about politics, and that politics is about power. Power, in the modern world, is primarily about control of the state. The central question, therefore, should be to relate nationalism to the objective of obtaining and using state power."[128] Although his identification of nationalism with state power is important, Breuilly confuses his analytical separation of political power from cultural and economic power with social reality.

Breuilly correctly explains why the colonized populations struggle for political power:"The creation of a genuine worldwide economic and political system has been marked by enormous disparities in wealth, power and values. These disparities have provoked attempts to get rid of subordination and exploitation or to sustain dominance and economic advantage. They have also involved painful adjustments to rapidly changing situations and the attempts to realise new objectives in ways which call for directed social change. All these responses have, to some extent, been related to nationalism."[129] However, those who believe the notion that politics can be separated from cultural and economic arenas in defining nationalism fail to grasp the complexity of nationalism. This work attempts to provide a corrective explanation to that approach by considering cultural, economic and political factors. Correctly explaining the connection between culture and politics, Smith explains that nationalism moves the subject people "from isolation to activism, from quietism to mobilization and from culture to politics."[130] Cabral captures the interplay between material and subjective forces and their impact on individual and collective identities. He also challenges both economic and cultural reductionism by demonstrating the dynamic interplay of material and subjective factors in developing revolutionary nationalism.[131]

Failing to grasp this dimension of nationalism and its material and subjective sources leads some scholars to claim that nationalism is a political principle that necessarily attempts to create a congruent political and cultural boundary to let "all nations have their own political roofs, and let all of them also refrain from including non-nationals under it."[132] Ernest Gellner and others who claim that nationalism necessarily attempts to create a congruent political and cultural boundary fail to observe what others have seen from history, that is, that oppressed nationalism is usually or often concerned with democratic and cultural rights, self-determination, and equal access to cultural and economic resources; it is not necessarily aimed at establishing an ethnonational state. Ignoring how despotism, colonialism, racial/ethnonational stratification, and imperialism facilitated the emergence of national movements by denying the subject populations their cultural and democratic rights, Elie Kedourie blames oppressed nationalism and the principles of national self-determination for political instability and wars in the modern world.[133] Since he confuses fascism, racism, and oppressor nationalism with oppressed nationalism of the colonized populations, Kedourie sees all forms of nationalism as an avoidable aberration. He seems to argue that oppressed nations go to wars and cause instability just to create their own respective states rather than living in harmony in multinational states. In reality, it is the lack of democracy, suppression of individual and group rights, cultural repression, and continued subjugation that force subjugated peoples to struggle for their rights, rather than what Gellner and Kedourie suggest.

Some scholars also have argued that ethnonationalism is facilitated by international factors.[134] This position locates the causes of the national struggle in external factors alone and, unfortunately, ignores how a racialized or an ethnicized state contributes to the development of oppressed nationalism by denying democratic and economic rights and by blocking all avenues for expression, thus forcing subjugated nations to engage in national movements. Since colonial and racial/ethnonational domination has reduced subjugated peoples to historical objects by disdaining their respective cultures and revering every aspect of the colonizing cultures, the anticolonial national movement attempts to achieve the cultural liberty and human dignity that are denied by the oppressive social system. According to Cabral, "The value of culture as an element of resistance to foreign domination lies in the fact that culture is the vigorous manifestation on the ideological or idealist plane of the physical and historical reality of the society that is dominated. . . . Culture is simultaneously the fruit of people's history and a determinant of history." [135] Racists and colonialists degraded the history and culture of the colonized to psychologically demoralize and socialize them into submissive free or cheap laborers unable to fight for their rights. National liberation movements emerged to restore "the inalienable right of every people to have their own history," culture, and human dignity that were wounded by racial/ethnonational domination and colonialism.[136]

Cabral notes that "the people are only able to create and develop the liberation movement because they keep their culture alive despite continual and organized repression of their cultural life and because they continue to resist culturally even when their politico-military resistance is destroyed. And it is cultural resistance which, at a given moment, can take on new forms, i.e., political, economic, armed to fight foreign domination."[137] Culture includes the material and nonmaterial aspects of a human group. The colonization of a human group denies dignity that is associated with freedom of development, democracy, free expression, self-respect, worldviews, and choices, and facilitates economic exploitation and underdevelopment. Colonialism impedes the development of productive forces in the colonized society. Cabral sees the national struggle of the colonized people "as the organized political expression of the culture of the people who are undertaking the struggle," and also as "necessarily a proof not only of *identity* but also of *dignity*."[138]

Oppressed nationalism emerges to change the nature of the existing oppressive state or to create a new state. Human groups, territorial or cultural, with the emergence of large-scale and long-term social changes invented or refashioned their respective states to deal with complex issues. Despite the fact that the modern states and their interstate structures are recent inventions, state elites and their supporters portray them as something "natural" that cannot be changed or modified. Bereciartu states that we must "eliminate scholarly myths that, from the perspective of the already-consolidated nation-states, speak to us of the sacred and indivisible unity of nation."[139] Since global political structures change constantly with socioeconomic and large-scale changes, there is not any reason to accept the assumption that the nation-state is the final form of political structure. The nation-state is not sacred; it is divisible or changeable. The same process that facilitated the emergence of the nation-state contributes to the development of oppressed nationalism. The collective grievances of the colonized nations and external factors must be combined in studying and understanding national movements. Recognizing that nationalism is a complex social phenomenon and that it has various forms,[140] the study specifically deals with the national movements of Oromos and African Americans.

Central Organizing Themes

The central theme of the book is that the national struggles of African Americans and Oromos developed in opposition to the racialized or ethnicized forms of state power that developed in the process of global capital accumulation. This form of state power is characterized by racial/ethnonational domination, colonial exploitation, and cultural repression or destruction. The African American and Oromo movements have been struggling to change fundamentally the racialization/ethnicization of state power in the United States and the Ethiopian empire respectively. This comparative study is specifically framed within the context of the modern world system because both African Americans and Oromos lost their rights by this system, and because the same system also produced the sociocultural conditions that facilitated the emergence and development of these two movements. "From an institutional perspective," Skocpol writes, "we should be looking for the cultural and ideological dimensions of *all* institutions, organizations, social groups, and political conflicts, so that we can integrate those dimensions into all aspects of our explanations and accounts of both the roots and outcomes of social revolutions."[141]

This study goes beyond a narrow definition of nationalism and considers the varied forms of struggles taken by the African American and Oromo movements. It touches upon the features of the African American and Oromo national movements as struggles for multicultural democracy, national self-determination, civil rights and social justice, and cultural rights and human dignity. Further, this study relates the African American and Oromo movements to the global forces that struggle to humanize and democratize the world by establishing a single standard for humanity. These issues have set the stage for Chapters II and III. Chapter II explores how Black nationalism developed in opposition to the American racial caste system. It also illustrates the features, causes, and outcomes of this movement. Chapter III introduces the reader to the Oromo people and their national struggle. It addresses the issues of Oromo nationalism—its emergence and development, its characteristics, outcomes, problems, and prospects.

Chapter IV examines the issues of race and racism in relation to U.S. foreign policy and the impact of this policy on the Oromo movement. Chapters III and IV prepare the reader for our comparative analysis. Organizing these chapters in this sequence makes possible close comparison and contrast of these two struggles. Using the comparative-historical and sociological approaches, chapter V compares and contrasts the African American and Oromo movements. All of the previous chapters are interconnected and their points further illustrated in this chapter. Chapter VI deals with the limitation of nationalism and the possibility of expanding the struggles of African Americans and Oromos to revolutionary multicultural democracy by challenging various forms of oppressive relationships and through forming alliances with antiracist, anticolonial, and popular democratic and progressive forces on local, regional, and global levels.

CHAPTER II

The Development of
African American Nationalism

We know through painful experience that freedom is never voluntarily given by the oppressor; it must be demanded by the oppressed.

—Martin Luther King, Jr.[1]

Power in defense of freedom is greater than power in behalf of tyranny and oppression, because power, real power, comes from conviction, which produces action, uncompromising action. It also produces insurrection against oppression. This is the only way you end oppression—with power.

—Malcolm X[2]

Black nationalism,[3] as an ideological, intellectual, political, and cultural manifestation of the African American movement, aimed to challenge American racist capitalist structures and to redefine the relationship between Black and White Americans so that American apartheid could be dismantled and Black America could be liberated and developed. It developed in opposition to White racial and colonial domination, cultural hegemony, exploitation, and poverty. This nationalism manifested itself in three overlapping forms: cultural, reformist and revolutionary. Too much emphasis has been given to its reformist aspect, which is the Civil Rights movement, and the cultural and revolutionary aspects of this movement have been suppressed by the media, politicians, and scholars ideologically, politically, and intellectually. The primary focus on the Civil Rights movement, without integrating it with cultural and revolutionary aspects of this nationalism, has limited our understanding of the Black national movement and its main objectives. The Black struggle for freedom had different forms, ideologies, tactics, and strategies in the nineteenth and twentieth centuries.[4] Over the past 35 years, scholars have dichotomized Black nationalism and the Civil Rights movement by focusing on their strategic and ideological differences and by ignoring the shared objectives of the Black freedom and development movements. Scholars such as Howard Brotz[5] and Harold Cruse[6] originated this dichotomizing tendency by emphasizing civil rights activism and separately focusing on Black nationalism, assuming that these were not related and not aspects of a single African American movement. According to Anthony Smith, "Nationalism . . . involves four elements: a vision, a culture, a solidarity and a policy. It answers to ideological, cultural, social and political aspirations and needs."[7] Since all forms of the Black struggle involved all these issues that Smith mentions, the Civil Rights movement was an integral part of Black nationalism.

The theoretical ideas and historical evidence presented in this chapter suggest a need for reassessment of the African American movement. We cannot understand comprehensively and critically the character of this movement without studying its cultural and revolutionary forms, and how these forms were connected to the Civil Rights movement, the movement that attempted to integrate African Americans into a larger society politically, culturally, and economically. The legal success of the Civil Rights movement had overshadowed the major issues that were raised by Black cultural and revolutionary nationalists. This chapter explores the three forms of the Black national struggle and demonstrates that the Civil Rights movement was an integral part of Black nationalism, a part that cannot be understood adequately by itself. It also reevaluates the features and impact of the Black movement in order to explain the complex problems of the Black community in America.

Redefining African American Nationalism

As the enslavement of Africans occurred in global capitalism, their struggle for liberation also developed as a part of the struggle of the enslaved and colonized ethnonational groups in the racialized capitalist world system. Through colonial expansion and racial slavery, global capitalism brought together various European, African, and indigenous population groups in a political unit that later became the United States. The European colonialists racialized this political unit to commit genocide and perpetuate the exploitation and oppression of the remaining indigenous Americans and enslaved Africans by establishing racist structures and policies and by denying to these population groups structural assimilation (access to political, economic, and cultural resources) and civil equality. However, the American racist capitalist structures and institutions could not totally crush the African American human spirit and cultural resistance. The creation of a racial caste system (slavery and later segregation) and the denial of structural assimilation and equal citizenship rights to the African American people based on the ideology of racism facilitated the emergence of Black nationalism.

Further, there were subjective and objective factors that dialectically interplayed and contributed to the development of this nationalism. Although the enslaved Africans were de-Africanized to a certain degree, isolated from their cultural roots, deprived of political and economic resources, and eventually dependent on White society, they maintained their cultural resistance and developed their nationalism because of social structural and conjunctural factors that dynamically interplayed with African American human agency. As we will see, the transformation in American social structures due to domestic and global economic and political changes, urbanization, and community formation, the development of indigenous institutions, and the emergence of Black intellectuals who helped politicize collective grievances through producing and disseminating social scientific and political knowledge facilitated the development of Black nationalism.

The literature on the Black struggle does not explain adequately the features and structures of the American racialized capitalist system and the different forms of response to the system by African Americans.[8] Studies of this struggle also fail to address comprehensively and critically the historical and sociological factors that necessitated the development of Black nationalism, the interconnection between the political economy of racism and poverty, and the persistent crises of the African American community. Most scholars in the area of African American studies also fail to explain the different forms of Black nationalism and the relationships among them. Furthermore, these scholars and others do not consider the Civil Rights movement as a form of African American nationalism.[9] This chapter demonstrates that since Civil Rights activists and revolutionary and cultural nationalists struggled for African American freedom, they were an integral part of the Black national movement, a movement that promoted an emancipatory ideological, intellectual, cultural, and political project[10] to challenge the racist capitalist establishment.

The African American movement took a political and cultural action and demanded to deracialize the American state so that African Americans would get equal access to state power and cultural and economic resources or to create an African American state. There is no question that White America delayed the development of Black national leadership for almost three and a half centuries by denying African Americans the opportunities necessary to develop an educated and organized leadership. When slavery was abolished after about two and a half centuries, White society and its institutions developed Jim Crow laws (segregation laws) and practiced apartheid by denying African Americans the structural assimilation that was necessary for upward social mobility. It prevented African Americans from sharing American economic, political, and educational institutions so that they would remain subordinated to and serve the interests of White society as servants and cheap laborers. Although Black nationalism developed as a mass movement in the first half of the twentieth century, it had first emerged in the 1700s.[11] It took almost one and a half centuries for this nationalism to develop and mature.

Within its cultural, ideological, and political components, Black nationalism manifested reformist and revolutionary tendencies. The Civil Rights movement can be seen as a reformist movement since its main objective was to achieve equal citizenship rights for African Americans within the existing social structure so that they would fully and equally participate in American institutions.[12] As the pillar of the Black struggle for freedom and civil equality, this movement focused on dismantling the legal infrastructure of American apartheid. Taking it one step further, the Black revolutionary movement struggled to gain autonomy or independence for Black America so that this people would determine their cultural, economic, and political rights. Practically speaking, both branches of the Black movement for civil equality and human dignity aimed at liberating African Americans from White supremacy, colonial domination, underdevelopment, and poverty. As we shall see, Black cultural nationalism was the foundation of the reformist and revolutionary forms of the African American struggle.

Black intellectual and professional groups established cultural, social, and civil rights organizations in order to engage their people in a political movement to seek civil rights or political power through legal and protest actions. The question of survival requires the colonized or oppressed ethnonation to "take on some of the attributes of nationhood, and adopt a civic model . . . rational political centralization, mass literacy and social mobilization."[13] Different brands of Black nationalists, whether they envisioned integration, separation, or cultural autonomy, struggled for desegregation, human dignity, and true equality.[14] Therefore, it is wrong to consider only those who struggled for separation or cultural autonomy as nationalists since all those who struggled against American apartheid were nationalists. Some revolutionary nationalists also demanded true equal citizenship rights and multicultural democracy that would empower African Americans. "Behind the revolutionary phrases of the black power militants," August Meier and Elliot Rudwick comment, "is usually a profound desire for an equal share and an equal status in American society."[15] Almost all scholars who have studied the Black struggle have not recognized the existence of different ways to be a Black nationalist. Whether they openly declared themselves as nationalists or not, all Blacks who fought for freedom, democracy, human dignity, and true equality are considered nationalists for the purpose of this analysis. Let us locate our discussion in a broad cultural, historical, and theoretical context.

The Foundation of Black Peoplehood and Nationalism

Without locating the enslavement, exploitation, and oppression of enslaved Africans and their struggle for emancipation in the context of the racialized capitalist world system, we cannot understand adequately the chains of historical and sociological factors that facilitated the emergence and development of their African American peoplehood and nationalism. The European-dominated capitalist world economy developed in Western Europe and then expanded to America and Africa and incorporated them throughout the sixteenth and seventeenth centuries. In this process of incorporation, some enslaved Africans were brought to America as slaves "to mine precious metals and to develop systems of mass crop production, which provided raw materials for European manufacturers."[16] According to Clovis E. Semmes, "The resulting triangular relationship between Europe, Africa, and the Americas gave a tremendous stimulus to Western capitalism and Europe's industrial revolution, while dooming African peoples to underdevelopment and dependency."[17] Racial slavery turned these Africans into commodities, robbed their humanity, and denied all forms of freedom for almost two and a half centuries.[18]

The collective identity of African American peoplehood developed as a response to the processes of racial slavery and cultural repression. The social construction of African American peoplehood did not take place in a vacuum, but occurred through revitalizing African cultural resources that had been carried over from Africa to America and through borrowing cultural elements from Native Americans and Europeans. The Africans who were captured by African and European slave hunters from different African ethnonational groups and shipped to America did not have a common culture, language, religion, and history when they arrived in North America as slaves. Sterling Stuckey notes that "slave ships were the first real incubators of slave unity across cultural lines, cruelly revealing irreducible links from one ethnic group to the other, fostering resistance thousands of miles before the shores of the new land appeared on the horizon."[19] The African American peoplehood was formed from the melting pot of various African and other ethnonational groups in America. Despite the fact that White slavers made various efforts to break existing social and cultural bonds and to prevent the formation of solidarity among enslaved Africans, they could not stop the development of the African American peoplehood and nationalism. Enslaved Africans developed their peoplehood and cultural resistance despite the fact that slavers and their institutions separated families and relatives and suppressed cultural communications among them.

African Americans are not a racial group, but rather an ethnonational group that developed through the imposition of the process of White cultural domination and racial oppression.[20] Martin Delaney called them "*a nation in themselves.*"[21] [original author's emphasis] The formation of the African American ethnonational group indicates how the boundaries of peoplehood can change depending on the sociopolitical milieu and basic structural features. Explaining similar conditions, Immanuel Wallerstein asserts that the group was "in no sense a primordial stable social reality, but a complex, clay-like historical product of the capitalist world-economy through which the antagonistic forces struggle with each other. We can never do away with peoplehood in this system nor relegate it to a minor role."[22] (However, as we will see in this book, the Oromo case indicates that peoplehood can develop in a precapitalist social formation.) The African American peoplehood developed in the racialized capitalist world system in general and that of America in particular.

Most enslaved Africans resisted slavery in many ways and kept their lingering memory of resistance in their minds and expressed it in folktales and other cultural activities: "That memory enabled them to go back to the sense of community in the traditional African setting and to include all Africans in their common experience of oppression in North America," and "tales of the traumatizing experience of the middle passage—as the voyage of a slave ship was called—have been retained in the folk memory" of African Americans.[23] Wallerstein notes that "pastness is central to and inherent in the concept of peoplehood. . . . Pastness is a central element in the socialization of individuals, in the maintenance of group solidarity, in the establishment of or challenge to social legitimation. Pastness therefore is preeminently a moral phenomenon, therefore a political phenomenon, always a contemporary phenomenon."[24] Without learning about the accumulated knowledge of the African American past, our understanding of African American peoplehood and nationalism is incomplete.

It is paradoxical that although the slaveowning class had firm control over the bodies of the enslaved Africans, they could not control their minds. As a result, this class and its institutions could not totally destroy African cultural elements that were engraved in the minds of these slaves. Stuckey notes that "for the slave, the retention of important features of the African cultural heritage provided a means by which the new reality could be interpreted and spiritual needs at least partially met, needs often regarded as secular by whites but often considered as sacred to blacks."[25] There is a large and rich literature that addresses the preservation of African cultural elements and the impact of these cultural elements on the formation of African American peoplehood.[26] African folktales and beliefs, linguistic forms and structures, religious philosophy, carving and sculpturing techniques in folk arts, and other cultural elements had been carried over from Africa to the United States by enslaved Africans and to a certain degree were preserved by the people of African descent. Scholars such as Carter G. Woodson have documented the survival of African cultural elements in forms of religion, music, dance, drama, poetry, oratory, technical skills, folklore, spirituality, attitudes toward authority, and a tradition of generosity.[27] The African American peoplehood was mainly formed through the merging of these several African cultural elements and identities.

The study of oral history and folklore reveal the extent of African cultural retention in some African American communities.[28] Other scholars have explored the impact of African languages on African American English and showed African linguistic retention.[29] For instance, Lorenzo Turner demonstrates how African linguistic elements are maintained in African Americans' speech, and Molefi Kete Asante explains how Blacks have retained certain African communication styles and linguistic structures.[30] Further, the exploration of African American kinship, ethnicity, family, linguistic forms, and other areas show African cultural retention.[31] These cultural elements helped Africans to maintain their cultural and historical memory and struggle to survive in the oppressive and degrading conditions in which they found themselves. By examining African American cultural elements in colonial America, Peter W. Wood demonstrates African contributions to medical practices, basketry weaving, agriculture and animal husbandry (such as cattle breeding, open grazing, rice cultivation), boat building, hunting, trapping, and fishing.[32] These cultural skills enabled Africans to carve a cultural space for themselves. In fact, Africans not only saved some elements of their African heritage, but they also influenced White Americans whenever they could. By going beyond the question of African cultural retention, John Edward Philips demonstrates how Africanisms influenced White American culture and provides some evidence from areas of agriculture, folklore, linguistics, religion, music, and cooking; he calls these cultural influences of Africans on White Americans "white Africanisms."[33] Enslaved Africans outnumbered their White owners in the South and influenced American culture through their music and dance, and their folk tales and religions.[34]

Enslaved Africans retained their African heritage and did not become totally acculturated: "But the possibility that whites might discover the guiding principles of African culture kept blacks on guard and led them, to an astonishing degree, to keep the essentials of their culture from view, thereby making it possible for them to continue to practice values proper to them. Such secretiveness was dictated by the realities of oppression and worked against whites acquiring knowledge of slave culture that might have been used to attempt to eradicate that culture."[35] While they knew that they came from different ethnonational backgrounds, enslaved Africans intentionally struggled to form a single people while resisting slavery and White cultural domination. Proto-African "nationalism provided the thrust toward autonomy, for diverse African peoples were represented and bent their efforts in pursuit of independence from their oppressors."[36] They were conscious of their Africanness, and when they created their separate church in 1821 in Charleston, they called it the African Church. One of their songs in 1816 in Charleston reflects their nationalist consciousness and recognition of Africa:

> Hail! all hail! Ye Afric clan
> Hail! Ye oppressed, ye Afric band,
> Who toil and sweat in slavery bound
> And when your health and strength are gone
> Are left to hunger and to mourn
> *Let independence be your aim,*
> Every mindful what 'tis worth.
> Pledge your bodies for the prize,
> Pile them even to the skies![37]

In an attempt to de-Africanize and depersonalize enslaved Africans, the slaveowning class called them "Negro" or "Nigger" in an attempt to erase Africanness and African culture. Despite the fact that since the thirteenth century the name *African* had been used to identify African people, White Americans called enslaved Africans *Negro* by borrowing the Spanish word meaning "black."[38] In this way, the color of their skin became their collective name, although African American "religious and educational organizations used the prefix *African* in their names, providing a sense of cultural integrity and a link to their African heritage."[39] At the turn of the nineteenth century, African Americans who worked as house servants as well as those who had European and African heritages called themselves "colored" to distinguish themselves from those Africans who worked in the field.[40] When the American Colonization Society intensified its racist activities to get rid of free Africans by returning them to Africa, the term *colored* was almost accepted by African American leaders to fight the plan of this society.[41] In this case, *colored* was used for a practical reason. These Africans used this name to disassociate themselves from Africa so that they would not be considered Africans and forced to immigrate to Africa.

Many names were designated to refer to this people in the nineteenth century including Negro, Nigger, colored, brown, African, Ethiopian, Free African, Children of Africa, Sons of Africa, people of color, Colored American, free people of color, Blacks, Anglo African, Afric, African-American, Afro-American, Afmerican, Aframerican, Africo-American, and Afro-Saxon.[42] According to Joseph E. Holloway, the debate over the name "has come to full circle, from *African* through *brown, colored, Afro-American, Negro,* and *black* back to *African,* the term originally used by blacks in America to define themselves. The changes in terminology reflect many changes in attitude, from strong African identification to nationalism, integration, and attempts at assimilation back to cultural identification. This struggle to reshape and define blackness in both the concrete and the abstract also reflects the renewed pride of black people in shaping a future based on the concept of one African people living in the African diaspora."[43] Stuckey suggests that "the crisis over names—like the larger identity crisis—was symbolized by the mark branded into thousands of Africans at the start of slavery. The branding iron proved two-edged, searing into the slave's consciousness and an awareness that his identity was under attack and triggering a recoil from the attempt to depersonalize that lasted, for large numbers of slaves, throughout history. . . . We must understand the African background to appreciate the emotional force behind the names controversy, the cultural loss and confusion it reflects, and the spiritual pain of those engaged in the controversy."[44]

Despite the fact that "the experience of domination has shaped and continues to shape the development of African Americans,"[45] the study of their issues should not be limited to racial oppression and economic exploitation and must explore the cultural process that dialectically connects social organizations with culture and affects institutional development. There is no doubt that slavery and cultural destruction debilitated African social organizations and dwarfed their institutional development for almost two and a half centuries. Plantation owners and their institutions imposed an alien cultural form on enslaved Africans and negated their cultures and histories. The efficient exploitation and social control of African labor required the destruction of African cultures and languages through imposing European cultural hegemony.[46] Clovis E. Semmes notes that cultural and historical "negation and distortion became central to the process of domination in order to weaken the ability of the victimized people to sustain a self-conscious and self-directed sense of origin, evolution, and purpose. The need was to force the victim to relinquish internal control (independence) in order to accept external control (dependence)."[47] Although Africans and Europeans both had influenced the formation of American culture since they arrived in America at the same time,[48] African Americans lacked "institutional power that would give them the ability to define and express their cultural needs and goals."[49]

The dominant group always attempts to impose its cultural hegemony on the dominated group so that the oppressed sustains its own oppression and exploitation by accepting the worldview of the former.[50] In addition to using physical violence in an attempt to shift the perspective of enslaved Africans, plantation owners and their institutions systematically attacked various African cultures, languages, and religions to replace them with European culture, Christianity, and languages. European Christianity "was central to the symbol of imperialism that became a foundation for the establishment of cultural hegemony."[51] When African languages and religions were systematically suppressed, enslaved Africans recognized that they were not allowed to practice their African heritages or to express memories of an African past. They were intentionally cut from their own historical roots so that their perspective would change to that of their oppressors. Cultural domination shifts the perspective of the dominated to that of the dominating structure and legitimizes the worldview of the oppressor and naturalizes subordination as a normative order. In this process the subordinated group accepts the worldview, historiography, sacred beliefs, knowledge, and social relationships that are defined by the dominating structure. White cultural domination negated Black self-development through limiting the intellectual and material production of African Americans; it introduced self-hatred and an inferiority complex, and it subordinated the Black world to that of White, promoting "efficient social control through differentiating a system of slave overseers and leaders selected and legitimated by the slave owners."[52] The slaveowning class used slaves to control those Africans who resisted slavery; those slaves who were totally de-centered became the tools of the slaveowning class and promoted the worldview of the dominant group.[53]

There is no question that, although not totally, African Americans were shaken from their cultural foundations through the imposition of White cultural domination. "The cataclysmic experience of chattel slavery, the basis of cultural hegemony," Semmes writes, "produced historical discontinuity and preempted normative cultural building through a decentering process."[54] However, without the total liquidation of the dominated people, it is impossible for the dominant group to completely de-center the perspective of the dominated group and stop its cultural resistance and revitalization.[55] Hence, short of the total destruction of enslaved Africans, plantation owners and their institutions could not eliminate African cultures. The same processes of oppression, exploitation, and cultural suppression that forced them to move from their African center also produced the conditions for the emergence of an African-centered consciousness. I agree with Semmes that "even though catastrophic oppression brought about a process of objectification and dehumanization, the absolute negation of humanity was not possible because a damaged human spirit seeks to resurrect and reconstruct itself; it also seeks self-consciousness. Culture building may be impeded, but it does not stop. Consequently, reconstruction involves renewed historiography and reflectivity."[56]

Culture provides a collective consciousness and a common center for every people through which and from which they observe their universe and understand others in terms of how they understand themselves and other phenomena external to their shared experience. The submerged African cultural elements and the common experience of oppression laid the foundation of African American culture that became the tool of resistance. "Social and revitalization movements," Semmes writes, "as well as the outpourings of creative intellectuals and artists, reflect varying degrees of a conscious and unconscious response to this [dehumanizing] problem [in order] to rehumanize one's existence and to transcend the dehabilitating and destructive capabilities of cultural hegemony."[57] Racial slavery, an ultimate denial of human freedom, and cultural hegemony could not destroy the cultural resistance and humanity of African Americans despite their destructive and enduring capabilities.

Although it took almost three centuries to blossom, African American protonationalism emerged with slavery: "The nationalism of the slave community was essentially African nationalism, consisting of values that bound slaves together and sustained them under brutal conditions of oppression. Their very effort to bridge ethnic differences and to form themselves into a single people to meet the challenge of a common foe proceeded from an impulse that was Pan-African—that grew out of a concern for all Africans—as what was useful was appropriated from a multiplicity of African groups even as an effort was made to eliminate distinctions among them."[58] Explaining how the ideology of Black nationalism was initially fashioned, Stuckey comments, "A conscious of a shared experience of oppression at the hands of white people, an awareness and approval of the persistence of group traits and preferences in spite of a violent anti-African larger society, a recognition of bonds and obligations between Africans everywhere, an irreducible conviction that Africans in America must take responsibility for liberating themselves—these were among the pivotal components of the world view of the black men [and women] who finally framed the ideology."[59] Despite the fact that White plantation owners and institutions and White society were determined to destroy African cultural elements and bonds to maintain tight control on enslaved and freed Africans, these Africans knew that it was essential to maintain their cultural solidarity and resistance to liberate themselves.

African American protonationalism attempted to challenge slavery and the cultural hegemony that had shaken the cultural foundation of enslaved Africans so that they would resist a world defined by their oppressor. Christianity that was imposed "to sustain a social order and a system of production based on the mutual cooperation of master and slave" became the arena of the struggle since it denied African Americans humanity by perpetuating slavery.[60] It became the religion of domination for White society and the religion of liberation for Blacks: "African Americans, slave and free, began to rediscover symbolic foundations for a redemptive African-centered consciousness. The irony of this discovery is that it occurred as a consequence of interpreting the biblical messages that were intended to bring conformity and docility. African American exegesis of biblical scriptures became the foundation for the rebirth of African-centered thought. Instead of learning to be good slaves by forgetting about Africa, some African Americans realized that many of the places discussed in the sacred text held in so high esteem by white oppressors were in Africa and that many of the people were quite properly African."[61]

When European and American racist scholarship distorted the social sciences and historiography to produce and preserve the myth of White superiority and African inferiority, "a countervailing struggle emerged to transcend the cognitive slavery of white supremacy."[62] In this process, an African-centered intellectual discourse emerged as the knowledge of liberation. African American scholarship that challenged White racism by straightening historical records was "based initially on African American historical research that established an African frame of reference, began in the early nineteenth century, reached maturity in the 1890s, and has continued with episodic prominence to the present."[63] African American intellectuals, such as Alexander Crummell, Robert A. Young, David Walker, Henry H. Garnet, Martin Delaney, and Frederick Douglass, mainly struggled in the North before 1860 for the end of racial slavery and freedom on cultural, intellectual, and political levels and laid the foundation of African American nationalism. The main issues that were raised and addressed by such scholars included the centrality of Africans to human groups, the antiquity of African civilizations, and the presence of Africans in Asia, Europe, and America before the modern era.[64] Slavery was seen as a temporary defeat and African civilizations were rediscovered through challenging the myth of White superiority and racist intellectual discourse. According to Stuckey, originally "Robert Alexander Young and David Walker speculated on the status of African peoples in a way which broke beyond the shackles which America sought to impose on the African mind. They created black nationalist ideology."[65] African-centered scholarship expanded during the Harlem Renaissance of the 1920s. During this decade, many African Americans overcame feelings of inferiority to a certain degree, became self-conscious, and intensified humanistic self-definition.

The Racialized Capitalist World System and Human Agency

The racialized capitalist world system incorporated the world populations primarily through two types of labor recruitment systems: wage labor and coerced labor (slavery).[66] The ancestors of African Americans were incorporated into this system through racial slavery. These enslaved Africans were forced to provide their labor freely to build American capitalism without getting any benefit for their generation and next generations. However, European workers who were incorporated into the capitalist system as wage laborers had better opportunities both in Europe and America because they had limited autonomy over their lives even if they were exploited by capitalists. Although they did not have equal access to major economic, political, and cultural institutions with elites and capitalists because of their class position, they had limited access to institutions that allowed them to have intergenerational upward mobility. For instance, diverse European immigrants who were indentured servants during colonial America became wage laborers after the American Revolution and obtained upward mobility, while African Americans were chained in the racial caste system for almost three and a half centuries (slavery and segregation).

Even with their emancipation during and after the American Civil War, African Americans were denied access to the cultural, economic, and political gains made during their abuse in the period of American apartheid. The denial was enforced through the criminal justice system and mob lynching. Those African Americans who obtained their freedom from slavery during the American Revolution and before the American Civil War were kept in the status of semislaves. They remained at the bottom of White society, were subjected to all kinds of abuses, and were seen as "slaves without masters."[67] According to Ira Berlin, "Segregation, black codes, the convict-lease system, and the various forms of peonage usually associated with the postbellum South all victimized the antebellum free Negro caste."[68]

The conditions of racial slavery, White cultural hegemony, segregation, and colonial domination were not enough to facilitate the development of Black nationalism. They were only the historical foundations of collective grievances from which this nationalism developed when other necessary conditions emerged. Scattered resistance and rebellions of slaves must not be confused with nationalism, but they were necessary foundations for the emergence of Black nationalism. They were chains of historical and sociological factors that led to the development of African American nationalism in the first half of the twentieth century. Racial slavery kept African Americans under the domination of White plantation owners. W. H. McClendon notes that racial slavery "was unwavering in its aggressiveness and determination to have blacks accept servitude without resistance. Black passivity was the theme of the slaves' socialization process."[69] Racial slavery imposed upon them a cultural hegemony by negating their cultural personality, and "the cultures of African peoples became . . . objects to be dismantled for the purpose of more efficient exploitation and control."[70] In order to change the African mindset and perspective through the imposition of cultural hegemony, enslaved Africans were forced to learn English and to accept Christianity, in the process discarding their African languages and religions.

Although this forced cultural assimilation had serious negative consequences for these Africans, they gradually learned how to reorganize these new cultural values and practices according to their new conditions. Further, this forced cultural assimilation could not totally eliminate the heritage of enslaved Africans. One important heritage of African Americans was the resistance struggle that they began against African and European slave hunters in the African hinterlands, on slave ships, and later on the plantations in the colonies as slave mutinies.[71] Some slaves spontaneously and culturally opposed slavery through day-to-day defiance, flight, and armed resistance.[72]

Discussing how slaves resisted in North America, John H. Clarke expounds that African culture "sustained the Africans during the holocaust of the slave trade and the colonial system that followed it . . . African culture, reborn on alien soil, became the cohesive force and the communication system that helped to set in motion some of the most successful slave revolts in history."[73] There were about 250 slave rebellions in the United States.[74] There were about 50 maroon communities formed by thousands of runaway slaves and their descendants between 1672 and 1864 in the forests and mountains of southern states.[75] Since most African Americans never accepted slavery, there were group arson attempts, runaways, violence against masters, and group attempts to organize rebellions.[76] According to St. Clair Drake, "The first 250 years of African impact on North America were years of struggle to restore freedom and to retain an African identity."[77]

Leon Litwack estimated that five thousand African Americans from the North fought for American independence.[78] Some former slaves who were freed between the American Revolution (1776) and the Civil War (1861–1865) with the support of a few antislavery Whites[79] struggled relentlessly also to liberate their fellow Africans from slavery.[80] A few former slaves and their descendants built independent organizations and religious institutions: The establishments of the Free African Society in Newport, Rhode Island and Philadelphia; the formation of the first Negro Baptist Church at Silver Bluff, South Carolina; and the African Methodist Episcopal Church; and the emergence of the National Negro Convention and separate antislavery societies, such as the Colored Female Anti-Slavery Society of Rochester, were the forerunners of Black nationalist institutions.[81] Rhoda Golden Freeman comments that "a group of active . . . highly intelligent Negro men [and women] worked unceasingly for full citizenship as indication of their belief in potential realization of the American ideal of equal opportunity for all."[82] Some free Blacks established independent churches, schools, and fraternal organizations in cities to worship, educate their children, protect themselves, and revitalize African culture. The freed men and women and their descendants continued to struggle after the abolition of slavery through building independent churches, mutual benefit societies, the press, and different movements.[83]

As the country that is called the United States today moved from colonial America to an independent country after the American Revolution, as it developed from an agrarian society to an industrial one and from a semiperiphery status to a world power, new political opportunities were created by emerging structural factors for an embryonic African American movement. As we will see in chapter V, the American Civil War, which resulted from the contradiction between core capitalism in the American North and slave-based peripheral capitalism in the American South and the disagreement on the strategy of national development between the northern and southern politicians, led to the end of racial slavery. The end of racial slavery and the intervention of the federal government in state policies on the side of former slaves between 1865 and 1877 created new hopes and opportunities. But after 1877 the federal government allowed the emergence of a new racial caste system called American apartheid to continue to deny African Americans structural assimilation and civil equality.

There were historical and immediate factors for the development of African American nationalism. The Anglo-American ruling class initiated two stratification systems with the emergence of colonial America: the class system and the racial caste system.[84] The systems flourished after the American Revolution, which legalized racism and racial slavery and eliminated or reduced indentured servitude. The class system was designed for White America while the racial caste system was mainly created for Black America. The class system allowed generational and intergenerational upward mobility for most children of poor whites. Because of this, most Whites gradually improved their economic and political positions in American society. While most White children got access to education to improve their social status, Black children were denied education and forced to remain illiterate and poor for many centuries. Discussing the impacts of such economic injustices, Richard F. America says, "Those injustices produced wrongful benefits that have been passed on to the present day, creating an imbalance that has damaged economic performance and caused social instability."[85]

While racial slavery and segregation denied African Americans the fruit of their labor, the class system allowed the White working class to obtain wages for its labor. By denying generational and intergenerational mobility, the racial caste system robbed Blacks of cultural and economic capital that was prerequisite for social development. After racial slavery was abolished, the White plantation owners "tried to consolidate their control by a modified version of the wage labor system in which they would organize gangs of wage laborers to work under overseers, as under slavery. Planters attempted to act in concert to keep wages down, but blacks refused to cooperate with this system which so resembled slavery."[86] They were denied access to public facilities. In American cities, European immigrants worked in the manufacturing and government sectors that provided high social mobility and better working conditions. These new immigrants kept the Blacks segregated by joining all-White labor unions.

Despite the fact that the Blacks contributed without gains to transforming America from an agrarian society to an industrial one, and from a British colony to a world power, they were kept at the bottom of White society by brutal violence, segregation, and racism until the 1950s and the 1960s, when they intensified their freedom movement. To impose cultural dominance, White southerners made the education of Blacks illegal. They considered "schools dangerous and revolutionary."[87] In 1860, less than 3 percent of African Americans were literate in the South.[88] Before the Civil War, only 28 African Americans were graduated from colleges and universities with bachelor degrees; in 1895 there were 1,100 Blacks who were college graduates.[89] Political and economic "modernization" during the last decades of the nineteenth century and the first half of the twentieth century transformed America from agrarian to industrial capitalism. These politico-economic changes created new conditions for racial relations.[90] The federal government engaged in what historians call the First Reconstruction (1865–1877) by sponsoring, with northern missionary societies, the establishment of Black higher educational institutions. Both the Freedmen's Bureau and northern missionary groups laid the foundation for the major colleges and universities, such as Atlanta, Howard, Morehouse, Dillard, Leland, Shaw, Fisk, and Hampton Institute.[91]

There were a few colleges founded before and after the American Civil War; for instance, Lincoln University was established in 1854 in Pennsylvania by the Presbyterian Church, and Wilberforce University was established in 1856 in Ohio by the Methodist Episcopal Church. Furthermore, African American religious institutions created schools, and between 1865 and 1869 in North Carolina, for instance, Black churches established 257 schools.[92] Although the Freedmen's Bureau coordinated and financed schools in cooperation with the educational activities of northern missionary groups, it was the northern missionaries that developed a formal system of schools and colleges for Blacks in the South. J. B. Roebuck and K. S. Murty demonstrate that "several benevolent societies sent missionaries into the South to uplift the freed slaves and their children through religion, education, and material assistance. The AMA [American Missionary Association] alone was responsible for founding seven black colleges and thirteen normal schools between 1861 and 1870."[93]

Furthermore, African Americans had a very strong commitment to educate themselves despite White hostility. They formed societies, raised money, and founded private schools. According to Roebuck and Murty, "After 1865, they formed a network of so-called Sabbath schools (also called African schools . . .) which were in session throughout the week. Classes in these and other private self-supported elementary African schools met in church basements, private homes, warehouses, pool rooms, and shacks. . . . Blacks desired to take full advantage of their freedom; to them, education, religion, and property were the means to gain personal respect, economic security, and social progress."[94] With the help of northern churches and missionary societies and the Freedmen's Bureau, more than two hundred Black private institutions were founded in the South between 1865 and 1890.[95] After the Freedmen's Bureau was dissolved in 1877, a number of philanthropic foundations joined missionary agencies in funding schools in the South. However, these philanthropic organizations never attempted to challenge White supremacy and financed programs that mainly benefited White society.[96] With the establishment of Black schools and colleges, professional and intellectual groups emerged and began to transform scattered resistance into the Black national movement.

Former slaves were not given the "forty acres [of land] and a mule" each that they were promised during the American Civil War; the system of segregation was legalized and institutionalized by the 1896 *Plessy v. Ferguson* Supreme Court decision that accepted the racist philosophy of "separate but equal." The federal government legally sanctioned the separation and exclusion of African Americans from cultural, political, and economic opportunities. This segregation denied Blacks citizenship rights that were provided with the Emancipation Proclamation by the thirteenth, fourteenth (assured due process), and fifteenth (extended franchise to Black males) amendments. Commenting on these conditions, Martin Luther King, Jr. wrote: "The pen of the Great Emancipator had moved the Negro [*sic*] into the sunlight of physical freedom, but actual conditions had left him behind in the shadow of political, psychological, social, economic and intellectual bondage."[97]

The federal government later abandoned its reformist policies of the First Reconstruction and allowed the emergence of White terrorist organizations, such as Ku Klux Klan, the Knights of Camellia, and the White League of Louisiana, which were determined to reestablish White supremacy. Southern Whites developed Black codes to disenfranchise and control African Americans. All Blacks were seen as servants by Whites. Whites for whom they worked were seen as masters. Black workers were not allowed to leave the premises without permission. They were only allowed to work as farm and domestic workers. They were not allowed to join the militia or possess firearms. African Americans needed special license to preach. They were not permitted to negatively react to Whites even if they were abused, insulted, hurt, or beaten. They were not allowed to testify against Whites. Black men were not allowed to look at White women.

White America enforced these Jim Crow laws through primitive kinds of social control, such as lynching, torture, terror, mutilation, rape, castration, and imprisonment. There were Black men, women, and children who were burned alive. Other Black men were castrated with axes or knives, or blinded with hot pokers or decapitated. Furthermore, African Americans were denied equal citizenship and suffrage rights. They were excluded from public facilities and the American political process by different measures, such as the poll tax, residential requirements, insufficient literacy to interpret a section of the Constitution, the "good character" test, registration procedures implemented through trickery, criminal records, having to produce a responsible White witness for worthiness, the "grandfather Clause,"[98] an all-White primary, and intimidation and violence. All these conditions and economic factors forced them to migrate to urban areas.

Migration, Urban Community Formation, and Nationalism

The great migration of African Americans from rural America to urban America and from the South to the North occurred between 1915 and 1960, when about five million of them moved due to economic problems, political and social repression.[99] Nicholas Lemann notes that this "migration was one of the largest and most rapid mass internal movements of people in history."[100] This great migration was seen by some scholars as the search for political and economic freedom. For example, Alferdteen Harrison argues that "the cause for the 'Great Migration' was the African-American's continuing pilgrimage in search of an acceptable status in America . . . because the status of the African-American as a slave and then as a 'Jim Crow' citizen were unacceptable, the migration was a continuation of the search."[101] Neil R. McMillen also considers this migration a "black protest against the outrages of lynching and injustice in the courts, protest against white notions of black character . . . protest against the disfranchisement, the discrimination, the exclusion, and the segregation that defined the black place in what was then often called 'a Whiteman's country.'"[102] The "push" factors for the migration were the reduction of the demand for Black labor due to the mechanization of agriculture and the competition with White labor, and lack of adequate income for Black tenant farmers, sharecroppers and farm laborers, and unequal financial support for White and Black schools, political abuses, and lynching.

Further, the invention of the mechanical cotton picker made obsolete the sharecropper system and reduced the demand for Black labor in agriculture. "The invention of the cotton picker," Lemann writes, "was crucial to the great migration by blacks from the Southern countryside to the cities of the South, the West, and the North."[103] Employment opportunities due to industrial expansion, the decline of emigration from Europe during World War I, and the shortage of workers in the war industries were the "pull" factors from the North.[104] This migration brought scattered people together in American ghettos to form social, geographical, and political communities. The development of Black nationalism was mainly facilitated by the massive migration of the Black people from rural to urban America, the emergence of the independent Black church, mosque and affiliated schools, the emergence of the educated class, and the formation of associations, and organizations. Further, the migration of other Blacks from the Caribbean and other places contributed to the development of African American nationalism.[105] For instance, as we will see below, Marcus Garvey and other Caribbean scholar activists and the workers who immigrated to the United States contributed a lot to the development of this nationalism.

Until the 1950s the base of a Black struggle was mainly in northern cities where African Americans enjoyed relative freedom of action because of their established communities and independent institutions and organizations. Out of 75 percent of rural African Americans, nine-tenths lived in the American South at the opening of the twentieth century under the total control of American apartheid and could not take organized political action.[106] In urban areas, African Americans were also confronted by racial segregation that disappointed and frustrated them. According to Kenneth B. Clark, "The dark ghetto's invisible walls have been erected by the white society, by those who have power, both to confine those who have no power and to perpetuate their powerlessness. The dark ghettos are social, political, educational, and—above all—economic colonies. Their inhabitants are subject peoples, victims of the greed, cruelty, insensitivity, guilt, and fear of their masters."[107] Before the great migration, race was mainly a Southern issue, but this migration "made race a national issue in the second half of the century—an integral part of the politics, the social thought, and the organization of ordinary life in the United States."[108]

The African Americans' main survival strategy in cities was the building of independent religious, economic, and social institutions. Black churches served as economic, social, educational, and recreational institutions. African American religious leaders emerged as educators and cultural and political leaders in the newly-emerging African American community. Various voluntary organizations helped in promoting and defending African American interests in economic, cultural, political, and educational arenas. Lennox Yearwood argues that these organizations "provided a major source of information and communication germane to the survival of urban Black communities. Organizations contributed to the social development of these communities in that they created some equilibrium, keeping ostracism from becoming total isolation. They provided avenues for challenge and competitiveness, and furnished opportunities for the development of individual and group public image."[109]

These mass-based associations and organizations became the main building blocks for African American nationalism. "For what we call nationalism operates on many levels," Anthony Smith writes, "and may be regarded as a form of culture as much as a species of political ideology and social movement."[110] Based on their own economic and cultural resources, African American nationalists recognized and emphasized the beauty of their blackness, the richness of their African and American traditions, and their stamina under the most deplorable and cruel racist system. Despite the fact that the ghetto has been the center of poverty and underdevelopment in affluent America, it brought Blacks together as an ethnonational community to build African American institutions, organizations, and cultural centers.[111] With the great migration the character of Black culture was transformed.[112] As we will see shortly, through Pan-Africanism, the Garvey Movement, and the Harlem Renaissance, African American culture started to reflect national and international characteristics.

The African American people widely formed their own geographical and social communities by creating institutions that became the fountains from which African American nationalism developed. African American nationalism had unleashed the potential, power, and humanity of the Black people who were suppressed by the American racial caste system. This nationalism "as a refutation of the racial ideology of slavery and segregation," James Turner writes, "is a direct challenge to white supremacy."[113] Collective grievances, political and economic modernization, urbanization, the expansion of independent institutions and organizations, and the consolidation of an educated class facilitated the development of Black nationalism. This nationalism manifested itself in three overlapping and interconnected forms.

Three Forms of African American Nationalism

Black nationalism cumulatively raised three important interrelated objectives: the redefinition of Black cultural identity, the liberation of Blacks from the racial caste system, and the economic, the political, and cultural transformation of the Black community. The objectives of Black nationalism manifested themselves in three overlapping historical forms that can be analytically separated. The first form of African American nationalism was manifested in cultural revitalization. The second form of this nationalism dealt with the issues of racial equality, citizenship rights, and social justice. This aspect of the Black national movement is popularly known as the Civil Rights movement. The third form of African American nationalism went beyond civil rights issues and attempted to address economic, political, and cultural rights that would allow the Black people to determine their historical destiny as people. This was the aspect of revolutionary nationalism.

Because of the suppression of the cultural and revolutionary aspects of African American nationalism and the lack of long-term cultural and political strategies for the Black community, the questions of cultural self-determination and economic development have not been adequately addressed in the literature on Black nationalism. The cultural and revolutionary forms of Black nationalism must not be ignored, since they in fact facilitated the legal success of the Civil Rights movement. The cultural and revolutionary aspects of Black nationalism were the powerhouses of the African American struggle. Without a cultural base there cannot be nationalism, and without militant revolutionaries there cannot be a fundamental social change since the dominant society always wants to maintain the status quo. Therefore, it is superficial to talk only about the Civil Rights movement without addressing both the cultural and revolutionary forms of the African American movement. Let us specifically look at the three forms of African American movement.

1. Cultural Nationalism: The Foundation of the Black Struggle

Black cultural nationalism has manifested itself in two forms. The first form is progressive, a part of the cultural awakening of resistance, and links cultural claims to structural social change. Another form of this nationalism is regressive, focusing on trivial cultural issues, while turning attention away from challenging the American racist capitalist order. This form of narrow cultural nationalism has at a time played a negative role in the history of the African American liberation struggle. For instance, the attempt to express cultural uniqueness without challenging various oppressive relationships within the African American community and a larger society is an aspect of the negative role of Black cultural nationalism. The glorification of African kings who participated in slavery in order to claim that Blacks had kings like Europeans is another example of trivial cultural nationalism. Our discussion here focuses on the first form of Black cultural nationalism.

African Americans not only lost the fruit of their labor in building America, they were also not allowed to practice some elements of their culture. The Anglo-American ruling class forced upon Blacks some of their cultural elements while denying them primary and secondary structural assimilation to maintain racial boundary mechanisms and impose cultural hegemony.[114] But, at the same time, to eliminate ethnic boundary mechanisms among different European ethnonational groups, the Anglo-American ruling class not only culturally assimilated other Whites, but it also vigorously promoted structural assimilation by allowing the sharing of educational, workplace, residential, political, and public and private facilities. The sharing of public and private facilities gradually led to primary structural assimilation (through close personal interactions) and marital assimilation among all Whites. The Anglo-American ruling class consolidated itself by gradually reducing or eliminating the cultural barriers that existed among all European immigrant groups.

But the Anglo-American ruling class strengthened the contradictions between Whites and Blacks by legalizing slavery, racism, and segregation. The American Constitution provided freedom for poor Whites and accepted Black slavery. That was why Bishop H. Turner said that the Constitution was "a dirty rag, a cheat, a libel and ought to be spit upon by every Negro in the land."[115] Gradually, White Americans, except a few of them, joined hand in hand to impose their racial hegemony on African Americans and others. While Blacks lost some elements of their culture for nothing except humiliation and degradation, White immigrant groups lost their respective native cultures for success and material gains. Most White social scientists and biologists tried their best to use "science" to prove the inferiority of Blacks in order to rationalize and justify their enslavement, segregation, and colonial domination. Bernard M. Magubane asserts that "between 1880 and 1920 at least, American thought lacks any perception of the black as a human being with potentialities for self-determination. Most of the people who wrote about the blacks accepted without question the idea that intelligence and temperament were racially determined and unalterable. They concluded, therefore, that the failure of Reconstruction, the low educational status of the black, his high statistics of crime, disease, and poverty were simply the inevitable consequence of his heredity."[116]

African American cultural nationalism developed in opposition to racist discourse and cultural hegemony. It included African heritage, black beauty, black literary activism, and psychological recovery. According to John H. Bracey, August Meier, and

Elliot Rudwick, "The half-century from about 1880 to 1930 witnessed the flowering of a clear-cut cultural nationalism. It was evident particularly in a rising self-conscious interest in the race's past and in efforts to stimulate a distinctively black literature."[117] Some Black intellectuals challenged racist discourses. The "New Negro" movement promoted the principles of ethnonational self-help, cooperation, ethnic heritage and pride, militancy and determination to struggle for constitutional rights.[118] Gradually, African Americans began to develop a positive attitude about themselves.[119]

Western world racism inflated the values of "Europeanness" and "Whiteness" in areas of civilization, human worth, and culture, and deflated the values of "African-ness" and "Blackness." This was intended to destroy Black cultural identity and Black psyche. Although the negative impact of deculturation and forced Anglo ideology were very serious, through developing their peoplehood and cultural identity, African Americans struggled to rebuild their historical continuity and humanity. Black cultural nationalists gradually challenged the negative images of Africanness and Blackness that were created by the Western world.[120] H. R. Isaacs comments that "transforming a negative into a positive identity, replacing self-rejection of the most literal kind with self-acceptance, has become the task of a whole new generation of black Americans coming up in politically and psychologically changed circumstances."[121] All peoples who have lived under colonialism and subjugation have experienced feelings of infe-riority and have accepted the definition of themselves given to them by their oppres-sors until they have politically and culturally become conscious and have begun to redefine their cultures and histories in their own terms.

All human groups use shared historical origins to define their identities, to defend their interests, and to assure their survival.[122] Gayle Tate notes, "One of the most prodi-gious efforts of Black nationalism was the restoration of the dignity of Afro-Americans through the retrieval of African history. This recovery was important to both the psy-chological and political consciousness of Afro-Americans."[123] Colonial domination dis-torts historical development by denying cultural development to the colonized population.[124] To overcome such historical distortion, the African American people embraced various ideologies in searching for their cultural roots, historical continuity, and development. Explaining the centrality of African civilization and culture to African Americans, Gene Marine says, "many excited blacks have begun to regain a sense of the value of their own past, an understanding of the fact that their roots run as deep and in soil as rich as those of Greeks or the Jews."[125] The three important move-ments that connected them to Africa were Garveyism, Pan-Africanism, and the Harlem Renaissance. According to Magubane, "Garvey's epigrammatic call, Back to Africa, was more a spiritual and psychological emancipation from the pervasive racism which af-flicted the black proletariat at every turn, than an actual effort to get blacks to emigrate. In contrast, the Pan-African Movement represented certain black intellectuals, most of whom could be described as farsighted fighters for black emancipation."[126]

Marcus Garvey brought to African Americans the idea of being themselves with-out imitating White Americans. He taught African Americans that they are Black and African. He convinced the urban Black masses that Africanness and Blackness are not inferior to Whiteness and Europeanness. As a result, the Black physical and cultural beauty and the term African American entered the psyche of Black Americans and be-came the foundation of modern Black nationalism. As King comments, Garvey's "movement attained mass dimensions, and released a powerful emotional response be-cause it touched a truth which had long been dormant in the mind of the Negro.

There was reason to be proud of their heritage as well as of their bitterly won achievement in America."[127] Similarly, the Harlem Renaissance reconnected African Americans to Africa and cultivated Africanization in art and made the Black artist turn to his or her African heritage.[128] The regeneration of Black culture and the ideological connection to Africa through Garveyism, Pan-Africanism, and the Harlem Renaissance manifested cultural, national, and international features of the emerging African American movement.

Exploring the impact of Garveyism, Magubane asserts, "The central theoretical assumption of black nationalism is that before the Negro can be truly free, he must effect a psychic separation from the idea of whiteness; that is, he must stop believing in it so much that he cannot believe in himself. The idea of separation, a part of the ideological armory of the nationalist movement, is a reiteration of this slightly more complex notion, which, by making it concrete puts it in terms the uneducated layman can understand."[129] The development of Black nationalism in the form of cultural awakening matured in the first two decades of the twentieth century. The Harlem Renaissance was "a precursor to the 'black consciousness' strivings of the 1960s."[130] Recognizing its importance, Nathan I. Huggins notes that Harlem became "a capital of the race, a platform from which the new black voice would be heard around the world, an intellectual center of the New Negro."[131] Prominent Black activist scholars, such as W. E. B. Du Bois, James W. Johnson, Marcus Garvey, A. Philip Randolph, Chandler Owen, and Charles S. Johnson, and literary activists, such as Langston Hughes, Claude McKay, Countee Cullen, and Zora Neale Hurston, moved to Harlem and made it a center of Black cultural and intellectual liberation.[132] As Smith asserts, an ethnonational "identity comprises both a cultural and political identity and is located in a political community as well as a cultural one."[133]

As we will see, various organizations emerged and started to build Black political and cultural life in Harlem. If migration provided a geographical and cultural space for Blacks, the Harlem Renaissance enabled them to have an intellectual, political, and a literary platform for the development of Black nationalism.[134] Black cultural revival expanded from its birth place, Harlem, to African American literary and historical circles of other American cities, such as Washington, D.C., Boston, Philadelphia, Baltimore, Los Angeles, and Topeka.[135] The Civil Rights movement evolved from African American cultural, intellectual and political experiences that developed in urban America.

2. The Civil Rights Movement: The Pillar of the Black Movement

The second form of African American nationalism focused on desegregation and civil rights issues. The opening of the last century witnessed African American protest actions in American cities. Although African Americans were less organized, they boycotted trolley car segregation in almost 30 cities, and these boycotts were led by businessmen and clerics.[136] Organized voices of the African American freedom movement, supported by progressive Whites, began to articulate the Black problem during the second half of the twentieth century. The migration movement of Blacks to urban areas, new allies, and the creation of Black institutions facilitated the development of the civil rights struggle.[137] In this process, various organizations and movements emerged. The Niagra Movement was founded in 1905 as the first of these organizations. However, between 1895 and 1915, as we will see, the accomodationist philosophy of Booker T. Washington overshadowed the Black struggle for freedom. The

Niagara Movement was founded by prominent Black leaders to oppose Washington's philosophy and to promote a Black struggle; it was led by W. E. B. Du Bois.

The Niagara Movement was the first modern Black organization that gave an organized forum for the struggle of freedom, equality, and multicultural democracy. It was organized mainly by well-to-do northern and educated urban African Americans. Its members numbered about four hundred.[138] This movement "placed full responsibility for the race problem squarely on the whites"[139] and demanded political freedom and equality and protested for political rights, suffrage, the right to equal treatment in public accommodations and access to equal opportunity. It denounced racial segregation, separate-but-equal racist doctrine, and disenfranchisement laws. The unofficial organ for this movement was a magazine known as *Horizon*.

W. E. B. Du Bois was the most influential opponent of Washington's policy; he severely criticized Washington's emphasis on industrial education at the cost of higher education. Du Bois attacked Washington for asking African Americans to give up the struggle for political power, civil rights, and higher education, and exposed the consequences of his policy that led to further disenfranchisement, civil inferiority, and withdrawal of aid from many Black educational institutions, specifically those offering liberal arts curricula.[140] It was William Monroe Trotter, the editor of the *Boston Guardian,* who convinced and helped Du Bois to attack Washington's policy. He was an uncompromising critic of racial segregation and accommodation and considered Washington "as the agent of oppression."[141] The Niagara Movement was the forerunner of the National Association for the Advancement of Colored People (NAACP).

The NAACP grew out of an interracial conference in 1909 on the Black status. The NAACP was formed by Black intellectual activists such as William Monroe Trotter, W. E. B. Du Bois, the noted antilynching crusader Ida Wells-Barnett, White progressives, and Christian socialists. Meier and Rudwick say, "The interracial character of the NAACP was essential to the success of its early work. The prestige of the names of well-known white progressives . . . gave the agitation for Negro rights better financial support and, more important, a wider audience. Except for Du Bois, who became director of publicity and editor of the Association's organ, the *Crisis,* all of the chief officials were at first white. Several of these white leaders seemed paternalistic and condescending in their dealings with Negro associates in the NAACP."[142] The principal tactics of this protest organization were persuasion, education, and legal action to achieve equal rights for Black Americans.

Another important civil rights organization was the National Urban League, which was founded by conservative Black leaders and White philanthropists in 1911 to improve the conditions of the Black masses in urban America. While the NAACP used legal approaches to fight against American apartheid, the National Urban League used moral persuasion to convince racist businessmen and labor unions not to discriminate against Black workers. Black and White conservatives did not like the legal approach that the NAACP was using to challenge American apartheid. Emphasizing the importance of industrial education, recognizing the potential of receiving financial support for their projects from White philanthropists, accommodationists like Booker T. Washington opposed the view of politically, morally, and legally challenging American apartheid. Born in slavery and educated at Hampton Institute in Virginia, Washington was taught "the doctrine of economic advancement with acceptance of disenfranchisement and with conciliation of the white South," and his ideology and strategy could not go beyond that of the racist White establishment.[143] He founded and became the principal of Tuskegee Institute, an industrial school in Alabama, and developed a "program of agriculture and industrial training that would make the education of Negroes palatable to the dominant elements of the New South."[144]

Washington internalized the notion of accommodation and emerged as an opportunist and pragmatist leader. Hence, he was favored by the White establishment. As a result, he became a rich man from the money he obtained from his White mentors and established Tuskegee Institute. Ignoring the importance of higher and liberal education for African Americans, Washington said, "Cast it down in agriculture, mechanics, in commerce, in domestic service, and the profession . . . it is in the South that the Negro is given a man's chance in the commercial world."[145] He publicly attacked the struggle for equality and citizenship rights: "The wisest among my race understand that the agitation of questions of social equality is the extremist folly, and the progress in the enjoyment of all the privileges that will come to us must be the result of a severe constant struggle rather than of artificial forcing."[146] For Washington, Blacks could not achieve social equality with Whites since they did not work as hard as Whites did. Meier and Rudwick argue that the compromising of the Black interest with that of racist Whites "satisfied those philanthropists and leading Southerners who opposed race equality yet liked to think that they were in favor of Negro uplift. Finally it enabled many Negroes to convince themselves that it was a way not only of obtaining money for Negro schools but also indirectly and ultimately elevating the race to the point where it would be accorded its citizenship rights."[147]

Washington convinced conservative Blacks and some protest organizations such as the Afro-American Council to adopt his philosophy.[148] "Though he covertly spent thousands of dollars fighting disenfranchisement and segregation laws," Meier and Rudwick assert, "he publicly advocated a policy of conciliation and gradualism."[149] Publicly, he blamed African Americans for their problems and saw the White man as their "best friend"; Washington "recommended economic accumulation and cultivation of Christian character as the best methods for advancing the status of blacks in America," "favored vocational training and working with hands at the expense of higher education and the professions" discouraged political activism, minimized the impact of racism and discrimination, and endorsed segregation.[150] Until his death in 1915, Washington limited the effectiveness of the NAACP and Black intellectuals because of his challenge to legal political action, his emphasis on economic development, and his access to American power and capital.[151]

After Washington's death, the NAACP gathered momentum and continued its legal attack on disenfranchisement and American apartheid. It challenged the "grandfather clauses" that limited the right to vote and municipal residential segregation ordinances in 1915 and 1917 respectively. The NAACP created its branch offices in the south in 1918 and linked its activities to the Black church and began to fight against lynching, segregated education and transportation, and political disenfranchisement.[152] It vigorously attacked the poll tax and school segregation between the 1920s and the 1950s. The NAACP provided organizational and management skills for the Black national struggle by recruiting and training ministers, lawyers, doctors, union organizers, and activists and teaching them how to organize themselves and establish working relationships among themselves.[153] Although its bureaucracy discouraged the participation of the Black masses in their struggle for freedom, the NAACP did serious preparatory work for the struggle of the 1950s and the 1960s.[154] The NAACP and its lawyers successfully challenged the legality of school segregation and, as a result, the Supreme

Court by its decision of *Brown v. Board of Education Topeka, Kansas,* ruled against the segregated public school systems in 1954. Commenting on this decision, Manning Marable says, "No one could realize completely the new phase of American history that would dawn on 17 May 1954, in a legal decision which would mark the real beginning of the Second Reconstruction."[155]

Historically, since the NAACP legal actions and the National Urban League moral persuasion against American apartheid had limited effects in solving the problems of the Black people during the 1920s, the masses paid more attention to the Garvey Movement. Marcus Garvey founded the Universal Negro Improvement Association (UNIA) in 1914 in Jamaica and established eight nationalist goals that he extended to the United States. The main goals of the UNIA were to establish a Black nation, to create "racial" consciousness, to fight for self-determination, to promote racial self-help, to make Blacks world conscious through the media, and to build "racial" respect and solidarity.[156] Because the Garvey Movement advocated the liberation of the Black peoples all over the world from White oppressors, more than three million individuals became members of this organization from more than 19 countries.[157] Hence, the UNIA was a manifestation of an implicit Black transnational collectivity. Magubane notes that this movement "arose and flourished in the conditions created by imperialism. It spread and became an anti-imperialist movement with incredible vigor and elan. At its peak [in the U.S.] in the early 1920s the Garvey movement was the greatest outbreak of black political activity since the Civil War."[158] Garvey also understood clearly the linkage between the economy and politics; hence, he encouraged the development of Black business. The UNIA organized a chain of restaurants, groceries, laundries, hotels, and printing plants and encouraged African Americans to support Black business. Although unsuccessful, the UNIA attempted "to establish a commercial link between the United States, the West Indies, and Africa" by influencing some Blacks to buy stock in the UNIA's Black Star Steamship Line.[159]

Although Garvey was criticized for his call, Back to Africa, he brought nationalist hope to the frustrated and disillusioned Black masses. Explaining why the Black masses were more attracted to the Garvey Movement than to the NAACP or the National Urban League, E. Franklin Frazier argues that the NAACP "has never attracted the crowd because it does not give the crowd an opportunity to show off in colors, parades, and self-glorification. . . . The same could be said of the Urban League. . . . Those who supported this movement pay for it because it gives them what they want—the identifications with something that makes them feel like somebody among white people who have said they were nobody."[160] For the first time, the Garvey Movement attempted to lead the Black struggle without depending on progressive Whites. This movement provided hope for the Black proletariat, but it could not provide freedom. However, Garveyism became the first ideological weapon for Black cultural and revolutionary nationalism.

In the 1940s and the 1950s, the Black people were further disillusioned and frustrated. African Americans were convinced that court actions could not destroy American apartheid without protest and revolutionary action. The founding of the Congress of Racial Equality (CORE) in 1942 by Black elites, White liberals, socialists, and pacifists contributed to the development of the nonviolent direct action strategy to fight against segregation in public facilities.[161] The direct actions of this organization included sit-ins and freedom rides to desegregate the interstate public transportation system. In the 1950s and the 1960s, CORE eventually combined its nonviolent struggle with the Southern Christian Leadership Conference (SCLC) and the Student Non-violent Coordinating Committee (SNCC).[162] Because of some legal successes of the NAACP against school segregation, White terrorist and racist groups, such as the White Citizens' Council, the American States Rights Association, the National Association for the Advancement of White People, and the Ku Klux Klan, intensified their organized attacks on the NAACP in the 1950s and weakened it by creating an organizational vacuum for the Black struggle in many Southern states.[163]

Then African Americans in Southern states turned to the Black church and made it the institutional center of their struggle. The Black church became the center of the struggle because it had an independent leadership of clergymen, financial sources, an organized mass base, and cultural and ideological foundations that were prerequisite for the Black liberation struggle. Using the Black church as their center, African Americans began to create what Aldon D. Morris calls movement centers in the South. The United Defense League was organized in 1953 in Baton Rouge, the Montgomery Improvement Association was formed in 1955 (see chapter V for details), the Inter Civic Council of Tallahassee was organized in 1956, and the Alabama Christian Movement for Human Rights was formed in Birmingham in 1956. The Southern Christian Leadership Conference (SCLC) was formed in 1957 as "the decentralized political arm of the black church" from these movement centers.[164] Taking the church as the center of protest movement and adopting nonviolent action as a main tactic, the SCLC began a mass boycott against the segregated buses; it also started to fight against political disfranchisement under the charismatic leadership of Dr. Martin Luther King, Jr.

One of these movement centers, the Montgomery Improvement Association, was deliberately organized by the efforts of community leaders from mass-based organizations, preexisting social networks, and social groups that participated in the Montgomery bus boycott of 1955. Activists such as Rosa Parks, E. D. Nixon, Ralph Abernathy, E. French, Jo Ann Robinson, and Mary Fair Bruks, as well as institutions and organizations such as the Black church, the local NAACP, and the Women's Political Council (WPC) had played key roles in mobilizing human resources in the form of money, skills, and knowledge of the community for this movement. The bus boycott that was initiated by Rosa Parks on December 1, 1955, when she refused to give her seat for a White man, defying Alabama segregation laws, triggered the formation of the Montgomery Improvement Association in the same month. Martin Luther King, Jr. was elected president of the movement on December 5, 1955. In this association "the visions of an uncharismatic and largely uneducated pullman porter [E. D. Nixon] and members of the WPC and other community organizations were thrust into the hands of a charismatic minister [King] who could play a key mobilizing role because he occupied a central position in the church."[165] Rosa Parks triggered this movement because she was well connected to community organizations that had the organizational capacity for mass mobilization. Similarly, E. D. Nixon was a militant activist who had rich organizational skills that he had accumulated from leading the local NAACP chapter and from heading the local Brotherhood of Sleeping Car Porters for more than 15 years. Like Parks, he was closely connected to community groups and organizations. These activists and others gave a lifeblood to the emergence of this movement, which became a model for the struggle of African Americans in the mid-twentieth century under the leadership of Martin Luther King. The bus boycott occurred for almost a year and became the watershed of the Black struggle by organizing and consolidating this movement center, facilitating the emergence of the charismatic leadership of King, achieving its objective of bus desegregation, and by laying the foundation of the Black movement.

King was a nonviolent, religious, and revolutionary leader who challenged the racist establishment, including the church. Explaining the conformist nature of the White church, King comments as follows: "The erstwhile sanction by the church of slavery, racial segregation, war, and economic exploitation is testimony to the fact that the church has hearkened more to the authority of the world than to the authority of God. Called to be the moral guardian of the community, the church at times has preserved that which is immoral and unethical. Called to combat social evils, it has remained silent behind stained-glass windows. Called to lead men on the highway of brotherhood and to summon them to rise above the narrow confines of race and class, it has enunciated and practiced racial exclusiveness."[166] He combined the social and otherworldly gospel in leading the African American struggle. King expressed that the church has an obligation to deal with moral issues in society as "the voice of moral and spiritual authority on earth" and as "the guardian of the moral and spiritual life in the community."[167] King criticized the White church for ignoring its social mission and sanctioning the racial caste system, colonialism, and apartheid.[168] King clearly understood the political and economic problems that confronted African Americans in particular and all the poor in general.

Despite the fact that most Black organizations were male-run, Black women actively participated in organizations and struggled against racial oppression.[169] Hence, it is no wonder that Rosa Parks ignited the bus boycott of Montgomery that led to the formation of the Montgomery Improvement Association and to the emergence of King as the national leader of the Black struggle in 1955. "What was once a liberal white and Negro [sic] upper-class movement," Meier and Rudwick note, "has become a completely black-led and largely working-class movement."[170] The mobilization of African Americans to participate in their freedom struggle facilitated the shift in strategy of the struggle. The struggle shifted from verbal agitation, legislation, and court litigation to direct action techniques to secure constitutional rights; by involving the masses the struggle went "beyond constitutional rights to demand specific efforts to overcome poverty of the black masses."[171]

King understood the vital role of the masses in bringing a progressive social change and developed the strategy of involving the masses and elites in massive direct action through boycotts, demonstrations, and marches. Recognizing the importance of an organized voice, Martin Luther King and his colleagues created the SCLC. King believed that when the oppressed "bury the psychology of servitude" within themselves no force can stop their freedom struggle.[172] He considered the Black struggle for freedom to be a "new expression of the American dream that need not be realized at the expense of other men around the world, but a dream of opportunity and life that can be shared with the rest of the world."[173] He dreamed and struggled to develop a just society where peoples from all sectors of American society can live together as brothers and sisters, where every person "will respect the dignity and worth of human personality."[174] Although the racist establishment did not positively respond to his religious, political, and social messages, he attempted to influence the White ruling class by using their religious philosophy: "You can use your powerful economic resources to wipe poverty from the face of the earth. God never intended for one group of people to live in superfluous inordinate wealth, while others lived in abject deadening poverty."[175] King's visions reflect democracy and distribution of wealth: "A dream of equality of opportunity, of privilege and property widely distributed; a dream of a land where men will not take necessities from the many to give luxuries to the few; a dream of a land where men do not argue that the color of a man's skin determines the content of his character; a dream of a place where all our gifts and resources are held not for ourselves alone but as instruments of service for the rest of humanity; the dream of a country where every man will respect the dignity and worth of all human personality, and men will dare to live together as brothers—that is the dream."[176]

Black students, supported by progressive White students, formed the Student Non-violent Coordinating Committee (SNCC) in 1960 and used sit-in tactics to desegre-gate hotels, coffee shops, restaurants, movie theaters, libraries, supermarkets, parks, and public transportation systems. The SCLC and other civil rights organizations, under the guidance of King, led effective desegregation campaigns in major American cities. According to Jack M. Bloom, "Nonviolence and mass participation in the freedom struggle became a central part of King's contribution to the cause of black freedom. Mass action transformed the character of the struggle itself—making it immeasurably stronger, with a much more rapid pace."[177] King used religion, the media, and a strat-egy of nonviolence, and mass participation to challenge the racist establishment. "White America," King remarked, "was forced to face the ugly facts of life as the Negro thrust himself into the consciousness of the country, and dramatized his griev-ances on a thousand brightly lighted stages."[178]

During this phase of the African American movement, two important laws were passed: the Civil Rights Act of 1964 and the Voting Rights Act of 1965. These laws were passed to eliminate segregation and integrate Blacks into American society. Then Black revolutionary nationalists and the leading figures of the Civil Rights movement began to assess the impact of these civil rights laws on those Blacks who did not have jobs, education, and decent housing. Recognizing that these civil rights laws could not fundamentally change the conditions of the Black majority, King tried to expand the scope of the Black struggle. He raised human rights issues and aimed at creating an al-liance with the poor and the working class in American society.[179] King was a very complex religious and national leader, and a pragmatist who challenged the racist cap-italist system on its territory by developing different strategies and tactics for the strug-gle. In his attempt to build an alliance of the oppressed groups, King started the Poor People's Campaign: "I am speaking of all the poor, I am not only concerned about the black poor; I am concerned about poverty among my Mexican-American brothers; I am concerned about poverty among my Puerto Rican brothers; I am concerned about poverty among my Appalachian white brothers, and I wish they would realize that we are struggling against poverty for everybody and would join in a movement to get rid of poverty."[180]

King called upon the church to challenge the status quo and to struggle to change an oppressive social order. He condemned racism, economic exploitation, and war as the three primary evils in American society.[181] He had a clear vision on the issue of integration. His main objective was to secure for African Americans access to state power. King said, "'Integration' is meaningless without the sharing of power. When I speak of integration I don't mean a romantic mixing of colors. I mean a real sharing of power and responsibility."[182] He also saw integration as access to social justice, human dignity, equality, and freedom.[183]

Since King recognized the connection between political power, wealth, and poverty, he not only struggled to gain access to state power but also to reduce or eliminate poverty. He was both nationalist and internationalist. The following quotation reflects King's complex ideological and political commitment: "Let us be dissatisfied until rat-infested, vermin-filled slums will be a thing of a dark past and every family will have a decent sanitary house in which to live. Let us be dissatisfied until the empty stomachs of Mississippi are filled and idle industries of Appalachia are revitalized. . . . Let us be dissatisfied until our brothers of the Third World—Asia, Africa and Latin America—will no longer be the victim of imperialist exploitation, but will be lifted from the long night of poverty, illiteracy, and disease."[184] Manning Marable comments that "King's unfinished search for more radical reforms in America may have been the central reason he was killed."[185]

King was assassinated before he completed his historical mission. The assassinations of Malcolm X in 1965 and King in 1968 and the limit of the civil rights laws to the conditions of Black masses clearly contributed to the consolidation of Black militancy and its crisis. Marable asserts, "After the assassinations of Malcolm and Martin, the modern black movement for biracial democracy had been crippled, to be sure, but it was by no means destroyed. Yet the absence of a widely-shared theory and strategy for black liberation was still missing; the political goal of black equality was still murky and ill-defined; opportunism and accommodation of many black militants and political leaders still raised unresolved questions for future struggles."[186]

The Nation of Islam, a religious national movement, appealed to the Black masses in the 1950s and the 1960s as the Garvey Movement had. This movement "evolved over a generation and only gradually became a well-known symbol of protest—at least in the black ghettos of America's principal industrial cities."[187] While other Black protest organizations attracted well-to-do African Americans and progressive Whites, like the Garvey Movement, the Nation of Islam mainly attracted lower-class Blacks.[188] This movement produced Malcolm X, who, after his death, "quickly became the fountainhead of the modern renaissance of black nationalism in the late 1960s."[189] As Malcolm X gradually evolved to become the revolutionary nationalist leader, his understanding of the Black question went beyond the comprehension of the other leaders of the Nation of Islam. Because of his militancy and vision, Malcolm was expelled from the Nation of Islam and created first the Muslim Mosque and then the Organization of African American Unity (OAAU) in 1964. His ideological and intellectual maturity and his increased commitment to the emancipation of his people shortened his life. Robert Allen argues that "Martin Luther King and Malcolm X were both assassinated at precisely the point at which they began working actively and consciously against the racism and exploitation generated by the American capitalist system, both at home and abroad."[190] The assassinations of these two prominent leaders further frustrated the Black masses and increased their militancy. Both King and Malcolm, although each emerged through a different route to lead the Black struggle, recognized the inability of the existing organizations to accomplish the objectives of the African American movement. Exploring this problem, William W. Sales notes, "While the existing institutional structure supported the early period of the Black insurgency, as the movement matured the existing institutional and organizational structures were inadequate to the new tasks at hand. Both men recognized that the further development of the movement required new organizational forms and for their supporters to relate to each other in new and different ways. King's 'Poor People's Campaign' represented this search while Malcolm X created the OAAU."[191]

3. Revolutionary Nationalism: The Wall of Black Struggle

A third pillar of African American nationalism that emphasized political, economic, and social transformation in Black America was revolutionary nationalism. Marable expresses that "militant nationalists of the post-war era were both anti-racist and anti-integrationist, in the sense that they opposed Jim Crow laws and simultaneously advocated all-black economic, political and social institutions."[192] African American nationalists, particularly revolutionary ones, did not want to be integrated into White society as subordinates. They struggled for Black human dignity and true equality. Reflecting on the tactical differences among Black leaders on the positions of integration and separation, Malcolm X argued "that our people want a complete freedom, justice and equality, or recognition and respect as human beings. . . . So, integration is not the objective nor separation the objective. The objective is complete respect as human beings."[193]

Among many, Malcolm X and Stokely Carmichael forcefully argued that Black America must have control of its political economy, life, and culture in order to survive and to fundamentally transform itself.[194] It was their position that this cannot be done without the mobilization of all social classes and groups in the Black community on a national level under a national leadership. As Sales notes, Black nationalism as an ideology "became a major force at a transition stage in the development of the Civil Rights movement: the stage requiring the accelerated institutionalization of formal movement organizations, the transformation of a regional movement into a truly national one, and the integration of previously inactive classes and social groups into the ongoing mobilization."[195] Discussing the importance of Blacks having control over their lives and attaining development, Malcolm X said, "Just because you're in this country doesn't make you an American. No, you've got to go farther than that before you can become an American. You've got to enjoy the fruits of Americanism."[196] During this phase, various militant and revolutionary organizations and the Black masses began to go beyond the civil rights demands.[197] Jack M. Bloom says, "The civil rights movement had won its victories because blacks had been able to assemble a coalition that altered the balance of power within the nation. That coalition had brought about structural change within the south; but that same coalition put limits on the extent of change it was willing to support."[198] Malcolm X recognized this reality and started to search for an organizational solution.

Malcolm X was a revolutionary democratic leader who combined the best elements of "the Charter of the United Nations, the Universal Declaration of Human Rights, the Constitution of the U.S.A. and the Bill of Rights" in the objectives of his new organization, the Organization of African American Unity (OAAU).[199] He attempted to revolutionize and internationalize the African American movement by creating the OAAU. According to Sales, "Due to U.S. fear of world opinion, internationalizing the struggle of African Americans would give Black people breathing room against the power of racism in the United States. Such breathing room could be used to organize for self-defense, aggressive electoral politics, and Black economic advancement."[200] Using the OAAU, Malcolm planned to form an African American united front based on the ideologies of Black nationalism and Pan-Africanism. He spread revolutionary Black nationalism to the masses.

Malcolm X mobilized material, intellectual, and ideological resources to challenge the racist establishment and to provide a new direction for the African American movement. He made the most important contribution in the ideological arena because he insisted that African Americans rethink their past experience in Africa and America by recognizing the significance of history and criticism.[201] In an attempt to increase the political consciousness of African Americans and lead their movement in a new direction, he struggled to expose "the confusion and inaction which resulted from the internalization of the racist ruling class's view of the world."[202] Malcolm X criticized civil rights leaders for not being critical enough in exposing the racist establishment and for their lack of vision in advocating an African American cultural identity: "Civil Rights thinkers never exposed the ideology of the ruling class itself to critical scrutiny. Behind the facade of racial equality, African Americans were frozen at the bottom of the political, economic, and social pyramid even though the structure of legal segregation and discrimination was being dismantled."[203]

Malcolm X criticized civil rights leaders for limiting the objective of the Black struggle to integration and civil rights, not challenging the ideological foundation of U.S. society, limiting the strategy of the struggle to nonviolence, refusing to recognize the African American peoplehood, and accepting "Americanness" uncritically.[204] Because of his militancy, dedication, oratory, fiery media appearance, and revolutionary character, Malcolm X was considered "an apostle of armed resistance," "the electronic man," "shining Prince," and "an uncompromising champion of his people."[205] With the increased militancy of Malcolm X and Martin Luther King and their assassinations, Black organizations like the SNCC also increased their social commitment to the Black struggle. According to Lester, Black revolutionary nationalists began to send a new message to White America: "This is their message: The days of singing freedom songs and the days of combating bullets and billy clubs with love are over. 'We Shall Overcome' sounds old, outdated. 'Man, the people are too busy getting ready to fight.'"[206]

Initially, SNCC emerged as one of the reformist civil rights organizations to fight against segregation. But after a few years it changed its position to militancy.[207] SNCC leaders coined the phrase "Black Power" to express the demand for self-determination. Clayborne Carson indicates that the late 1960s "had awakened dormant traditions of black radicalism and racial separatism by fostering among black people a greater sense of pride, confidence, and racial identity. Through their increasing positive response to the concept of black power, Afro-Americans . . . indicated their determination to use hard-won human rights to improve their lives in ways befitting their own cultural values."[208] Black militancy became the order of the day in the late 1960s. According to Emily Stoper, "By 1966, SNCC was a radical organization; it believed that it could not achieve success without a fundamental change in American institutions."[209] Although it was led by young educated Black elites, it attracted progressives and the other oppressed groups and classes. Stoper notes that "it mobilized the young and the dispossessed into a group that challenged directly first conservatives and then liberals and finally all those who were not dissatisfied with the status quo. By its activism and self-sacrifice, it rebuked those who saw some evils but contented themselves with passive and untaxing remedies."[210]

Some SNCC groups began to advocate forming African American independent institutions and racial separation. Carson explains, "Believing that they should not only stimulate Black militancy but also create black-controlled institutions to secure lasting social gains, SNCC workers gradually abandoned strategies based on assistance from the federal government or the emerging New Left. A group of

SNCC activists began to see racial separation as an ideal that would awaken the consciousness of black people and began a new phase of the black struggle."[211] With SNCC in decline because of its internal organizational contradiction and because of the opposition from and suppression by the White establishment, the Black Panther Party emerged as the leading Black nationalist organization among youth. It was formed in 1966 in Oakland, California, and in 1969 it created an alliance with new left radical communist Whites.[212] It advocated revolutionary nationalism and a strategy of self-defense. Explaining the essence of Black Power, Huey Newton, one of the prominent leaders of this organization, says, "When black people start defining things and making it act in a desired manner, then we call this Black Power."[213]

The OAAU, the SNCC, and the Black Panther Party struggled to bring about a fundamental social change in American society. The new Black revolutionaries believed "that black dignity and liberation are not possible in the United States without profound changes in the system—changes which run so deep that only so strong a word as 'revolutionary' will do to describe them."[214] One of the Black revolutionary organizations, the Black Panther Party, developed a ten-point program in 1966. This program included the demands for political power, national self-determination, full employment, decent education, housing, food, justice to end police brutality and unfair trials, and economic development.[215] The Black Panther Party picked up the gun for self-defense.[216] Another movement that advocated armed struggle was the Revolutionary Action Movement (RAM): "RAM represented the wing of the Civil Rights movement most committed to revolutionary guerrilla warfare in the United States. It had direct ties to Robert Williams, then exiled in Cuba, and the nationalist wing of the southern student movement and its northern groups. RAM also had a grounding in Marxist-Leninist ideology which gave to its variant of Black nationalism a particular leftist character."[217] Furthermore, the formation of the Republic of New Africa in 1967 to create an independent African American state in the Deep South of the United States was another expression of Black revolutionary nationalism.

The Black masses began spectacular rebellions and set fire to millions of dollars of property in big cities. Marable estimates that "the ghetto rebellion from 1964 to 1972 led to 250 deaths, 10,000 serious injuries, and 60,000 arrests, at a cost of police, troops, other coercive measures taken by the state and losses to business amounting to billions of dollars." [218] The White establishment could not tolerate the revolutionary aspect of Black nationalism. The government developed a double-edged policy to deal with Black militancy. On one hand, by using civil rights laws, the government integrated Black reformist elites into the American system. On the other hand, it suppressed the Black masses and Black revolutionaries. Several hundreds of Blacks who participated in a series of rebellions were either killed or imprisoned. Robert Allen reports, "the FBI had organized a secret nationwide conspiracy . . . to 'expose, disrupt, misdirect, discredit, or otherwise neutralize' black freedom organizations and their leaders. The tactics employed in this illegal FBI program included everything from sending 'anonymous' poison-pen letters to red-baiting, planting agents and provocateurs in organizations, using illegal telephone taps and burglarizing files, provoking violent confrontations between different groups, and assassinating militant leaders."[219] As reformist approaches limited the capacity of the Black struggle to broaden mobilization and to facilitate fundamental social change, revolutionary strategies invited repression from the White establishment.

Conclusion

The Black struggle for self-determination, democracy, social justice, and development partially succeeded in achieving its objectives: the institutions of the racial caste system were legally defeated. Several laws were passed to legally protect the political and economic rights of the Black people. But mainly the African American elites have benefited from these changes, although there is structural limitation to what they can achieve. The interest of the Black masses was suppressed with the suppression of Black revolutionary and cultural nationalists. In practical terms, individual, institutional, and structural racism has remained intact in American society despite the fact that it is illegal to discriminate based on race or national origin. Because of the opposition from the White establishment and the lack of a long-term cultural and political strategy among the African American community, the struggle for cultural identity and multicultural democracy has not yet achieved expected goals. The objective of transforming Black America fundamentally has failed since the majority of Blacks are still at the bottom of society; African Americans still do not have equal access to political, economic, and cultural resources of the country.

By focusing on the Civil Rights movement, most scholars and politicians have denied a historical stage for the revolutionary and cultural aspects of the Black national movement. However, cultural nationalism and the revolutionary wing of the Black nationalist movement and the Black masses were the backbone of the Civil Rights movement. Revolutionary and militant Black organizations supported in practice the movement and at the same time went beyond it in demanding a fundamental social change. With the success of the Civil Rights movement in dismantling the legal infrastructure of American apartheid and the suppression of revolutionary nationalism, African American cultural nationalism lost its centrality and more attention was given to integration. Of course, as the result of the Black struggle, the size of the Black middle class grew from about 15 percent to 37 percent of the Black population from 1960 to 1980.[220]

But cultural assimilation since the seventeenth century and integration since the mid-1960s did not fundamentally transform Black America. In 1966 Meier and Rudwick asked the following question: "Will the civil rights organizations be able to harness this political potential [the growing middle-class blacks] and thus help the black masses in the ghetto to secure for themselves the power with which to compel society to provide them with adequate employment, education, and housing?"[221] Presently, because of the absence of organizations that can effectively articulate the demands of the Black majority, existing civil rights organizations and Black elites could not obtain adequate goods and services for the Black community. As a result, the majority of the African Americans have been left in ghettos and exposed to all social ills, such as poverty, illiteracy, disease, unemployment, crimes, police brutality, and drugs. Alphonso Pinkney argues, "Public support for black progress virtually disappeared, and blacks were once again being blamed for their plight in a society where racism has historically been an integral part of all of its institutions and has served to maintain and protect white privilege."[222] The suppression of revolutionary nationalism and the incorporation of Black elites into the White racist capitalist establishment since the mid-1960s have perpetuated the dependency that does not allow Blacks to have political and cultural power, which is required to facilitate a fundamental social transformation.

Both structural and institutional racism and the intensification of globalization have increased the problem of the African American masses. With the intensification of globalization, the racist capitalist economic restructuring has shifted the Black population from being incorporated into the capitalist economy as the lowest of the most super-exploited sector to being *discarded* and *marginalized* from participation in the capitalist production process. White flight to suburbia mainly to undermine desegregation laws after the mid-1960s and the intensification of globalization have created a functional transformation in large American cities where the Black people live. These cities have become the centers of knowledge-intensive service industries, such as administration, information, finance, law and health, insurance, colleges and universities, transportation and communication technologies, and management consulting. At the same time, labor-intensive jobs that require fewer skills and less education in manufacturing and retail have been declining because of industrial relocation and capital flight to suburbia and peripheral countries. According to J. D. Kasarda, "The simultaneous transformation and selective decline of the employment and residential bases of these cities have contributed to a number of serious problems, including a widening gap between urban job-structures and the skill levels of disadvantaged residents (with corresponding high rates of structural unemployment), spatial isolation of low-income minorities, and an intractable high level of urban poverty. Accompanying these problems have been a plethora of social and institutional ills further aggravating the predicament of people and places in distress: rising crime, poor public schools. . . ."[223]

These social ills, particularly unemployment and poverty, have forced some Blacks to depend on the welfare economy and the underground economy. Rather than promote development and transformation, these economies perpetuate dependency, hopelessness, despair, drug abuse, family dissolution, and crime. Referring to the underdevelopment of Black America, Roger Wilkins argues, "The state of helplessness, debility, and cultural deprivation imposed for centuries on millions of blacks in the United States did not prepare them, their children, or their grandchildren for the transition into a modern high-tech society."[224] Currently, Black ghettos are controlled by two main forces: the police and gangs. These are not forces of development. When police are the force of social control, gangs are forces of social destruction. Because of these problems and the availability of opportunities in suburbia, the Black elites left these cities, leaving behind the Black masses. This makes the future of the Black struggle complex.

The Black masses in inner cities have lost control of their educational, social, political, and economic institutions. The subordination of Black America to White America for centuries has arrested African American cultural and economic development. Since the Black movement legally challenged American apartheid laws, the future struggle can use these successes and engage in developing cultural, political, and intellectual strategies that are required in developing Black America and promoting multicultural democracy. Further, the complex features of the previous struggle, such as Black mass militancy, resilient cultural and institutional resources, the sophisticated political and ideological pragmatism of Martin Luther King, the cultural and revolutionary heroism of Malcolm X, the organizational knowledge of various grassroots leaders, and the accumulated liberation knowledge of Black intellectuals, can be the foundation of the future African American struggle for total emancipation and development.

CHAPTER III

The Oromo National Movement

I do not die in vain. My blood will water the freedom struggle of the Oromo people. I am certain that those who sentenced me to death . . . will receive their due punishment from the Ethiopian people. It may be delayed, but the inalienable rights of the Oromo people will be restored by the blood of their children.

—Mamo Mazamir[1]

We Oromos must capture state power by any means necessary. . . . In order to do this we must clandestinely organize all sectors of our society. It is the responsibility of young educated Oromos like you to disseminate this spirit of Oromo nationalism when you return to your respective communities. We can only change the deplorable condition of our people by being tolerant to one another and reestablishing Oromo unity. In this way we can build a strong organization, capture state power, and take actions that facilitate a fundamental social transformation.

—Baro Tumsa[2]

The Oromo national movement emerged as a cultural, intellectual, ideological, and political movement in opposition to Ethiopian settler colonialism and its particular institutions that denied Oromos either historical space or autonomous cultural, political, and economic development. It was Ethiopian colonial and racial/ethnonational domination, political disenfranchisement and exclusion, cultural destruction and repression, and massive human rights violations that stimulated Oromo nationalism. This movement attempts to rediscover Oromo cultural heritage and strives to combine it with a "modern" ideological discourse in its struggle against Ethiopian colonial domination. Collective historical and contemporary grievances and the heritage of cultural resistance combined with urbanization and formal education to facilitate the birth of Oromo nationalism. Like other national liberation movements that have gained political legitimacy because they base their struggle on the grievances of collective memory[3] to regain for the colonized peoples economic, political, and cultural rights the Oromo movement also used these devices to reject national subordination and cultural assimilation.[4]

Colonialism not only creates collective grievances, but often it also creates a condition in which indigenous intellectual and professional groups emerge. Some elements of these groups gradually recognize the irreconcilability of the contradictions between the colonizing structure and the colonized peoples and begin to rediscover the cultural heritage of the colonized peoples. When this happens, as it did with the Oromo, these groups identify themselves with the colonized peoples in the social process that Amilicar Cabral calls the "return to the source," and Gurtuz Bereciartu calls "national revindication."[5] Through this social process these nationalist elements assist the colonized peoples to reclaim and attempt to restore their lost cultural, political and economic rights and to develop the collective consciousness of nationalism. This "national revindication" or the "return to the source" involves ethnoclass consciousness due to the fact that the colonized peoples are culturally suppressed and economically exploited.[6]

This kind of nationalism is a form of liberation politics[7] that challenges colonial or racial/ethnonational domination. Hence, the Oromo struggle for self-determination is a form of liberation politics that challenges Ethiopian "ethnocratic"[8] politics and attempts to overthrow Ethiopian settler colonialism. The ethnocratic nature of the Ethiopian state and its racist ideology has prevented this state from transforming itself into a multicultural democratic and civic state that can protect the interests of all peoples it governs regardless of their racial/ethnonational origins. The main objectives of Oromo nationalism are: a change in the status of Oromos from historical obscurity to global recognition; the liberation of the Oromo nation from Ethiopian colonial domination; the restoration of central aspects of the Oromo democratic heritage; and the fundamental transformation of Oromia (the Oromo country) through establishing autonomous or independent institutions.

Now we will identify and examine the chains of historical, sociological, and cultural factors that have facilitated the emergence and development of Oromo nationalism, and then its main features, phases, objectives, and problems.

Historical and Cultural Background

With the help of European colonial powers, Ethiopians colonized Oromos during the last decades of the nineteenth century; killed such a large proportion of the Oromo population that most scholars of the Oromo consider it a genocidal campaign; expropriated the natural and economic resources of Oromia; destroyed or suppressed Oromo culture; and negated Oromo history.[9] European imperialism and Ethiopian colonialism in collaboration imposed on Oromos oppressive institutions such as the *nafxanya-gabbar* system[10] (semislavery), slavery, garrison cities, the *balabat* system (the collaborative class), and colonial capitalism.[11] According to Bonnie Holcomb and Sisai Ibssa, "Advisers who represented various capitalist countries were initially involved at every stage in forming the empire, and then at every level of government. These advisers were the conduits through which the capitalist ideology, embodied in strategy, was implemented in shaping Ethiopia."[12] The relationship between these European powers and Ethiopian colonialists was embodied in the exchange of raw materials on one hand, and modern technology, armed forces, and administrative expertise on the other. William Robinson expounds, "the world capitalist system made possible the *creation* of the Ethiopian state, *and also* made possible Abyssinian conquest of Oromia and other groups. . . . The socioeconomic and class structure in Abyssinia was reoriented toward integration into world capitalism. In this stage Oromia was captured by world capitalism as a subordinate segment of the Ethiopian social formation. Oromia provided the labor and resources for the rapid transformation of Ethiopia's socioeconomic and productive structure to feed the needs of an intermediary Ethiopian ruling class and dominant groups in the core of world capitalism."[13] Oromos have been resisting two structures that are linked together by the global capitalist system—global imperialism and Ethiopian settler colonialism. The Oromo collaborative class has served the interests of each of these systems by facilitating the operation of both structures.

Most Oromos who fought against Ethiopian colonizers were either killed or enslaved or impoverished by the expropriation of their lands. Since the remaining Oromos could not defend their homeland from European-sponsored Ethiopian settler colonialism, they were defeated and turned into landless people or semi-slaves. In the process of obtaining an intermediate status in the global capitalist system, the Ethiopian colonial ruling class and its state expropriated three-fourths of the Oromo lands and built garrison cities as their political centers in Oromia. From these centers they implemented colonial domination through the monopoly of the means of coercion, wealth and capital accumulation, and cultural destruction.[14] By claiming absolute rights on the Oromo lands and providing portions of these lands to its followers, the Ethiopian colonial state consolidated itself. Oromos were forced to become slaves or semislaves to provide raw materials that were needed in regional and international markets. The colonial state controlled the process of forced recruitment of labor through slavery and the *nafxanya-gabbar* system. Ethiopian colonialists frequently raided Oromos to use them as domestic slaves or sell them as commodities.[15] Slavery existed in the Ethiopian empire until the 1930s, when Italian fascists colonized Ethiopia and destroyed slavery and the *nafxanya-gabbar* system to get adequate cheap wage labor for their agricultural plantations in the Horn of Africa.

As Ethiopian colonial settlers and their state controlled Oromian political economy, their European advisers and European, Indian, and Arab merchants controlled commercial activities in Oromia.[16] After the Second World War, Great Britain and the United States both sponsored Ethiopian colonialism and facilitated the development of colonial capitalism and extraction of Oromo produce. These two world powers "modernized" the Ethiopian colonial state and enabled the intensification of colonial exploitation in Oromia until the early 1970s.[17] Similarly, by replacing U.S. sponsorship and involving itself in Ethiopia between 1974 and 1991, the Soviet Union further consolidated Ethiopian colonialism and the subjugation of Oromos. The U.S. returned to Ethiopia by assisting the emergence of a new regime which has claimed since 1991 that it would support the promotion of democracy.[18] But in practice the new regime has emerged as a Tigrayan ethnonational dictatorship, which has been able to replace that of the Amhara only through the support of the West, particularly the United States.[19] Oromo nationalism developed as a national liberation movement in order to oppose all these colonial practices and the dehumanization of Oromos and to promote Oromian self-determination.

Oromo historical and cultural foundations have served as storehouses for Oromo nationalism. Oromos were independent people prior to their colonization by Ethiopia and Great Britain. They were colonized and partitioned during the last decades of the nineteenth century, when Africa was divided among the European colonial powers in "the Scramble for Africa."[20] Oromos were never dominated by other peoples prior to the last decades of the nineteenth century; they called their homeland "Biya Oromo," and their culture was respected by their neighbors.[21] The German missionary, geographer, and researcher J. Lewis Krapf called this homeland "Ormania" in the 1840s; Oromo nationalists named this homeland Oromia[22] in the early 1970s. Oromos have lived in a geographical place and in cultural milieus.[23] But Ethiopians who have a colonial design on the space and who wish to impose an Ethiopian culture have tried their best through political and intellectual discourses to deny this society a historical homeland and historical and cultural space. For *Habasha* (Amhara-Tigray) politicians and intellectuals and their Euro-American supporters, Oromos have been depicted in politically motivated writings as "newcomers" and "invaders" of "Ethiopia,"[24] despite the fact that they were one of the original peoples who settled in this region.[25] The emergence of the Oromos as one of the dominant peoples in the Horn of Africa in the sixteenth century has led many scholars to conclude that they came from another continent and "invaded" nonexistent Ethiopia. Others have hypothesized that they were expelled in the tenth century by the Somalis from their original homeland and invaded "Ethiopia."

The name *Ethiopia* was originally associated with the regions where Black peoples lived in Asia and Africa. This name originated from the Greek word *Aethiopes*, which meant burned face. This name came to be associated with Abyssinia through the process of translating the Bible from Hebrew to Greek and from Greek to Geez (the ancient Abyssinian language). Since Abyssinia has been mainly the homeland of Amharas and Tigrayans, it was only small part of the Black world, which was called Ethiopia. Recognizing the political significance of the name Ethiopia, Abyssinian leaders claimed Ethiopian identity and named their country and the regions they colonized, including Oromia, "Ethiopia" in the 1930s. Despite the fact that the historical meaning of Ethiopia is applicable to all Black peoples, its current meaning applies mainly to the Amharas and the Tigrayans. Recognizing this historical implication and rejecting *Habasha* racist claims, Oromo nationalists say, "We are Oromians, not Ethiopians."

The Ethiopian elites and their Euro-American supporters believed that Oromos should be regarded as primitive people and argued that Oromos could not contribute to human civilization.[26] The Oromo people who have been condemned as people without a homeland and history by some Ethiopian and Ethiopianist knowledge elites are engaged in political and cultural reconstruction to determine their destiny. The cultural resistance to colonialism can develop into political and armed struggles provided that there are other necessary conditions. The colonization of a human group denies human dignity and suppresses the material and nonmaterial elements of culture that are necessary for survival and development. Hence, the national movement is "the organized political expression of the culture of the people who are undertaking the struggle."[27] The understanding of the Oromo national struggle requires the study of the conditions of the people before and after their colonization.

The Oromo institutional heritage has become the ideological foundation of the Oromo nationalist discourse; therefore, it is essential to explore the character and significance of these institutions. These institutions laid the foundations of Oromo political, economic, cultural, and political structures.[28] Since Oromos have been an oral society and since their culture and civilization have not yet been adequately studied, we have only partial data on Oromo institutions. The Ethiopian political and knowledge elites have discouraged the thorough study of this society.[29] However, with the consolidation of the Oromo struggle since the 1970s, despite all these obstacles, a few scholars have begun to study seriously some aspects of Oromo culture and institutions and broadened our knowledge of Oromo society.

Ethiopian settler colonialists had essentially committed cultural genocide by eliminating Oromo cultural experts and replacing Oromo institutions with those of

Ethiopians, and by creating an alienated and Ethiopianized Oromo intermediate class. Colonialism can only be maintained by organized cultural destruction or repression and the assimilation of a sector of the colonized population.[30] Ethiopian colonialism repressed the Oromo cultural identity by denying Oromos the freedom of having and developing their cultural institutions for the span of a century. Colonialism also denied Oromos opportunities for developing the Oromo system of knowledge and worldview by hindering the transmission of Oromo cultural experiences from generation to generation.[31] The exploitation of Oromo resources was facilitated by uprooting the Oromo identity. But Ethiopian colonialism could not totally destroy Oromo traditions since "*gada* [Oromo democratic] symbols and some practices went underground and survived until the present time."[32] As we will see below, the ideological expression of the Oromo national movement has centered in *gada* (Oromo democracy) since it "represents a repository, a storehouse of concepts, values, beliefs and practices that are accessible to all Oromo."[33] Oromos have already fashioned their ideology of national liberation based on their civil and political culture. As Benedict Anderson explains, "Nation-ness, as well as nationalism, are cultural artefacts of a particular kind. To understand them properly we need to consider carefully how they came into historical being, in what ways their meanings have changed over time, and why, today, they command such profound emotional legitimacy."[34] Now let us explore the Oromo cultural identity and its relation to Oromo nationalism.

The Cultural Bases of Oromo Identity and Nationalism

In contrast to the ancestors of African Americans who were taken away from their geographical and cultural milieus and placed in the country that is called the United States, most Oromos were enslaved and colonized in their own homeland, Oromia, and tightly controlled and exploited by Ethiopians. Oromos were not exposed to complex global multicultural centers as the African Americans were. Despite the fact that their cultural institutions were dismantled, Oromos have maintained more of their cultural elements than have the African Americans. Unlike African Americans, Oromos have even maintained some elements of their precolonial institutions in certain Oromo regions, and the majority of Oromos still speak in their language, *Afaan Oromoo.* Further, as we see shortly, all Oromo groups share common cultural and historical roots in the form of kinship, political philosophy, worldview, and ritual. Lambert Bartels notes that most Oromos "speak a mutually intelligible language of their own. Kinship relations and marriage customs are much the same, and so their attitude to leadership on one hand and to freedom of the individual on the other, the position of nuclear family, their concept of man and society, and their modes of experiencing the divine—all things which still find expression in many rites, ceremonies and forms of social intercourse."[35] Although Oromos have a biologically and socially constructed complex kinship system, the formation and expression of Oromo peoplehood are culturally shaped.[36] The Oromo kinship system on macro and micro levels has been the basic social structure for defining common interests in resource management and utilization, for establishing political and religious leadership, and for forming leagues or confederations within Oromo society.[37]

Oromo political and social institutions have been built on the kinship system; Oromos call the largest grouping of the system *gossa,* which is subdivided into moiety, sub-moiety, and *qomo* (clan). These subdivisions have lower-order branches known as *mana* (lineage), *balbala* (minor lineage), and *warra* (minimal lineage or extended family). Wherever Oromos were divided into submoieties and clans, there is "clear distinction between clans and lineages. The clan (*qomo*) is first of all a social group, consisting of several descent groups who need not all be Oromo. The heart of every clan is compounded of a cluster of lineages tracing their descent to the ancestor who gave his name to the clan."[38] All Oromo branches claim a single ancestral origin and trace their genealogies to two moieties, or confederations, known as Barentu and Borana. However, practically it is not possible "to trace in detail the manner in which further division and the formation of" these moieties, submoieties, clans, and lineages occur.[39] However, Gemetchu Megerssa notes that the names of the two moieties, Barentu and Borana, "were . . . not originally the names of specific groups but conceptual categories standing for the division of the Oromo into east and west, or right to left, constituting the lateral or horizontal form of classification of the people into two halves."[40] Politically, this has important implications, because the classification of duality is a basic structural requirement for balancing and maintaining democracy and peace in Oromo society.[41]

Despite the fact that Oromos claim that they descended from the same family stock, Oromo, they do not define or limit kinship to biological ancestry alone. Oromos recognize social ancestry and avoid the distinction between the biological and social descent since they know that the formation of Oromo peoplehood was based on a biological and social kinship. Oromos have had a long history of cultural contacts with non-Oromos through war, marriage, economic relationship, and group adoption.[42] When there were wars and conflicts between Oromos and their neighbors over economic and cultural resources such as land, water, trade routes, and religious and political issues, the former imposed specific cultural policies in order to structurally and culturally change the conquered people and to Oromoize (*Oromeesu*) them to consolidate Oromo society before their colonization. Consequently, it is impossible to recognize the difference between original and assimilated Oromos today. Oromo customs and laws strictly forbade the distinction between social and biological descent.[43]

Through the processes of group or individual adoption known as *moggaasa* and *gudifacha* respectively, non-Oromos were adopted into Oromo *gossa* and were structurally and culturally Oromoized. These assimilated Oromos trace their descent to Oromo moieties, lineages, and to the original Oromo.[44] Non-Oromo neighbors who were defeated at war or who wanted to share resources with Oromo groups also would be adopted to the Oromo *gossa*: "The adopted groups now become collectively the 'sons' of *gossa*. . . . This arrangement was inspired by political, military and economic considerations, though clearly it is couched in the symbolism of kinship affiliation."[45] There was no doubt that through the process of Oromoization, Oromos increased their population. The main two moieties of the Oromo, Barentu and Borana, had originally one overall political structure called the *gada* system that helped fashion Oromo relations with each other and with outsiders.[46] Further, there were five sets of submoieties that extended from the Borana and Barentu moieties: the Sabbo and the Gona, the Macha and Tulama, the Raya and Assabo, the Siko and the Mando, and the Itu and Humbana.[47] To maintain the principle of balanced opposition there must be the same number of leaders from the two moieties. Whenever members of these moieties are asked to identify their descent, they always provide the name of their moieties, rather than their lineages. The existence of similarly named putative descent groups on the macro and micro kinship levels across the whole spectrum of Oromo society[48] shows the complexity of the Oromo kinship system. Based on this brief sketch of this kinship system, let us explore the characteristics of Oromo religion, worldview, and political philosophy that are relevant in understanding Oromo peoplehood and nationalism.

Oromo Worldview and Philosophy

Central to Oromo cultural identity is the relation of society to nature and the existence of a Supreme Being, *Waaqa,* which regulates the connection between nature and society. The Oromo knowledge of society and the world can be classified into two types: the cultural and customary knowledge. The cultural knowledge is known as *beekumssa* or *seera aada,* and the knowledge of laws is known as *beekumssa seera.*[49] There have been two sets of laws in Oromo society. Oromos recognize the first set of laws as *seera Waaqa* (the laws of God), and *seera nama* (the laws of human beings). Oromos believe that the laws of God are immutable, and the laws of human beings can be changed thorough consensus and democratic means. The Oromo customary knowledge is a public and common knowledge that guides and regulates the activities of members of society; some elements of this customary knowledge can develop into rules or laws depending on the interest of society.[50] Every able person is expected to learn and recognize *seera aada;* however, since everyone may not know the important rules or laws of society, there are Oromo experts who study and know them. These Oromo experts know the organizing principles of the Oromo worldview and culture that reflect Oromo cultural memory and identity both temporally and religiously.[51]

Oromo religious and philosophical worldviews consider the spiritual, physical, and human worlds as interconnected phenomena and believe that *Waaqa,* the creator, regulates their existence and functions in balanced ways. Aneesa Kassam expounds that the "image of creation has important consequences for the Oromo vision of the universe as a whole. It has influenced among other aspects its traditional culture, its political and economic thought, and determined its traditional system of government and modes of production."[52] Oromos use three concepts to explain the organization and interconnection of human, spiritual, and physical worlds. These three concepts are *ayaana* (spirit), *uuma* (nature), and *saffu* (moral and ethical order). Oromos believe that through *ayaana, Waaqa* (God) created and regulates human and physical worlds in balanced ways. This *ayaana* also maintains the connection between the creator and the created. Oromo society has organizing principles for its known and unknown universe like any society; *ayaana* is a major organizing principle of Oromo cosmology through which the concepts of time and creation are ordered.[53] *Ayaana* establishes the connection between the creator *Waaqa* and the created (nature and society) by differentiating and at the same time uniting them.[54] Gemetchu Megerssa argues that "*ayaana* is a religious and philosophical construct which represents the principles of temporality and spirituality . . . [and] also serves as an ordering device according to which the entire universe is organized and classified."[55]

Oromos believe in *Waaqa,* a monotheistic God, that created the world through its *ayaana.* They believe that this Supreme Being created *ayaana* and uses it to organize scattered things into order. Megerssa explains that "*ayaana* is the mechanism by which the creator propels itself into becoming its own opposite, and dwells in that which it creates. This is then transposed to explain the basic principles that embed themselves in the diverse Oromo institutions, since there is no distinction between the laws of thought, the laws of nature, history and society."[56] As a religious and philosophical construct, *ayaana* provides meanings of the complex universe: "Faced with the concrete reality of existence and the contradictions, Oromo seem to have been compelled to look for a creator, who not only creates, but also holds the opposing forces in balance, and represents permanence behind the flux of existence."[57]

The second concept, *uuma,* includes everything created by *Waaqa* including *ayaana.* The third concept, *saffu,* is an ethical and moral "code that Oromos use to differentiate bad from good and wrong from right. . . . [S]affu 'constitutes the ethical basis upon which all human action should be founded; it is that which directs one on the right path; it shows the way in which life can be best lived.'"[58] Oromos claim that the understanding of laws of *Waaqa,* nature, and society, both morally and ethically and living accordingly is necessary. Oromos believe in God's law and the law of society that they establish through the *gada* system of democracy to maintain *nagaa* (peace) and *saffu* among Waaqa, society, and nature to achieve their full human destiny known as *kao* or *kayyo. Kayyo* "represents the degree to which individuals have achieved the ideal state of peace and the rewards which flow therefrom. When a man has many cattle and children and an abundance of food his *kayyo* is good. It is also good when his relations with others are peaceful and he has achieved respect and high office."[59] Most Oromos believe that they had full *kao* before their colonization since they had freedom to develop their independent political, economic, and cultural institutions. The Oromo national movement struggles to restore full *kayyo* for individuals and the Oromo nation.[60] Oromo nationalists believe that their nation will restore its *kayyo* and *finna* [61] (development) through liberation and recreation of *naga Oromoo* and the *gada* system.

Oromo institutions can be better understood by learning about the Oromo concept of social development known as *finna* (sustainable development). As in any society, social changes occur in Oromo society by combining the cumulative historical experiences with the contemporary condition. Hence *finna* "represents the legacy of the past which each generation inherits from its forefathers and which it transforms; it is the fertile patrimony held in trust by the present generation which it will enrich and bequeath to future generations. . . . It describes a movement emanating from inside, a developing of the inner potential of society based on the cultural roots it has already laid down."[62] The Oromo theory of social development is constructed in seven interconnected phases: *Guudina, gabbina, ballina, badhaadha, hoormata, dagaaga,* and *dagahoora.* Whereas *guudina* indicates an improvement in cultural life due to the introduction of new experiences to Oromo society, *gabbina* involves the process of integrating cumulative cultural experiences with contemporary social conditions through broadening and deepening knowledge and the worldview. "This can only be achieved through the full knowledge, consent and active participation of all members of the community. This implies the existence of a political organization, the forum for debate and the democratic means of reaching consensus on all decisions affecting the common good. This should be obtained without force or coercion, without excluding the interests of any group, within the Oromo society and outside it, in the broader context of the national or international arena. To this end, the Oromo evolved a political process of power sharing reputed for its highly egalitarian nature: *Gada.*"[63]

Without *gada* there cannot be *finna,* peace, social justice, and *kao* (success and happiness), and *saffu.* As we will see below, *gada* has been the foundation of Oromo civilization. *Gabbina* emerges through democracy, peace, cooperation, and consensus of all members of Oromo society of different levels to improve economic, cultural, and political conditions. After *gabbina,* there is a *ballina* phase. *Ballina* involves the expansion of enriched cultural and political experiences from Oromo society to another society through reciprocal cultural borrowing and resource sharing and interdependence, based on the principles of democracy. This is the phase that focuses on foreign relations. It allows Oromo society to engage in cultural exchange and cooperation with neighboring peoples. The cumulative experiences of *guudina, gabbina,* and *ballina* lead to the phase of *badhaadha* (richness). Theoretically, *badhaadha* is a phase at which Oromos and their neighbors who accept their philosophy of social development obtain peace, prosperity, and wholeness since there is no conflict, poverty, disease, or natural calamities. This phase of development can only be achieved when there is peace among *Waaqa* (God), *uuma* (nature), and society. According to Paul Baxter, human beings "must keep right with each other in order to keep right with God, and they must keep right with God to keep right with each other. Good social relationships and proper ritual relationships are reflexes of each other."[64] The development of this stage facilitates the emergence of the *hoormata* phase. During this phase, animals and people reproduce and multiply because of availability of abundant resources and peace. Following this phase there is a development phase known as *dagaaga;* this is the stage at which development cycles are assessed and integrated to maintain even and sustainable development. At the final stage of development, called *daga-hoora,* Oromo society expands its cumulative cultural experiences of development to neighboring peoples through different mechanisms depending on a given condition.[65] Oromo democracy has allowed these different phases of Oromo development.

Oromos have had the *gada* system as a political, economic, social, cultural, and religious institution, although its political, cultural, social, economic, and religious roles have not been clearly differentiated.[66] Although Oromos were under one *gada* administration during the sixteenth century, they developed autonomous *gada* councils after they increased their territory and the size of their population.[67] Bonnie Holcomb notes that the *gada* system "organized the Oromo people in an all-encompassing democratic republic even before the few European pilgrims arrived from England on the shores of North America and only later built a democracy."[68] This system has the principles of checks and balances (such as periodic succession of eight years and division of power among executive, legislative, and judiciary branches), balanced opposition (among five parties), and power sharing between higher and lower administrative organs to prevent power from falling into the hands of despots.[69] Other principles of the system include balanced representation of all clans, lineages, regions, and confederacies; accountability of leaders; the settlement of disputes through reconciliation; and the respect for basic rights and liberties.[70]

There are five *miseensas* (parties) in *gada;* these parties have different names in different parts of Oromia as the result of the expansion of Oromos and their establishment of different autonomous administrative councils.[71] All *gada* officials are elected for eight years by universal adult male suffrage. The rule of law has been the key element of the *gada* system; those leaders who have violated the law or whose families cannot maintain the required standards of the system are recalled before the end of their tenure in the office.[72] *Gada* leaders implement the laws made by the representatives of the people.

Oromo democracy allowed the Oromo people to make, change, or amend laws and rules ever eight years. The *gada* system accepted the general assembly as the ultimate source of authority, and nobody was above the law. This system as an integrative social system combined political and civil culture in this society.[73] All Oromos had spiritual, moral, and political leadership before their colonization: "The possession of . . . [qaallu] and the common gada government seems to have been the 'special mark' of the Oromo nation."[74] Gada as an integrative social and political system organized male Oromos according to hirya (age-sets) and luba (generation-sets) for social, political, and economic purposes.[75]

Studying how the gada system works under Ethiopian colonialism in the Borana region of Oromia, Legesse reconstructs the system as the following: This system "is a system of classes (luba) that succeed each other every eight years in assuming military, economic, political, and ritual responsibilities. Each gada class remains in power during a specific term (gada) which begins and ends with a formal transfer ceremony."[76] The word gada has three related meanings: it is a period of eight years during which elected officials take power from the previous ones; it is the phase during which a class of people are in power by having politico-ritual leadership; it is the institution of Oromo society.[77] For their known history, Oromos have had the gada institution to regulate their economic, political, military, cultural, ritual, and other social activities.

Despite the emergence of various autonomous gada councils[78] with the increased Oromo population and territories between 1522 and 1618, the central principles of the overall system remained intact. The organization of males based on age and generational roles reflect the principle of balanced opposition. The Borana Oromo is "a society that is . . . [organized] into two distinct but cross-cutting systems of peer group structures. One is a system in which the members of each class are recruited strictly on the basis of chronological age. The other is a system in which the members are recruited equally strictly on the basis of genealogical generations. The first has nothing to do with genealogical ties. The second has little to do with age. Both types of social groups are formed every eight years. Both sets of groups pass from one stage of development to the next every eight years."[79] Whereas Oromo males are involuntarily assigned to age-sets on the basis of age, they are recruited to gada classes involuntarily on the basis of genealogical generations. Male children enter into the system of gada grades 40 years after their fathers, but they join age-sets as newly born infants. Since one grade is eight years, fathers and sons are five grades apart. Male children can join advanced grades at birth, and may join men or old men who are considered to be members of their gada grades. Older men mentor young males, teaching rules and rituals, but the former treat the latter as equals since there is no status difference between the two groups in a gada class. Members of a gada class share the same status and roles and perform their rights of passage from one grade to another collectively.

A key Oromo religious institution played an indirect role in the Oromo political system. The leader of this institution is known as qallu; H. A. Kelly notes that this leader "is thought to possess sacred characteristics that enable him to act as intermediary between the people and Waq [Waaqa]. The qallu had no administrative powers, but could bless or withhold blessings from gada leadership, and had an extraordinary power to curse anyone who threatened the well-being of the entire community by deviating from Waq's order."[80] The criteria to be a qallu included seniority in lineages, respectability in the community, expertise in ritual practices, moral qualification, respect for cultural taboos, sound social status, and other leadership qualities.[81] The leader of all qallus was known as Abba Muuda (father of the anointment), who was considered to be the prophet and spiritual leader of Oromo society. Oromo pilgrims traveled to the residence of *Abba Muuda* to receive his blessing and anointment to be ritual experts in their respective regions.[82] *Abba Muuda* served as the spiritual center and symbol of Oromo unity and helped all Oromo branches to keep in touch for several centuries; "as the Jews believe in Moses and the Muslims in Muhammad, the Oromo believe in their *Abba Muda* [*sic*]."[83] *Abba Muuda* and other *qallu* leaders had a moral authority to oppose tyrants and support Oromo democracy, and encourage harmonious and democratic relations in this society. According to the *qallu* mythology, the original Oromo religious leader was descended from heaven.[84]

Abba Muuda used to serve as the symbol of Oromo unity before the Ethiopian colonial system undermined its role; all Oromo groups kept in touch through this institution for hundreds of years. When Oromo representatives went to him from far and near to receive his blessings, *Abba Muuda* commanded them "not to cut their hair and to be righteous, not to recognize any leader who tries to get absolute power, and not to fight among themselves."[85] Original Oromo religious leaders had a moral authority and social obligation to oppose tyrants and support popular Oromo democracy and *gada* leaders based on the principles of *saffu, kao, Waaqa,* and *uuma.*

The *qallu* and his institution were committed to social justice, the rules of God and the law of society, and fair deliberation; "his residence was considered politically neutral ground, suitable for debating controversial issues and for adjudicating highly charged disputes, although he himself might not take a prominent role in proceedings."[86] The *qallu* institution has played an important role in protecting the original Oromo culture, religion, worldview, and identity. When those Oromos who were influenced by this institution kept their Oromo names, most Oromos who were converted to Islam or Christianity willingly or by force abandoned their Oromo names and adopted Muslim or Christian names depending on their borrowed religion.

In its modified form, this religious institution exists in some parts of Oromia, such as in the Guji and Borana areas. It still protects an Oromo way of life, such as dispensing of local justice based on Oromo customs and providing solutions to problems created by changing social conditions.[87] The *qallus* of Guji and Borana are ritual leaders, advisors, and experts in the *gada* system. The *qallus* "possess the exclusive prerogative of legitimizing the different *gada* officials, when a new *gada* group is initiated into the politically active class."[88] Oromos still practice some elements of Oromo democratic values in the areas where the *gada* system was suppressed a century ago. The *gada* system is still practiced in the Borana and Guji regions under the control of the Ethiopian colonial system in its modified form; it helps maintain peace, exchange knowledge, and practice rituals between some clans and regional groups.[89] The current *gada* of Borana and Guji cannot fully reflect its original political culture under Ethiopian colonialism; probably that is why scholars such as Hinnant, Baxter, Bassi, and others emphasize the ritual function of the system and ignore its political culture.[90]

Before Oromos were fully incorporated into the global capitalist world system through Ethiopian and British colonialism, they were pastoralists, farmers, and a few of them were merchants. In certain territories, a few Oromo kingdoms known as *moti* (tributary kingdom) emerged because of class, ethnonational, and gender stratification in the first half of the nineteenth century. However, the two dominant religious and political institutions were *qallu* and *gada,* respectively. Some elements of these institutions have survived in Oromo society, particularly in southern Oromia. Although the *qaallu* institution has survived in a changed and modified form,[91] *gada* rituals still exist in all parts of Oromia.[92] Baxter explains that the relationships "between the ritual welfare of a family and its stock and the national rituals of *gaada* [*sic*] are linked by the use of prayers and blessings which utilise the same rich store of metaphors and symbols. The adult members of each village or camp usually come together daily to offer prayers, as a duty and a joy; but they will not do it if they are quarreling or if the family head cannot provide coffee beans for sacrifice."[93] The *qallus* in the Boran and Guji regions still practice some of their original roles; these roles include election officer, ritual leader and expert, and advisor in the *gada* system. The *qallu* leaders play important roles in the domain of the sacred and in the election and legitimation of *gada* leaders. In the Borana region, the *qallus* and other leaders of the Sabbo and Gona moieties and clans directly participate in the recruitment of leadership, and the *qallus* of the two moieties "have responsibility and the power to organize the election of *gada* leaders."[94]

Global capitalists used Ethiopian warlords to incorporate Oromos, and, in the process, Ethiopian colonialists suppressed or destroyed some Oromo cultural elements and institutions by imposing their culture and institutions on Oromo society with the support of global structures. However, the Ethiopian colonizing structure was not fully successful "despite over one hundred years of colonial domination, in bringing about a structural change in the Oromo view of the world. The custodians of the Oromo oral tradition were able retain intact to a large degree the system of knowledge."[95] Although some Oromos accepted Islam by force or as resistance to Ethiopian colonial domination, and others were forced to accept Ethiopian Orthodox Christianity or willingly accepted other forms of Christianity, their worldviews "are still hidden under the surface,"[96] according to Lambert Bartels, who was a Catholic missionary in Oromia. Oromo prayers, blessings, and greetings manifest the Oromo worldview. "The words of prayers, blessings and greetings continuously create and recreate connections between the organizational and the cosmological structures," Baxter writes, "such as the moieties and *gaada* [*sic*], and workaday."[97] Discussing the original system of Oromo thought and world view, Bartels asserts that it "is these things which constitute their most precious heritage and their identity as a people, and in this they can enrich other people."[98] For Bartels, "Whether they became Christians or Muslims, the Oromo's traditional modes of experiencing the divine have continued almost unaffected, in spite of the fact that several rituals and social institutions in which it was expressed have been very diminished or apparently submerged in new ritual cloaks."[99]

In the whole Borana community, where some elements of the *gada* system still exist, the assembly known as *Gumi Gayo* (the assembly of multitudes) brings together almost every important leader, such as living *Abba Gadas,* the *qallus,* age-set counselors, clan leaders and *gada* councilors, and other concerned individuals to make or amend or change laws and rules every eight years. The *Gumi Gayo* assembly has the highest degree of ritual and political authority, higher than the *gada* or other assemblies because it "assembled representatives of the entire society in conjunction with any individual who has the initiative to come to the ceremonial grounds," and "what *gumi* decides cannot be reversed by any other assembly."[100] The 37th *Gumi Gayo* assembly was held in August 1996 to make or amend or change three kinds of laws that the Borana Oromo classify as cardinal, customary, and supplementary laws.[101]

Oromo leaders have been elected to office based on certain criteria: "There is a general understanding among the electors and among the men competing for office that *personal qualities, achievements, mystical attributes,* and *public service* are the most important factors. . . . It should be stressed that it is not the candidate himself who is being judged but rather his whole lineage and in particular, his lineal ancestors. Specifically, the candidate's father is the one most closely scrutinized."[102] Despite the fact that kinship, *gada* grades, and age-sets are the foundation of political and ritual behavior in Oromo society, those who are elected to office "are expected to serve . . . without regard to kinship ties. Custom prescribes that they abandon their paternal settlements and establish a new band consisting of the councilors and their assistants."[103] Baissa Lemmu mentions that the *gada* system "as a whole provided . . . the machinery for democratic rule and enjoyment of maximum liberty for the people. It was the suppression of the system . . . that dehumanized the Oromo for the past hundred years."[104]

Despite the fact that *gada* was an egalitarian social system, women were excluded from active political and military participation, except in supporting roles. When males were passing through age-sets and generation-sets, females were married to men without belonging to these sets. *Gada* effectively enforced a gender-based division of labor in Oromo society, although it allowed two equally important separate and interdependent economic domains. Qabbanee Waqayyo asserts that "men have controlled the mobile resources—those that required going out from the homestead—herding, defense of livestock and land, tilling new fields, plowing, etc. Women have controlled the stationary resources—the house, the grain and other products of the fields once they are brought into *gotara* for storage, etc. Even the cattle around the house are under their control; women milk them, decide how much milk goes to the calves, how much to the people in the household for drinking, how much for butter or cheese to eat or sell, how much to guests who bring valuable information, become friends in time of need, etc."[105] The balancing of the domains of women and men and maintaining their interdependence have been a precondition for keeping peace between the sexes and for promoting *saffu,* moral and ethical order in society.[106] "By exercising a real day-to-day control over the disposition of the resources at every point of the decision-making process in ways that are protected by the value system of society," Waqayyo writes, "the woman wields determinative influence in the society as a whole."[107] Oromo women have participated in several *gada* rituals and in the domestic sphere, and "women have *de facto* control over the most important resources."[108]

The value system of Oromo society has been influenced by the *gada* and *siiqqee* institutions. In the precolonial Oromo society, Oromo women had the *siiqqee* institution, a parallel institution to the *gada* system that "functioned hand in hand with the *Gadaa* [*sic*] system as one of its built-in mechanisms of checks and balances."[109] These two institutions helped to maintain *saffu* in Oromo society by enabling Oromo women to have control over resources and private spaces, social status and respect, and sisterhood and solidarity by deterring men from infringing upon their individual and collective rights.[110] If the balance between men and women was broken, a *siqqee* rebellion was initiated to restore the law of God and the moral and ethical order of society. When there were violations of their rights, women left their homes, children, and resources and traveled to a place where there was a big tree called *qilxxu* and assembled there until the problems were solved through negotiation by elders, both men and women.[111] Kuwee Kumsa notes, "Married women have the right to organize and form the *siiqqee* sisterhood and solidarity. Because women as a group are considered *halaga* [non-relative] and excluded from the *Gadaa* grades, they stick together and count on one another through the *siiqqee* which they all have in common . . . in the strange *gosa* where women live as strangers, *siiqqee* represents the mother and they even address each other as 'daughters of a mother.' They get together regularly for prayers as well as for other important individual and community matters. If men try to stop women from attending these *walargee* (meetings), it is considered against *saffu*."[112]

Oromo women used different *siiqqee* mechanisms to maintain their rights; such mechanisms included the law of *muka laaftu* (soften wood), the *abaarsa* (curse), *iyya siiqqee* (scream), and *godaana siiqqee* (trek). Kumsa comments that "Because of their liminality, women wield a special religious power where they draw an enormous moral and ritual authority. Men, therefore, try to avoid their curse and seek their blessings. . . . 'Women in general are symbolically and politically liminal and correspondingly enjoy special sacred power as a class.' . . . People respect and revere a woman because *Waaq* made her to be respected and revered. . . . [I]nterference with a woman's sacred authority is regarded as violating *seera Waaq* and *saffu*."[113] A man who violated women's individual and collective rights could be corrected through reconciliation and pledging not to repeat the mistakes or through women's reprisal ritual: A group of women "ambush the offender in the bush or on the road, bind him, insult him verbally using obscene language that they would not normally utter in the direct presence of an adult male, pinch him, and whip him with leafy branches or knotted strips of cloth. In extreme cases, they may force him to crawl over thorny or rocky ground while they whip him. . . . They demand livestock sacrifice as the price to cease their attack. If he refuses, they may tie him to a tree in the bush and seize one of his animals themselves. Other men rarely intervene."[114]

With the colonization of the Oromo people and the destruction of *gada* and *siiqqee* institutions, Oromo women have been subjected to three levels of oppression: racial/ethnonational, class, and gender oppression. However, it is necessary to recognize that internal factors such as class and state-formation processes, with their articulation with external factors, such as Turko-Egyptian colonialism, European and Ethiopian colonialism, the emergence of an Oromo collaborative class, and the spread of Islam and Christianity, undermined the political and military roles of the *gada* system in the nineteenth century.[115] However, these changes could not totally uproot Oromo values and traditions. Some elements of Oromo democratic values are still exist in areas where the *gada* system was suppressed. Nevertheless, in its modified form, the system is still in practice in southern Oromia, such as in the Borana and Guji regions, under Ethiopian colonialism; *gada* still helps to maintain peace, exchange knowledge, and practice rituals among some moieties and groups in southern Oromia.[116] Today some Oromo nationalists attempt to mobilize these cultural and political values, recognizing that Oromos can easily understand the objective of the Oromo national movement through these cultural devices.

Although the Oromo struggle mainly started as a political movement, it gradually mobilized a few Oromo intellectuals and other students of Oromo society to study Oromo culture and history. Particularly, a few Oromo intellectuals in the diaspora and other students of Oromo society, who were later prevented from studying Oromo society in Oromia by successive Ethiopian regimes, started to explore the main features of Oromo culture. In the 1980s and 1990s, intellectuals from the left and right found themselves on a shaky foundation in addressing the problems of indigenous peoples like that of Oromia. At the same time, when a few Oromo intellectuals and other students of Oromo society were engaged in studying Oromo culture, Oromo revolutionaries who initiated the political and armed struggle in Oromia discovered that the Oromo nationalist ideology that was based on a Marxist-Leninist-Maoist approach was not attractive to the Oromo people. This style of leftist approach was alien to

Oromo culture, and the Oromo people did not find any reference point in it. In addition, the Ethiopian military regime and the Ethiopian left misused and abused this Marxist paradigm to continue the exploitation and oppression of the Oromo nation. Gradually, Oromo nationalists started to realize that they did not capture the hearts and the minds of the Oromo, whom they struggled to liberate by using the Marxist-Leninist-Maoist approach. Since then, at least on ideological level, the Oromo political discourse has started to manifest Oromo cultural values and the Oromo democratic tradition. Recognizing that the Oromo democratic tradition had the potential to mobilize their people, "The Oromo national liberation fronts had chosen to champion specific components of popular democracy identified with the pre-colonial *Gada* system of government" when they joined the Transition al Government of Ethiopia between 1991 and 1992.[117]

The OLF, the main Oromo liberation organization, began to realize the power of Oromo culture and values, such as *gada,* after it failed to mobilize Oromos by using the alien ideology of Marxism-Leninism-Maoism. Some Oromo farmers accepted the OLF and its objectives after this organization used *gada* political discourse, which is engraved in their minds.[118] OLF officials and cadres learned through trial and error that embracing the principles of the Oromo democratic tradition and using symbols, such as the *odaa* (sycamore) tree, were necessary to mobilize the Oromo nation. When the OLF became part of the Transitional Government of Ethiopia, most Oromos saw the *odaa* symbol on its flag and accepted this organization, believing that it would restore the Oromo democratic tradition that would allow the Oromo to have the power of decision making to determine their destiny as a nation. Holcomb writes, "The overwhelming positive response of the Oromo population to the call for democracy was stimulated by seeing the symbol of *Gada,* the *odaa* tree under which Oromo formally deliberated and fashioned their law, flying on the flag of the largest of the independent Oromo organizations (OLF), as these once-underground organizations were invited and then welcomed into the Transitional Government of Ethiopia."[119] Because of the symbol of the *odaa* on the OLF flag and because of the articulation of the Oromo democratic tradition by some Oromo nationalists, most Oromos openly asserted, "Kun dhaba Keenya."[120] Literally, this means: "The OLF is our organization." The OLF that was known to only a few activist circles before 1991 became the popular national front, mobilizing the entire Oromo nation by using the Oromo democratic tradition and symbols.

Before the OLF was pushed from the transitional government by the Tigrayan-led government in 1992, as will see, OLF leaders, cadres, and community leaders and elders established a common political reference point by using Oromo democratic traditions and by openly discussing what Oromos should do to determine the future of their nation, Oromia.[121] The blossoming of Oromo nationalism, the re-emergence of Oromo unity, and the potential of Oromo cultural and political power angered the Tigrayan minority regime.[122] Consequently, the Tigrayan People's Liberation Front (TPLF) and its surrogate organization, the Ethiopian People's Revolutionary Democratic Front (EPRDF), abolished the transitional government by violently suppressing the Oromo struggle and by establishing the Tigrayan ethnocratic state with the help of the imperial interstate system, particularly the United States. Despite the suppression of the Oromo national movement by this racialized state, the Oromo national struggle and its democratic discourse have continued both in Oromia and in the world. The Oromo scholarship that was unleashed by the Oromo national struggle has mobilized Oromo cultural resources and started to develop a liberation knowledge that has challenged Ethiopianist scholarship by exposing the fallacy of its discourse.[123] Oromo scholars and other students of Oromo society agree that the Oromo democratic heritage still exists in Oromo cultural memory, language, religion, folklore, ritual, and custom and influence Oromo lives in private and public affairs. That is why Oromo nationalism cannot be understood adequately without its cultural foundations.

The emergence of Oromo nationalism and the attempt the Ethiopian state made to destroy it forced some Oromos to flee their homeland and disperse in Europe, the United States, Australia, the Middle East, and elsewhere.[124] Some Oromo refugees and other Oromos who left Oromia for education started to organize themselves in foreign countries. Politically conscious elements of the Oromo diaspora started to break down the isolation imposed on the Oromo nation by the alliance of Ethiopian colonialism and global imperialism; they organized themselves in groups such as the Union of Oromos in North America, the Union of Oromo Students in Europe, the Oromo Studies Association, the Oromo Relief Association, and Oromo community and support organizations. This new condition brought Oromos of diverse backgrounds "in the world beyond Oromia where communication was unrestricted" at the same time that globalism was intensifying revolutions in communication, technology, transportation, and finance.[125] The Oromo diaspora has begun to have access to political and cultural opportunities by being beyond Ethiopian state censorship and by producing and disseminating liberation knowledge via books, journals, pamphlets, newspapers, telephones, e-mail, the Internet, and the fax machine.

The issue of the return to the culture's sources is debated openly and routinely among the diaspora Oromos. As Holcomb says, "For the first time, Oromo in Europe and America have experienced the freedom of openly forming organizations and expressing themselves. . . . The Oromo started getting to know one another and working together in the outside world in ways that had never been allowed in Ethiopia. These organizations, through different mechanisms and media available to them, enabled the old and new arrivals to express their *Oromumma* [Oromo nationalism] and, in concert with others from all over Oromia, they raised the voice of the Oromo in the First World."[126] The Oromo diaspora has the potential to create a durable bridge between the Oromo nation and the world community, provided that it can develop an organizational capacity. This process may help to challenge the isolation imposed on the Oromo and their culture by the alliance of Ethiopian and global structures. Despite the fact that most Oromo intellectuals and activists and liberation organizations lack a profound knowledge of Oromo culture and democratic traditions, a few thinkers, activists, and artists have initiated the Oromo cultural movement. This movement embodies concepts such as *Oromumma* (Oromo cultural identity), *gootuma* (bravery and patriotism), *bilisumma* (emancipation), *gada* (Oromo popular democracy), *mootumma* (government), *nagaa* (peace), *kayyo* (fullness and richness), and *finna* (sustainable development).[127] These cultural and historical ideas must be linked to other chains of factors, as we shall see, that facilitated the development of Oromo nationalism.

The Development of Oromo Nationalism

The first factors to facilitate the emergence of Oromo nationalism were a collective grievance and the hope of freedom. However, colonization, dehumanization, subjugation, cultural destruction, and suppression by themselves cannot cause the emergence of nationalism. Between the 1860s and the 1900s, different Oromo groups resisted Ethiopian colonialism and fought several wars against Ethiopian colonial settlers and their collaborators.[128] Various Oromo branches, such as Wallo, Arssi, Tulama, Hanbana, Borana, Macha, Raya, and Yejju, fought bravely against the Ethiopian occupying forces.[129] Mentioning that his people were defeated because of lack of alliance with Europeans and modern weaponry, one Oromo leader said, "The hour has not come, but it will come; perhaps our children will see the departure of the oppressor."[130] The resistance also took varied ideological expression; some Oromos accepted Islam,[131] and others accepted Protestant Christianity to resist the imposition of the Ethiopian religion, Orthodox Christianity.[132] Islam and Protestant Christianity helped to draw a cultural boundary between Ethiopian colonizers and some colonized Oromos, although, as we will see, Oromo nationalism originally was initiated by elements of educated Oromo who were forced to accept Orthodox Christianity and assimilate to Ethiopian culture.

Different Oromo groups continued their resistance struggle during the first half of the twentieth century; there were numerous local uprisings in the Arssi, Hararghe, Qellem, Borana, Gibe, Wallo, Raya, Azabo, Yejju and other regions.[133] Northern Oromos, such as the Raya and Azabo, allied with the enemies of the Ethiopian government, including the Italian fascists who occupied Ethiopia between 1935 and 1941, to eliminate Ethiopian colonialism and create their own freedom.[134] Other Oromos used the opportunity of Italian colonialism to liberate themselves from Ethiopian colonialism. According to Baxter, "The Italian invasion led to local outbreaks of violence and there were some attempts to create locally autonomous units. In Arussi [Arssi] and Bale the people seem to have been content to chase away or kill local naftaanya [colonial settlers]. In Wallaga and Jimma, there was a series of attempts to create a Western Oromo Federation which would break away and place itself under British mandate."[135] In 1936, thirty-three Oromo leaders held several meetings and decided to form a Western Oromo Confederacy and expressed the desire of Western Oromos to become the protectorate of the League of Nations with the assistance of the British government until Western Oromia could achieve independence.[136] Since the British government and the League of Nations did not listen to this Oromo voice, Fascist Italy occupied western Oromia.

In 1941, the British government helped the restoration of the Haile Selassie government, although one of its officials openly admitted that it was wrong to restore the corrupt Amhara rule over the Oromo and other colonized nations. The Chairman of the British Committee on Ethiopia, Lord Moyne, after the Italians were defeated, commented, "we have a moral duty to see that the people of the country are not oppressed and enslaved. When we are fighting for freedom in Europe, how can we restore the Gallas [Oromos] and other subject races to Amharic tyranny?"[137] The British government ignored this important comment and restored the corrupt Haile Selassie regime which, immediately eliminated reforms that the Italian fascists introduced to win Oromos to their side. The Italian fascists abolished slavery and the *nafxanya-gabbar* system, restoring some rights to their lands and introducing the wage system and an Oromo-language radio station, but all these were eliminated when Ethiopian colonialism was restored. One Oromo aphorism captures how Ethiopian colonialism was as degrading and exploitative as that of Italian fascists: "Ha'adatu shashi gabi waya, ha'aamatu Xaliyani waya." (This means even if Italians were cruel they were not worse than the Ethiopians in their treatment of Oromos.) After Italians were expelled and the Haile Selassie government was restored under the auspices of the British government, Oromos continued their resistance struggle. In the 1940s and 1950s, a series of local resistance actions occurred in the effort to expel the colonialists. For instance, the Oromo in Hararghe took up arms against the regime in 1947 and 1948. The Raya, Azabo, and Wallo Oromos rebelled in 1947 but were crushed by the British Air Force. Furthermore, the Oromo of Dawe in Wallo rose up in arms and were brutally suppressed.

The Ethiopian colonial ruling class was initially successful in creating a collaborative Oromo class and in Ethiopianizing this class through marriage, education, and providing some privileges. A few elements of this class even gained higher status in Ethiopian bureaucracy. At the same time the Ethiopian system also made sure that these elements carried a badge of shame for being of "Galla" background. These Ethiopianized elements were constantly reminded that Galla elements could not be totally civilized.[138] Even if those Ethiopianized Oromos acted as Ethiopians or Amharas, the Ethiopian elites, by using racist discourse and some subtle discriminatory practices, made these kinds of Oromos humiliated and frustrated at the same time that they kept them away from key decision-making positions.[139] In addition to their cultural racism,[140] Ethiopians have feared and at the same time degraded Oromos as a people and assimilated those whom they wanted to use against Oromo society through the policy of divide, conquer, and dominate. The presence of *Habasha* fear can be demonstrated by examining their actions against Oromo culture and identity.

In addition to destroying and repressing Oromo culture and cultural leaders, successive *Habasha* governments have ensured that Oromos were denied educated cultural leaders. The colonization of Oromos denied them the opportunity to develop their language and literature; the Ethiopian government prevented Oromos from developing their language, *Afaan Oromoo,* as a literate language until the 1970s, when the Oromo national movement challenged the Ethiopianization/Amharization policy by adopting *qubee* (Latin alphabets).[141] Successive Ethiopian governments "have not only neglected, but have also actively suppressed the development of Oromo literature. The purpose of *Amharization* was to create a homogeneous Ethiopian society and identity through the medium of Amharic, the language of a dominant minority. Amharic was to be spread among the non-Amhara majority, through the school system, the Church—including the foreign missionaries—administrative institutions and not the least, settlement of Amharas in non-Amharic regions."[142] Formal study of the Oromo language had started in the first half of the nineteenth century in Europe, but the colonization of Oromia halted its progress.

Karl Tustschek, a German scholar, was hired by Prince Maximilian of Bavaria in 1938 to tutor former slaves (four Sudanese and one Oromo). He developed an interest in *Afaan Oromoo* because of "the simplicity and euphony and grammatical formation of the Oromo language which became evident, but after a very short study."[143] By studying *Afaan Oromoo* through communicating with more Oromo former slaves, Tustschek learned this language and wrote the manuscript of the Oromo-English-German dictionary in 1843. Since he died before publishing his manuscript, his brother, Lawrence Tustschek, edited and published two books, *The Dictionary of the Galla Language* and *A Grammar of the Galla Language* in 1944. Another German, J. L. Krapf, went to Oromia and studied this language. In 1840 he published his work, *An Imperfect Outline of the Elements of the Galla Language;* he also translated the Bible into *Afaan Oromoo.* Mekuria Bulcha asserts that "during the second half of the 19th century, Oromos in the diaspora (ex-slaves) continued to play an important role in the development of written *Afaan Oromoo*. Among these, the works of Onesimos Nasib and his Oromo language team came to constitute the basic literature of the Oromo language until the present day."[144] The scholarly team that worked with Onesimos Nasib included Aster Ganno, Lidya Dimboo, and Feben (Hirphee) Abba Magaal. These scholars translated biblical scriptures into the Oromo language.[145]

These scholars, under the guidance of Onesimos Nasib, laid the foundation of modern education in western Oromia by producing religious and secular books, developing the Oromo language, and opening schools, despite the opposition and repression they faced from the Ethiopian government and church.[146] Onesimos Nasib and his team pioneered the development of Oromo literature in western Oromia. Similarly, Sheik Bakri Sapalo initiated modern education in eastern Oromia, invented an Oromo alphabet in 1956, and produced several works on Oromo history and culture.[147] The brutality of Ethiopian colonialists did not allow such Oromo scholars to develop literary culture in Oromo society. Onesimos Nasib was imprisoned and banned from teaching Oromo children. Sheik Bakri Sapalo was put under house arrest for ten years and later forced to flee to Somalia, where he died in a refugee camp in 1980.[148] According to Mohammed Hassen, "What the two examples of Onesimos Nasib and Shaykh Bakri Sapalo clearly show is that educated Oromo both Christians and Muslims emphasized the importance of education for their people and the production of literary material in their language. Onesimos Nasib and Shaykh Bakri Sapalo are clear proof of the existence of Oromo national consciousness and of their concern with the Oromo language."[149] The literary works of Onesimos Nasib and his team and that of Bakri Sapalo indicate the existence of the first phase of nationalist cultural activities in Oromo society: "In the first phase, learned and culturally-minded individuals such as teachers, students . . . and writers turned their attention to their people's language, history and culture, though without arousing in society at large any great excitement about things national for the time being."[150]

Ethiopians face three dilemmas related to how to deal with Oromos. The first dilemma is a historical one. *Habasha* and Oromo societies fought each other over territory, land, water, religion, and civilization for almost four centuries without one dominating the other and establishing permanent colonialism, because both of them were at similar technological stages. As discussed earlier, this problem was solved by the alliance of European imperialism with Ethiopian colonialism in the second half of the nineteenth century.[151] Of course, this could not eliminate the potential threat of the Oromos to *Habasha* power. The second dilemma is the minority *Habashas'* attempt to assimilate the Oromo numerical majority without risking a political problem. Margery Perham clearly articulates the need for assimilating the Oromo majority into Ethiopian society, when she says "that they are estimated to outnumber the Amharas and the Tigrayans, and that they quite literally embrace half of the empire" and "there seems every possibility at this date that a development [of Oromo nationalism] that would be so disastrous to Ethiopia may be avoided."[152] She suggests that the spread of the Amhara language and *Habasha* culture amongst Oromo society as soon as possible would prevent the emergence of disastrous Oromo nationalism.[153] Perham failed to understand that Oromo cultural assimilation without structural assimilation (i.e., access to state power and cultural and economic resources) could not prevent the emergence of Oromo nationalism.[154] Global historical evidence demonstrates that those ethnonational groups who are denied cultural and economic development and access to state power develop a collective national consciousness to challenge the dominant ethnonations.[155] Because of the Oromo numerical weight, Ethiopian elites feared to structurally assimilate Oromos.

The third dilemma is that the major economic resources on which Ethiopians depend are located in Oromia. Ethiopian elites know that Oromos are aware of their second-class status in Ethiopia, their numerical weight, and the richness of Oromian resources. They fear the Oromo political potential, and hence they are determined to prevent Oromo access to state power by any means necessary.[156] The Ethiopian colonial ruling class and its state have aspired to maintain an ethnonational class hierarchy by culturally assimilating Oromos as second-class citizens, dominating the Ethiopian political economy through preventing structural assimilation of the majority population. As a result, Oromos are not integrated into Ethiopian society. Since assimilated Oromos have not been accepted as equals by Ethiopians and since they have been rejected by Oromo society as collaborators, they cannot become an effective force except when promoting their class interests and that of the Ethiopian and global colonizing structures. As we will see shortly, a few elements of this class initiated Oromo nationalism by rejecting their collaborative status, siding with the exploited and oppressed Oromo majority, and transforming the Oromo resistance to Ethiopian colonialism into a national movement.

Urbanization and formal education played key roles in transforming Oromo resistance to Ethiopian colonialism into Oromo nationalism in the early 1960s. A few young Oromos, who either moved voluntarily or were brought to garrison cities from different areas of Oromia as students and soldiers, gradually became bureaucrats, politicians, professionals, and intellectuals and "able to see more clearly the similarity of their experiences and commonality of their aspirations."[157] As the development of colonial capitalism intensified in Oromia, the processes of urbanization, education, and communication increased.[158] As a result, two interlinked and contradictory social processes developed. One is the process of subordination and Ethiopianization or Amharization. The second one is the process of resistance to subordination and the development of Oromo political consciousness. The Ethiopian colonial ruling class assumed that Oromo identity could be dissolved through cultural assimilation. According to Herbert Lewis, "By claiming that Oromo ethnic identity is unauthentic, that it never existed, that Oromo have too many different local and cultural varieties to ever agree on anything and have no overarching sense of 'nationhood,' or that they are inextricably mixed with many other peoples, the opponents believe that they can divide, destroy, or, perhaps, wish away Oromo nationalism."[159] Successive Ethiopian regimes have tried to destroy or suppress Oromo national identity through different colonial policies. Oromo nationalism emerged in opposition to Ethiopian colonial policies and ethnocratic politics that targeted their identity and cultural and economic resources.[160] Originally, Oromo politics emerged as reform nationalism, which had as its goal to change the status of Oromos within the Ethiopian context. The organization that manifested this aspect of Oromo nationalism was the Macha-Tulama Self-Help Association.

The Macha-Tulama Self-Help Association

The Macha-Tulama Association was formed as a social movement in 1963 by urban-based Oromo intellectuals, army officers, soldiers, students, and merchants who were frustrated by their status of second-class citizenship, colonial mistreatment, and discrimination due to their ethnonational origin. The year 1963 was a turning point in Oromo history because prominent Oromos such as Haile-Mariam Gamada, a lawyer, and Colonel Alemu Qixxeesa facilitated the merging of three small self-help associations—the Meta-Robbi, Jibat-Macha, and Tulama Shawa self-help associations—to create the Macha-Tulama Self-Help Association in the Shawa administrative region.[161] However, this regional self-help association, because of its objectives, emerged as an Oromia-wide organization and centrally led movement by attracting members from all regions. There were two sets of objectives of the association. The first one was the establishment of schools and health clinics and the construction of roads wherever they were needed in Oromia. The second set of objectives was the construction of churches and mosques for the Christian and Muslim believers who did not have them and the provision of financial and legal assistance for disabled and unemployed persons. The first set of objectives was aimed at improving the welfare of the Oromo nation. The second set was aimed at mobilizing the Oromo nation toward a common goal, thus undermining the colonial policy of divide and rule on the bases of religion, class, and region.

It was only in the 1950s that the Ethiopian government allowed the formation of associations by its revised Constitution.[162] Before this time it was a political crime to form an association or an organization. Using the opportunity that was provided by this revised Constitution, those few Oromo individuals who joined colonial institutions such as schools, the army, and administration, as well as merchants, started to promote Oromo national development by forming this association. According to Baxter, "As more Oromos became civil servants, army officers and NCO's and more Oromo schoolboys became undergraduates, and as more Oromo members of Parliament managed to get elected, the various Oromo groups found that, in addition to humiliating experiences, they shared a common language and similar values. The new pan-Oromo consciousness was largely generated by the army, the university and parliament itself."[163] Both individual experiences and the exploitation and dehumanization of their people made such Oromos politically aware. Such Oromo individuals were brought together in urban areas by the same colonial institutions that discriminated against them and attempted to use them as members of a collaborative class.

Because of its objectives and popularity, within three years, the membership of the association reached more than two million.[164] There were also 26 leaders from other ethnonations, such as Afars, Issas, Adares, Bella Shanguls, Gamos, Gimiras, Kulo Kontas, Sidamas, and Walayitas, who joined and held important positions within various committees of this association.[165] A core of nationalist leaders, such as Haile-Mariam Gamada, Alemu Qixxeesa, Taddasa Biru, and Mamo Mazamir, clearly articulated to Oromos the objectives of the association and expanded its branches all over Oromia. Whereas scholars like Onesimos Nasib and his team and Bakri Sapalo had attempted to restore Oromo culture and develop Oromo literature through their written works, these nationalists attempted to mobilize Oromos politically and culturally. Explaining similar conditions, Peter Alter said, "The second phase, in political mobilization, comes when the learned interest of the minority, spreads to the other sectors of the population, when it is transformed into channeled political agitation by a minority that thinks in terms of the nation."[166]

When Brigadier General Taddasa Biru, who hesitantly joined the Macha-Tulama Association, discovered that the Ethiopian government and its top Amhara officials intentionally designed mechanisms that would restrict a constant influx of Oromo into Ethiopian institutions, he became very angry and started to promote the objectives of the association.[167] As a result, he emerged as the leader of the association and started openly to agitate for the Oromo cause. He was the Commander of the Rapid Force (riot battalions), Deputy Commissioner of the Ethiopian Police Force, Commander of the Territorial Army, and Chairman of the National Literacy Campaign. When this influential Ethiopianized Oromo turned to the Oromo cause and appeared in several mass meetings to champion the political, cultural, and economic rights of Oromos with other Oromo leaders, the Ethiopian government feared that this would promote Oromo nationalism. When such mass meetings were held at Gulale, Kachis, Jeldu, Kalacha, Bishoftu, Bako, and Dheera, local government branches attempted to disperse these meetings.[168] As A. P. Wood puts it, "Although nominally a self-help association, it began to articulate the dissatisfaction of the Oromo with the government and particularly with their position in society. This position . . . caused much government concern and . . . the association was banned" in 1967.[169]

Another reason for the government concern was the linkage of the association with the Bale Oromo armed struggle (1963–1970). Leaders such as Adam Buna and Haji Adam Sado had established a strong link between the two; this armed struggle liberated almost 75 percent of the Bale administrative region in 1967 and expanded to other regions.[170] Captain Mamo Mazamir, who was the most revolutionary element of the association, encouraged the Bale Oromo armed struggle and expressed: "The history of mankind shows that a people who rise in the struggle for freedom and independence, in defiance of death, is always victorious. . . . The life and death struggle of the oppressed masses in the Ethiopian Empire against the hegemony of the Amhara and their allies headed by American imperialism is a sacred liberation struggle of millions of oppressed and humiliated people."[171]

Furthermore, these leaders' interest in Oromo history, culture, and language annoyed Amhara elites and the government because the latter thought that the Ethiopianized Oromos would reject Oromo history, culture, and language that were targeted for destruction. Baxter notes, "Oromo was denied any official status and it was not permissible to publish, preach, teach or broadcast in Oromo. In court or before an official an Oromo had to speak Amharic or use an interpreter. Even a case between Oromos, before an Oromo speaking magistrate, had to be heard in Amharic."[172] Since the association, both leaders and members, defied the position of the Ethiopian government regarding the Oromo, the Haile Selassie government targeted the association and its leaders. The crime of this association and its leaders was mainly to attempt to reform Ethiopia so that Oromos and other oppressed peoples would be equal to Amharas and Tigrayans by restoring their respective histories, cultures, and languages.

It was only Mamo Mazamir and Haji Robale Ture who indicated the need to go beyond reforming Ethiopia. When Mamo Mazamir noted that "the militant members are working now on the means of organizing a nationwide people's movement which is based on realizing the aspirations of Oromo people as a whole," Robale Ture asserted that as "streams join together to form a river, people also join together to be a nation and to become a country."[173] As we will discuss below, the position of these two leaders has emerged as the mainstream in the Oromo national movement because of the opposition and cruelty of Amharas and Tigrayans to this movement. The government banned the association, labeling it a "tribal association," and imprisoned the top leaders and severely tortured and dehumanized them. It also killed some of these leaders. The government sentenced Taddasa Biru and Mamo Mazamir to death and later changed Taddasa's death sentence to life imprisonment. Mamo was hung in 1968.

Mamo's predictions were partially fulfilled; those who sentenced him to death were killed by the military regime in 1974. Although the liberation of Oromos has not occurred, the Oromo movement has been transformed into a mass liberation struggle. Haile-Mariam Gamada, the secretary of the association, who eventually was tortured to death, also said: "Neither the imprisonment and killing of the leaders nor banning of the association will deter the [Oromo] nation's struggle. What we did is like a snake that entered a stomach. Whether it is pulled out or left there, the result is one and the same. It has spread its poison."[174] Oromo nationalism has become poison to the Ethiopian empire, as this prominent leader predicted. Realizing that a peaceful and open movement was not to be allowed in this empire, revolutionary Oromo nationalists who were schooled in the Macha-Tulama Association and other nationalists created the Oromo Liberation Front (OLF) in the early 1970s to engage in armed struggle.

The Birth of the Oromo Liberation Front

After the Ethiopian colonial government denied Oromos any channel through which to express their ethnonational interest, a few Oromo nationalist elements established an underground political movement and transformed reform nationalism into a revolutionary one. When Oromo nationalism aimed at reform was forced to go underground through the destruction of the Macha-Tulama Association, some nationalists joined the Bale Oromo armed struggle while others fled to Somalia, Sudan, and the Middle East to continue the Oromo struggle from a distance. The nationalist elements who remained in Oromia established a clandestine movement and organized secret political study circles. They produced political pamphlets such as *The Oromo: Voice against Tyranny* and *Kana Beekta?* The central mission of this underground movement was expressed as a national liberation struggle.[175] *Voice* states that an Oromo nationalist is "ready and prepared to pay any sacrifice and oppose any person or groups that in any way hinder his mission for liberation from all forms of oppression and subjugation. An Oromo has no empire to build but a mission to break an imperial yoke, that makes this mission sacred and his sacrifices never too dear."[176] For the first time, this underground movement started to use the name Oromo in writing, instead of Galla (the name of contempt and derogation), thus defying Ethiopian and Ethiopianist historiography. Besides restoring the original name of the people, this underground movement continued to expose the distortion of Oromo history in its writings. Its members and those Oromo students who were influenced by them began to study and reconstruct Oromo history according to an Oromo perspective. "For the peoples and nations in struggle for their effective liberation," C. Wondji asserts, "history provides a valuable understanding of earlier patterns of development in these societies; it thus clarifies the problem of development in the present as well as analyzing of the past."[177]

These Oromo nationalist elements understood from the beginning the importance of the reconstruction of Oromo culture and history for the survival of the Oromo national identity and for the development of Oromo nationalism. Therefore, they influenced young Oromo nationalists to engage in an Oromo cultural renaissance by challenging the Ethiopian and Ethiopianist scholarship that attacked Oromo peoplehood, culture, and history. The emergent Oromo studies have replaced colonial history with a history of liberation and have refuted historical myths that had been produced to justify Ethiopian colonialism. Since the theories of Western civilization, such as modernization and Marxism, had failed to explain adequately the problem of the Oromo, emerging Oromo intellectuals returned to study the traditions of their society.

The Oromo nationalist nucleus originally found its active audiences mainly among Oromo university students, students who had joined the Haile Selassie I University from different regions of Oromia.[178] They were already exposed to the brutality and dehumanization of Ethiopian colonialism through the experiences of their families and local elementary and secondary schools that glorified Ethiopian culture, history, civilization, and language while denigrating that of the Oromo. These students discovered that the Ethiopian knowledge elites, with the support of the Ethiopian state and the imperial interstate system, produced "official" history that completely denied historical or cultural space for the Oromo and other colonized peoples. Oromo students had two choices: They were either to ignore their denigrated Oromo identity and accept the Ethiopian identity or to challenge the falsehood about Oromos by siding with the underground Oromo movement. If they chose the latter, it was at the cost of risking their professions and their lives. Those who accepted the Ethiopian identity and joined Ethiopian political groups took the position that the Oromo movement was a "narrow nationalist" movement.

Since most Ethiopian teachers and professors taught the superiority of Ethiopian culture and civilization and the inferiority of Oromos in educational institutions, it was not difficult to recruit clandestinely some students and educate them about the plight of Oromos through secret study circles. These students studied philosophy, Marxism–Leninism, political economy, social history, revolution, and nationalism. As a result, some of these students started to gain a critical understanding of the Oromo question. Further, the one-sidedness of most teachers and professors and their ignorance of Oromo culture, civilization, and history increased the commitment of some students to learn more about their people and to struggle to liberate them. Hence, university education allowed some Oromo students to understand and articulate the accumulated collective grievances of their people. With their increased political consciousness and political maturity, they first used the Ethiopian student movement as a platform to express Oromo grievances. They did this without rejecting, as Ethiopianized Oromos, the Oromo identity; that is, at the same time, they began to build the Oromo independent student movement in the early 1970s. These students worked closely with the underground nationalist nucleus and helped in transforming the Oromo resistance into an organized revolutionary movement. Higher education helped Oromo revolutionary intellectuals and students to learn about "modern" organization, methods of organizing people, and historical and current ways of engaging in protracted guerrilla warfare against a formidable enemy.[179]

The new Oromo nationalist leaders produced political pamphlets and expanded their sphere of influence by organizing different political circles in different sectors of Oromo society, such as professionals, workers, farmers, high school students, and the army. Those Oromos who fled to foreign countries and received military training returned to Oromia to initiate armed struggle. A committee to organize a liberation front was formed and the guerrilla armed struggle started in 1973 under the leadership of Elemo Qilixxu. As Cabral says, "With a strong indigenous cultural life, foreign domination cannot be sure of its perpetuation. At any moment, depending on internal and external factors determining the evolution of society in question, cultural resistance (indestructible) may take on new forms (political, economic, armed) in order fully to contest foreign domination."[180] With the official birth of the OLF in 1974, the Oromo nation consolidated its challenge to Ethiopian colonial domination ideologically, intellectually, politically, and militarily.

The birth of the OLF introduced a new direction for Oromo nationalism; conscious Oromos had started to talk about the formation of a liberation front before the birth of the OLF.[181] The OLF's stated objectives were to create Oromo national power, to overthrow Ethiopian settler colonialism, and to decide Oromia's political future democratically through a referendum. OLF asserts that it is only the Oromo nation that can decide whether to create "an independent republic of Oromia," or to build a multicultural democracy by joining "other peoples in a federal or confederal arrangement."[182] The OLF emphasized that "the right of self-determination is an inalienable right of our people to the fulfillment of which our front is committed as a matter of priority and it holds that it is the Oromo people and only the Oromo people who should determine its own political future."[183]

An Oromo armed group initiated its first military operation in the Charchar mountains of Hararghe in November 1973. Since this group had connections with the underground Oromo movement that later emerged as the OLF, the OLF claims this military operation as its own, although it declared itself as a front in 1974. This operation was not successful. Its leader, Elemu Qilixxu, was martyred in 1974, and the guerrilla unit was suppressed. This occurred when the military regime, the *Derg*, "deployed a special force in the area . . . and carried out mass genocide on an innocent civilian population."[184] Similarly, General Taddasa Biru, who escaped from prison when the Haile Selassie government was overthrown, initiated unsuccessful armed struggle in Ambo, central Oromia, in December 1974 and declared land to be owned by those who farm it. Since the General took popular measures and won several followers within a very short time, the Mengistu regime panicked and hurriedly declared the nationalization of rural land, mobilized its military and security personnel, infiltrated the rank and file of his followers, and captured and arrested him on March 13, 1975.[185] His associate, Colonel Hailu Ragassa, and the general were executed by the military regime on March 19, 1975.

These unsuccessful armed struggles, the revolutionary crisis of the Ethiopian empire, and the land reform put the Oromo underground movement in turmoil. Some Oromo intellectuals, in order to influence the direction of the emerging revolutionary crisis in Ethiopia, joined different organizations, such as the Ethiopian People's Revolutionary Party (EPRP), All Ethiopian Socialist Movement (MEISON), and Ethiopian Oppressed Revolutionary Struggle (ECHAT). Of all the Ethiopian organizations, it was only ECHAT that did not oppose the independent Oromo voice, because it was mainly organized by the members of the colonized ethnonations. At this time the majority of Oromo intellectuals thought that the Oromo question could be solved by these Ethiopian organizations and consequently joined them. It was a minority of Oromos at that time who insisted in maintaining the independent Oromo voice.

The military regime destroyed these Ethiopian organizations one by one ostensibly because of their political immaturity, lack of interest in the questions of the oppressed classes and the colonized nations, adventurism, opportunism, Ethiopian chauvinism, and lack of political unity. The independent Oromo voice survived and reorganized the Oromo Liberation Front in 1976, revising its program and reinitiating armed struggle.[186] The Front's underground papers, such as *Warraaqaa* and *Bakkalcha Oromo,* popularized the activities of the movement. There were also independent underground papers, such as *Oromia* and *Gucaa Dargagoo,* that agitated for the Oromo national movement. The Oromo armed struggle that resumed in Gara Mulata, Hararghe, in 1976 faced major problems because of the lack of sanctuary and the confrontation between Somalia and Ethiopia over eastern Oromia. Just as Ethiopia wanted to assimilate and destroy Oromo peoplehood and to claim Oromo resources as Ethiopian, Somalia attempted to Somalize Oromos and claim Oromo resources as Somali within the vision of a greater Somalia. According to Ernest Gellner, the Somali viewed "the Oromo as a kind of human population without a set of form, a pre-ethnic raw material, waiting to be turned either into Amharas or into Somalis by the turn of political fortune and religious conversion."[187]

The Somali government applied the term "Somali Abbo" to Oromo refugees in Somalia, claiming that Oromos in Bale, Arssi, Sidamo, and Hararghe were "Somali Abbo" who did not know their identity and called themselves mistakenly Oromos.[188] From the beginning, the OLF faced strong opposition from both the Ethiopian colonialists and the Somali expansionists. As a result, the development of the OLF was slowed because it lost some leaders, fighters, supporters, and sympathizers. The Somali government created the Somali Abbo Liberation Front (SALF) in 1976 to serve as a branch of the Western Somalia Liberation Front (WSLF) for incorporating eastern and southern Oromia. Some Somali elites have remained the enemy of Oromo nationalism. Comparing the opposition of Somali and Amhara elites to Oromo nationalism, Hassen states, "Whereas the Amhara elites saw the danger to their empire in the growth of Oromo nationalism, the Somali elites perceived the frustration of their ambition in the birth of Oromo nationalism. The Amhara attitude was nourished by the spectre of the disintegration of their empire for, without the resources of Oromia, Ethiopia cannot exist as a viable state. The attitude of the Somali ruling elites was nourished by the untenable ambition to build greater Somalia."[189] Despite the brutality of both the Ethiopian and Somali governments against the OLF, it survived and extended its influence.

In 1981, the OLF launched an operation in Wallaga, Western Oromia. It built its military sources through a series of surprise attacks on the Ethiopian forces and the capture of their weapons and other materials.[190] During the Ethio-Somali war of 1977–1978, OLF fighters captured some weapons and ammunition from both sides.[191] Since the OLF did not have international assistance, it depended on the local population for food, intelligence, and supplies.[192] Due to lack of international support and sanctuary, Ethiopian brutality, Somali opposition to Oromo nationalism, and internal disagreement within Oromo elites, the growth of Oromo nationalism was very slow in the 1970s and the 1980s. However, as the Ethiopian military regime of the *Derg* intensified its political pacification through its villagization schemes, its economic concentration through the expropriation of Oromo properties, and its de-Oromization of Oromia through settling Amharas and Tigrayans there, thousands of Oromos began to recognize the importance of armed struggle. As the OLF intensified its agitation through its radio station, the Voice of Oromo Liberation, and various political networks, its areas of influence expanded. Then, to frustrate and weaken an Oromo urban connection, the military regime imprisoned or murdered prominent Oromo intellectuals, students, and merchants in the 1980s. Baxter notes why successive Ethiopian governments have been seriously concerned about Oromo nationalism, and says, "The crucial dependence of Ethiopia on the Oromo inclines the central . . . government to strike out at any manifestation of Oromo consciousness."[193]

The OLF's longevity is due, less to its military strength than to its public commitment to and defense of Oromian self-determination and the restoration of Oromo culture, particularly aspects of the Oromo democratic heritage. When the OLF expanded its sphere of influence and began to consolidate its army in the late 1980s and the early 1990s, new conditions started to emerge in the Ethiopian empire. These new situations were indicators of the deep crisis and disintegration of the Amhara-led military regime in response to internal, domestic, regional, and global politics. These politics raised new opportunities and new challenges for the Oromo national movement.

The Current Status of the Oromo Struggle

The current Oromo national struggle cannot be clearly understood without explaining it in relation to the structural problems of the Ethiopian empire and the global imperial interstate system. The Ethiopian military regime headed by Colonel Mengistu Haile-Mariam (1974–1991) emerged as the result of the structural and revolutionary crises of the early 1970s. This government took several policy measures, such as land reform and nationalization of industries and financial institutions, then allied with Soviet-bloc countries to solve the crises that subsequently arose. Depending on Soviet military assistance and expertise, the military regime attempted to solve political problems largely through military violence and terrorism. It also tried to reduce the problems of politics, poverty, and famine through controlling farmers by forcing them into cooperatives, resettlement, and villagization schemes. Further, thousands of able-bodied farmers were conscripted into the army to fight against the OLF, the Eritrean People's Liberation Front (EPLF), and the Tigrayan People's Liberation Front (TPLF). Despite all these attempts, the military regime failed to eliminate the political, economic, and social problems that it inherited from the Haile Selassie government. Further, its misguided policies led to the severe internal crisis of the regime that brought on the unsuccessful military coup of 1989. The top leaders of the army who were involved in this coup were murdered or imprisoned by Colonel Mengistu and his faction. As a result, the military lost its experienced leadership and was debilitated. It could not fight effectively against the national liberation fronts in the late 1980s and the early 1990s.

At the same time, the Soviet Union began new initiatives known as *glasnost* and *perestroika* (openness and restructuring) under the leadership of Gorbachev to change its domestic and international policies.[194] Since the Soviet Union was changing its cold-war politics, it informed the Ethiopian military regime that it would not continue its military assistance after 1992. Between 1977 and 1991, the USSR provided military equipment estimated at U.S. $12 billion, but this could not guarantee the survival of the regime.[195] When the USSR notified Ethiopia that after 1992 it would not renew its arms transfer agreement, Ethiopia began to look to the United States for assistance. The U.S. government agreed to act as a broker between the military regime and the EPLF, the strongest liberation front, and continued its support to the TPLF, viewing it as an alternative to the Mengistu regime. Domestic crises, global politics, and assistance from the U.S. and the EPLF encouraged the TPLF to prepare itself to replace the Mengistu government and rule over a collapsing empire. The ambition of the TPLF to reorganize Ethiopian colonialism by replacing the Mengistu regime was also supported by Sudan and Libya. All of these forces ignored Oromos and their primary front, the OLF. Although the EPLF had a friendly relationship with the OLF, it demonstrated its favor for the TPLF by helping it in "recycling" Oromo-speaking Ethiopian soldiers who were captured at various war fronts and by assisting the TPLF in creating the Oromo People's Democratic Organization (OPDO) to undermine the OLF and Oromian national self-determination.[196]

Because of shared ethnonational affinity, geographical proximity, and political interest, the EPLF-trained TPLF fighters coordinated their operations with the EPLF against the army of the *Derg*'s military regime. Sudan provided sanctuary and territory to import weapons, ammunition, provisions, and other necessary materials without intervention.[197] Libya provided ample military and financial assistance to the TPLF, too.[198] Furthermore, during the famine (1984–1985) and after, the TPLF formed a strong relationship with the United States and received economic assistance that helped it to build itself militarily, organizationally, and diplomatically. The TPLF mobilized famine-stricken Tigrayan farmers as its fighters and organized its affiliate organizations from prisoners of war by using U.S. financial and political assistance. It merged the Ethiopian Officers Revolutionary Movement (EORM), the Ethiopian People's Democratic Movement (EPDM), and the Oromo People's Democratic Organization (OPDO) to form the Tigrayan-led Ethiopian People's Revolutionary Democratic Front (EPRDF).[199] As Agency France Press states, the U.S. government backed the TPLF "for several years in their struggle against Lieutenant-Colonel Mengistu's regime and it was on American advice that the TPLF became the EPRDF, though former Tigrayan guerrillas are still dominant in the movement."[200] Both the EPLF and the United States essentially ignored the Oromo, the largest ethnonation, and its primary liberation front, the OLF, and prepared the Tigrayan elites and their liberation front, TPLF, to reorganize Ethiopian colonialism under Tigrayan leadership. The EPLF fought side-by-side with the TPLF-led EPRDF in capturing parts of Oromia and later recolonizing Oromos by fighting against the OLF. The EPLF army was in Oromia as late as 1997 defending the Tigrayan regime.[201]

When the Colonel Mengistu regime was paralyzed because of its internal, domestic, and international structural crises, the United States attempted to bring together the EPLF, the TPLF/EPRDF, the OLF, and the Ethiopian government at the London Peace Conference on May 27 and 28, 1991. Before this conference was held, Mengistu, on U.S. advice, left his power to Tesfaye Gebre Kidane and fled to Zimbabwe. Then the organization of Mengistu's troops dissolved and they turned on one another and stopped fighting. The TPLF/EPRDF replaced the Mengistu regime with the blessing of the EPLF and the United States without establishing "a broadly based provisional government that would prepare the country for election."[202] Hoping that the Oromo question would be solved peacefully and democratically and that attendance would give the Oromo people and its main front media recognition all over the world, the OLF participated in the aborted U.S.-sponsored London Conference and the Addis Ababa Peace Conference of July 1–5, 1991. The OLF also invited and convinced other independent Oromo political organizations such as the Islamic Front for the Liberation of Oromia (IFLO), the United Oromo People's Liberation Front (UOPLF), and the Oromo "Abbo" Liberation Front (OALF) to participate in the Tigrayan-dominated Transitional Government of Ethiopia.

The OLF participated in the formulation and adoption of a Transitional Charter, which was to govern relations among the parties during an interim period. This charter theoretically endorsed the Universal Declaration of Human Rights of the United Nations, the right of nations to self-determination, freedom of association and expression, and the formation of a multinational federal democratic state. However, in reality the adoption of the charter and the formation of the Transitional Government "was more an exercise in bringing more groups under the mantle of Tigrean People's Liberation Front than in open democracy."[203] Using its surrogate organization, EPRDF, the TPLF dominated a Council of Representatives and a Council of Ministers and controlled the policy and decision-making process; it reduced the influence of the OLF in government "by filling all key government posts with EPRDF"[204] and by establishing its shadow government in four ministerial positions it provided to the OLF.[205]

While the Tigrayan rulers had opposed the *Derg* out of an interest in capturing and consolidating Ethiopian state power and keeping the Ethiopian empire under their control, Oromos were struggling for the dismantling of the Ethiopian colonial system. "If we accept that national liberation demands a profound mutation in the process of development or productive forces," Cabral notes, "we see that this phenomenon of national liberation necessarily corresponds to a revolution."[206] The Oromo national movement has sought to promote the processes of decolonization, democratization, transformation, and national self-determination. According to then OLF General Secretary Galasa Dilbo, Oromos and their organizations participated in the transition to give a democratic transition a chance and to further mobilize the Oromo nation culturally and politically.[207] The OLF has officially taken the position preferring a democratic conflict resolution, and it engages in armed struggle only where democracy is not working.[208] Implicitly to avoid war and give peace and democracy a chance, the OLF leaders during this period downplayed its objective of the creation of an independent republic of Oromia.

The participation of the OLF in the Tigrayan-dominated transitional government for almost one year enabled the Oromo leadership to realize some of its ideological, cultural, and intellectual objectives. Evidence suggests that a majority of Oromos accepted the OLF during that transitional period and declared the necessity of the unity of Oromos, of the OLF leadership, and of the creation of Oromo national power.[209] Michael Hiltzik said in 1992, "Any unwitting observers who happened upon a public ceremony . . . recently could be forgiven for thinking they had strayed across the border into another country. Speaker after speaker evoked the name of the 'nation of Oromia.'"[210] The revival of Oromo culture astonished many observers. For example, Ben Barber observed in 1994, "Ordinary Oromo people are savoring the return of cultural freedom."[211] He also commented, "The challenge faced by Ethiopia today is whether allowing an Oromo language and cultural revival will go deep enough to convince nearly half of its people to remain part of the nation. The allure of self-determination could well lead to conflict such as has convulsed Hutus and Tutsis in nearby Rwanda."[212] One of the cultural achievements of the OLF was to enable Oromos to use *qubee,* an Oromized Latin Alphabet, which transformed Oromo society from an oral to literary society. Because of the Oromo national movement, Oromia has become a political and geographical reality, despite the fact that parts of it have been partitioned off and given to other regions by the Tigrayan-led regime in order to minimize the influence of Oromos.

The OLF extended its politics from the periphery to the center; this new condition temporarily allowed Oromos to send their representative to Habro, Arssi, Finfinne, Naqamte, Ambo, and other regions to discuss and develop a strategy for the Oromo national struggle.[213] OLF cultural and musical troupes articulated the nature of Ethiopian colonialism and the necessity of liberation through traditional and modern music, poems, and speeches. The OLF expressed its commitment to guarantee Oromos the right to develop their culture, language, and education; to create Oromo national power; to guarantee Oromia the right to build its own army to defend its national interests; and to enable Oromos to achieve their right to national self-determination under Oromian national assembly.[214] Through their representatives the Oromo population demanded that five Oromo organizations, including the OPDO, join the independent Oromo national movement.[215] However, it took almost a decade for the independent Oromo organizations OLF, IFLO, UOPLF, OLC (Oromiya Liberation Council, OPLF (Oromo People's Liberation Front), and OPLO (Oromo People's Liberation Organization I & II) to form the United Liberation Forces of Oromiya. The blossoming of Oromo nationalism within short time, the re-emergence of Oromo unity, the operation of the OLF in particular "above the ground for the first time," its popularity among Oromos, and its fierce competition with the TPLF/EPRDF for political power annoyed the Meles regime.[216]

The TPLF/EPRDF regime feared that Oromo nationalism would explode like a social volcano and would destroy it. Therefore, it began to practice state terrorism to suppress the independent Oromo national movement and replace it wherever possible with EPRDF's own OPDO. Opposing the violations of Oromo national and individual rights, various representatives of the Oromo charged that the TPLF/EPRDF forces looted the economic resources of the Oromo nation; divided Oromia and gave parts of it to the regions of other peoples; organized minority ethnonational groups against Oromos; involved itself in the internal affairs of Oromia through its army and surrogate organization, the OPDO; conducted a series of wars of aggression against Oromos; and violated the Transitional Charter by intimidating, killing, imprisoning, and torturing Oromos for supporting the OLF.[217] When the Meles regime realized that it was highly unlikely that the Oromo majority would democratically put the TPLF/EPRDF in state power, it opted for the continuation of Ethiopian colonial domination under its leadership. It attacked Oromos, the OLF, and other independent Oromo organizations such as IFLO and UOPLF, militarily. The regime's attempt to consolidate a Tigrayan version of Ethiopian colonialism increased the popularity of the OLF and facilitated the further development of Oromo nationalism.

These problems—the blockage of regional elections in June 1992, and the declaration of war on the encamped OLF army—forced the OLF to withdraw from the election process. The regime then intensified its war of aggression against the Oromo people, the Oromo Liberation Army and other Oromo organizations, and ordered OLF leaders to leave the country. To discourage the populace, the regime intensified its state terrorism and the practice of ethnic cleansing[218] with little opposition from the world, particularly the United States. Since 1992, the Meles regime has murdered thousands of Oromos and created several concentration camps, such those as at Hurso (Hararghe), Didhesa (Wallaga), and Bilate (Sidamo), where pregnant women, children, elders, and sick Oromos have perished.[219] The hopes for Oromian national self-determination and democracy that emerged with the demise of the military regime in 1991 were dashed in the 1992 elections, when the EPRDF, dominated by TPLF (with the Oromo out of the way), consolidated a minority Tigrayan-based authoritarian government. Originally in order to obtain political legitimacy, the TPLF-led regime had invited different fronts, the largest and most prominent of which was the OLF, and other political organizations and established a transitional government. The EPRDF had persuaded the others that it would prepare a ground for the formation of a multi-national federal democratic government of Ethiopia. However, in less than a year, this regime had expelled all coalition partners by using war and terrorism and established an ethnic-based party dictatorship without any opposition from the United States and other Western countries that support the regime.[220]

The financial and grain assistance that the TPLF had received, mainly from the United States, enabled this liberation front to mobilize hungry Tigrayan peasants in the mid-1980s to become fighters. Unfortunately, using their fear of famine, of poverty, of Oromo and of Islam, the Meles regime converted these former freedom fighters into state terrorists in order to assassinate or murder, intimidate and control Oromos and others, and loot their economic resources.[221] Oromos are mainly targeted by the TPLF/EPRDF regime because of their national struggle, numerical strength, and economic resources. The Tigrayan colonial regime is still in power mainly because of the financial and military assistance it receives from the United States and other industrialized countries. For example, *Impact International* notes that the U.S. government "agreed in July 1996 to supply Ethiopia 50 fighter aircraft and a number of helicopter gun ships. After signing the agreement, a Pentagon spokesman described Prime Minister Meles Zenawi as 'a trusted and important friend of America . . . the Ethiopian leader was the only one in the region' whom they could depend upon to counter the menace of fundamentalism."[222]

The United States, other Western countries, and Israel use the discourse of Islamic fundamentalism to support the Meles regime and to suppress the struggle of Oromos for national self-determination and democracy.[223] Despite the fact that the U.S. government officially promotes a democratic discourse, it practically supports the subordination of Oromos to Tigrayans on the pretext of suppressing the expansion of Islamic fundamentalism and maintaining the territorial integrity of Ethiopia.[224] However, the majority of Oromos, regardless of religious affiliations—Christian, Muslim, non-Christian, and non-Muslim Oromos—support independent nationalist organizations that lead the Oromo national movement in their struggle for national and democratic rights. Oromos are labeled "Islamic fundamentalists" and their liberation fronts are labeled "bandits" or "terrorists"[225] without evidence or justification with the result that the violation of Oromo rights generates no sympathy for them in the world. As the Mengistu regime utilized a "socialist" discourse to ally itself with the Soviet bloc and to consolidate its power, the Meles government uses a "democratic" discourse to make its authoritarian rule legitimate and acceptable, and also to continue to get financial and military support from the West. "Although Meles and the EPRDF leaders continued to speak in the language of freedom and democracy," Theodore Vestal argues, "their performance was [is] sharply condemned as authoritarian by Ethiopian and foreign critics."[226] Therefore, Christianity, socialism, and democracy have been used in a political discourse by successive *Habasha* ruling classes to legitimate Ethiopian state power without changing its authoritarianism and terrorism.

To hide the true nature of the TPLF/EPRDF regime, John Sorenson claims that the regime adopted "democratic capitalism" and contends that it achieved "an overwhelming victory" in national elections of 1995.[227] Similarly, scholars such as John Young, who ardently supports the Meles regime, claim that the regime granted the right of national self-determination to the colonized ethnonations. This implies that Tigrayans, Oromos, Amharas, and others have equal rights and can politically, economically, and culturally determine their destinies equally.[228] Sandra Fullerton Joireman sees the Meles regime as "a parliamentary system of government" and blames the opposition political organizations for the Ethiopian political problem: "By refusing to engage in an electoral contest the opposition is, with intention, denying legitimacy to the EPRDF-led regime and preventing the consolidation of democracy."[229] In an attempt to delegitimize the Oromo struggle for democracy and self-determination, Joireman also argues, "The Oromo have been given their own region to administer and, theoretically, the right of self-determination up to, and including, secession through the 1995 constitution. The OLF has refused to renounce violence and therefore cannot legally be recognised as a political party."[230] These scholars take at face value the Tigrayan-led regime's assertion that it is committed to national self-determination and democracy. Consequently, they conclude that any group opposing the regime is against democracy and self-determination. This position is irresponsible. These scholars naively or intentionally promote the ideological discourse of the Tigrayan-led regime and its international supporters and blame the victims for the crises of the Ethiopian empire. These statist intellectuals cannot see beyond the discourse of the rulers and, in effect, legitimize human rights violations and state terrorism in the name of democracy and self-determination. Any state policy must be evaluated not only for what it proclaims on paper but for what it practices on the ground. Responsible scholars must at the very least examine the evidence beyond claims of the state.

The development of the Oromo national movement has prevented the new colonial ruling class from establishing ideological and political hegemony over the empire. States that fail to establish ideological hegemony and political order are unstable and insecure. Hence, they engage in state terrorism.[231] The main assumption of such regimes is that they can control populations by destroying their leaders and culture of resistance. The Meles regime accepts state violence against Oromos and others as a legitimate means of establishing political stability in order to control Oromo territories and to exploit Oromo economic resources. State terrorism is associated with the issues of control of territory and resources and the construction of political and ideological domination.[232] Since there has been no Ethiopia without Oromia, the Tigrayan elites are determined to violently destroy the Oromo national movement. What Annamarie Oliverio expresses about state terrorism in general captures the essence of Ethiopian state terrorism:

> First, the state reinforces the use of violence as a viable, effective, mitigating factor for managing conflict; second, such a view is reinforced by culturally constructed and socially organized processes, expressed through symbolic forms, and related in complex ways to present social interests. Within increasing economic and environmental globalization . . . and the resurgence of nationalities within territorial boundaries, the discourse of terrorism, as a practice of statecraft, is crucial to the construction of political boundaries. As such, terrorism is invoked in the art of statecraft when multiple, often conflicting versions of the past are produced and, at particular historical moment, become sites of intense struggle.[233]

After controlling Oromos and their country, Oromia, for almost one century, the *Habasha* elites are being challenged by an organized Oromo national movement. The Meles regime, with the support of the West, carries out state terrorism against Oromos because Oromos are in the process of radically redefining the relationship between Oromos and Ethiopians (particularly Amharas and Tigrayans), which is to ideologically, culturally, and intellectually challenge Ethiopian cultural and ideological hegemony.

Since the Tigrayan-led regime survives primarily on Oromo economic resources internally, its terrorism has targeted the Oromo people. According to the *Oromia Support Group,* "Because the Oromo occupy Ethiopia's richest areas and comprise half of the population of Ethiopia, they are seen as the greatest threat to the present Tigrean-led government. Subsequently, any indigenous Oromo organization, including the Oromo Relief Association, has been closed and suppressed by the government. The standard reason given for detaining Oromo people is that they are suspected of supporting the OLF."[234] The *Oromia Support Group* reported in 1997, "The current wave of arrests appears to be concentrating on all prominent Oromo, whether or not they are associated with the OLF."[235] Despite the fact that state terrorism is practiced in the forms of war, assassination, murder (burying alive, throwing off cliffs, hanging), castration, torture, rape, confiscation of properties by the police and the army, firing professionals from their jobs without adequate reasons, forcing people to submission by intimidation, beating, and disarming citizens,[236] the U.S. Department of State declared, "There were no confirmed reports of extrajudicial killings by government security forces" in Ethiopia.[237]

Several interviews conducted by Bruna Fossati, Lydia Namarra, and Peter Niggli reveal that since 1992 several thousands of Oromos have been killed or arrested on suspicion of being OLF supporters or sympathizers or for refusing proposed membership of the EPRDF. Based on their field research, these three scholars report that former prisoners testified that their arms and legs were tied tightly together on their backs and their naked bodies were whipped; larger containers or bottles filled with water were fixed to their testicles, or bottles or poles were pushed into their vaginas; there were prisoners who were locked up in empty steel barrels and tormented with heat in the tropical sun during the day and with cold at night; there were also prisoners who were forced into pits so that fire could be made on top of them.[238] Umar Fatanssa, an elderly Oromo refugee in Djibouti, says, "We had never experienced anything like that, not under Haile Selassie, nor under the Mengistu regime: these people just come and shoot your son or your daughter dead in front of your eyes."[239]

Explaining how systematic terrorism takes place through a tightly organized party that functions from the central government to the grassroots committee, The *Oromia Support Group* asserts, "Testimonies of victims of abuse by rural security personnel persistently pointed to the role of security committees, consisting of local officials, political cadres of the EPRDF and its affiliates and army officers, in control of the peasant militias. The committee system made the militia an integral part of the national political structure and placed them under the control of the central government through the ruling party apparatus. They provided the interface between local authorities, the militia, the army and the ruling party, in practice subordinating local security structures to the federal authorities."[240] Being misled or intentionally accepting the Ethiopian Constitution at face value, U.S. officials praise the Ethiopian government for its goal of a "decentralized system that brings justice closer to the people"[241] and reject the idea that "real power is retained at the center and used repressively."[242] It is paradoxical that when Oromos and others assert that the Meles regime has brought terrorism and intimidation to their neighbors and families, U.S. officials argue that it has brought justice closer to the people. As the Oromo national movement has been intensifying its struggle for national self-determination and democracy, the Tigrayan-led minority regime has been increasing its repression and state terrorism.

Conclusion

We have established that the Oromo national movement emerged and developed in opposition to Ethiopian settler colonialism and associated ethnocratic politics. Its goal is to enable Oromos to determine their cultural, economic, and political destiny as people through national self-determination. Like successive Amhara-dominated regimes, the Tigrayan-dominated government has racialized/ethnicized the Ethiopian state by placing Tigrayan ethnicity at its core, by denying Oromos and others national self-determination, and by preventing the construction of a legitimate state that can reflect a multicultural society through accountability and democracy. Without an accountable, democratic, and legitimate state, Oromos and other ethnonations may soon face a more disastrous condition. If the current Ethiopian state terrorism and massive human rights violations continue to be ignored by the United States (and other Western countries that back the regime), these conditions may soon result in ethnocidal conflict and war. The crises facing the Ethiopian empire since the early 1970s has already destroyed social and cultural systems of peoples who traditionally opposed incorporation into the empire.

The Tigrayan-led Ethiopian government has penetrated Oromo society and others through repression and terrorism, and key positions at all levels are now controlled by Tigryan elites. Even those Oromos who have chosen to collaborate with the regime, the OPDO, are not trusted. The Tigrayan-dominated government has been killing or chasing or imprisoning all opposition political movements and their supporters. Today we find structural and conjunctural problems in the Ethiopian empire that facilitate the radicalization of racist prejudice. Although the Tigrayan elites took power from their ethnonational cousins, the Amharas, they could not establish their cultural and ideological hegemony in the empire mainly because of the Oromo national movement. As a result, the Tigrayan-dominated state has targeted the Oromo people using subtle racist and public democratic discourses to maintain its ethnocracy. The racist discourse helps to facilitate the intra-Tigrayan alliance against Oromos and others, and its formal democratic discourse is used to hide Tigrayan ethnocracy and racism. Because the discourses of "democracy," "ethnonational federalism," "development," and the "social revolution" have failed to convince Oromos and others, the Meles regime uses state terrorism to violently subordinate civil society and to maintain the kind of political order that keeps EPRDF in power.

As all of these discourses and political practices are an integral part of global politics, they must be located and further explored in the context of the global world system. Since the incorporation of Oromia into the Ethiopian empire, the colonization of Oromos by *Habashas,* and the continued subjugation of the Oromo nation have taken place within the logic of the racialized capitalist world system, it is necessary to pay more attention to these issues in the next chapter. By focusing on the racist role of the United States and its commitment to help maintain the Ethiopian empire at the cost of Oromos by supporting the TPLF/EPRDF, the next chapter also explores the challenge the Oromo national movement has faced in the racialized capitalist world system.

CHAPTER IV

The Impact of U. S. Foreign Policy on the Oromo National Struggle[1]

This chapter critically examines the impact of U.S. foreign policy on the Oromo national movement, focusing on its racist practices. The application of racist values to the Oromo issue by Ethiopian and U.S. foreign policy elites makes possible the economic exploitation and political oppression of Oromos and facilitates judgments and policy based upon stereotypes and unexamined, preconceived ideas about Oromos. Just as other Western and Eastern bloc countries discriminated against Oromos and other colonized nations in their dealings with Ethiopia, U.S. foreign policy elites and the U.S. government have approached the Oromo issue with a racist mind-set that serves its imperialist interests. This racist mind-set fosters institutional and individual discrimination by treating Oromos unfairly and undemocratically. It avoids critical investigation by introducing and accepting false information and by closing off options for either democratic policy making or finding solutions to the contradictions between Oromos and *Habashas* (Amharas and Tigrayanns).

Specifically, this chapter questions why the West, particularly the United States, sees *Habashas* as "Semitic," Christian, and "advanced" peoples, and Oromos as "savage," "Muslim fundamentalists," "pagan," "backward," and, most recently, "terrorist."[2] This false dichotomy leads the United States and other Western countries to provide successive *Habasha* state elites with political, financial, technological, diplomatic, and military assistance and to ignore the voice of Oromos. Noting how European colonial scholars misused political power and social scientific knowledge by characterizing Africans as savages, V. Y. Mudimbe argues, "The novelty [of explorer's text] resides in the fact that the discourse on 'savages' is . . . a discourse in which an explicit political power presumes the authority of a scientific knowledge and vice-versa."[3] A racist ideological discourse has enabled successive Ethiopian elites and their governments to dominate and exploit Oromos, who comprise more than half of the population of the Ethiopian empire.

Several scholars have studied the impact of U.S. foreign policy on the Oromo national movement but have not addressed the racist ideological base of this policy[4] that prevents policy experts from objectively examining the Oromo question. By siding with the Tigrayan ethnocratic minority regime, the U.S. government still enables the massive violation of the human rights of the colonized Oromo ethnonational majority.[5] Because of its imperialist economic and strategic interests and clearly racist assumptions about Oromos, the U.S. government and its foreign policy elites allied with the Tigrayan ethnocratic elite to form a government and to suppress the Oromo national movement. Douglas Hellinger comments, "What is missing from U.S. policy toward Africa is a basic respect for the people, their knowledge and their right to collectively determine their own future."[6] This discussion draws on the works of several critical scholars in the fields of African American and Native American studies and other areas. Since these scholars have brought several significant insights into their fields of studies, their observations and conclusions are particularly useful in analyzing the condition of Oromos. Since Native Americans and African Americans have suffered under the racist domestic policies of the United States,[7] and since Oromos have been suffering under the racist foreign policies of the same country, it is helpful to use the insights of scholars who critically study the experiences of these two groups under the racial oppression and the capitalist exploitation of the United States.

Background

Between the early 1950s and the 1970s, the United States introduced its "modernization" programs to the Ethiopian empire and supported the Haile Selassie government.[8] Several scholars demonstrated that the U.S. foreign policy toward Ethiopia consolidated the racial/ethnonational hierarchy that was formed by the alliance of Ethiopian colonialism and European imperialism.[9] When the Haile Selassie regime was overthrown by the popular revolt of 1974, a military leadership emerged to protect and extend the interests of *Habasha* settlers in Oromia and other colonized regions. This leadership allied with the Soviet Union,[10] which also adopted *Habasha* views toward Oromos as part of its colonizing role in Ethiopia. At the end of the 1980s, a structural crisis that manifested itself in national movements, famine, poverty, and internal contradictions within the ruling elite factions eventually weakened the Amhara-dominated military regime and led to its demise in 1991.[11] The U.S. government, as the dominant global power, reestablished its relations with the Ethiopian empire by allying with the emerging Tigrayan ethnocratic elites. Recognizing that this Amhara-based state power had lost credibility, the United States supported the Tigrayan People's Liberation Front (TPLF) in the 1980s and prepared it financially, ideologically, and militarily to replace the Amhara-led military regime by creating the Ethiopian People's Revolutionary Democratic Front (EPRDF).[12] With the use of Western relief aid and financial support, the TPLF and its leaders converted the Tigrayan peasants into guerrilla fighters in the 1980s.[13]

One of the major reasons why the U.S. government chose the TPLF was that the Tigrayan ethnocratic elites were perceived as a legitimate successor to an Amhara-led regime because of the racist assumptions of the West. Paul Henze, one of the architects of the American–Tigrayan alliance, argued in the mid-1980s that the Tigrayans "as much as the Amhara, are an imperial people who, despite their loyalty to tradition, think of themselves as having a right—and perhaps even a duty—to play a role in the larger political entity of which they are a part."[14] While promoting the Tigrayan interest, the same scholar dismissed the political significance of Oromos by arguing that Oromo grievance "is both territorially and politically diffuse and unlikely to coalesce into a coherent ethnic resistance movement."[15] In a multicultural empire like Ethiopia, to identify one ethnonation and support it so it can dominate and exploit other ethnonations is racist. In justifying his position, Henze asserted that the Tigrayans recognize "the need to reconstitute Ethiopia and establish a just government recognizing regional rights and ethnic distinctions" as "a natural outgrowth of . . . [their] view of Ethiopian history."[16] Just as they are justified to rule and dominate other peoples by their sense of "fairness," Tigrayans are also seen as pro-West because "they do not try to claim they are Arabs and they do not seek the support of Arab governments," according to Henze.[17] Implicit in these arguments is that other peoples similar to Oromos are pro-Arab and anti-West and lack a sense of fairness to deal with other peoples. Based on these false assumptions, U. S. foreign policy experts like Henze advised the American government to invest in the TPLF and dismissed the relevance of the Oromo Liberation Front (OLF). In Henze's words, "The claims of the Oromo Liberation Front of widespread organization and effectiveness inside Ethiopia cannot be substantiated by firm evidence. *Oromia* as a territorial entity has no meaning inside Ethiopia. It is an exile construct."[18] Based on false information about Oromos and the OLF or because of his support for the Tigrayans and the TPLF, Henze made these erroneous conclusions. The American effort to overthrow the government of Mengistu Haile Mariam and support of the TPLF between 1976 and 1991 was influenced by such biased assumptions.

With the assistance of several forces, such as the United States and the Eritrean People's Liberation Front, the Tigrayan-led Ethiopian People's Revolutionary Democratic Front overthrew the weakened military regime in 1991 and formed a transitional government by signing a Transitional Charter with other political organizations, of which the OLF was the largest and most prominent. But within less than a year, the Tigrayan-led regime violated the Charter and established a Tigrayan ethnocratic minority government, justifying its action through the discourse of "democracy"[19] and "ethnic federalism." Since 1991, the United States has cemented its relationship with Tigrayan state elites at the cost of the colonized Oromo ethnonational majority and other groups who have been systematically denied meaningful access to Ethiopian state power. Consequently, the U.S. foreign policy toward Ethiopia has had a serious negative impact on the Oromo struggle for self-determination and democracy.

By signing the Transitional Charter in 1991 with the Tigrayan-led regime, the Oromo political leadership tacitly—or effectively—accepted the U.S. policy of polyarchy or elite democracy.[20] However, by ignoring the Oromo leadership, the U.S. government endorsed the violation of this Charter in 1992 by the Tigrayan-led Ethiopian People's Revolutionary Democratic Front. Ignoring the human rights violations of Oromos and other nations, George E. Moose, former Assistant Secretary of State, argued in 1994 that the Meles regime "for the first time in decades, has brought general peace and stability to Ethiopia. Though not sufficient, these conditions are essential for progress in many areas, including human rights."[21] Despite the fact that the Oromo national movement does not have any support from Arab and African countries, U.S. foreign policy elites have tried to link the Oromo national struggle to Muslim forces that they consider "terrorist" to discredit the Oromo struggle for self-determination and democracy.[22] Despite the fact that the offices of the OLF and the Oromo Relief Association have been closed since 1992 in the Sudan by the collaboration between the Ethiopian government and the Sudanese government, Susan Rice, then Assistant Secretary of State for African Affairs, argued that the Oromo movement is supported by the Sudanese National Islamic Front regime and destabilizes Ethiopia. This regime has been against the Oromo national struggle, because the Oromo leadership does not accept any religious ideology. When the Sudan supported the TPLF and EPLF full-heartedly, its support for the OLF was minimal. Susan Rice attempted to include the OLF in the terrorist camp, thus denying legitimacy for the Oromo national struggle for self-determination and democracy, and has endorsed the Tigrayan ethnocratic regime. Ignoring the national struggle of Oromos and the massive violations of their human rights, former Secretary of State Madeleine K. Albright claimed in 1997 that under the leadership of Prime Minister Meles, "Ethiopia is again earning the world's admiration, this time for its strides in reforming, rebuilding, and re-uniting at home and its leadership for peace and unity across Africa."[23]

Michael Sealy observes, "Africa's many dictatorships despite their characteristic gross economic mismanagement and severe abuses of human rights have been able to endure for so long because they have been actively supported by external agents, the most notable and hypocritical of which is the United States of America."[24] Ethiopia is an example of such a dictatorial regime. Despite the West's acceptance of the Tigrayan-led Ethiopian regime as democratic, convincing arguments have been made that the regime is ethnocratic, colonial, and terrorist.[25] The Meles regime has racialized the Ethiopian colonial state more than have successive Amhara-led governments. Two layers of colonial administration in Oromia run this ethnocratic state. The first layer consists of Tigrayan colonial officials, military commanders, and cadres who have absolute power over Oromos.[26] Operating above the rule of law, these officials, commanders, cadres, policemen, and soldiers have the power to imprison, torture, murder, mutilate, rape, and confiscate property in an attempt to suppress or destroy Oromo nationalism.[27] Marginalized Oromo intermediaries are also used by the Tigrayan-led regime to violently suppress Oromo nationalists.[28]

The second layer of colonial administration is occupied by members of the Oromo People's Democratic Organization (OPDO). This organization was created by the TPLF from Oromo prisoners of war, Oromo-speaking colonial settlers in Oromia, and marginalized Oromo intermediaries who abandoned the collective interests of the Oromo people.[29] The officials of the OPDO appear to be Oromo representatives who have power to plan and implement policies on development and political affairs. In reality, the actual power is in the hands of a core of Tigrayan officials and cadres from local to central administration.[30] As Theodore Vestal asserts, "The tightly organized and firmly disciplined EPRDF cadres infiltrated and eventually manipulated many of the institutions and mass organizations of public and collective life, such as trade unions, peasant commissions, professional bodies, grassroots action committees, workers' grievance committees, and local government."[31] Members of the OPDO are the foot soldiers of the TPLF/EPRDF in Oromia; they facilitate the transfer of resources from Oromos to Tigrayan elites and from Oromia to Tigray through suppressing Oromo nationalism and killing or imprisoning Oromo nationalists.[32] If any member of the OPDO raises any question in relations to Oromos, he or she is suspected as sympathetic to Oromo nationalism. Suspicion may lead to removal from position, demotion, imprisonment and torture, or death.[33]

Those Oromo individuals who continue to serve the interests of Tigrayans and are engaged in the Ethiopian colonial project of suppressing or destroying Oromos do so because they have been shifted from their Oromo identity and marginalized. The marginality that has been imposed on these Oromos by Ethiopian colonialism reflects the quality of psychic acculturation that ties the self-image and self-worth of these individuals to the dehumanizing worldview imposed on Oromos by Ethiopian racist culture.[34] Because of their psychic enslavement, such Oromos support the Ethiopian colonial project rather than assisting the Oromo struggle for freedom and democracy.

According to Luana Ross, "One of the main motives of colonialism is economic exploitation, and cultural suppression almost invariably accompanies colonialism. . . . Cultural suppression is a legal process that involves deculturation—eradication of the indigenous people's original traditions—followed by indoctrination in the ideas of the dominators so the colonized may themselves assist the colonial project. The process, in which the colonized are removed from their cultural context through enslavement or transplantation, involves the abandonment of culture and the adoption of new ways of speaking, behaving, and reasoning."[35]

Since these decultured and marginalized Oromos accept jobs that work against the Oromo national interests and their own interests coincide with those of the Ethiopian colonizing structure, the majority of Oromos have rejected the OPDO and called them "maxanne,"[36] "Gobana," or traitors. These Oromo OPDO members play the classic intermediary role described so well by Frantz Fanon when discussing the dynamics of colonialism: "The intermediary does not lighten the oppression, nor seek to hide the domination; he shows them up and puts them into practice with the clear conscience of an upholder of the peace, yet he is the bringer of violence into the home and into the mind of the native."[37] Ethiopian colonialism not only has facilitated the transfer of resources from Oromos to *Habashas* through the physical domination of Oromia and destruction of indigenous Oromo culture, but it also has domesticated the minds of a few elements of Oromo society. Such Oromo intermediaries serve their own class interests and the interests of the Ethiopian colonizing structure at the cost of Oromo society.

With the help of the West, particularly the United States, the Meles regime has attempted to destroy the OLF and other independent Oromo organizations so that it can freely control and exploit Oromia through the OPDO, its puppet organization. Oromos have been targeted because of their economic resources and their political opposition.[38] Since the majority of Oromos have supported the Oromo national movement, the Meles regime has been targeting Oromo nationalists and the Oromo people. The Oromo movement is the only national movement in the Horn of Africa that has been denied assistance from the West, the Middle East, and Africa. Yet Oromo nationalists have never endorsed any dogmatic ideology, and their stated objective is to restore their indigenous Oromo democratic tradition, which they believe provides the foundation for a future form of Oromo self-determination and democracy.[39] Following this background information, we now briefly explore how the United States was founded as a country in the capitalist world system in order to account both for the evolution of the racist ideology in its domestic and foreign policy and for its wholesale adoption of a racist Ethiopian colonial ideology in its dealings with Ethiopia and Oromia.

Global Capitalism, Racism, and the Formation of the United States of America

A better understanding of racism in U.S. domestic and foreign policy requires an examination of the global capitalist system and its impact on the formation of the United States, and as well as the historical relationships among racial/ethnonational groups in the United States. The United States emerged in the process of the colonial expansion of the European-dominated capitalist world system.[40] The global capitalist system hierarchically organized world peoples through the processes of slavery and colonialism, which led to the racialization/ethnicization of a global division of labor. This hierarchical organization of peoples served to transfer resources from subjugated population groups to dominant groups in the West and to their intermediary groups in the Third World. In founding the United States, European colonial settlers rationalized the colonization and destruction of Native Americans through racist discourse. They described Europeans as hard workers and more disciplined than Native Americans.[41] The discourse of racism, work, discipline, and whiteness were combined to rationalize the destruction of Native Americans.[42] While all European settlers were considered hardworking whites, all Native Americans were considered lazy. European settlers invented "Indian savagery" through the ideology of whiteness.[43] Based on these racist assumptions, schools were introduced to assimilate some Native American children—Christianizing and "civilizing" them and teaching the superiority of Europeans and the inferiority of Native Americans.

This educational policy was intended to create an educated intermediate class in Native American society that European settlers could use to implement their colonial policies. According to Bobby Wright and William Tierney, "The earliest colonial efforts to provide Indians with higher education were designed to Christianize and 'civilize' the Indians, thus saving them from the folly of their 'heathenish' and 'savage' ways. The hope was that educated Indians, as schoolmasters and preachers, would become missionary agents among their own brethren."[44] Later, the ideology of whiteness was used to commit genocide and/or to create reservations for the remnants of Native Americans and to transfer the resources of the indigenous people to European settlers. One U.S. general wrote in 1868, "The more I see these Indians the more convinced I am that all have to be killed or be maintained as a species of pauper. Their attempts at civilization are simply ridiculous."[45] Today Native Americans are the most oppressed, exploited, and underdeveloped part of American society because of the racist political and economic attack that historically targeted them and currently continues to do so. Ross explains that historical evidence "reveals the process of how the 'savage' was invented. Racial oppression, then as now, is not a discrete phenomenon, independent of larger political and economic tendencies. Twentieth-century laws and their enforcement can readily be seen as instruments for creating and maintaining social and economic stratification created centuries before. Indeed, past deeds illuminate present treacheries."[46]

The United States emerged through establishing settler colonialism, practicing genocide, and intensifying two types of labor recruitment systems: wage labor for Whites and coerced labor for enslaved Africans. The White Anglo-Saxon Protestant group that founded the United States developed two major stratification systems: class and racial caste systems.[47] While the class system and gender hierarchy were maintained to protect the power of rich White males in an emerging White society, the racial caste system was invented to keep African Americans at the bottom of White society so that they would provide their labor and other resources freely or cheaply.[48] As the ideology of whiteness was used to exterminate Native Americans and to transfer their resources to White society, it also justified slavery for about two and a half centuries and segregation for about one more century. Through the racial caste system, White Americans imposed on African Americans slavery, segregation, cultural hegemony, and colonial domination to keep them at the bottom of a society in which Whites were on the top.

"The conception of race," Michael Hunt writes, "defined by the poles of black and white, carried over into American foreign policy."[49] White racism was invented and refashioned with the changing times to prove the mental inferiority of Blacks and other colonized peoples and to rationalize their mistreatment by Whites.[50] Recently, an infamous book titled *The Bell Curve* revived "scientific racism" and rehashed nineteenth-century arguments of Social Darwinism. We can conclude from the popular acceptance of this publication that the Black struggle of the mid-twentieth century did not uproot White racism. Instead it forced racism to go underground. Despite national liberation movements in general and the African American struggle in particular that "made untenable a hierarchy cast in explicitly racial terms,"[51] since the mid-twentieth century indirect institutional racism and discrimination remained strong in the United States.

A racist ideology that hierarchically organizes various peoples based on skin color and/or cultural attributes to justify colonialism, slavery, genocide, imperialism, and dictatorship corrupts U.S. institutions. According to Hunt, "The idea of a racial hierarchy proved particularly attractive because it offered a ready and useful conceptual handle on the world. . . . Rather than having to spend long hours trying—perhaps inclusively—to puzzle out the subtle patterns of other cultures, the elite interested in policy had at hand in the hierarchy of race a key to reducing other peoples and nations to ready comprehensible and familiar terms. . . . Races were different and unequal. Some were civilized or progressive, others were more barbaric or backward."[52] The challenge to this racist ideology mounted by a few White intellectuals and progressives, Black scholars, and national liberation movements could not overthrow this ideology. Therefore, racism in different forms continues to influence U.S. policy elites who deal with the issues of the oppressed racial/ethnonational groups in the United States and the Third World. The mistreatment of Oromos by U.S. policy elites and the U.S. government in siding with Tigrayans clearly shows this reality. As we will see, the racist views of U.S. foreign policy elites toward the Oromo people are being solidified by the racist discourse in Ethiopian studies and by U.S. support for racism in Ethiopian society.

Racist Views in Ethiopian Studies and Ethiopian Society

As the names of different African peoples who were enslaved and brought to America were changed to *Negro,*[53] and as the names of various peoples in America were changed to *Indian*[54] with their colonization and destruction, Oromos were given the name *Galla*. The names *Negro, Indian,* and *Galla* were the products of the fifteenth and sixteenth centuries, and they were externally imposed by slavers and colonizers. These names were invented in the process of removing these peoples from their respective cultural and historical centers and making them the target of destruction, enslavement, colonialism, and continued subjugation. The appellation *Galla* was given to Oromos as a name of contempt and derogation. It characterized them as slave, pagan, uncivilized or barbaric, inferior, and ignorant.[55] The name *Galla* was invented to destroy Oromoness and to devalue Oromo culture, history, and tradition. John Sorenson asserts that "the Oromo were known as the Galla, a term they do not apply to themselves and one that carries 'overtones of race and slavery' as well as the imputation of a lack of civilization; according to myth, the Oromo were descendants of 'a high-born Amhara lady and a slave.'"[56] *Galla* is the name of racist ridicule in academic and popular discourse.

In Ethiopian discourse, Oromos have been depicted as "somewhat darker" than Amharas and Tigrayans[57] although it is difficult to differentiate the former from the latter by just looking at their skin color or physical appearance. By using the discredited racist categorization of human groups, such as Semitic, Hamitic, Negroid, and Cushitic, *Habashas* place Oromos between themselves and the people that they wrongly call *Shankallas*, whom they consider Negroid.[58] Despite the fact that *Habashas* are black, they consider themselves Semitic to associate themselves with the Middle East and dissociate themselves from Africa whose peoples they consider both racially and culturally inferior. For instance, when Haile Selassie, the emperor of Ethiopia, was interviewed by the *Nigerian Daily Times* about Ethiopian racial identity in the 1930s, he said "that Ethiopians were not, and did not regard themselves as negroes [*sic*], as they were a Hamito-Semitic people."[59] Sorenson expresses this racist attitude as "a multiplicity of Ethiopians, blacks who are whites, the quintessential Africans who reject African identity."[60] Since the concept of race is a sociopolitical construct, it is essential to critically understand a historical context in which Ethiopian racism is produced and reproduced to denigrate colonized peoples to deny them access to Ethiopian state power. In Ethiopian discourse, racial distinctions have been invented and manipulated to perpetuate the political objective of *Habasha* domination of the colonized population groups. "The fact that racial distinctions are easily manipulated and reversed indicates," Sorenson notes, "the absurdity of any claims that they have an objective basis and locates these distinctions where they actually occur, in political power."[61]

Habasha elites recognize the importance of racial distinctions in linking themselves to the Middle East, Europe, and North America to mobilize support for their political projects. Jews, Arabs, Europeans, and Americans see *Habashas* as closer to themselves than the peoples whom they consider "real black." Also, the West, particularly the United States, places *Habashas* at "an intermediate position between whites and blacks" and considers them to be closer to "the European race" or members of "the great Caucasian family."[62] There are Europeans who consider *Habashas* a very intelligent people because of their racial affinity with the "Caucasian race."[63] There are also those who see *Habashas* as "dark-skinned white people" and "racial and cultural middlemen" between Black Africa on one side and Europe and the Middle East on the other side.[64] One German scholar admired the intelligence of *Habashas* and noted that he never saw such mental capability among Negroes, Arabs, Egyptians, and Nubians.[65] These racist discourses are unchallenged in academic and popular discourse because they help reproduce Ethiopian ethnocratic and colonial state power. U.S. foreign policy elites, diplomats, and other officials recognize and defend such "racial pretensions of Ethiopia's ruling class."[66]

Habasha racism prevents the peaceful coexistence of different cultures as shown by the destruction of the Gafat and other peoples. *Habashas* see themselves as a Semitic people who are racially and culturally superior to others in the Horn of Africa. Paul Baxter explains that they "used to stress their Middle Eastern rather than African cultural roots, as is so obvious in the reiteration of the Solomonic legend, taught in schools as history and justification of imperial rule. Just as the expansion of the European empire in Africa coincided with that of Abyssinian, so the latter took on some of the same sanctimonious assumptions of bringing civilization to the savages. Menelik and his courtiers became honorary, if second-class, bearers of the 'white man's burden in Africa.'"[67] *Habashas* have effectively used cultural racism[68] in destroying or suppressing other peoples. Cultural racism and its contradictions may result in the extermination or/and continued subjugation of the dominated population group. Racism does not necessarily manifest itself in the discourse of biological difference. Usually it combines the discourses of biological and cultural differences to justify unequal treatment of different population groups. The extermination of Jews by Germans, the continued subjugation of Palestinians by the Jews, the ethnic cleansing of Bosnians by Serbians, the destruction of Tutsis by Hutus, and the suppression of Hutus by Tutsis are examples of extreme forms of cultural racism.

As Eurocentric scholars have intellectually separated the original Black civilization of Kemet (Egypt) and Kush or Nubia and then linked it to the Middle East to prove the racist notion of superiority of non-Blacks to Blacks,[69] some Ethiopianists tried to prove the racial and civilizational superiority of Amharas and Tigrayans by Semitizing and linking them to the Middle East and Europe. Baxter notes that "evolutionists and racist assumptions, mostly unvoiced, have contributed to the belief that a Christian, Semitic culture with Middle Eastern leanings had to be superior to a black Africa."[70] Recognizing the political and diplomatic significance of the name *Ethiopia* (the old name for the Black world), the Abyssinian state elites replaced the name *Abyssinia* with that of *Ethiopia*. The Ethiopian ideological history claims "the modern Ethiopian state as the direct heir to the Ethiopia mentioned in biblical and classical sources. Ethiopian and Western scholars presented Ethiopia as an entity that had existed continuously as an integrated and independent state for three thousand years."[71] Successive Ethiopian state elites use the African and Semitic discourses both regionally and globally. Globally, they use the Semitic discourse and the discourse of Christianity to mobilize assistance from Europe, North America, and the Middle East.

Skillfully, they have used their blackness to mobilize other Africans, the African diaspora,[72] and Black U.S. policy elites against Oromos and other colonized peoples. By confusing original Ethiopia (the Black world) with contemporary Ethiopia (former Abyssinia), *Habasha* elites misled some historically naive people in Africa, Europe, North America, and the world. Most people do not know the difference between ancient Ethiopia and present Ethiopia. Because of this historical misinformation, Africans who were colonized and enslaved by Europeans, except those who were enslaved and colonized by contemporary Ethiopians, wrongly considered contemporary Ethiopia (former Abyssinia) as an island of Black freedom since they maintained formal political power. Most Blacks "knew very little about the social and political conditions of Ethiopia. What they wrote or said about Ethiopia was at best a manifestation of their emotional state."[73] Other Africans were unaware that Ethiopia's political power came from allying with the colonizing European powers. In reality, the Ethiopia that participated in the slave trade and the "Scramble for Africa" was not an island of Black freedom. Instead, it has been a "prison house" in which Oromos and other colonized and enslaved populations were and are still brutalized.

One would expect that the African American policy elites in the U.S. State Department, including George Moose, Irvin Hicks, and Susan Rice, would think differently from their White counterparts and genuinely promote social justice and democracy in Africa. But African American policy elites, because of the distorted historical knowledge, and/or because of their class interests, have accepted the ideological discourse on Ethiopia that presented this empire as the home of Black freedom—when all Blacks were under Euro-American colonialism and slavery—and endorsed the racist U.S. policy toward Ethiopia and Oromia. As some African kings and chiefs participated in the slave trade with European slave merchants to commodify some Africans and ship them to North America and other parts of the world, these African American elites collaborate with racist structures that dehumanize African peoples. It is an irony of history that the lack of critical historical knowledge and the ideological confusion built into this racist policy has brought an alliance between the biological or ideological descendants of slavers and the descendants of slaves to victimize people like Oromos, who have been victimized by colonialism and slavery. Current *Habasha* elites are the ideological or actual descendants of Emperors Yohannis and Menelik, who participated in the massacre and enslavement of millions of Oromos and others.

While glorifying the culture and civilization of *Habashas,* racist scholars such as Edward Ullendorff advanced the notion that Oromos as a barbaric people did not possess "significant material or intellectual culture" that could allow them to "contribute to the Semitized civilization of Ethiopia."[74] To demonstrate the civilizational and cultural superiority of Amharas and Tigrayans, racist scholars downplayed the Africanness of Ethiopia and emphasized its similarities to European societies.[75] Sorenson expounds that "along with the emphasis on a Great Tradition in Ethiopian history, came a specific configuration of racial identity. As in other discourses of race, this configuration merged power with phenotypical features in order to devalue the Oromo and other groups as both 'more African' and 'more primitive' than the Amhara [and Tigray]. The Oromo were presented as warlike, essentially 'people without history' and without any relationship to the land."[76] In Ethiopian studies, Oromos were depicted as "crueller scourges" and "barbarian hordes who brought darkness and ignorance in the train" to Ethiopia.[77] They were also depicted as evil, ignorant, order-less, destructive, infiltrating, and invasive.[78]

Oromos were also seen as "a decadent race" who were "less advanced" because of their racial and cultural inferiority. Therefore, their colonization and enslavement by the alliance of Ethiopians and Europeans were seen as a civilizing mission.[79] Since in the racist and modernist thinking historical development is linear, and society develops from primitive, or backward, to civilized, or advanced, Oromos who have been seen as primitive people are also considered as a collection of tribes or a single tribe or a 'cluster' of diverse groups that cannot develop any nationalist political consciousness except tribalism.[80] Racist and modernist scholars have also denied the existence of a unified Oromo identity and argued that Oromos cannot achieve statehood because they are geographically scattered and lack cultural substance.[81] Since the creation of the Ethiopian empire, *Habasha* elites have claimed that they have a superior religion and civilization, and even sometimes expressed that they were not Black and saw other Africans as "baryas" (slaves); in Abyssinia proper, "Galla" and "barya" have been used interchangeably.[82] Alberto Sbacchi asserts that the *Habashas* "have traditionally looked upon the dark skinned people as inferiors and given them the name of *'Shankalla'* [sic]. . . . The Black Americans were known as negro [sic], which in Ethiopia was associated with slavery. Hence to the Ethiopians the Afro-Americans were *Shankallas.*"[83] William R. Scott, an African American who participated in a student work-camp in Ethiopia in 1963, expresses his painful encounter with *Habasha* racism: "I was called *barya* (slave) by young, bigoted Ethiopian aristocrats, who associated African-Americans with slavery and identified them with the country's traditional servant class."[84] The participation of *Habashas* in the scramble for Africa and in the slave trade and the commodification of millions of Oromos and others encouraged them to associate themselves with Europe and the Middle East rather than Black Africans. "Western discourse . . . duplicated many of the assumptions and ideologies that had been put in place by the ruling elites of Ethiopia," Sorenson writes, "constructing the latter as the carriers of a Great Tradition which was engaged in its own Civilizing Mission with respect to what it regarded as other uncivilized Groups in Ethiopia."[85]

The popular discourse on Oromos is full of racist prejudices and stereotypes. When *Habashas* want to show the inferiority of Oromos on a racial/ethnonational hierarchy, or to deny the humanity of Oromos, they debase an Oromo and his nationality by asking "sawu nawu Galla?" (Is he a human being or a *Galla?); this query shows that *Habashas* consider Oromos as inferior human beings. Because of such racist views the Ethiopian Orthodox Church publication denounced sexual relations between *Habashas* and Oromos, saying that Jesus would punish those who had sexual intercourse with "the cursed, the dumb, the Moslems, the Galla, the Shankilla, the Falasha, the horse, the donkey, the camel and all those who committed sodomy."[86] This religious tract was written in *Geez* (an old Abyssinian language) and was translated into Amharic in 1968, but its original date of writing and its author were not known. But the piece was popular and widely recited by literate *Habashas.* Oromos, Ethiopian Jews, Muslims, and various peoples were categorized with beasts, such as horses, donkeys, and camels. Of course, the implicit intention of the Orthodox Church was to draw a racial/ethnonational boundary between *Habashas* and non-*Habashas* to maintain the racial/ethnonational purity of the former.

Habasha stereotypes depict Oromos as dirty people; the expression "Galla na sagara eyadare yigamal" compares Oromos to feces and claims that Oromos continue to stink like feces with passing days. This expression warns that the closer you get to Oromos, the more you find they are bad and dirty. This racial insult is used to create suspicion between Oromos and *Habashas.* Another expression depicts Oromos as a rotten people ("timbi or bisbis *Galla*"). Yet another expression explains that Oromos cannot be clean even if they wash themselves again and again; it says that "*Galla* na Shinfila ayitaram," which literally means, "Even if you wash them, stomach lining and a Galla will never come clean." Oromos have been depicted as barbarians and backward people in popular discourse, too. A *Habasha* expression claims that Oromos' attempt to be civilized cannot be successful since Oromos are predestined to fail in civilizational projects. The saying "*Galla* sisaltin bacharaqa jantila yizo yizoral" attempts to show that even if he is civilized, an Oromo does not know the true essence of civility. Literally, this saying means, "When an Oromo is civilized he stretches his umbrella in moonlight and walks around so that he can be seen by others." Simply put, since Oromos are stupid, they do not know how to behave in a civilized way. The expression "Ye *Galla* chawa, ye gomen choma yelewum" depicts Oromos as a society that does not have respected and notable individuals. Literally, this expression means, "As there is no fat in vegetables or greens, there is no gentleman in the *Galla* community." Oromos have been seen as a useless people who do not deserve respect.

Oromos have been insulted for even trying to assimilate to Ethiopian culture by speaking in an Ethiopian language. *Habasha* racists have expressed their anger toward Oromos who have mispronounced Amharic words by saying, "Afun yalfata *Galla;* tabitaba *Galla*" (an Oromo who cannot express himself clearly). To psychologically demoralize Oromos, the *Habasha* discourse also depicts Oromos as cowardly people who cannot resist subordination; the saying "aand Amhara matto *Galla* yinadal" clearly shows the essence of this discourse. Literally it means "one Amhara can force one hundred Oromos to submission or subordination." However, historical evidence indicates that until they allied with Europeans and obtained modern weapons, *Habashas* saw Oromo fighters as their nightmare. Even a poor *Habasha* or a leper claims that he is better than a *Galla.* The expressions "Even if I am poor, I am not a *Galla,*" and "Even if I am a leper, I am not a *Galla*" clearly show how most *Habashas,* including the sick and the poor, claim racial/ethnonational superiority. Generally speaking, *Habashas* have "looked upon and treated the indigenous people as backward, heathen, filthy, deceitful, lazy, and even stupid—stereotypes that European colonialists commonly ascribed to their African subjects."[87]

Habasha social institutions, such as family, school, media, government, and religion, reproduce and perpetuate these racist prejudices and stereotypes among Ethiopian society.[88] Explaining how racial insults wound the colonized people, Richard Delgado says, "The racial insult remains one of the most pervasive channels through which discriminatory attitudes are imparted. Such language injures the dignity and self-regard of the person to whom it is addressed, communicating the message that distinctions of race are distinctions of merit, dignity, status, and personhood. Not only does the listener learn and internalize the messages contained in racial insults, these messages color our society's institutions and are transmitted to succeeding generations."[89] These prejudices and stereotypes consciously or unconsciously influenced Ethiopian society and Ethiopian studies. Ethiopians, and particularly those Ethiopian scholars and Ethiopianists who have been influenced by these racist assumptions, never respected Oromo culture and also opposed the Oromo struggle for social justice and human rights under different pretexts.

Some assert that since Oromos are dispersed among other peoples, the question of national self-determination is not applicable to their cause; others argue that the assimilation of Oromos to *Habashas* both biologically and culturally prevents them from having a cultural identity that enables them to have national self-determination.[90] Further, since Oromos are considered "invaders" of Ethiopia, some Ethiopian elites contest that they do not deserve self-determination because the region that they call Oromia does not belong to them.[91] This assertion implicitly assumes that Oromos must accept their subjugation and second-class citizenship, or they must leave Ethiopia before they will be totally annihilated for continuing to demand self-determination and democracy. The political agenda of the destruction of Oromo society is not a new phenomenon. This political agenda has been supported by the West. The massive killing of Oromos during Abyssinian colonialism was never condemned as genocide. Leenco Lata notes that "despite its unparalleled brutality, Menelik's conquest escaped condemnation as the only positive historical development in the Africa of the late 1800s. To achieve this, the Oromo were made to appear deserving to be conquered."[92] Just as genocide committed by Menelik and his followers escaped world condemnation, so does the ethnic cleansing that is systematically committed by the Meles regime.[93] According to Lata, "Massacres of Oromos by any one of the Ethiopian forces rarely gets mentioned in Ethiopian or Euro-American writings. The slightest threat to the Abyssinian by the Oromo, however, can throw up a storm of protest and condemnation."[94]

Denying the reality that contemporary Abyssinia/Ethiopia was a product of neo-colonialism that was invented by the alliance of Ethiopian colonialism and European imperialism, the West praises Abyssinia (later Ethiopia) as the country that was never colonized in Africa. The idea that Ethiopia was not colonized laid the cornerstone for the ideology of "Greater Ethiopia." This Ethiopia was seen as "a civilized nation of an immense intelligence, the only one that is civilized without wearing trousers and shoes."[95] Since the U.S. policy toward Ethiopia builds upon the European policy established before the United States became involved, it is necessary to briefly consider the essence of European policy toward Ethiopia. The ideology of Greater Ethiopia that has been accepted and developed by European and American policy elites and their governments have been the bedrock of racism on which Ethiopia was built and is still maintained.[96] When the French and British could not decide which of them would get this key region, and were not willing to go to war with each other over it, each backed a different proxy leader; the British chose Yohannis of Tigray, and the French chose Menelik of Amhara. But when Yohannis died in 1889, the British and the Italians devised a different solution for sharing access to the region.

The British and Italians struggled at Menelik's court to advise and control him and seek his favor; because of Menelik's failing health in 1906, France, Great Britain, and Italy devised the policy behind the Tripartite Treaty without Menelik's even knowing about it. This treaty states, "We the Great powers of Europe, France, Great Britain, and Italy, shall cooperate in maintaining the political and territorial status quo in Ethiopia as determined by the state of affairs at present existing and the previous [boundary] agreements."[97] The foreign policy experts of Western countries not only provided technology and expertise in different fields, but they have been playing a critical role in formulating and promoting racist mythologies to justify the colonization and continued subjugation of the colonized subjects. For instance, the notion of claiming Abyssinia/Ethiopia as an ancient kingdom was originally suggested by an Italian expert in 1891: Francisco Crispi instructed an Italian agent in Addis Ababa "to inform Menelik that the European powers were establishing their boundaries in Africa and that the emperor should, with Italian assistance, circulate a letter defining his borders in order to guarantee the integrity of his empire. Crispi suggested that in the letter, Menelik ought to point out that Ethiopia was an ancient Kingdom which had been recognized as independent by the Christian states of Europe."[98]

The racist idea that *Habashas* were different from the rest of the Africans lay at the core of the European justification for empowering them to colonize and rule Oromos and other nations, who were seen as being like other colonized Africans. In the 1930s, when Haile Selassie went to Europe and became the darling of the Western media, the ideology of Greater Ethiopia was refined and celebrated in Europe, America, and Ethiopia.[99] He was praised in *Manchester Guardian* (July 8, 1924) for his "extraordinary handsome face, next door to black, with high standing curly hair, a crisp black beard, a fine hawkish nose, and large gleaming eyes"; he was also glorified in *The Times* for his "devotion to modernization."[100] The Ethiopian empire that was created with the alliance of European imperialist powers and *Habasha* warlords has maintained itself through an alliance with successive imperial superpowers, namely, Great Britain, the Soviet Union, and the United States, that have provided protection to successive Ethiopian state elites and their governments.[101] After colonizing Oromos and other nations with the help of European technology and expertise, Abyssinian colonial settlers in Oromia and other regions justified their colonial domination with racist discourse. With the establishment of their colonial authority, *Habasha* settlers "assumed that their own innate superiority over the local residents accounted for this accomplishment."[102] Since then *Habashas* and their Euro-American supporters have contributed to "Ethiopian mythology [which] consists in part of the erroneous notions that [Abyssinian] society had reached a superior evolutionary stage at the time of conquest, making them able to move in and take over Oromia and others. . . . The illusion plays a critically important role in holding the entire complex together, the ideology of Greater Ethiopia."[103]

The ideology of Greater Ethiopia[104] claims that: Ethiopia was not colonized like other parts of Africa because of *Habasha* bravery and patriotism that made this empire unique in Africa; Ethiopian boundaries are sacred since they were established for three thousand years; Abyssinian "society represented an advanced level of social and economic organization" that enabled it to defend itself from European colonialism by eliminating slavery and protecting "all the peoples of greater Ethiopia from falling prey to European imperialism";[105] and Ethiopia played a significant civilizing mission by colonizing and dominating Oromos and other nations who were backward, pagan, destructive, and inferior. These racist mythologies of Greater Ethiopia helped the Haile Selassie government gain admission to the League of Nations in 1924. As a result, Ethiopia began to enjoy more recognition in Europe and North America, and "there was extended public discussion of Ethiopia's place in the world community and a great elaboration of the Ethiopian mythology initiated by European writers for the European public."[106] By joining the League of Nations, the Ethiopian empire, according to Evelyn Waugh, "had been recognized as a single state whose integrity was the concern of the world. Tafari's own new dynasty had been accepted by the busy democracies as the government of this area; his enemies were their enemies; there would be money lent him to arm against rebels, experts to advise him; when trouble was brewing he would swoop down from the sky and take his opponents unaware; the fabulous glories of Prester John were to be reincarnated."[107]

These essential components of racist discourse of Greater Ethiopia have remained intact. "Socialist" and then "democratic" discourses have been introduced by successive *Habasha* state elites and accepted by their Euro-American supporters without changing the colonizing and racist structure of Ethiopian society. As we will see shortly, Ethiopian racism and White racism have conveniently intermarried in the U.S. policy formulation and implementation in Ethiopia. When policy issues are discussed in relation to Ethiopia, the issues of Semitic civility, Christianity, antiquity, bravery, and the patriotism of Amharas and Tigrayans are retrieved to valorize and to legitimize *Habasha* dominance and power. Moreover, the barbarism, backwardness, and destructiveness of Oromos are reinvented to keep Oromos from access to state power. The combined racist views about Oromos and the racist assumptions of U.S. foreign policy elites effectively mobilize the U.S. State Department against the Oromo people.

U.S. Foreign Policy Elites and the Oromo

The U.S. Department of State claims that the Meles government protects human rights and promotes democracy. Rarely admitted weaknesses of this government are attributed to the local government officials.[108] Stevens Trucker, democracy and governance advisor to the U.S. AID Mission to Ethiopia, claims that the Meles regime is committed to the establishment of "a functioning multiparty democracy within a federal structure"[109] despite the fact that the Ethiopian transition period that, as Terrence Lyons concluded, "began with a broadly inclusive national conference ended . . . with a single-party-dominant political system."[110] Despite the rhetoric of democracy, the United States and other Western countries openly endorsed the emergence of Tigrayan ethnonational dictatorship under one-party rule.[111] At the same time Prime Minister Meles engineers the killing of thousands of Oromos and the creation of several concentration camps in Oromia,[112] U.S. Secretary of State Madeleine K. Albright argues that he promotes human rights in Ethiopia and Africa. Albright says, "The United States strongly supports the Prime Minister's initiative at the OAU to create an eminent persons group to study the recent genocide in the Great Lakes, examine the international community's response, and propose ways we can all do better in the future."[113]

Her remark that the Meles regime has "a good human rights record"[114] refuses to recognize reports by human rights organizations regarding Ethiopia's violations of human rights.[115] In 1997 Meles Zenawi was "regarded as one of Africa's 'new leaders': he recently won an award in the United States for good government. . . . Their [Western] governments tend to give priority to the Prime Minister's economic reforms rather than his record on human rights."[116] Susan E. Rice, Assistant Secretary of State for African Affairs, announced the end of wars in the Horn of Africa and the emergence of a democratic form of government in Ethiopia[117] despite the fact that almost all ethnonational groups in the Ethiopian empire charge that they suffer under the Tigrayan ethnocratic and terrorist regime.[118] She claimed that the United States facilitates "Africa's full integration into the global economy" through the promotion of "democracy and respect for human rights" and resolving conflict and promoting peace.[119] There is no question that the globalization of Africa is being intensified; but, as the conflict between Oromos and the Tigrayan regime indicates, the United States has failed to promote even its policy of "democracy promotion." A gap exists between what U.S. policy elites claim as their policies and what they practice.

Albright has emphasized the importance of democracy for development, saying, "It is essential to sow the seeds of prosperity if Africa is to become a full participant in the world economy. It is necessary to build democracy. In this decade, people everywhere have learned that democracy is a parent to development. For people who are free to choose their leaders, publish their thoughts, organize their labor and invest their capital will build richer and more stable societies than those shackled by repression."[120] One of former President Clinton's four goals for his trip to Africa was to promote democracy in Africa,[121] but the U.S. government policy does not promote democracy in Ethiopia and Oromia. Oromia has been integrated into the global economy without its own political leadership and democracy; consequently Oromos have been brutalized and peripheralized. Unfortunately, the U.S. government contributes to the peripheralization and misery of Oromos by supporting a regime that violates human rights through state terrorism. Most Americans have no sympathy for the enslaved and subjugated peoples since they see them as inferior or uncivilized peoples who do not have the capability to be like them. Since this mind-set flourished with the ideologies of whiteness and cultural superiority that caused the destruction of Native Americans and enslaved Africans, and since these ideologies also have been "recycled" by American institutions, Americans do not realize that U.S. foreign policy can have detrimental effects on a people like the Oromo. American President Theodore Roosevelt openly justified colonial violence and expansion in a racist discourse. Considering Native Americans to be an inferior race, Roosevelt argued that the elimination of Native Americans was necessary "for the benefit of civilisation and in the interest of mankind."[122] Further, since the ideologies of whiteness and cultural superiority devalued the humanity of Native Americans, the treaties that were signed with them were not respected. In 1830, one U.S. politician said that "treaties were expedient by which ignorant, intractable, and savage people were induced without bloodshed to yield up what civilized peoples had a right to possess."[123] Probably the reason that the U.S. government ignored the violation of the Transitional Charter of Ethiopia and supported the emergence of the Tigrayan ethnocratic minority regime was that it made the same sort of assumption, that is, that Oromos were negotiating their defeat and destruction "to yield up what civilized peoples had a right to possess."

Marc Baas, U.S. Charge d'Affaires, on November 14, 1991, said that "Oromos have been 'niggers' of this society."[124] Subsequent policy reveals that U.S. foreign policy elites and the U.S. government do not believe that these "niggers" of Ethiopia can play a decisive role in determining the essence of the Ethiopian state despite the fact that the so-called niggers are a numerical majority and possess the major resources on which Ethiopia depends for existence. This racist mind-set allows the U.S. government to ignore the Oromo people. Accordingly, Oromos who are considered as "real black" and "less advanced" deserve less than *Habashas* who are considered as less black in the thinking of U.S. foreign policy elites. These foreign policy elites do not even bother to reconcile the contradiction that there is no skin color difference between *Habashas* and Oromos, only cultural and political differences. In the thinking of most White Americans, blackness denies rights and power. Since racism is a means of phenotypically and culturally categorizing people to justify their unequal treatment, Oromos are seen as darker and less advanced than *Habashas.*

Because of imperialist economic and strategic interests and these racist assumptions, the U.S. government does not recognize the struggle of Oromos for self-determination and democracy despite the fact that the Oromo political leadership endorsed its policy of "democracy promotion." Since the biological concept of race can be easily challenged, U.S. policy elites mainly apply "development theory" rather than racist biological notions when they deal with countries like Ethiopia. They do this without changing the long-established American views on race. According to Michael Hunt, "Policy makers, whose impulse to see the world in terms of hierarchy was even more at odds with the need for political direction, found their way out of their bind by recasting the old racial hierarchy into cultural terms supplied by development theorists. No longer did leaders dare broadcast their views on barbarous or backward people, race traits, or skin color. It was instead now the attributes of modernity and tradition that fixed a people's or nation's place on the hierarchy."[125] The concepts of tradition, modernity, and development are used by U.S. foreign elites to support Ethiopian state elites despite the fact that *Habasha* and Oromo societies are at similar levels of economic and technological development. Oromos are assigned to serve the interests of Ethiopian and global elites at their own cost. Hence, through the process of racialization/ethnicization of the division of labor, Oromos must be poor farmers, servants, and soldiers and not state elites, intellectuals, policy makers, and traders.

Only a few Oromos who have subordinated their interests and the interests of the Oromo people to that of *Habashas* are allowed to become intermediaries between *Habasha* elites and Oromo society. The Tigrayan-led regime, with the tacit agreement of the West, particularly the United States, has targeted for destruction Oromo intellectuals and business elites who attempt to play a decisive role in regional and global politics through promoting the Oromo struggle for self-determination and democracy.[126] The Oromos' current refusal to accept the racialization/ethnicization of the division of labor and their attempt to achieve freedom and democracy have annoyed *Habasha* and U.S. policy elites. Therefore, it is tacitly accepted by the West, particularly by the United States, that the Tigrayan government suppress the Oromo national movement by destroying its leadership and Oromo activists. Despite the fact that the OLF agreed to form a federal democratic Ethiopia, during the transition period, the West and the Meles regime rationalized their actions by labeling the organization as separatist or terrorist. Neighboring countries like the Sudan, Kenya, Djibouti, Yemen, and some factions in Somalia could not resist financial incentives and/or political pressures from the West, particularly the United States, to deny sanctuary to the OLF and to deport many Oromo nationalists to Ethiopia even if it meant breaking international laws. Further, Oromo refugees have been threatened with *refoulement* from Yemen, Germany, Israel, Djibouti, Sudan, and Kenya since the United Nations High Commission for Refugees (UNHCR) is "staffed by apologists for the Ethiopian government" that do not protect Oromo human rights.[127] The *refoulement* of hundreds of Oromo refugees has taken place from Djibouti since the early 1990s with the "protection" of the UNHCR that ignores the violation of Oromo human rights.[128]

The United States ignores the violation of human rights of Oromos and other colonized nations. According to *Human Rights Watch/World Report 1999:* "With about $30 million in development aid and $66 million in food aid, bringing the total to about $97 million, Ethiopia remained the second largest recipient of U.S. aid in Sub-Saharan Africa, after South Africa. The U.S. failed to use its privileged relations with Ethiopia as a leverage for human rights improvements. . . . The only public statement involving human rights came on August 6, [1998] when the U.S. government expressed deep concern at the detention and expulsion of Eritreans in and from Ethiopia."[129] The U.S. government is only concerned about the human rights violations of Eritreans, ignoring the ethnic cleansing that the Tigrayan-led regime commits against Oromos and other colonized nations. When Oromos presented their cases to the U.S. government that it should support the struggle of Oromos for self-determination and democracy rather than supporting Tigrayan ethnocracy, they did not get a positive response. They were ignored. U.S. foreign policy elites seek advice from scholars who have accepted without inspection the racist assumptions implicit in the construction of Ethiopia when they formulate a policy toward Ethiopia. They never have taken into consideration Oromo scholarship and Oromo studies that have successfully exposed the deficiency in Ethiopian Studies.[130] The State Department and its elites who deal with Ethiopian issues ignore the voices of Oromo scholars and politicians and other students of Oromo society.

Conclusion

Racism in U.S. foreign policy has discouraged the success of an alternative leadership that can solve the problems of Oromos and other population groups who suffer under Ethiopian colonialism and global imperialism. Both the generous support the successive *Habasha* elites headed by Menelik, Haile-Selassie, Mengistu, and Meles received from the West, particularly the United States, and from the East, and the institutionalized distinctions in the Ethiopian empire have mobilized Amharas and Tigrayans against Oromos and other colonized peoples and eliminated the possibility of forming a common political platform against the Ethiopian colonizing structure. The distinction between *Habashas* and Oromos is the outward expression of the fundamental subjugation of Oromos and other nations upon which Ethiopia is built. To challenge this basic contradiction is to shake the very foundation of Ethiopian colonialism.

Combined Ethiopian policies and U.S. policies have frustrated Oromos from democratically getting access to Ethiopian state power or from creating their own independent state by keeping them in the position of second-class citizens. Because of this, the Oromo national movement must broaden its political base both regionally and globally by forming an alliance with antiracist, anticolonial, and democratic forces to expose and remove all impediments to self-expression through educational mechanisms and organized struggle. As Oromos consolidate their national movement in Oromia, Oromos in the diaspora and the friends of Oromos in the world must build a global network through which they can expose ideologies that have had a serious negative impact on the Oromo struggle. The next chapter directly compares and contrasts African American and Oromo nationalisms.

CHAPTER V

Comparing the African American and Oromo Movements

In this chapter I explain how the racialized capitalist world system that produced modern slavery, colonization, genocide or ethnocide, cultural destruction and repression, and continued subjugation also facilitated the emergence and development of the African American and Oromo movements. Both African Americans and Oromos resisted slavery and colonization first without systematically organizing themselves. Their cultural and political resistance continued after their enslavement and colonization because these two peoples were assigned to the status of slaves and colonial subjects and second-class citizens by the United States and Ethiopia, respectively. In the case of the Oromo, the United States has been also involved on the side of the Ethiopian state to suppress Oromo society since the early 1950s.[1] This comparative chapter historically situates the emergence and development of these two movements by focusing on their similarities and differences.

The Rise of African American Nationalism

African American nationalism developed as a mass movement during the mid-twentieth century as a cultural, intellectual, ideological, and political movement whose purpose was to achieve civil equality, human dignity, and development by overthrowing White racial and colonial dictatorship. This development was facilitated by the cumulative struggles of the previous generations, social structures and processes, and conjunctures. As we discussed in chapter II, there were various forms of individual and group resistance struggles and protonationalism in African American society prior to the twentieth century. The ancestors of African Americans both individually and collectively resisted enslavement in Africa and fought against slavery on slave ships and later on the American plantations.[2] Some of the slaves engaged in revolts[3] while others formed maroon communities after running away from slavery.[4] For 250 years, African Americans influenced North America through their resistance struggle, which aimed to retain an African identity and restore their freedom.[5] American racial slavery absolutely denied human freedom to the ancestors of African Americans. It was during this period that African American peoplehood developed from the enslaved Africans of various ethnonational origins.[6] This peoplehood developed from the past African cultural memory, the collective dehumanization of slavery, and the hope for survival as a people in the future. All these and other forms of ideological and cultural resistance established a strong social foundation from which cultural memory and popular historical consciousness emerged to facilitate the development of African American nationalism.[7]

The freed and segregated African Americans in the urban North established autonomous self-help and fraternal associations, churches, schools, small businesses, media, and cultural centers between the American Revolution and the Civil War. According to W. J. Moses, "Classical black nationalism originated in the 1700s, reached its first peak in the 1850s, underwent a decline toward the end of the Civil War, and peaked again in the 1920s, as a result of the Garvey Movement."[8] Although freed Africans and their children helped the emergence of black nationalism between the 1770s and the 1860s by building institutions and organizations, the persistence of racial slavery until the mid-1860s, denial of formal education, the repression of African culture, and the absolute denial of freedom to African Americans had delayed the development of African American nationalism.

However, the Black indigenous institutions later provided "a favorable structure of political opportunities"[9] for the African American struggle. Antebellum freed African Americans developed "organizational infrastructure" that evolved from these indigenous organizations and institutions that helped develop the African American movement during the first half of the twentieth century. D. McAdam argues that "the ability of insurgents to generate a social movement is ultimately dependent on the presence of an indigenous 'infrastructure' that can be used to link members of the aggrieved population into an organized campaign of mass political action."[10]

The antebellum African American scholars wrote several books, magazines, newspapers, and journals that later helped build Black cultural memory and popular historical consciousness. These scholars and activists, while fighting against racial slavery and segregation, also attempted to capture intellectually the past African cultural experience, evaluated the negative and positive experiences of Africans in the New World, and rejected American racist cultural elements and structures. Through reconnecting African Americans to the African cultural past and showing various African civilizations to the world, they challenged White supremacy and Eurocentric historical knowledge that claimed that Blacks were backward, primitive, pagan, and inferior intellectually to Whites.[11]

By explaining that African civilizations and cultures prior to the sixteenth century were equal to and in some respects more advanced than those of Europeans, they refuted the claim of the natural superiority of the White people. Despite the fact that these scholars sometimes manifested elitist and "modernist" positions, they produced an alternative knowledge that laid the foundation of an Afrocentric scholarship, the paradigm that promotes the idea of multicultural society. Freed and freeborn Blacks struggled to free their Black brothers and sisters from slavery and to gain civil equality, and consolidated the cultural and ideological foundations for African American political consciousness and nationalism between the eighteenth and nineteenth centuries. Politically conscious freedmen and their children used different platforms to fight against racial slavery and to promote civil equality. For instance, the nation's first African American newspaper, *Freedom's Journal,* was established by Thomas Paul and Samuel Cornish in 1827. The editors of this newspaper provided a critical social, political, and cultural commentary that "invoked the common African ancestry on which the earlier pamphleteers had drawn to shape a moral community. Yet the African American press pursued an explicitly political rather than implicitly moral agenda, manipulating the symbolism of common ancestry to unify public opinion and mobilize collective action."[12]

Similarly, David Walker published the *Appeal, in Four Articles,* in 1829 declaring that "the greatest riches in all America have arisen from our blood and tears," and demanded that White Americans "make a national acknowledgment to us for the wrongs they have inflicted on us."[13] E. B. Bethel comments on the essence of the *Appeal* as follows: "Reverberating with passionate energy, setting aside the civility previously used to address white audiences, no longer needing to mask their frustration and anger with a veneer of rhetorical reserve, within the freedom movements African Americans spoke to each other in a vocabulary of race unity and cultural autonomy; and from those movements an ethnic identity grounded in a common mythic African heritage welded from a blend of autobiographical and generational memory emerged and crystallized."[14] In his manifesto, David Walker demanded civil equality and cultural integrity by condemning racial slavery, White racism, and the corruption of Christianity and other institutions. William Lloyd Garrison also founded a magazine called *Liberator* on January 1, 1831. Gradually, some politically conscious elements started to build a collective movement. With the suggestion of Hezekiah Grice, a Baltimore ice dealer, Richard Alen convened a clandestine meeting of 40 self-selected delegates in September 1830 in Philadelphia and founded the National Convention Movement, the first civil rights movement in the United States. This movement met only twice, in 1830 and 1835, and shaped the future African American political agenda:

> The architects of the movement transformed race identity for free African Americans into a political resource upon which two major twentieth-century liberation movements would draw to fuel their agendas. Within the National Convention Movement, African American concerns about emigration in general, and about the Canadian refugee settlements and opportunities for resettlement in Hayti [sic] in particular, anticipated the impulse for cultural unification of people of color that would also drive twentieth-century Pan-Africanism. At the same time, and complementing the focus on citizenship and the improvement of the status of free African Americans, the movement aimed to eradicate structural and legal sources of racial oppression. In this way it foreshadowed the political and economic agendas both of post - Civil War Reconstruction in the Southern states and of the 1960s Civil Rights Movement.[15]

Further, the Haitian Revolution that led to the formation of a Black republic in 1804 "extended African American consciousness beyond the borders of the United States."[16] The dehumanizing experiences of racial slavery and the struggle for freedom and civil equality were reflected in both personal and cultural memories of the antebellum African American scholars: "The welding of past to present and the crafting of a political agenda informed by that union took place at a revolutionary intersection of social movements and demographic shifts in antebellum America. In particular, the numerical growth of the free African American population in the Northern states, and the expansion of a literate public within that population, combined with two great civil rights movements—the (biracial) antislavery movement and the (African American) Convention Movement. The resulting political climate nurtured an intellectual and literary tradition."[17]

This intellectual and literary tradition "redefined the boundaries as well as the content of a collective past by grounding that in historical consciousness rather than autobiographical memory and by subordinating the particularized and individualized to larger explanations of events and processes."[18] The emergence of a few intellectuals helped to lay the ideological foundation of African American nationalism by developing African American collective consciousness from politicized collective grievances and personal experiences expressed through autobiographical and cultural memory. "The popular historical consciousness that resulted from these *lieux de memoire*—a body of shared beliefs, myths, and images—connected a New World past to an American present and validated a vision of the future that would inform the African American political and cultural agenda into the twentieth century."[19] The struggle of freedmen had a few sympathizers and supporters in White American society. The antislavery movement was a biracial movement that brought together Black activists and White reformers to fight against American slavery.[20] Quakers dominated the antislavery movement until the nineteenth century by providing large numbers of members and effective leadership.

However, some of these abolitionists were racists who wanted to get rid of freed Blacks: "In 1816, a group of reformers who sought the end of slavery as a great evil—but who at the same time rejected as a similar evil the prospect of the Black's remaining in America—formed the American Colonization Society."[21] Although the early abolitionists for the most part failed, they succeeded in persuading the Congress to pass gradual emancipation laws in the North and to end the foreign slave trade in March 1807.[22] M. L. Dillon argues that these abolitionists had "great moral courage and independence of mind to venture to subvert the dominant practices and values of their age."[23] During this period, complex social structural changes were taking place in the United States because this country was changing from agrarian to industrial and from a semiperipheral to a core country. During the political confrontation between the North and the South on several political, economic, and strategic issues, abolitionists provided an ideological ammunition for the Northern leadership that wanted to establish its class hegemony by developing core capitalism through removing the obstacles created by the planter class that strived to maintain racial slavery.

The development of core capitalism in the North and the persistence of peripheral capitalism in the South led to contradictions in the strategy of national development and facilitated class struggle in the antebellum United States.[24] The class forces of core capitalists and their allies and peripheral capitalists contended to control federal state power. This gradually resulted in civil war. The South's control over the federal state crumpled when the alliance between the farmers of the West and the planters of the South was broken, and when the Northern and Southern Democrats were divided, and when the Republicans captured the federal state by the election of Abraham Lincoln to the office of Presidency in 1860.[25] C. Chase-Dunn states, "The crumpling of this alliance provoked the Civil War even though the Republicans never advocated the abolition of slavery but only prevention of its expansion to the West. Southern peripheral capitalism was expansionist because of its extensive nature and the quick exhaustion of the soil, but this was not the main reason why the South desired the extension of slavery to the West. The main issue for the South was control over the Federal state. Planters opposed the creation of free states because the alliance with free farmers was tenuous and they felt they would have less and less power in the Federal state."[26]

The Civil War was initiated by the slave-owning states that seceded from the federal union, and the Northern core capitalists and their allies entered into the war to maintain the union and to impose the strategy of core capitalist development.[27] The

United States achieved upward mobility from semiperiphery to core by the alliance among the classes of Northern core capitalists, some workers, and farmers who opposed the expansion of slavery to the west of the country: "It was not slavery that was the main issue but the question of who would dominate the Federal state. Free farmers and workers found themselves at odds with the interests of the peripheral capitalists of the South on the issue of the frontier, and so cast their lot with core capital. In so doing, they destroyed the plantocracy and created a strong core state. The Civil War and reconstruction firmly established the hegemony of core capitalism and core labor over the Federal state."[28] Slavery was abolished mainly to dismantle the power of the slave-owning class that was against the interest of core capitalists.[29] Challenging the misconception that the American Civil War was mainly fought to end slavery, Dillon asserts that the issues of slavery and the welfare of African Americans were secondary: "Such motives for abolition bore slight resemblance to the moral and religious imperatives that had inspired abolitionists during their long crusade. The new kind of antislavery had little to say about the rights of black people and about justice for freedmen. It was, finally, an emancipation policy derived from enmity generated by the strategic errors of slave holders rather than from a recognition of the evils inherent in slavery itself."[30]

Although the abolitionists might have had some impact on some leaders, the Lincoln government started the idea of emancipation as a political measure after the Civil War began mainly to weaken the Confederacy by depriving it of Black manpower, to stop the English and French support to the South, and to get support from the Radical Republicans in the Congress.[31] Despite the fact that Black and White abolitionists had made an ideological contribution against slavery, the institution of racial slavery was dismantled mainly because of the contradictions between core and peripheral capitalism, the strategic mistake of the South, and the alliance of some workers and farmers with core capitalists to control the federal state. Although most of these forces were not abolitionists, they indirectly contributed to the abolition of slavery for political and economic expediency. The historical contradiction between the core capitalism of the North and peripheral capitalism of the South resulted in the Civil War that created conducive social structural and conjunctural factors that later contributed to the development of Black nationalism. It released the control that the slave owners had over the enslaved Africans. In other words, the Civil War, the defeat of the planters, and the abolition of slavery transformed the nature of the African American struggle. For almost a decade the federal government intervened in the South on the side of freed Africans after the Civil War; however, after establishing its political hegemony in the South the federal government left the fate of this people to Southern states that established Jim Crow laws to segregate and continue to dominate, exploit, and oppress Blacks. The "push" factors—such as Jim Crow laws, racial dictatorship, oppressive social control mechanisms, lawlessness, denial of political and cultural rights, poverty, lack of education and other opportunities—and "pull" factors from the North, such as availability of jobs and the possibility of freedom, facilitated the great migration of the Black folk to Northern and other cities.

This mass migration transformed African Americans from rural and agricultural workers to industrial and urban workers. As a result, they formed communities, associations, fraternities, churches, mosques, schools, organizations, and other kinds of urban relations. The educated class and other activists who were previously isolated from the slaves found a fertile social ground in which they would sow their ideas of social change and struggle. African American activist intellectuals, such as Du Bois, politicized collective grievances and mobilized White activists and reformers who participated in the antislavery movement and their children and others. Some White reformers and radicals supported the struggle to legally dismantle racial segregation; this struggle received some White assistance in several forms from some foundations, clergy, and student volunteers. J. C. Jenkins and M. Eckert call these supporters "conscience constituencies."[32] At the turn of the century, several African American organizations, such as the Niagra Movement (1905), which evolved into The National Association for the Advancement of the Colored People (NAACP) (1909); the National Urban League (1911), and others emerged and promoted the African American movement. Social structural factors and processes and conjunctures in the form of war, migration, economic and political changes, urban community formation, and human agency in the form of the consolidation of the activist intellectual bloc, politicized political grievances, and the formation of independent institutions and organizations facilitated the development of Black nationalism in the first half of the twentieth century.

Movement scholars explain that "the level of infrastructure in a given population is itself shaped by the type of macro factors. . . . Broad macro-processes, such as industrialization, urbanization, mass migration, and the like, largely determine the degree to which groups in society are organized and the structure of that organization. The extent and structure of that organization in turn imply very different potentials of collective action."[33] The majority of Blacks moved to cities and became members of the urban working class during the first half of the twentieth century. This created conducive conditions for the development of Black institutions and organizations. Then African Americans started to be connected together through social networks, the media, transportation, and communication networks and technologies by overcoming their dispersion in rural areas. The geographic concentration in cities increased the density of interaction among them and facilitated recruitment in various movement organizations. The indigenous institutions and organizations became the foundation of professional social movements and political organizations. According to D. McAdam, J. D. McCarthy, and M. N. Zald, "The key concept linking macro- and micro-processes in movement emergence is that of the *micro-mobilization context*. A micro-mobilization context can be defined as any small group setting in which processes of collective attribution are combined with rudimentary forms of organization to produce mobilization for collective action."[34]

The African American movement blossomed and galvanized the African American people and their supporters for collective action in the urban setting. Explaining how urbanization and collective action were related in African American society, McAdam, McCarthy, and Zald expound that "the rural to urban migration of blacks within the South greatly enhanced the prospects for collective action by transforming an impoverished, geographically dispersed mass into an increasing well organized urban population."[35] Similar types of socioeconomic conditions, and historical, cultural, and political factors and conjunctures facilitated the development of Oromo nationalism.

The Rise of Oromo Nationalism

Oromo nationalism only developed into a mass movement in the early 1990s.[36] This development occurred after a long period of resistance. Like African Americans, initially Oromos resisted slavery and colonization without systematically organizing themselves. The Oromo cultural and political resistance continued after their enslavement and colonization because they were assigned to the status of slaves and colonial subjects and second-class citizens by the Ethiopian state. Because of the seriousness of Oromo resistance to slavery and colonialism, it took more than 30 years to establish Ethiopian settler colonialism and its institutions in various Oromo regions. Oromo groups continued to challenge Ethiopian settler colonialism in attempts to regain their freedom and independence. There were numerous local uprisings in different parts of Oromia. Sometimes these local groups expelled the Ethiopian colonial settlers from their country.[37] Although unsuccessful, some Oromo groups tried to use European powers, such as Italy and Great Britain, to regain their independence.[38]

Despite all these resistance struggles, it took a long time to develop Oromo nationalism when nationalism in different parts of colonial Africa emerged between the 1920s and the 1950s. The denial of formal education, the structure of Ethiopian colonialism such that almost all Oromos lived in rural areas, limiting their economic participation to agriculture, and tight political repression—all delayed the development of Oromo nationalism. The Ethiopian colonial state and its institutions prevented the emergence of Oromo leadership by coopting many of the intellectual elements and liquidating the nationalist ones, by suppressing Oromo autonomous institutions, and by erasing Oromo history, culture, and language. According to Mohammed Hassen, "From the 1880s to the early 1960s, the Oromo suffered a great deal from the lack of central leadership. It should be remembered that in the 1880s during the conquest and colonization of Oromo territory, a large number of the Oromo people, together with their leaders, were decimated. . . . Other Oromo leaders were coopted into the Ethiopian political process. The basis for independent Oromo leadership was destroyed."[39] Despite the fact that Oromo individuals and various Oromo groups resisted and fought against the combined forces of Ethiopian settler colonialism and global imperialism, a few Oromo elites and urbanites started to develop and manifest Oromo collective consciousness and nationalism by the early 1960s.

The destruction "of Oromo national leadership, the tight control of the government, the meagerness of a modern educational establishment, lack of transport and communication systems and mass media, the absence of written literature in the Oromo language and the limited nature of interaction among the Oromo in different regions . . . may have contributed to retarding the growth of an Oromo national consciousness before the beginning of the 1960s."[40] For a considerable length of time, Oromo lacked formally trained and culturally minded intellectuals. The Christianized Oromo scholar and former slave, Onesimos Nasib, who was trained in Europe, and his team Aster Ganno, Lidya Dimbo, and Feben (Hirphee) Abba Magaal, as well as another religious scholar, Sheik Bakri Sapalo, pioneered the production of written literature in *Afaan Oromoo* and tried to introduce literacy to Oromo society in the first half of the twentieth century. To deny formal education to Oromos, the Ethiopian colonial government and the Orthodox Church suppressed the efforts of these scholars. It was not only the Ethiopian government and its international supporters that hindered the progress of Oromo society. The opposition of Somalia to Oromo interests also contributed to the slow development of Oromo consciousness and nationalism. The Somalia state that emerged with the liberation of Somalia in 1960 tried its best to Somalize some Oromos and incorporate a part of Oromia to Somalia. While the Ethiopian elites "feared Oromo nationalism as a major threat to the disintegration of the Ethiopian Empire, Somali ruling elites regarded it as a dangerous movement that would abort the realization of the dream of greater Somalia."[41] All these obstacles hampered the development of Oromo nationalism for some time.

The development of colonial/peripheral capitalism in Oromia, the emergence of a few conscious Oromo intellectuals and bureaucrats, the cumulative experiences of struggle, and politicized collective and individual grievances—all facilitated the development of Oromo nationalism.[42] Since the 1960s, some Oromos started to move to cities where colonial settlers were concentrated. As the Oromo people flowed from rural areas into cities, the condition of urban areas began to change. While a few were successful and became petty traders, most became laborers or were unemployed. These groups and students brought the Oromo language and culture to urban areas where the colonialists were concentrated. An example of this was the formation of musical groups, such as the Arffan Qallo and Biftu Ganamo musical groups in Dirre Dhawa. It was not only the Oromo masses who were mistreated by the Ethiopian colonizers. Those Oromo elites who joined the Ethiopian colonial institutions were not treated as equal citizens. Since the colonial government ignored them, those few Oromo individuals who joined colonial institutions (such as schools, parliament, the army, and the administration) and Oromo merchants began to think about ways to improve the Oromo living standard. Despite their relative achievements, these individuals had inferior status to Ethiopians due to their Oromo national identity.

Paradoxically, the idea of developing the collective consciousness of Oromo and Oromo nationalism was initiated by a few Oromos who were educated to be members of an Ethiopianized Oromo collaborative class, but who were not treated as equals with Ethiopians. "Exclusion breeds failed assimilation," Anthony Smith writes, "and reawakens an ethnic consciousness among the professional elites, at exactly the moment when the intellectuals are beginning to explore the historic roots of the community."[43] Since there has been a fundamental contradiction between the interests of Ethiopian colonizing structures and the colonized Oromos, Ethiopian society could not culturally and structurally assimilate the Oromo elites. The formation of the Macha-Tulama Self-Help Association in the year 1963–1964 marked the public rise of Oromo nationalism.[44] Since the Ethiopian Constitution did not allow the establishment of political organizations, emerging Oromo leaders formed this association in accordance with Article 45 of his Imperial Majesty's 1955 revised Constitution and Article 14, Number 505 of the Civil Code as a civilian self-help association. These Oromo elites, through forming this association in Fifinnee (Addis Ababa), the capital city of the Ethiopian empire, started to articulate the collective grievances of the Oromo people and formulated programs to solve some economic, social, and educational problems of Oromo society. Since the association was open to all interested ethnonational groups in Ethiopia, it embraced the principle of multicultural diversity.[45] According to Hassen, within a short time, the association "transformed itself from a self-help development association in Shawan administrative region, into pan–Oromo movement that coordinated peaceful resistance, and in turn gave birth to Oromo political awareness. This means that since their conquest in the 1880s, the Oromo developed a single leadership . . . for two interrelated purposes: economic, educational and cultural development and to establish the political equality of the Oromo with other peoples of Ethiopia."[46]

Despite the fact that Oromos provided resources to build Ethiopian infrastructure and institutions, they were denied access to social amenities. Reflecting on this reality, in May 1966, the association at its Itaya meeting expressed that: "(1) less than one percent of Oromo school age children ever get the opportunity to go to school; (2) . . . less than one percent of the Oromo population get adequate medical services; (3) . . . less than fifty percent of the Oromo population own land; (4) . . . a very small percentage of the Oromo population have access to [modern] communication services. [And yet] the Oromo paid more than eighty percent of the taxes for education, health, and communication."[47] When the Ethiopian government and Ethiopian elites continued to mistreat these Oromo elites, conspired to deny Oromos educational and professional opportunities, and even attempted to destroy the leadership of the association, the association under its charismatic leader, Taddasa Biru, intensified its mobilization for struggle.[48] The Oromo nationalist elements of the 1960s recognized what C. Greetz describes: "The one aim is to be noticed; it is a search for identity, and a demand that identity be publicly acknowledged. . . . The other aim is practical: it is a demand for progress for a rising standard of living, more effective political order, great social justice, and beyond that of 'playing a part in the larger arena of world politics,' of exercising influence among the nations."[49]

The Ethiopian colonial state and the Ethiopian settlers in Oromia did not tolerate any manifestation of Oromo consciousness. The Haile Selassie government banned the association in 1967,[50] and its leaders were imprisoned or killed. The Ethiopian government did not even tolerate the existence of the Arffan Qallo and the Biftu Ganamo musical groups because they expressed themselves in the Oromo language and culture. They were banned like the association. Similarly, the Bale Oromo armed struggle that started in the early 1960s was suppressed with the assistance of Great Britain, the United States, and Israel between 1968 and 1970.[51] The global capitalist structure that created the Ethiopian empire through the colonization of Oromia has continued to make sure that Oromos remain subordinated to *Habashas* by any means necessary. Unlike African Americans, who have struggled against the racist American capitalist structure, Oromos have to fight against the racist Ethiopian colonial structure and its sponsor, global capitalism. The banning of the Macha-Tulama Self-Help Association, the destruction of the Arffan Qallo and Biftu Ganamo musical groups, and the suppression of the Bale Oromo armed struggle forced Oromo nationalism to go underground. The Macha-Tulama "movement marked the beginning of a new political experience that was crucial to the growth of Oromo nationalism in the 1970s, an experience that taught the Oromo elites that they needed a liberation movement that would marshal the resources of their people, harmonize their actions and channel their creative activities and innovation against the oppressive Ethiopian system."[52]

The suppression of Oromo reform nationalism forced some Oromo nationalists to go underground in Oromia; others went to Somalia, the Middle East, and other countries to continue the Oromo national movement. When Oromos were denied the right to express themselves in the late 1960s and the early 1970s, a few Oromo militant elements produced underground political pamphlets, such as *Kana Bekta* (Do you know this?), and historical documents, such as *The Oromos: Voice against Tyranny*. The denial of individual, civil, and collective rights and the suppression of all forms of Oromo organizations and movements forced Oromo nationalists to pursue their objectives in clandestine forms. Explaining how the Ethiopian National Liberation Front (ENLF) was formed in 1971 and the Oromo Liberation Front (OLF) in 1974, Bonnie Holcomb and Sisai Ibssa note that "intellectuals who had survived the banning of Macha-Tulama had gone underground to find a new approach. Those who had been able to leave the country were also searching together for alternative tactics and strategies to achieve the objective they had espoused and to find a new model for effective organization."[53]

The ENLF's main objectives were to reform Ethiopia, introduce democracy, and bring civil equality for all peoples by removing the imperial structure of Ethiopia.[54] However, most Oromo nationalists did not endorse these objectives, which seemed to accept the nature of Ethiopian elites, but rather determined to develop revolutionary nationalism that attempted to dismantle Ethiopian settler colonialism and to establish a people's democratic republic of Oromia; it is left open whether this was to find expression as an independent or as an autonomous state within a federated multicultural democratic society.[55] Oromo revolutionary nationalism emerged with the birth of the OLF in the early 1970s. The OLF states that the main "objective of the struggle is the realization of national self-determination for the Oromo people and their liberation from oppression and exploitation in all their forms. This can only be realized through the successful consummation of the new democratic revolution . . . and the establishment of the people's democratic republic of Oromia." This organization also recognizes the significance of creating a multinational democratic state through voluntary association by dismantling colonial, dictatorial, and racist structures. The more that Oromos intensified their national struggle, the more the crisis of the Ethiopian state and its terrorism increased.

A few Oromo revolutionary elements established an underground political movement and transformed reform nationalism into revolutionary nationalism after the Ethiopian colonial government systematically denied Oromos any channel through which to express or pursue their individual and collective interests. The revolutionary Oromo leaders produced political pamphlets and expanded their sphere of influence by organizing different political circles in different sectors of Oromo society, such as students, professionals, workers, farmers, soldiers, students, and the army. Those Oromos who fled to foreign countries and received military training returned to Oromia to initiate armed struggle. The group that initiated the Oromo armed struggle in 1973 and other revolutionary elements together created the OLF in 1974. As soon as the OLF began to challenge Ethiopian colonial domination ideologically, intellectually, politically, and militarily, the Ethiopian state initiated terrorism against Oromo nationalists and the Oromo people. Due to lack of international support and sanctuary, Ethiopian terrorism, Somali opposition to Oromo nationalism, and internal disagreement within Oromo elites, the growth of Oromo nationalism was slow in the 1970s and the 1980s.

In the late 1970s, almost all members of the OLF central committee, including Margarsa Bari, (Chairman), Demise Techane (vice chairman), Aboma Mitiku, and Omer Abrahim, were wiped out on their way to Somalia to attend an important organizational meeting. The Ethiopian regime of the *Derg* targeted prominent Oromo nationalists and arranged for the assassination of veteran leaders like Tadassan Biru and Hailu Ragassa. In 1980, it imprisoned or murdered top OLF leaders and activists. Despite all of these problems, the Oromo movement played a role in overthrowing the Ethiopian military regime headed by Mengistu Haile Mariam in May 1991.

With the demise of the Mengistu regime, the Ethiopian People's Revolutionary Democratic Front (EPRDF), dominated by the Tigrayan People's Liberation Front (TPLF), came to power mainly with the support and endorsement of the U.S. government, and then later established a minority Tigrayan-based authoritarian government. To obtain political legitimacy, at the beginning the new regime invited

different liberation fronts, the most prominent of which was the OLF, and other political organizations and established a transitional government. The new regime persuaded these fronts and organizations that it would prepare a ground for the
formation of a multicultural federal democratic government of Ethiopia. However, in
less than a year, this regime had effectively expelled all coalition partners by using intimidation, terrorism, and war, and had established an ethnic-based party dictatorship
without any opposition from the United States or other Western countries.[56] The
United States, other Western countries, and the Organization of African Unity called
the sham elections this regime used to legitimize its power satisfactory, fair, and free.[57]
As we shall see below, the feat was accomplished through systematic intimidation and
outright terrorism.

States, such as the Ethiopian state, that fail to establish ideological hegemony and
political order are unstable and insecure, and hence, they engage in terrorism.[58] State
terrorism is the systematic policy of a government through which massive violence
is practiced to impose terror on a given population in order to change their behavior of political struggle or resistance.[59] The Tigrayan-led Ethiopian government has
practiced state-sponsored violence against Oromos and others as an acceptable
means of establishing political stability and order. Since this regime mainly survives
on Oromo economic resources, it uses terrorist actions mainly against the Oromo
people.[60] The activities of this regime have proved to be terrorist as manifested in
its plans and actions, such as systematic assassinations of prominent Oromos, open
and hidden murders of thousands of Oromos, reinitiating of villagization and evic-
tion of Oromo farmers and herders, expansion of prisons in Oromia, forcing of
more than 45,000 Oromos into hidden and underground detention camps, and
looting of economic resources of Oromia to develop the Tigrayan region and enrich Tigrayan elites and their collaborators.[61] A video smuggled out of Ethiopia in
1997 shows horrifying mass graves in Easter Oromia (Hararghe).[62] Without any
doubt Oromos are exposed to systematic state terrorism so that their lands and natural and economic resources can be used by Tigrayan elites, their collaborators, and
transnational corporations.[63]

History repeats itself in different forms and contexts. The Amhara elites systematically exterminated an independent Oromo leadership with the help of European
colonial powers. Later they used so-called socialism and the Soviet bloc to suppress the
Oromo national movement. Currently, state terrorism manifests itself in this empire in
yet a different form: its obvious manifestation is violence against its opponents, primarily against Oromos.[64] Since 1992 several thousands of Oromos have been killed
or arrested on suspicion of being OLF supporters or sympathizers or for refusing proposed membership in the EPRDF via OPDO.[65] Despite all these inhumane and criminal activities, U.S. officials deny the existence of torture in Ethiopian prisons or
camps.[66] Another form of state terrorism is economic violence. The government has
confiscated the properties of some Oromos and others who have been imprisoned.
Those who were released from prisons paid a huge amount of "ransom money" col-
lected by relatives for TPLF/EPRDF soldiers and agents.[67] The Ethiopian government
attempts to destroy Oromo merchants and intellectuals by labeling them "narrow nationalists" and "the enemy of the Ethiopian Revolution."[68]

Oromos are not even allowed to have a meaningful relief association in Ethiopia
and neighboring countries. Realizing that the Ethiopian government and international organizations pay little attention to the welfare of Oromo society, a few Oromo

leaders created the Oromo Relief Association (ORA) in exile as an independent humanitarian Oromo association in the late 1970s to assist Oromo refugees in the Horn of Africa.[69] Assuming that the political change of 1991 would allow a peaceful and democratic political resolution for the Oromo problem, ORA moved its head office to Finfinne and shifted its program from relief work to rehabilitation and settlement activities, developing projects that included health, education, agricultural, and afforestation activities.[70] One thousand three-hundred fifty-two ORA orphans moved to Oromia from Sudan, when ORA decided to locate its headquarters in Oromia in 1991; some of these children were killed by TPLF soldiers or drowned by big rivers while being chased by these soldiers, and others were captured and taken to the Didessa concentration camp where they were beaten, tortured, raped, and where some died of hunger and infection.[71] The regime closed ORA regional offices in August 1995 and its headquarters in February 1996, confiscating all its properties. ORA activities were banned not only in Ethiopia, but also in Djibouti, Sudan, Somalia, and Kenya. Explaining the banning of ORA in Djibouti, B. Fossati, Namarra, and P. Niggli comment, "The only organization that for some years looked after the Oromo refugees, the Oromo Relief Association (ORA), was banned . . . in June 1995 by the Djibouti government at the request of the Ethiopian government."[72] Most international humanitarian organizations did not object.[73]

Using the leverage of Western countries, the regime pressures neighboring governments to return or expel Oromo refugees from their countries. The alliance of the West with this regime has frightened neighboring countries such as Djibouti, Kenya, and Sudan and turned them against the Oromo struggle and Oromo refugees. The United Nations High Commission for Refugees (UNHCR) has even failed to provide reasonable protection for thousands of Oromos in Djibouti. "The Oromo refugees are generally regarded by the Djibouti authorities as unwelcome aliens or illegal immigrants, despite the fact that Djibouti is a signatory to the Geneva Convention on Refugees. Every day the refugees fear being caught in one of the frequent police raids and forced back across the border. Only a small minority has legal refugee status."[74] The burdens of Oromo women refugees are heavy; many of them are raped while crossing the border on the way to Djibouti or they are forced to work as slaves by Djibouti households or the Djibouti police. Sebida Musa says, "They take the women home and treat them as their personal property. If one of the women gets pregnant, she is mercilessly thrown out into the street, where she and her unwanted child have to try and survive by begging."[75] Oromo refugees have been abused by the Djibouti authorities and the Ethiopian government, and ignored by international organizations, such as UNHCR. Fossati, Nammarra, and Niggli note: "The Oromo council of elders told us they believed they were entitled to a small portion of the international aid available to refugees, but did not even get a glass of water from the UNHCR and had been completely forgotten."[76] Some refugees also faced terrorism and forced repatriation.

The TPLF/EPRDF forces have entered into Kenya, murdering and looting the economic resources of some Kenyan Oromos by accusing them of harboring the Oromo Liberation Army. Oromos are even denied a sanctuary from neighboring countries and are denied the right to be refugees. Oromos have been assassinated or murdered by the regime in their own country, Kenya, South Africa, and Djibouti. They have been denied burial rites and eaten by hyenas and other wild animals. Since Oromo refugees are not welcomed by neighboring countries and international organizations, there are also thousands of "internal" Oromo refugees in Oromia and

Ethiopia. Fleeing from Ethiopian state terrorism, these internal refugees hide in the bush and in remote villages.[77] Democratic discourse has been used by the government and its international supporters to hide the state terrorism and the massive human rights violations. The emergence of war between Ethiopia and Eritrea in May 1998 and the intensification of the guerrilla-armed struggle by the OLF and other liberation organizations have created a very dangerous condition for the Oromo and other colonized peoples.

Similarities and Differences Between the Two Movements

The specific interplay of several social, structural, and historical factors in the global capitalist system affected the emergence and development of the two movements: the inability of the slavers or colonizers to completely control or crush the human spirit, individual and collective resistance to colonial or racial/ethnonational domination, the immortality of certain cultural memories, economic and political changes, urbanization and community formation, the emergence of an educated class, politicized collective grievances, and the dissemination of social scientific and political knowledge through global and local networks. The development of these movements cannot be adequately understood without linking them to ideological formation and cultural revitalization, institutional and organizational manifestations, and alternative knowledge production and dissemination.

As slavery and racial segregation destroyed most African American cultural elements for almost two and a half centuries, Ethiopian settler colonialism and its institutions have facilitated systematic and organized cultural destruction and repression of Oromo culture for more than a century. Cultural destruction and repression have occurred in these two societies to deny free cultural spaces and political voices that are essential to create and build institutions that can facilitate autonomous social development. A free cultural space is an "environment in which people are able to learn a new self-respect, a deeper and more assertive group identity, public skills, and values of cooperation and civic virtue."[78] The White slave owners and American institutions during slavery and American society during racial segregation imposed White cultural domination on African Americans. As a result, African Americans were denied access to state power and prevented from having institutions during slavery, except for a few freed Blacks in Northern cities. After slavery ended between 1863 and 1865, they were also denied access to the American government and other public institutions as well as private institutions until the 1960s. However, they were allowed to have separate religious, economic, cultural, and educational institutions during the American apartheid. These institutions laid the foundation of African American nationalism.

Ethiopian colonialists and their institutions, with the support of the imperial interstate system, have attempted to destroy Oromo cultural identity by denying Oromos the freedom of having their own cultural institutions and developing an authentic Oromo culture. While dismantling Oromo cultural, religious, and governmental institutions, the Ethiopian colonizing structures established the *nafxanya-gabbar* system (semislavery), garrison cities, a collaborative Oromo class, and colonial landholding.[79] Oromo economic resources were expropriated by the Ethiopian state and its agents; Oromo institutions were destroyed or suppressed and lost their economic and political significance. As a result, Oromos lost their decision-making capacity and were silenced. They were prevented from organizing themselves on central, regional, subregional, and community levels. Oromos have maintained their cultural legacy through ritual practices and political and cultural memory. They are tightly controlled by the institutions of the state and their collaborators.

Oromo modes of communication, including movement, are still restricted. Oromos have been denied opportunities necessary for developing their own regional and national institutions and the Oromo system of knowledge that would facilitate the transmission of accumulated cultural experiences from generation to generation. Therefore, Oromo culture and tradition are only survived on family and local levels. Oromos have been denied the freedom of association, organization, education, and expression through the media. They have even been denied the right to organize cultural groups, such as musical groups, and prevented from using their own language in public and business arenas. Bonnie Holcomb explains that the institutionalization of colonialism and racial/ethnonational hierarchy occurred

> in such a way that the identity of the incorporated peoples was erased from public life and from formal and historical record. Abyssinia [Ethiopia] became the intermediary representative in the outside world for all peoples contained within the empire. In addition, the Oromo, an expansive and mobile people, were not only isolated from the outside world, they were isolated from one another inside the empire. Most of the sectors of Oromo society whose communications cut across geographical, religious, economic and trade categories were denied access to one another through their own channels and prevented from transferring people, information or goods along routes that had significance for their development and self-expression. When the Oromo political system with its overarching integrative republican mechanism of public assemblies was officially dismantled and replaced by centralized Ethiopian administrative policies in Oromia, the isolation of the Oromo was complete.[80]

However, Ethiopian colonialism was less effective in destroying Oromo cultural elements than American racial slavery was in destroying African American culture. During slavery, African Americans were forced to abandon their various African cultural elements, religions, and worldviews and to accept the English language, Christianity, and to some extent European worldviews although they sometimes used these imposed cultural elements for resistance. Whereas African American peoplehood and nationalism developed from the process of intense oppression that caused the loss of previous social bonds and networks and the creation of new ones, Oromo peoplehood and nationalism developed from oppressive colonial and racial structures in the presence of long-lasting social bonds and structures.

Although the Ethiopian colonial government imposed its Orthodox Christianity on Oromos, a few Oromo groups accepted it. The majority of Oromos accepted Islam and other forms of Christianity in opposition to the Ethiopian colonizing structures. Similarly, despite the fact that Ethiopian colonizers tried to impose their language on Oromos, the majority of Oromos still speak their own language known as *Afaan Oromoo*. What Amilcar Cabral asserts about the colonized society is applicable to the Oromo condition. There has been an Oromo collaborative class that betrayed and compromised with Ethiopian colonialism by abandoning the Oromo interest, culture, and language. Amilcar Cabral asserts that oppressed, "persecuted, humiliated, betrayed by certain social groups who have compromised with the foreign power, culture took refuge in the village, in the forests, and in the spirit of the victims of domination. Culture survives all these challenges and through the struggle for liberation blossoms forth again."[81] Although there were house slaves and field slaves, and later there were a few African elites who were compromising with the world-view of the White establishment, American society could not until recently produce an effective collaborative class like the one produced by Ethiopian colonialism. The organized destruction and repression of the cultural elements of the two societies could not prevent the struggle for cultural revival and nationalism. Based on the collective struggle of former slaves, "an ethnic identity grounded in a common mythic African heritage welded from a blend of autobiographical and generational memory emerged and crystalized. For African Americans, that identity anchored a cultural world separate and apart from the nation that oppressed them."[82] Elizabeth Bethel asserts that when the majority of African Americans were slaves, those few who achieved their half-freedom in the urban North crafted "a metaphorical homeland within the nation of their birth and [constructed] a civic culture that buttressed the daily realities of social, economic, and political oppression."[83] Similarly, Oromo urbanites formed self-help associations and musical groups in the 1960s reflecting on Oromo collective grievances and cultural memory. The idea of developing Oromo political consciousness and nationalism appeared subsequent to the 1960s with the emergence of Oromo political and cultural organizations.

Without totally killing the colonized or enslaved population, the force of domination cannot have complete control over the spirits and the minds of the subordinated population. This population maintains its existence through cultural memory and popular consciousness and the hope of freedom. Richard Couto suggests that "the community of memory nurtures individuals by carrying on a moral tradition that reinforces the aspiration of their group. . . . The test of community is its sense of a common past. . . . There are stories of suffering 'that sometimes create deeper identities. . . . 'These stories approximate a moral tradition and turn community of memory members 'toward the future as communities of hope.' Such communities of hope sponsor transforming social movements."[84] Subjugated peoples like African Americans and Oromos have faced tensions between a lost past and uncertain future that forced them to forge popular historical consciousness through common forms of rituals, symbols, historical sites, and so forth. The lost past is preserved in ancestral memory in skills, rituals, habits, religion, and other forms of cultural memory. Torn away from their ancestral past, African Americans and Oromos constructed and celebrated a mythological past by imagining a preslavery and a precolonial era.

African Americans had forged an ethnonational identity from common mythic African heritages, collective grievances, and autobiographical and generational memories that passed from generation to generation mainly through oral discourse. Particularly, freed African Americans and their descendants in Northern states organized local churches, mosques, schools, and mutual aid and fraternal societies by proclaiming their mythological ancestry in the name of their institutions and organizations, such as African churches, Free African schools, and African Benevolent Societies, when the majority of their sisters and brothers were suffering under racial slavery in the American South. In 1830, forty self-selected delegates from these elements of African Americans met at Bethel Church, Philadelphia, and formed the National Convention Movement, the original civil rights movement in the United States. Explaining how African Americans survived under racial slavery and segregation, Lawrence Levine expounds that "in the midst of the brutalities and injustice of the antebellum and post-bellum racial systems black men and women were able to find the means to sustain a far greater degree of self-pride and group cohesion than the system they lived under ever intended for them to be able to do."[85]

By systematically examining African American folktales, proverbs, songs, aphorisms, jokes, verbal games, and narrative oral stories and poems, Levine demonstrates how this people developed their culture through maintaining kinship networks, love and marriage, raising and socializing children, and building religion, and nurtured a rich expressive culture to articulate their feelings, pains, dreams, and hopes.[86] Both in African and Oromo societies where the rights of political expressions and demonstrations were denied, songs, proverbs, stories, and other means of expression were used to articulate the dehumanization of collective oppression and exploitation and the aspiration of freedom. Addisu Tolesa explores how Oromos used their expressive culture, like *geerarsa* (folk song), to explain their conditions under Ethiopian colonialism and to remember their past glory under the Oromo democratic tradition that they wished to reinvent with their liberation.[87] The cultural memories and popular historical consciousness of these two peoples have emerged from their respective cultural foundations. Such memories and consciousness pass from generation to generation. "The soul of each generation . . . emanates from the soul of the (collective) 'body' of all the preceding generations," Dubnow writes, "and what endures, namely, the strength of the accumulated past, exceeds the wreckage, the strength of the changing present."[88]

Cultural revival and nationalism help the dominated population group to use its suppressed cultural elements and popular historical memory to organize and struggle for its liberation. The dominated ethnonational group develops a nationalist ideology that promotes the idea that its culture and peoplehood are everlasting by surviving the onslaught of slavery or colonialism. "Anchored in the assurance of the immortality of the community and sustained by the beliefs and traditions of its culture," Maciver notes, "the individual members share an inner environment that blankets them."[89] As the structure of oppression marginalizes and weakens the colonized population, the dominated population develops its human agency based on its cultural traditions and popular historical consciousness to dismantle the structure of domination. The struggles of African Americans and Oromos demonstrate this reality. The demand for the freedom of the colonized or enslaved "included the right to worship in dignity and the right to an identity that incorporated memories of a lost homeland and imaginings of life freely lived. Claims to spiritual and psychological autonomy were inevitable parallels to physical freedom."[90]

Sociologist Elizabeth Rauh Bethel explains how former slave Africans in Northern and Western states consolidated their collective identity between the American Revolution and the Civil War based on their collective grievances, cultural memories, and popular historical consciousness: "Torn away from an ancestral past, African Americans constructed, preserved, and celebrated a mythological past. Prevented from exercising the full prerogative of citizenship, and lacking the material and symbolic resources to develop viable pressure groups that might penetrate the formal machinery of politics, African Americans forged a cultural identity and an agenda for community action that blocked or at least softened the disadvantages of race. The infrastructures of African-American material communities revolved around helping each other and combating the seemingly impenetrable wall of American racism. Both had become defining features of African-American identity."[91] These Africans, a marginalized group, neither slave nor free, developed an African American ethnonational identity based on their collective past that influenced their aspirations. Bethel explores how the transition from individualized and autobiographical memories had laid the foundation of this ethnonational identity through forming a movement, celebrating festivals, and participating in different public events to reshape and develop politicized collective identity. African Americans forged their ethnonational identity from different African ethnonational groups, based on remote African ancestry and cultural heritage and popular consciousness, and developed their political and cultural consciousness to liberate themselves from the American racial caste system.

The ill-equipped Ethiopian state, with the help the imperial interstate system, has kept the Oromo under tight control through denying them educational, cultural, and economic opportunities. The denial of formal education prevented Oromos from developing an educated class with the skills and knowledge needed in building strong national institutions and organizations. Therefore, Oromos have not yet developed an organizational capacity that can transform their cultural heritage into Oromo political and cultural consciousness. Like African Americans, Oromos needed urbanites and educated elements, political and cultural organizations, and political opportunities in order to develop Oromo nationalism and to struggle to dismantle Ethiopian settler colonialism. Although Oromos could rely on a whole series of shared values and culture, the nature of the Ethiopian political system does not allow them to build national institutions that are needed in consolidating the Oromo national movement. Oromos are denied autonomous or independent educational, economic, cultural, and political institutions under Ethiopian settler colonialism. This has delayed the development of Oromo nationalism when compared with other African nationalisms. Several factors have prevented Oromos from mobilizing their cultural resources to develop Oromo nationalism. Similarly, African Americans who were under slavery were denied the opportunity of developing autonomous institutions. Free Blacks, however, could have their autonomous institutions in spite of segregation. After slavery was abolished, African Americans were allowed to develop segregated autonomous cultural, educational, religious, and economic institutions. Despite the fact that these institutions could not fully flourish since they were under internal colonial domination, they had free space that enabled them to contribute to the development of Black nationalism.

What Anthony Smith says about culture and nationalism correctly reflects the conditions under which African American and Oromo nationalisms emerged: "If nationalism is part of the 'spirit of the age,' it is equally dependent upon earlier motifs, visions and ideals. For what we call nationalism operates on many levels and may be regarded as a form of culture as much as a species of political ideology and social movement."[92] The emergence of Oromo nationalism has facilitated the demand for restoration of the Oromo democratic tradition known as *Gada*.[93] According to Ben Barber, an American photojournalist, "Oromo—with its unique *Gadaa* [sic] system of organized social responsibilities according to distinct age-groups [and generation-sets]—is coming back to life."[94] Oromo nationalists have refuted the ideologies of colonialism and racism by returning to their rich cultural traditions and declaring the everlasting nature of Oromo peoplehood and cultural history. Similarly, although they were torn away from their African roots for several centuries and although the restoration of their African heritages has been mainly symbolic and ideological, African American peoplehood and nationalism have been historically and culturally grounded in their African historical memory and their experiences in the United States.

African Americans lived under racial slavery and segregation for almost three and a half centuries; Oromos have been suffering under Ethiopian settler colonialism, which practiced slavery, semislavery (the *naftanya-gabbar* system), tenancy and share-cropping, forced villagization, and collectivization for a little over one century.[95] In the capitalist world economy, only those peoples who have state sovereignty or meaningful access to state power enjoy relatively various political, economic, and cultural advantages. They are recognized internationally and regionally by the imperial interstate system, by multinational organizations and corporations. Business and state elites who get resources from these linkages and who control domestic resources suppress the colonized peoples and deny them meaningful access to state power.[96] During slavery, African Americans were under the firm control of plantation and slave owners and the White government and its various institutions. After slavery was abolished, they were totally dominated and controlled by White society and its government. Similarly, Oromos have been dominated and tightly controlled by Ethiopian colonial settlers and their government and other institutions.

The incorporation of Oromia into Ethiopia made Oromos invisible in the world. Oromos were identified with Ethiopians, the very colonizers who suppressed an Oromo identity, and robbed of their cultural and economic resources. As a result, the existence of Oromos and their national liberation struggle were largely hidden until the early 1990s.[97] The situation of African Americans was different. Their enslavement, segregation, and struggle were widely known to the world. Particularly the Soviet Union and its bloc and China, and almost all revolutionary countries, exposed the fallacy of American democracy by citing the condition of African Americans. The media in the world paid great attention to the struggle of the Black people because they struggled against the United States, one of the hegemonic world powers. Although they have been racist, the American "democracy" and the media made the African American organizations and leaders known nationally and globally. But the Ethiopian racist/ethnonational dictatorship and its media tried its best to hide Oromos and their organizations and leaders in order to destroy them. Let alone known to the world, it took a long time for the Oromo organizations and leaders to be known to their own people whom they attempt to liberate. While Oromos still lack sympathizers and allies because of the lack of recognition, African Americans enjoyed sympathy and support from the oppressed people and revolutionary and democratic forces. The same instruments of American media that spread racist stereotypes also contributed to the recognition of the African American movement. Until recently, however, the world media did not even recognize the existence and the struggle of the Oromo people. Even today Oromos in the diaspora are having difficulty introducing themselves and their peoplehood to the world. The lack of media (television and newspapers) and the absence of communication technologies (telephone, direct mail, etc.) have negatively affected the Oromo movement, whereas African Americans used them to "play an important role in movement efforts to attract members, discredit opponents, and influence . . . the general public."[98]

Both White and Ethiopian societies and their institutions have justified the hierarchical organization of peoples and the firm control of African American and Oromo societies with racist discourses.[99] As explained above, both the African American and Oromo movements were produced by similar social structural and conjunctural factors. According to McAdam, McCarthy, and Zald, "While broad political, economic, and organizational factors may combine to create a certain 'macro potential' for collective action, that potential can only be realized through complex mobilization dynamics that unfold at either the micro or some intermediate institutional level. At the same time, these mobilization processes are clearly collective, rather than an individual phenomenon."[100] Although comparable conditions facilitated the emergence and development of these two movements, the duration and the way these two societies developed their collective identities, political consciousness, nationalism, human agencies, and outcomes varied because of their respective social and political environments. The foundation of African American consciousness and nationalism was laid by slaves and later by some former slaves and their freeborn children between the American Revolution and the American Civil War. But for African American nationalism to develop fully new historical conditions that would change the status of enslaved Africans were required. As explained, the historical contradiction between the core capitalism of the North and the peripheral capitalism of the South resulted in the Civil War, which created conducive social structural and conjunctural factors that later contributed to the development of African American nationalism.

Oromos have been under Euro-American sponsored Ethiopian settler colonialism for almost a century. Oromo nationalism developed faster than African American nationalism. But the development of Oromo nationalism was slower than that of other Africans who were colonized directly by the European powers at the same period Oromos were also colonized. Oromos were colonized by minority settlers that aimed to destroy Oromo peoplehood through ethnocide and selective assimilation. Despite the fact that the settlers were successful in gradually coopting some Oromo elites and in destroying Oromo political, religious, and cultural institutions, they could not destroy totally Oromo culture and language. But the development of Oromo culture and language has been stagnated. The effective imposition of colonial institutions, the development of an Ethiopianized Oromo collaborative class, and the denial of formal education hindered the development of Oromo nationalism until the 1960s. While African Americans have been dominated by the Euro-American majority, Oromos have been dominated by the numerical-minority Ethiopian settler colonialists. This happened because of the support Ethiopians have been receiving from the capitalist world system.

Technologically underdeveloped and organizationally suited to a different mode of production, the Ethiopian colonial settlers established their main geopolitical centers in Oromia, through which racist and colonial policies have been formulated and implemented to keep the majority Oromos as second-class citizens and to exploit their economic and labor resources by denying them access to state power. These geopolitical centers are garrison cities surrounded by the Oromo rural masses who are denied health, educational, and other social services, despite the fact that these colonial settlers and their collaborators depend on the economic and labor resources of the Oromo majority. For instance, in the early 1990s, one source estimated that less than 0.01 percent of Oromos received modern education out of the total population of about 30 million Oromos.[101] These garrison cities were geopolitical headquarters from which Ethiopian soldiers were dispatched to impose colonial rule through enslavement, subjugation, and expropriation of the basic means of production, such as cattle, land, and other valuables. Through these centers expropriated goods flowed for local consumption and an international market. The Ethiopian state introduced the process of forced recruitment of labor via slavery and the *nafxanya-gabbar* system. "The gun (from Europe) and the gun carrier (from Abyssinia) arrived in the colonies as one unit," Holcomb and Ibssa note, "and this unit basically expresses political alliance that created the neftenga-gabbar [*sic*] relationship, the relation that lay at the heart of the emerging Ethiopian colonialism."[102] Millions of Oromos were enslaved, and most of Oromos were reduced to the status of semislaves.[103] The Ethiopian colonialists continued to depopulate Oromia through slave trade until the 1930s when the Italians abolished slavery to recruit adequate labor for their agricultural plantations in the Horn of Africa.[104] Emperor Menelik, the founder of the Ethiopian empire, and his wife at one time owned 70,000 slaves, and he was considered "Ethiopia's greatest slave entrepreneur."[105]

After expropriating three-fourths of Oromo lands, the Ethiopian settlers gave the remaining one-fourth to these Oromo intermediaries who were integrated into the colonial system and who acted against the interest of the Oromo majority. As a result, the majority of Oromos became landless *gabbars,* tenants, and sharecroppers. Although the major objective of the local *balabbat* system was to ensure the maintenance and reproduction of the Ethiopian colonial system, the immediate purpose was to facilitate the continuous supply of grain, labor, and other necessary materials for the settlers. A few Oromos who gave up their Oromo identity were Ethiopianized (Amharized) and became collaborators and served the interests both of their class and of the settlers. This was not possible for African American collaborators since the racial caste system totally excluded them until the 1960s. However, Ethiopian colonialism and its institutions had kept the Oromo majority under tight control and in darkness by denying them formal education and information, and by suppressing Oromo institutions.

Just as the American Civil War had created new conditions for the African American struggle, the arrival in the 1930s of Italian Fascist colonialism in Ethiopia created a more conducive atmosphere for the future of the Oromo struggle. Paradoxically, Italian Fascist colonialism of the Ethiopian empire created new conditions by removing all the archaic Ethiopian institutions of slavery and *nafxanya-gabbar* systems between 1935 and 1941. By abolishing the *nafxanya-gabbar* system and slavery and by introducing wage labor and colonial capitalism, Italian colonialism created social structural and conjunctural factors that would allow Oromos to express their grievances and Oromoness. The Italians attempted to win Oromos and mobilize them against the Ethiopians by broadcasting in the Oromo language, using this language in the court and schools,[106] and by giving "many of them full rights to the land they had cultivated under Amhara landlords."[107] Using these opportunities, Oromos attempted to expel their Ethiopian enemies and achieve autonomy for themselves. Although the Ethiopian state was restored in 1941 with the help of the British government, Italian colonialism laid an economic and physical infrastructure that facilitated the development of colonial capitalism in Oromia. Italian colonialists built roads and bridges that connected Oromos from different parts of Oromia. Further, the development of colonial capitalism gradually produced structural and conjunctural factors for the emergence of Oromo consciousness and nationalism: The new social forces that emerged with the development of capitalism began to develop Oromo political consciousness. In the 1960s Oromia began to produce a centralized leadership linked to a farmer rebellion, despite the barbaric nature of Ethiopian colonial rule, which restricted leadership development in Oromo society.

African American nationalists of the eighteenth and nineteenth centuries had the right to develop segregated religious, economic, and cultural institutions in urban areas, although they did not have access to state power. However, they were not allowed to influence the slave population. The American racial and sexist democracy at least allowed free Blacks and their children to develop their separate institutions, such as churches, schools, self-help associations, and fraternities. These indigenous institutions and organizations later provided organizational infrastructure from which the African American movement developed during the first half of the twentieth century. [108]

But Oromos were not allowed to develop autonomous institutions under Ethiopian colonial rule. The Ethiopian colonial government has imposed absolute control on both Oromo nationalists and the Oromo masses. It allowed Oromo elites to establish a self-help association only in 1963, and banned it in 1967, when this association tried to provide educational and health services to Oromo society. The indigenous Oromo institutions and organizations have been suppressed and denied freedom of development; as a result, Oromo society still lacks organizational infrastructure. Explaining the condition of the African American movement, McAdam, McCarthy, and Zald comment that "the strength and breadth of indigenous organizations was the crucial factor in the rapid spread of the movement."[109] State violence and tight control have disabled Oromo society by maintaining what McCarthy calls "infrastructure deficits."[110] As African American classical nationalists and White abolitionists were prevented from having access to the slave population, Oromo activists have been prevented from educating and helping the Oromo masses. But while the Black classical nationalists had the right to organize themselves, Oromo nationalists are still denied the right to openly organize themselves. Since Oromo society has been penetrated by Ethiopian agents and spies, their informal groups or associational networks, which McCarthy claims "serve as the basic building blocks of social movements,"[111] have been tightly controlled. The Oromo national movement has been struggling under this dangerous condition.

Despite the fact that the American Constitution was racist and endorsed racial slavery, it had provided limited political opportunities to freed Blacks. During the 1950s and the 1960s, African American leaders and activists used effectively this Constitution to obtain some rights for the Black people. Further, a few White reformers and radicals supported the struggle to abolish slavery and later to dismantle racial segregation. The African American movement received support from some White foundations, clergy, and student volunteers. According to J. C. Jenkins and M. Eckert, "The Kennedy administration's interventions on behalf of the Civil Rights movement were rooted in at least two concerns: controlling volatile protests, and securing black votes. . . . Jewish support for the civil rights movement reflected both universalistic concerns about civil liberties and particularistic concerns about racial discrimination. . . . The United Auto Worker Union sponsored civil rights activists. . . . the National Organization for Women out of the staff's ideological commitments as well as a political stake in the left - labor political coalition."[112] Of course, White reformers mainly supported the reformist wing of Black nationalism. But almost all Ethiopians are against the Oromo national movement. Even the Ethiopian left opposes Oromo nationalism. Oromo nationalists have been facing a very different condition from that of African Americans. Oromos still live under political slavery since they are denied both individual and group rights. The Ethiopian state is racist and absolutist, and it has only a limited space for an Ethiopianized Oromo intermediate class.

The Ethiopian state operates above the rule of its own laws, and it has liquidated most Oromo nationalists and other activists without any hesitation. The international community has rarely blamed this state for this misconduct. That is why the Oromo national movement has been an underground movement in Oromia while that of African Americans was legal and open. Comparatively speaking, the course of the Oromo struggle has been more difficult and dangerous, with several thousand leaders, activists, and sympathizers killed or imprisoned since the 1960s. African American scholars had intellectual freedom to write several books, newspapers, magazines, and journals that later helped build African American cultural memory and popular historical consciousness. These scholars laid the foundation for Black cultural nationalism, the Civil Rights movement, and revolutionary nationalism. They produced an alternative knowledge that laid the foundation for an Afrocentric paradigm, the paradigm that helped develop Black cultural nationalism by challenging Eurocentrism. Although they have some weaknesses, Afrocentric-paradigm scholarship and research have challenged the racist and Eurocentric intellectual paradigm. With democratic or revolutionary Euro-American scholars and other intellectuals, some African American cultural nationalists, Civil Rights activists, and revolutionary scholars played a leading role in critical cultural studies that helped challenge the knowledge of domination. The African American Civil Rights activists and revolutionary nationalists formed various organizations during the first half of the twentieth century to marshal Black human, financial, and intellectual resources to fight for Black freedom by dismantling American apartheid. This development began in urban settings.

The majority of African Americans moved to cities and became members of the urban working class during the first half of the twentieth century. This created conducive conditions for the development of Black institutions and organizations. The indigenous organizations and institutions became the foundations of professional social movements and political organizations. As a result, the African American movement blossomed in the first half of the twentieth century and began to galvanize the African American people for collective action. With the freedom of the press, association, organization, and communications several Black leaders and organizations emerged and openly articulated Black consciousness and nationalism and began to fight for the rights of the Black people. On the other hand, because Ethiopia itself is so underdeveloped, there is little infrastructure in the empire. Oromos still lack opportunities that African Americans have had, since they are geographically dispersed and impoverished rural people, and since they do not have political freedom to organize and express themselves. More than 90 percent of Oromos are poor farmers and herders. In garrison cities in Oromia, Oromos are in the minority, since Ethiopian settlers dominate these cities. In addition to the suppression of the Oromo institutions and organizations, these conditions created serious obstacles for the development of Oromo nationalism and collective action. Because of the lack of modern communication and transportation networks, and domination of the media (television, radio, newspaper) by the Ethiopian colonial government, Oromos have limited communication among themselves. Oromos are even denied operation of their own independent media. The Ethiopian colonial system did not leave any cultural space in which Oromos could develop their institutions and educate their children—in the same way that the American racist system denied a cultural space to the enslaved African population. But the latter left a limited cultural space for former slaves and their children to develop their institutions and educate themselves, even though they were denied public resources that were necessary to facilitate institutional growth.

Those few Oromos who had an opportunity of formal education were forced to be Amharized or Ethiopianized and to reject their Oromo identity. Those educated elements that did try to maintain their Oromo identity and promote the interests of their people were systematically suppressed or liquidated. A few journals and magazines (*The Voice, Kana Bekta, Bakkalcha Oromo, Oromia, Warraqa,* and *Gucca Dargago*) that emerged in the 1960s and 1970s were produced clandestinely. Explaining how writing about Oromo by Oromos in Ethiopia can lead to death, Hassen says: "Mamo wrote History of the Oromo, which was confiscated by the government when his house was searched in 1966. In addition to writing history, Mamo prepared a plan for a new government, a new constitution and distribution of land among the landless tenants. This was too much for the ruling Amhara elites, and Mamo Mazamir was martyred for producing that document."[113] The denial of intellectual freedom still prevents Oromo scholars and Oromo society from developing freely an alternative knowledge in Oromia. The Oromo literature that started to mushroom when the OLF joined the Transitional Government of Ethiopia between 1991 and 1992 was suppressed. Oromo scholars, journalists, and musicians who tried to express themselves at that juncture and today have perished in Ethiopian prisons or have been assassinated. Today Oromo scholars in the diaspora produce and disseminate an alternative knowledge that is considered illegal in Ethiopia and Oromia.

Challenging how the Ethiopian knowledge elites and Ethiopianists treated Oromos, diaspora publications on Oromo cultural and social history challenge a top-down paradigm of historiography and make the Oromo subjects rather than objects of history. Studying people as subjects or agents helps scholars avoid producing false knowledge. The Ethiopian elites and the Euro-American scholars who supported them erased Oromo history and culture from the world map. Therefore, until Oromos intensified their struggle between the 1960s and the 1990s, the world did not even recognize the existence of 30 million Oromos. "The lack of critical scholarship has inadvertently distorted the human achievements of conquered peoples like the Oromo," W. A. Shack notes, "including transformations of their social, cultural, and political institutions."[114] Oromo nationalism influenced several Oromo scholars and friends of Oromos to produce and disseminate an alternative knowledge in Oromo studies. The emergence of Oromo studies in North America and Europe and the creation of the Oromo Studies Association in the late 1980s in the diaspora attest to this reality.[115] The Ethiopian colonial elites and their state are keeping Oromos in the darkness of ignorance and political slavery to maintain the Ethiopian colonial system. The conditions in which the Oromo struggle takes place in Oromia have been hostile and brutal. The intensification of globalization and the maturation of the Oromo struggle may change these conditions fundamentally.

Even if they were segregated and oppressed and even if they were terrorized by organizations like the Ku Klux Klan, freed African Americans could openly organize themselves and engage in peaceful struggle for their rights. Oromos in Oromia still have no such rights because of the dictatorial and violent nature of the Ethiopian state. The colonial government allowed organizations, such as "Galla Gaday," the killer of Oromos, to assassinate prominent Oromo activists. Since Oromo organizations are secret organizations, they cannot practice democracy within themselves and among themselves. The idea of tolerating diverse ideologies and diverse approaches and forming a unity of purpose is just getting started in the Oromo movement. But African Americans had the freedom among themselves to talk freely and openly and form a unity of purpose among most of the forces of the African American struggle. Whereas the African American movement reached its peak in the 1950s and the 1960s and won some legislative measures, the Oromo movement is still lagging behind. By legally dismantling American apartheid, the African American "movement succeeded in institutionalizing significant gains during the early 1970s. Blacks became an important voter bloc, participating at higher rates than whites of the same socioeconomic status and the number of black office holders rose rapidly. . . . Although the socioeconomic gap between blacks and whites remained glaringly wide, significant progress against the most overt forms of racial discrimination in education and employment gradually became evident."[116]

Since the 1980s there has been a political backlash against the Black movement. Most Whites do not like the emergence of Black intellectuals and professionals because they think that these African Americans have become successful only at the expense of White society.[117] Consciously or unconsciously, most Whites believe that most Black professionals get jobs because of affirmative action since they are considered less qualified than Whites.[118] This shows that the idea of White cultural and ideological supremacy is still alive and strong despite the fact that African Americans have achieved substantial progress. Manning Marable asserts that racism "is still a destructive force in the lives of upper-middle-class, college-educated African-Americans, as well as poor blacks, and programs designed to address the discrimination they feel and experience collectively every day must be grounded in the context of race."[119] Since members of the Black middle class are concentrated at the lower end of the spectrum of higher status professional jobs, the material success of the Black elite has remained marginal. Considering the complex problems of the Black community, Marable states the following points:

> Black America stands at a challenging moment in its history: a time of massive social disruption, class stratification, political uncertainty, and ideological debate. The objectives of black politics in the age of Jim Crow segregation were relatively simple: full social equality, voting rights, and the removal of "white" and "colored" signs from the doors of hotels and schools. Today's problems are fundamentally more complex in scope, character and intensity: the flight of capital investment from our central cities, with thousands of lost jobs; the deterioration of the urban tax base, with the decline of city services; black-on-black violence, homicide and crime; the decline in the quality of our public schools and the crisis of the community's values. To this familiar litany of problems one more must be added: the failure to identify, train and develop rising leaders within the African-American community who are informed by a critical and scientific understanding of the needs and perspectives of their own people.[120]

As we discussed in chapter III, the majority of African Americans have been left in ghettos and exposed to all social ills.

The Oromo movement has a long way to go to achieve its main objectives. However, as a result of the Oromo movement the geographical location of Oromia is named and recognized within the Ethiopian territory. This is progress, even though some territories have been partitioned and annexed into neighboring regions. The Oromo language has been recognized and made the medium of instruction in elementary school. It is taught in an Oromo alphabet known as *Qubee*. Hoping to halt the development of Oromo nationalism, the Meles government has recently started to revoke *Qubee*. Since the Tigrayan-dominated government does not want the flowering of the Oromo language, literature, culture, and Oromo nationalism, it targets Oromo intellectuals, politicians, and other leaders, silencing all Oromos connected with *Urjii,* an independent Oromo newspaper, by imprisoning or killing them, even though *Urjii* has been officially recognized. Oromos have gained some cultural, intellectual, and ideological success in Oromo society and in the diaspora. Oromia, the Oromo country, and the Oromo nation emerged out of historical obscurity in one century. The Oromo people have achieved some level of cognitive liberation because of the development of Oromo nationalism. Further, Oromo organizations have officially recognized the Oromo democratic tradition known as the *Gada* system. By recognizing the importance of a unity of purpose, Oromo organizations have started to work toward building a united front known as the United Liberation Forces of Oromia (ULFO). The formation of the ULFO is encouraging, because pressure from the Oromo people made it happen.

By challenging Ethiopian ideological and cultural hegemony, the Oromo movement has introduced political instability to the Ethiopian empire. The empire survives by sheer military force. "Generalized political instability destroys any semblance of a political status quo," McAdam writes, "thus encouraging collective action by all groups sufficiently organized to contest the structure of a new political order."[121] But still Oromos are under political slavery, and their land and its resources are owned by the Ethiopian state that sells them to Ethiopian elites, their collaborators, and multinational corporations. Oromos are still landless people, and they do not have control over their lives and resources. In other words, they remain colonized. For example, whenever there is a war they are forced to go to war and die in defending the Ethiopian racist state. During the Ethiopian Eritrean War between 1998 and 2000, it was estimated that more than one hundred thousand soldiers were killed on the Ethiopian side. The majority of these dead soldiers were Oromos. Since the Ethiopian government does not allow a peaceful struggle, the only avenue now open to Oromos is armed struggle.

The alliance of the West, particularly the United States, and some African countries with the Tigrayan-dominated Ethiopian government has weakened the Oromo movement since 1992. The destruction of the emerging indigenous Oromo associations and organizations, such as the Oromo Relief Association, the Oromo Human Rights League, newspapers, musical groups, and various professional, political, and economic organizations, negatively affected the expanding political opportunities for the Oromo national movement. But the war between Eritrea and the Ethiopian empire, though technically settled, has created new political opportunities for the Oromo struggle. Oromo political leaders and organizations attempt to capture these emerging opportunities by reinitiating their friendship with Eritrea and by mobilizing Oromo nationalists for collective action. Oromo leaders have convinced Eritrean leaders that they made a serious strategic mistake in enabling the TPLF to capture Ethiopian state power and rebuild an empire and in supporting the Tigrayans in weakening the Oromo liberation organizations, particularly the OLF. Oromo liberation organizations have to recognize that the diversity and unity of the Oromo people are important because "people who participate in collective action do so only when such action resonates with both an individual and a collective identity that makes such action meaningful."[122] Collective identities are not automatically given, but they are "essential outcomes of the mobilization process and crucial prerequisites to movement success."[123] Through tolerance and critical and democratic discourse, African Americans maintained their diversity and collectivity by creating a unity of purpose among various organizations for collective action.

This can be an important lesson for the Oromo movement. "One critical intervening process which must occur to get from oppression to resistance," S. M. Buechler asserts, "is the social construction of a collective identity which unites a significant segment of the movement's potential constituency."[124] Like that of the African Americans, the Oromo collective identity has been constructed from past cultural memory, political grievances, popular historical consciousness, and the hope for freedom and democracy. Oromos also have different religions, various cultural and economic experiences, class divisions, and different ideologies, as do African Americans. "If the social construction of a collective identity is an ongoing, never-completed task in social movements," Buechler writes, "this is because movements are often composed of diverse and heterogenous individuals and subgroups. . . ."[125] The African American movement to a certain degree recognized the importance of collective identity and diversity, which contributed to its legal success during the first half of the twentieth century. However, the Oromo movement has only focused on collective identity and paid less attention to movement diversity until now.

This comparative study demonstrates that in the capitalist world system, one of the central contradictions is the racialization/ethnicization of state power. The racialization of state power undermines accountability and multicultural democracy. In the United States and Ethiopia, African Americans and Oromos respectively have been struggling to dismantle racial/ethnonational hierarchy, colonial domination, racial hegemony, and those institutions that have been legitimated by the ideology of racism. The movements of African American and Oromo peoples show the necessity of the construction of a legitimate state that can be accountable and democratic and that reflects a multicultural society. The solution for racial/ethnonational problems in the global system lies in recognizing cultural diversity, genuinely promoting self-determination, and expanding genuine multicultural democracy by eliminating the racialization/ethnicization of state power in the world. Although small steps have been taken toward these goals in the United States mainly because of the Black movement, the forces of reaction are currently active in destroying this important progress. As for Ethiopia, because of the violent nature of the Ethiopian elites and their racialized state and due to the alliance these forces have with the West, particularly the United States, the Ethiopian empire is empowered to conduct more state terrorism, leading to crisis and disintegration.

CHAPTER VI

Beyond Nationalism:
The Challenges of a Genuine
Multicultural Democracy

This concluding chapter highlights the important lessons we can draw from the experiences of the struggles of African Americans and Oromos, the role of oppressed nationalism and its limitations, and the necessity of a genuine multicultural democracy to challenge and to solve the problem of the racialized/ethnicized state and to promote peace and justice. It also addresses the issue of the appropriate professional ethics that scholars need to embrace in order to establish a single standard for humanity and to promote social justice, egalitarianism, and popular democracy.

This comparative study has utilized an analytical framework that draws from theories on nationalism, the world system, globalization, and social movements to critically understand the dynamic relationship between global racist capitalist structures and societal agencies. As the experiences of African Americans and Oromos show, the struggle to challenge and transform a racialized state is very complex and difficult. Social changes in colonized societies and structural transformations in the capitalist world system always facilitate the development of revolutionary forces.

We can better understand these changes by listening to the voices of the subjugated population groups in the world. The experiences of African American and Oromo movements demonstrate the long-term and large-scale consequences of the dialectical interplay between oppressive social structure and human agency. There were racist capitalist social structural and conjunctural factors that led to colonialism, racial/ethnonational dictatorship, underdevelopment, poverty, and ultimately, the emergence and development of national movements. *"Human beings produce society,"* Anthony Giddens notes, *"but they do so as historically located actors, and not under the conditions of their own choosing"* [Giddens' emphasis].[1] The current study addresses the attempts of the subjugated oppressed human groups to change their subaltern positions within available political opportunities and the structural limitations of oppressive institutional structures imposed upon them.

The African American movement reached its highest point in the 1960s and declined due to institutional violence and the internal crisis of the movement. But these setbacks came after it legally dismantled racial segregation. Its objectives of cultural self-determination and the transformation of the African American community have not yet been achieved or abandoned. However, the Oromo struggle is a movement in a different stage. Because of the institutional violence of the Ethiopian state and the support that this state secures from the imperial interstate system, the Oromo movement faces a very difficult situation. Both of these movements have been progressive and revolutionary in the march toward human liberation; they have been attempting to dismantle colonialism, underdevelopment, and racial/ethnonational hierarchy and to promote social justice, self-determination, and multicultural democracy.

Both the enslaving and colonizing groups and the enslaved and colonized groups interacted within a single capitalist world system. In this process, Euro-Americans and their descendants created and maintained institutions of racial dictatorship and racial hegemony. In the same global process, Oromos were also enslaved and colonized by an alliance of European and Ethiopian colonizing structures. As historical actors, these globally linked oppressors have been producing and reproducing the racialized capitalist world system to maintain their group and class privileges, and the privileges of their collaborators. But they do not have absolute and permanent control over the process of societal reproduction. When the dominant Euro-Americans and their collaborators, such as Ethiopian elites, consciously attempt to maintain their privileges, the colonized, enslaved, and oppressed groups seek total liberation from racial dictatorship and hegemony. The African American and Oromo movements have been the products of these processes. "For very long and very short time spans, and from very deep and shallow perspectives," Immanuel Wallerstein comments, "things seem to be determined, but for the vast intermediate zone things seem to be a matter of free will."[2]

The collective identity of African American peoplehood that was formed through racial domination and oppression, and a new set of political opportunities that built on preexisting forms of social institution and organization in African American society, facilitated the expansion and consolidation of the Black struggle in the mid-twentieth century. African Americans have played decisive roles in challenging various forms of racialized capitalist social structures and the racialized U.S. state, although they have not yet reached their final destination of emancipation and development. However, the contradiction between the core capitalism of the North and the peripheral capitalism of the South created conducive conditions during the 1860s to give a final death blow to racial slavery. The resistance against slavery by slaves, freed African Americans, and the abolitionists provided ideological and moral justification for core capitalists and their leaders to outlaw slavery. The end of slavery was the first step in African American history toward liberation. Without the end of this system, the Black movement could not have developed.

In the decade between 1866 and 1877 during the First Reconstruction, the dominant forces tried to reform racial relations, but after they established their hegemony in the South they allowed the emergence of racial segregation. The Civil Rights Act of 1866, which stated, "All persons within the jurisdiction of the United States shall have the same right in every State and Territory, to make and enforce contracts, to sue, be parties, give evidence, and to the full and equal benefit of all laws and proceedings for the security of persons and property as is enjoyed by white citizens,"[3] reflected some aspects of the First Reconstruction. But with the emergence of Jim Crow laws, this Civil Rights Act was abandoned and racial segregation was institutionalized without the opposition of the U.S. government until the 1950s and 1960s, when the Black movement challenged it. Because of the structural limitation that the federal government and Southern states imposed, the abolition of racial slavery did not bring full freedom for the Black people. They were neither slaves nor free. However, the elimination of slavery created political opportunities that later allowed the African Americans to develop the autonomous institutions and organizations that became the foundation of the Black movement.

Further, the gradual emergence of the United States as the hegemonic world power, large-scale social and economic changes that provided more political opportunities for the development of indigenous institutions and organizations, and the emergence of Black intellectuals—all strengthened the Black struggle for liberation. As a result, the Black movement was able to legally dismantle racial segregation in the 1950s and the 1960s. But it fell short of removing indirect institutional racism, poverty, and underdevelopment. Both domestic conditions and international politics were conducive for the development of the Black struggle in the first half of the twentieth century. During the first half of the same century, the capitalist world system faced serious crises because of two world wars and the struggle of the colonized peoples. All these factors together challenged "America's domestic praxis of white supremacy."[4] With the emergence of the U.S. as the hegemonic global power in the capitalist world system after World War II, its racist domestic policy was exposed globally, and the U.S. government recognized that it was increasingly difficult to overtly defend White supremacy at home.[5] As the United States became the global power, international opinion started to support the Black movement against racial segregation. Swedish sociologist Gunnar Myrdal advised that "America, for its international prestige, power, and future security, needs to demonstrate to the world that American Negroes [sic] can be satisfactorily integrated into its democracy."[6]

The U.S. government never paid serious attention to hiding its true face of racism prior to the time when the international media started to expose it by reporting accounts of racial violence and discrimination against nonwhites, particularly against African Americans, foreign diplomats, and visiting dignitaries from the Third World.[7] Since the Black movement made school segregation its target of legal attack in the 1940s and early 1950s, the international media also focused on it and seriously criticized school segregation as a racist policy.[8] Some U.S. policy makers who were not committed to racial justice supported the efforts of the Black struggle to desegregate school legally in 1954 because of pragmatic political interests and criticism from the world audience of racial segregation.[9] The 1954 U.S. Supreme Court ruling known as *Brown v. Board of Education of Topeka* on school desegregation was defined as a cold war imperative since it occurred within the politics of both the Black movement and global political pressure.[10] Gerald Horne comments, "The fact that the *Brown* ruling campaigned against international and domestic communism is one of the most overlooked aspects of the decision."[11]

By realizing its foreign policy benefits, U.S. officials "used the *Brown* decision as an impression management strategy in their attempts to convince the world that problematic race relations were regional, not national. Legally ending U.S.-sanctioned support of segregation at the national level helped redefine race relations as a regional problem. Resistance at the state level occurred in part because state governors were less concerned with an international audience."[12]

With the intensification of the Black movement in the 1950s and 1960s, racial violence, police brutality, and the ugly nature of White supremacy were increasingly reported by domestic and international media. As a result, some U.S. officials who engaged with the world audience "supported eliminating overt, legal racial discrimination in social institutions in hopes of limiting black radicalism at home and of expanding U.S. influences in the world."[13] Gradually, overt racism and institutional violence were legally challenged. But, again, the racialized social structure limited the impact of the Black struggle by intellectually, ideologically, and militarily suppressing the transformative aspects of the struggle, such as the cultural and revolutionary wings of the movement. However, in the process of the struggle, racial dictatorship was replaced by racial hegemony, and the reformist wing of the Black movement was incorporated into the White establishment.[14]

There were other outcomes of the Black struggle. The Black middle class expanded. The gap between the Black middle class and the poorer masses widened. Institutional violence and discrimination flourished in the forms of the prison industrial complex, crisis, unemployment, poverty, and underdevelopment. Prior to the African American struggle of the 1960s, racial segregation forced all African Americans to live in the same geographical areas and to feel a sense of collective oppression and group identity. The African American movement and the Civil Rights laws changed these conditions and expanded "the potential base of the African-American middle class, which was located primarily outside of the neighborhood confines of the old ghetto. By 1989, one out of seven African American families had incomes exceeding $50,000 annually, compared to less than $22,000 for the average black household. Black college-educated married couples currently earn 93 per cent of the family income of comparable white couples."[15] Manning Marable asserts that "affirmative action was largely responsible for a significant increase in the size of the black middle class; it opened many professional and managerial positions to blacks, Latinos and women for the first time. But in many other respects, affirmative action can and should be criticized from the left, not because it was 'too liberal' in its pursuit and implementation of measures to achieve equality, but because it was 'too conservative.'"[16] The Civil Rights Act of 1964, the Voting Rights Act of 1965, and the affirmative action programs were the main outcomes of the Black movement. Civil Rights laws legally dismantled racial segregation and allowed middle- to upper-class Blacks to access economic, educational, and political opportunities to a certain degree. This had the impact of diffusing the movement. Consequently, the progress of the movement was stopped.

While Civil Rights laws were passed to legally destroy racial segregation, affirmative action programs were designed to allow qualified Blacks, other minorities, and women to get access to education, employment, and other economic opportunities. Since it was not intended to uproot institutional racism and White privileges, affirmative action "sought to increase representative numbers of minorities and women within the existing structure and arrangements of power, rather than challenging or redefining the institutions of authority and privilege."[17] Affirmative action "was . . . a series of presidential executive orders, civil rights laws and governmental programs regarding the awarding of federal contracts, fair employment practices and licences, with the goal of uprooting bigotry. Historically, at its origins, it was designed to provide some degree of compensatory justice to the victims of slavery, Jim Crow segregation and institutional racism."[18]

Of course, the Civil Rights Act of 1964, the Voting Rights Act of 1965, and affirmative action programs that followed them could not solve the problems of the Black majority, as the following indicators demonstrate. In the 1990s, the infant mortality rate was 17.7 deaths per 1,000 births. Children who live in poverty account for 43.2 percent. The functional or marginal illiteracy rate was about 44 percent. Explaining how the condition of inner-city Blacks was worse in the 1990s than in the 1950s, D.

Schwartzman said that during "the early 1950s the unemployment rate for black males was only 5.4 percent—about half the current rate. Black unemployment was higher than white unemployment, but the early 1950s was a golden age for blacks compared to today. Things have gotten even worse for black youths. The unemployment rate among young men and women 16 to 19 years of age in 1995 was 37.1 percent, compared to 16 percent in the early 1950s."[19]

These figures do not exactly reflect the magnitude of Black unemployment, because they do not include those who are imprisoned and those who have stopped searching for jobs after trying many times. Despite the fact that the Black population is only about 13 percent of the total American population, about half of murder victims are Black, and the main cause of death for young Black males is homicide. Out of two million men in American prisons in 1998, 51 percent were Black men, and one out of three black men between the ages of 20 and 29 was under some form of criminal justice supervision in 1994.[20] All these crises and problems show that the objective of fundamentally transforming Black America has not been reached. With the intensification of globalization, Black people face more challenges and manifest the characteristics of the peripheral nations. Noam Chomsky captures this reality by asserting, "A corollary to the globalization of the economy is the entrenchment of Third World features at home: the steady drift toward a two-tiered society in which large sectors are superfluous for wealth-enhancement for the privileged. Even more than before, the rabble must be ideologically and physically controlled, deprived of organization and interchange, the prerequisite for constructive thinking and social action."[21] Racial and class contradictions and institutional racism, which have evolved through change and continuity for centuries, have hindered the transformation of inner cities, where mainly Black people live.

Just when the African American community is again facing serious crises, "scientific racism" is reemerging to explain why the problems of this community are not yet solved. Richard J. Herrnsten and Charles Murray wrote an infamous book, *The Bell Curve: Intelligence and Class Structure in American Life,* in 1994, claiming that unemployment, crime, unwed motherhood, school failure, workplace accidents, welfare dependency, and broken families are caused by low intelligence and heredity. The central theme of the book is that the United States is a polarized society in which a "cognitive elite," made up mainly of Whites, are at the helm of society, and a sociopathic "cognitive underclass," made up mainly of Blacks, are at the bottom.[22] The authors of the book advocate that it is useless to attempt to provide opportunities for the Black masses and other poor since they are genetically disabled. This book reinvents old racial theories to prove the "mental inferiority" of Blacks and other colonized peoples and to rationalize their underdevelopment and denial of opportunities. The popular acceptance of this publication indicates that the Black movement of the mid-twentieth century has not uprooted White racism and institutional discrimination.

Robert Allen comments that without providing an alternative public policy, White conservatives and their Black clients have recently begun to attack the limited rights that Black people obtained through the struggle:

> Reactionary forces in the mass media and academia launched a propaganda campaign to convince middle-class and working class whites that their economic troubles were being caused by the alleged massive gains the black people had made in the public sector, such as government employment, public educational institutions and social welfare programs. . . .

> The new racism asserts that racial discrimination is no longer a serious problem in American society. That is, those blacks who are "qualified" are succeeding in climbing the economic ladder and making it into the middle-class; and it is only those blacks who are "unqualified" who are falling behind. The purpose of this ideology was to convince whites (and middle-class blacks) that the black masses were being held down, not by racism and capitalist exploitation, but by their own individual cultural deficiencies: lack of thriftiness, lack of work ethic, lack of respect for education, and broken families.[23]

The conservative Whites and Blacks argue that the current tragic problems of the Black majority are caused by the effects of welfare work disincentives, a ghetto-specific culture, Black nationalism, lack of traditional American values, and Black self-doubt.[24] In their attempts to exonerate the racist American capitalist system and its institutions, conservative scholars and politicians blame the Black community and those leaders who have struggled to liberate this community from racial domination and exploitation. These conservatives assert that Black problems are perpetuated by Black culture and the ineffectiveness of the civil rights leaders. They criticize the strategy of group rights and reliance on political power rather than on individual initiative and traditional values.[25] For instance, S. Steele comments that Black nationalism does not "help us much in this challenge because it is too infused with defensive grandiosity, too given to bombast and posturing."[26] For conservative politicians and intellectuals, the Black problem is internally created by the unconscious replaying of oppression and racial self-doubt.

These conservatives ignore chains of external factors, such as the political economy of racism and institutional discrimination, that have contributed to Black poverty and underdevelopment. For instance, Steele suggests that to overcome their current problems, African Americans should abandon their Black collective identity and deal with their individuality.[27] There is no society that has abandoned its collective cultural identity, including White society, because individuals cannot exist outside of collective cultural identity. Based on the ideology of individualism, which conservative and liberal White elites falsely promote, conservative Blacks and some liberals reject the notion of reaching back and supporting the struggle of the less fortunate Blacks. This self-serving ideology justifies burning the bridge on which these conservative and liberal Blacks crossed to the side of the privileged groups and classes. All conservatives and some liberals promote the ideology of individualism, which creates a superficial dichotomy between group and individual identity and claims the primacy of the latter over the former. Only Black elites who are determined to promote their personal and class interests at the expense of the Black majority accept this position. Molefi K. Asante notes that "black super conservatives negate history because they refuse to accept the source of their problem. Their lack of historical consciousness underscores their inability to approach a problem scientifically."[28]

The Black conservatives are compensated for attacking Blacks, and "they are given high profiles by the white conservatives who created them."[29] By sponsoring and providing privileges for conservative Blacks, White conservatives have established a base of political support within African American society. By attacking the principles of the Black movement, some conservative Blacks can easily climb to political power, as Associate Justice Clarence Thomas did by being appointed as a Supreme Court judge. Marable argues that "given the profound level of confusion in both the strategic and ideological perspectives of the African-American middle class, its present inability to transcend the bankrupt politics of liberal integrationism, it is probable that we will witness more Clarence Thomases in the near future."[30] Integration as it has been practiced since the 1960s only helped middle-class Blacks, and it could not improve the condition of the Black majority. The idea that integrationism can solve the problems of the entire Black community must be abandoned since the interests of a few well-to-do Blacks do not necessarily coincide with those of the Black masses. "The fundamental contradiction inherent in the notion of integrationist 'symbolic representation' is that it presumes that a degree of structural accountability and racial solidarity binds the black public figure with the larger masses of African-Americans."[31]

In reality, once Black public figures join White institutions, the Black majority have no mechanisms to influence their behavior and to make them accountable to the Black community. Conservative and some African American liberal elites can get access to positions of power and privilege without being accountable to the Black community and without compensating for the sacrifice the Black masses and activists paid to dismantle racial segregation. Despite the fact that liberal integrationism failed to solve the problems of the Black community, most "black liberal intellectuals, whose world-views and political perceptions were hardened by the turmoil of the 1960s and the heroic struggles against legal segregation, implicitly accept the notion of symbolic representation, and the totality of the ideological baggage of liberal integration."[32] These Black liberals, like their White counterparts, do not recognize the connection between wealth and poverty and consciously or unconsciously endorse the status quo that maintains and reproduces the poverty and underdevelopment of the Black majority. According to Marable, "The moral poverty in contemporary American society is found, in part, in the vast chasm which separates the conditions of material well-being, power and privilege of some from the others. The evil in our world is politically and socially engineered, and its products are poverty, homelessness, illiteracy, political subservience, race and gender domination."[33] Those Whites who claim adherence to the ideology of individualism create, re-create, and maintain the ideologies of racism, sexism, and classism to protect their class and group privileges through capturing and maintaining institutional power.

The Black struggle for individual and group rights, cultural identity, and multicultural democracy has not yet reached its desired goals. The suppression of revolutionary nationalism, the denial of self-determination for the Black community, and the imposition of the politics of law and order on the Black masses and revolutionaries have perpetuated the underdevelopment of Black America. Because of the absence of a national organization that can effectively mobilize and organize Blacks to articulate the demands of the Black majority, presently existing Civil Rights organizations and Black elites cannot obtain adequate goods and services for the Black community. Black elites have been incorporated into the White establishment, and they do not have the institutional and organizational power to facilitate meaningful social change in the African American community. In creating and socializing a global intermediate class by destroying multicultures in the name of science, the dominant elites and groups in the capitalist world economy use the ideologies of individualism and cultural universalism to look at the world from their own cultural centers and to control the economic and cultural resources of the dominated people.[34] Different people have different authentic cultural centers that allow them to freely develop.[35] The destruction of these cultural centers through colonization and globalization promotes underdevelopment.

That is why serious studies take the African American experience in the New World as their center and study it within the global context to critically understand the problem of this society and to find an appropriate solution. Therefore, these approaches recognize a pluralism of cultural and historical centers to critically understand historical and social relations within a community, region, and the world. The critical aspects of these approaches develop through "an earth-wide network of connections, including the ability partially to translate knowledges among very different—and power-differentiated—communities."[36] The complexity and contributions of the African American movement were intellectually and politically undermined by the White establishment, its institutions, and collaborators. Those who minimized the importance of the cultural and revolutionary aspects of the Black movement have started to attack even the contributions of the Civil Rights movement. As we have seen, they even argue that Black cultural identity, nationalism, and Civil Rights leaders undermined the development of the Black community by making it dependent on government and by undermining individual initiatives.

The sophisticated attack on the Black movement, its contributions, and its leaders needs an organized and sophisticated response, and planned long-term political, cultural, intellectual, and ideological strategies. Such strategies must draw lessons from the past struggle of many centuries and must reflect the concrete conditions of the African American people. Critical understanding of the concrete conditions of African American society requires critical scholarship and discourse. The conservative White and Black knowledge elites have treated African Americans as historical objects because of their subordination and powerlessness. Critical studies challenge a top-down paradigm to either historiography or cultural studies and make African Americans subjects rather than objects of history. Such studies challenge false knowledge regarding this society and other communities.[37]

When the institution of racial slavery was dismantled, Black nationalists and activists and their supporters continued to struggle against racial dictatorship and colonialism. Because their African American ancestors fought against racial slavery, segregation, and colonialism to advance the collective interest of the Black community, the Black middle class and their children who have benefited from those efforts have a moral and intellectual responsibility to mobilize and organize the Black majority to solve the problems of this community. If the crisis in the Black community continues, the success that some Blacks made can be attacked and undermined. Therefore, to struggle to change the conditions of the Black majority is not only an issue of moral and intellectual responsibility, but also of the advancement of self-interest for all African Americans. Those who wish social death for the Black community undermine the importance of Black collective cultural identity, institutions, organizations, and movements and create obstacles for the future struggle of Black people.

To forget all the achievements of Black heroines and heroes promotes the ideology of individualism, consumerism, and individual luxury, and causes African Americans to become disorganized and isolated people who cannot solve their common problems by common efforts and struggles. Serious scholars need to critically reassess the significance of the Black collective identity, nationalism, diversity of movement centers, and the importance of leaders. The future struggle of the Black people needs to draw some lessons from the past movement. Specifically, the incorporation of the best elements of King's ideological and political sophistication and pragmatism, Malcolm X's cultural heroism, and mass militancy are absolutely necessary for developing the future strategy of the Black struggle. The future Black movement also will need to broaden its political foundation on national, regional, and international levels based on the principle of revolutionary democratic multiculturalism. This will require to form an alliance with antiracist, anticolonial, and other progressive forces in order to expose and remove obstacles to social justice, popular development, and self-determination through educational mechanisms and organized struggle. Since the African American and Oromo movements have different experiences and outcomes, they can learn from each other a lot.

Because the Oromo movement is militarily, intellectually, and politically suppressed, it has not yet forced the Ethiopian colonial state to pass and implement laws that would improve the condition of the Oromo people. Since there is no rule of law in Ethiopia in actual practice, the rulers do not have any obligation to enforce or implement laws that restrict their tyrannical rule. Because successive Ethiopian governments have come to power through the barrel of the gun that they received from their international supporters, the current ethnocratic state will most likely be replaced through the barrel of the gun. Although popular forces created conducive conditions for overthrowing the Ethiopian governments in 1972 and 1991, the regimes that emerged through these processes have not been different from the previous regimes except that they used "socialist" and "democratic" discourses while they imposed ethnic-based dictatorships. The Oromo people are still under political slavery and denied the freedom of organization, association, and expression, and the right to bear arms.

We have established that successive Ethiopian regimes and their global supporters claim that Ethiopia is unique in Africa due to Ethiopians' presumed linkage to the Middle East, with racial and cultural superiority to that of the peoples whom they conquered and dominated, a feat they could not have accomplished without the assistance of the West. Nevertheless, Ethiopia is actually known for recurrent famine crises, institutional violence and war, underdevelopment, and poverty from the time of its creation. The current rulers of Ethiopia, the TPLF/EPRDF, have not solved these fundamental problems.

Although they have attempted to hide their true nature behind "socialist" and "democratic" discourses, they have remained racist and dictatorial like their forefathers, and have continued to pursue destructive policies that intensify state terrorism, war, underdevelopment, and poverty. Successive Ethiopian ruling classes have been "pimps" and "parasites." They have conspicuously consumed the available wealth brought from colonies. In order to maintain the status quo and their privileges, they have also invested meager resources in military and administrative expenditures. The Oromo people were forced to transfer most of their wealth to these global pimps and structural parasites. As a result, today Ethiopia is one of the three poorest countries in the world and its per capita income is only 100 U.S. dollars; Niger and Sierra Leone are the only two countries below Ethiopia in the level of their life expectancy, education, and per capita income.[38]

Economic and health indicators of Ethiopia show the hardship that Oromos and others face in this empire.[39] Life expectancy is only 49 years. The mortality rate for children under five years is 177 per 1,000 live births. The infant mortality rate is 113 per 1,000 live births. The maternal mortality rate is 1,400 per 100,000 births. Less than half of the population (about 46 percent) has access to basic health service, only 19 percent of the population has access to basic sanitation, and only 25 percent of the population has access to clean water.[40] Further, Ethiopia has only 85 hospitals, 187 health centers and 2,470 health stations[41] for more than 60 million people. Because of economic, political, and geographical reasons, most Oromos do not have access to these public facilities. More than 90 percent of Oromos live in rural areas, and almost all of them have been made landless. Since urban areas in Oromia are mainly populated by Ethiopian colonial settlers and their collaborators, they are the ones that have access to the limited public facilities, such as schools and hospitals, that are found in Oromia. At the beginning of the twenty-first century, the Oromo are one of the colonized population groups of the world that are exposed to the vagaries of nature and the cruelty of colonial exploitation.

Oromo nationalists unsuccessfully attempted to change the ethnocratic and colonial character of the Ethiopian state in the 1960s, 1970s, and the early 1990s. Without being discouraged by the negative experiences of the Macha–Tulama Association, some Oromo leaders who lived in the Middle East in exile created the Ethiopian National Liberation Front (ENLF) in 1971 under the leadership of Sheik Hussein Suura. Simply because this organization was created by Oromos, Ethiopians attacked it, branding it as "narrow nationalist." Since it was created on the eve of the 1974 unsuccessful Ethiopian Revolution, and since it was not also endorsed by some Oromo nationalists and other reasons, the ENLF was not successful. Most Oromo nationalists rejected the notion of reforming Ethiopia after they tried many times and failed. The toppling of the Haile Selassie regime by the popular demand of workers, students, farmers, soldiers, and other sectors of society brought hopes for democracy, self-determination, and social justice for all oppressed ethnonations and classes. Influenced by these changes, some Oromo nationalists and Ethiopian intellectuals returned to Ethiopia from exile to participate in the emerging popular revolution.

The military group of 120 members known as *Derg* in Amharic, meaning "committee," captured state power by using the political opportunities of the popular demands and crises and started to take popular actions, such as the "nationalization" of both urban and rural lands and financial institutions. The policies of the military regime were also influenced by the politics of leftist intellectuals who embraced a socialist ideology. Haile Fida, a prominent Oromo leftist intellectual, and his associates in the organization he led, All Ethiopian Socialist Movement, played a central role in influencing some leaders of the new regime, particularly Colonel Mengistu Haile Mariam. This man gradually emerged as the head of the state. Assuming that the nationalization of the land would make the land collective property of the farmers, and since most Oromos were landless and poor, Oromo intellectuals supported the popular policies of the regime until they later discovered that the regime was against their fundamental interests. Zegaye Asfawu, a progressive Oromo lawyer, was appointed as the minister of Agriculture and Land Reform and played a leading role in the formulation and implementation of land reform policies until they were subverted by the regime and he was sent to prison. Two prominent Oromo nationalists, Fakadu Waqijira and Dima Noggo, also played important roles in policies related to land reform. By failing to understand the true nature of the Ethiopian state, Oromo socialists paid with their lives while trying to reform Ethiopia. Indirectly, these Oromo socialists undermined the role of the Oromo national movement by opposing some of its objectives.

After replacing the previous ruling class, the military regime intensified its institutional violence against various liberation fronts, such that of Oromos, Sidamas, Ogaden-Somalis, Eritreans and Tigrayans, and the Amhara-dominated Ethiopian People's Revolutionary Party (EPRP). Although the regime successfully suppressed the EPRP, the national liberation movements survived and continued their struggles that led to the overthrow of the regime in 1991. The regime destroyed the All Ethiopian Socialist Movement by killing or imprisoning its leaders. Prominent Oromo socialists such as Haile Fida, Birhanu Gamada, Hailu Garbaba, Abdullai Yosuf, Lama Fida, Mitiku Tarfasa, Makonen Jote, and Tarafe Waldasadik were murdered by the regime because they attempted to promote an independent political line and refused to be subservient to Mengistu and his political party. Similarly, hundreds of prominent Oromos who tried to build the Oromo national movement were either imprisoned or killed or forced to join an armed struggle. Prominent Oromo nationalists such as Reverend Gudina Tumsa, Negussie Nagassa, Imiru Ibssa, Gazhigne Kassahun (Beka), Biru Warqu, Argawu Dinka, Mohe Abdo, and others were murdered by the regime, and others spent about a decade in prison.

The assassination of Baro Tumsa, the central figure in the Oromo national movement after the banning of the Macha-Tulama Association, denied the Oromo struggle a visionary and charismatic leadership. The circumstance of his assassination is not yet adequately explained. He was murdered when he was in the liberated area of Oromia. Baro Tumsa informally established a complex informal network among Oromo nationalists that gradually led to the formation of the Oromo Liberation Front (OLF). Further, the assassination of Magarsa Bari (OLF Chairman), Demise Techane (Vice Chairman), Aboma Mitku, Omer Abrahim, Yigazu Banti, and others attacked the central nervous system of the Oromo national movement and armed struggle. Further, in the 1990s, thousands of OLF leaders, fighters, and supporters or sympathizers of the Oromo national struggle were assassinated by the Tigrayan ethnocratic regime or killed at war fronts. The OLF executive committee members who sacrificed their lives for the liberation of their people included Gutama Hawas, Gammachis Dhaba, Nadhi Gamada, Milkessa Gadaa, Gutu Chali, Nagasa Kumsa, Buriso Boru, Waqigari Ayana, Boru Dheressa, and Mulis Abba Gada. Due to the problem of space I cannot list the names of all Oromos[42] who were assassinated or killed in this process. Since these people were the best and the brightest of the Oromo people, had they survived and continued to lead the Oromo struggle, the Oromo might have been liberated or close to liberation. Probably there is no other national liberation organization that has lost its leadership and fighters to the same extent as has the OLF. Further, members of other Oromo liberation organizations also lost their lives while struggling to liberate Oromia from Ethiopian colonial occupation.

The Ethiopian elites and their government never tolerated or found means to accommodate Oromo leaders who refused to be blatantly subservient to them. Without being discouraged, Oromo leaders tried several times to transform Ethiopia from a colonial empire to a genuine multicultural democratic society. In 1991, Oromo liberation organizations joined the Transitional Government of Ethiopia, which was dominated by the Tigrayan People's Liberation Front. By joining the transitional government, the Oromo liberation organizations, particularly the OLF, positioned themselves to popularize the Oromo struggle openly among the Oromo people and introduce it to the international community.[43] This helped in developing Oromo awareness crucial to nationalism. As a result, the feeling of Oromoness penetrated Oromo society.[44] The world community recognized a national entity called Oromia, although its boundaries are not correctly established to include all Oromo. *Afaan Oromoo,* the Oromo language, and its alphabet, *qubee,* were officially recognized. The

Oromo language became an official language in Oromia. By participating in the transitional regime between 1991 and 1992, the OLF increased the awareness of Oromoness culturally, politically, and ideologically.[45] Unfortunately, these achievements alarmed the Tigrayan-led minority regime and turned it against the Oromo people and their struggle.

Despite the fact that the Amhara-led regime was replaced by a Tigrayan-led regime, the character of the Ethiopian state remained almost the same except for some cosmetic changes. As the Ethiopian military regime attempted to camouflage its true identity with "socialist" and "revolutionary" discourses, the Tigrayan-dominated regime camouflaged itself with "democratic" and "revolutionary" discourses while establishing itself as a Tigrayan ethnocratic state and calling it a "federal democratic Ethiopia." Explaining how these successive regimes have been the same in character, Bonnie Holcomb asserts that "the ponderous state machinery of the ostensibly 'socialist' *Derg* has been revived virtually intact to serve the purpose of the ostensibly 'democratic' EPRDF government. This development raises questions concerning the nature of the social formation in which two supposedly different governments have operated. On the one hand, it reveals that the Soviet-backed *Derg* did not function as a socialist system, but rather administered an outpost of a form of state capitalism emanating from the Soviet Union. On the other hand, the speed and apparent ease with which an U.S.-sponsored administration has stepped in utilizing the same repressive apparatus with no significant alteration belies its 'democratic' nature."[46] The Tigrayan regime created a fake federation by denying the Oromo people their own leadership and self-determination and imposing OPDO where independent groups might have participated.

The TPLF/EPRDF has systematically attempted to exterminate the independent Oromo movement. Thousands of Oromo intellectuals, professionals, teachers, journalists, farmers, merchants, fighters, musicians, and others still languish in prisons and concentration camps without due process. Successive Ethiopian governments have been determined to destroy an independent Oromo leadership in order to control and exploit Oromo resources, and to keep Oromos as second-class citizens by keeping them in the system of political slavery. The Oromo land is owned and controlled by the Tigrayan ethnocratic state that leases or sells it with impunity to *Habasha* elites and multinational corporations.[47] Gobena Huluka expounds that the Tigrayan-dominated regime "adopted what it proclaims a 'free market economy' in order to privatize the common property of the Ethiopian people nationalized during the preceding regime. The privatization actually personalized the common goods for exclusive use of mainly ethnic Tigrean aristocrats since the government controls the state power apparatus and the economic sector. In addition, the TPLF government put all resources of the Ethiopian Empire up for sale to the highest bidder in the name of a 'free market economy.'"[48] In order to liberate themselves, the Oromo must dismantle these arrangements.

The majority of the Oromo people are outraged by their continued dehumanization. They are also angry and dissatisfied that the Oromo liberation organizations have not yet developed the capability to effectively change the Oromo position. An effective Oromo national organization must have the capacity to mobilize Oromos in all their different organizations, associations, civic and religious institutions, and formal and informal social networks on macro- and micro levels in order to ensure the creation of an Oromo national power strong enough to form a revolutionary democratic state. This revolutionary step must be an initial stage for the Oromo to participate in creating and building a democratic multicultural society in the Horn of Africa. Since all Oromo liberation organizations have not yet developed the capability to effectively change the condition of the Oromo, it is time for serious Oromo nationalists and activists to critically ask themselves why infrastructure and organizational deficits could not yet be removed with the development of Oromo nationalism. Most Oromo leaders and intellectuals do not openly and honestly confront the Oromo organizational problem. They like to raise issues informally, and they do not take serious social responsibility by openly and publicly debating serious policy and political issues. There has never been any open and public policy debate among Oromo leaders and intellectuals on the essence of the Oromo struggle and the future of Oromia. Hence, it is no wonder that Oromo leaders and intellectuals have not yet solved the Oromo organizational problem, a task which will require combining politics, research, and policy formation.

The Oromo movement has two alternative options: The first one is to continue to have a movement that is less participatory, more prone to negotiate with the enemies of Oromos, and ready to impose its elitist decision on the Oromo people. The second option is to develop a participatory Oromo movement in which the Oromo people, political and intellectual leaders, cadres, and activists at every level play a decisive role by mobilizing, organizing, and managing Oromo resources (including labor, money, skills, knowledge, information) and implement the will of the Oromo people. The Oromo movement has different centers that must be linked together both vertically and horizontally. If the Oromo liberation organizations adopt the second option by changing their old attitudes and approaches and promoting a grassroots movement, they can play a central role in the Oromo movement by linking together diverse Oromo movement centers through consensus building and democratic discourse. It is also the responsibility of all Oromo activists and nationalists to change their attitudes and approaches by returning to the Oromo democratic tradition in order to coordinate and centralize the Oromo national struggle. If the Oromo movement is to be participatory, it must mobilize all sectors of Oromo society, particularly women and youth. Without effectively mobilizing these two key groups, the Oromo movement cannot be participatory. Oromo democracy and its principles must lay the foundation of this participatory mobilization. Further, Oromo nationalists can draw lessons from the experiences of other movements, such as that of the African American struggle, for their mobilization and organization efforts.

The Oromo movement can learn a lot from the experiences of the African American struggle. Different African American movement centers, associations, institutions, and organizations mobilized different sectors of the society and coordinated their struggle on local, regional, and national levels. Since African Americans had obtained legal rights, they openly organized themselves and coordinated their struggle for emancipation. But Oromo nationalists and activists and their organizations do not have similar political opportunity because of the lack of the rule of law and basic rights in Oromia and Ethiopia. Whereas African American leaders could openly mobilize and organize their people, Oromo leaders are forced to do so clandestinely. In addition, the legacy of Ethiopian political slavery weakened Oromo political leadership and crippled its organizational capacity. Although Oromos in the diaspora have political opportunity and technological and financial means to overcome the legacy of political slavery, they spend their energy on trivial issues and remain less effective. Conscious elements of the Oromo in the diaspora can gain substantial lessons from the African American struggle and organize Oromos on international level by linking them to the Oromo national movement in Oromia. Oromo liberation organizations in Oromia and abroad can understand the significance of combining various movement centers and taking collective political action by looking at the experience of the African American struggle.

Oromo activists, leaders, and organizations are faced with overcoming the legacy of Ethiopian political slavery by any means necessary in order to unify different Oromo movement centers, institutions, and organizations in order to develop a united movement. The participation of all sectors of Oromo society in the Oromo movement is true to the Oromo democratic tradition. It is also appropriate in the new global era for the Oromo in the diaspora to play a key role because they are beyond the rigid political limitations of the Ethiopian system. Western political culture, despite its racist, elitist, and sexist values, permits the development of this participatory approach. Broad participation also forces Oromo leaders and intellectuals not only to teach, but also to learn from their fellow citizens in order to change their outlook and approaches. In a revolutionary movement, all participants need to change together to facilitate a fundamental social transformation.

Despite the fact that there has been expanding political opportunities in the 1990s, Oromo nationalists and liberation organizations have not yet effectively utilized them. At the same time, thousands of Oromos have been sacrificing their lives to maintain the ongoing Oromo revolution. Oromo organizational and infrastructure shortcomings have exposed these revolutionaries to Ethiopian state terrorism. During the 1990s, Oromo liberation organizations could have changed their organizational condition, particularly in the diaspora, because of the changing circumstances of Oromos and the revolution in communication technologies. Several Oromo political leaders could have freely interacted with Oromos in the diaspora. They have rarely tried to openly and frankly discuss with Oromos in the diaspora what should be done. Similarly, most Oromos in the diaspora have been less interested in building mechanisms that will help them to take concrete action. Most Oromo intellectuals, in particular, are passive in these areas. Open and frank discussion, persuasion, consensus building, examining competing views and approaches, and accepting the best views and approaches have yet to be practiced by Oromo in the diaspora.

Oromo leaders and intellectuals in the diaspora have more opportunities than Oromos in Oromia to build Oromo organizational readiness, to increase the level of Oromo political consciousness, and to expand the structure of political opportunities for the Oromo struggle. Oromo leaders, intellectuals, and all nationalists must be able to build a more enduring organizational structure that can assume the centralized direction of the Oromo national struggle. This organizational structure must develop mechanisms that can deal with Oromo issues on three levels: macro-, meso-, and micro levels. On the macro level, flexible goals and tactics must be formulated and implemented. On the meso level, this structure needs to build a formal body that can build a consensus among all Oromos and existing organizations. The enduring organizational structure must link all formal organizations and small, informally organized groups, churches, mosques, civic organizations, and friendship networks both horizontally and vertically to facilitate the process of micro mobilization for collective action. This micro mobilization includes increasing cognitive liberation, contributing money for the Oromo cause, creating a lobbyist group, campaigning for Oromo human rights, and creating political and intellectual fora, seminars, workshops, and town meetings. If Oromos start to believe that the internal structure of the Oromo population determines whether they can use available political opportunities, they will take collective action to determine their destiny as people. Particularly, Oromos in the diaspora must start to overcome their infrastructure and organizational shortcomings by effectively mobilizing resources such as members, communication networks, leaders, money, skills and knowledge, information, and friends.

In this era of globalization, Oromos need to build an effective national organization that can mobilize resources and use the media and communication technologies to effectively attract members and friends, discredit enemies, and influence the public through framing new meanings, ideologies, and programs and packaging and disseminating them. Since the Oromo struggle is the Oromo national project, every Oromo must take action through macro-, meso-, and micro mobilization. At the same time, Oromo liberation organizations must continue to build alliances with other colonized ethnonations and oppressed groups and classes that are determined to create a revolutionary multicultural democracy.

Nationalism is a transitory social process that emerges to solve certain problems of an oppressed or colonized society. Oppressed nationalism as an ideology plays a limited purpose by helping the efforts of cultural reclamation and liberation struggle. Once cultural reclamation and national liberation are achieved, nationalism proves itself to be inadequate and "neglects the integration of that earned and achieved consciousness of self within 'the rendez-vous of victory.'"[49] In *The Wretched of the Earth*, Frantz Fanon explains the pitfalls of national consciousness and the failure of postcolonial societies to transform nationalism into true liberation, and recommends the necessity of transforming nationalism into "social consciousness" while overthrowing colonial domination. In his words: "National consciousness, instead of being the all-embracing crystallization of the innermost hopes of the whole people, instead of being the immediate and most obvious result of the mobilization of the people, will be in any case only an empty shell, a crude and fragile travesty of what it might have been. . . . We shall see that such retrograde steps with all weaknesses and serious dangers that they entail are the historical result of the incapacity of the national middle class to rationalize popular action, that is to say their incapacity to see into the reasons for that action."[50]

Nationalism is revolutionary when it fosters all forms of social consciousness to dismantle race-, class-, and gender-based oppressive social relationships. The struggles of oppressed people, groups, and classes have a foundation of revolutionary democratic multiculturalism: "The ferment in minority, subaltern, feminist, and postcolonial consciousness has resulted in so many salutary achievements in the curricula and theoretical approach to the study of the humanities as quite literally to have produced a Copernican revolution in all traditional fields of inquiry."[51] With the intensification of globalization and the development of communication technologies, cultural borrowing and integration will increase. Since collective identities are socially and culturally constructed, depending on structural conditions and human actions, progressive integration is inevitable among all humanities. Asmarom Legesse states that "every culture has something vital to offer. Man's [and woman's] wider cultural identities must be allowed to grow, not by the predatory expansion of one civilization but by the complementary integration of many diverse cultures. No human community, however humble, should be forced to give up its cultural identity without making a critical contribution to the larger reality of which it becomes a part."[52] In precapitalist and precolonial societies, most human groups had localized and small-scale identities. Global capitalism and imperialism brought large-scale identities, such as ethnonational groups, and regional identities, such as African-ness, European-ness, American-ness, Asian-ness. Whether they are smaller or larger identities, they are not biologically given since they have been formed and re-formed depending on the circumstances in which they have found themselves. Since there have been cultural overlapping and cultural borrowing among all human groups, it is impossible to have clear cultural boundaries among them. Hence, while fighting against racism, classism, and sexism, revolutionary democratic multiculturalism must promotes progressive integration of all humanity.

With the development of capitalism and the nation-state, those cultural groups that dominated the political economy of a given territory or a country tried to destroy the cultures and identities of those groups who were conquered and dominated in order to form a "nation" with their own images. This objective was successful in limited degree when cultural and structural assimilation was combined. However, in most cases, the objective was not successful since the dominant group only wanted to impose its culture without structurally assimilating the dominated group by subordinating them as second- or third-class citizens to exploit their economic and labor resources. These conditions led to the development of ethnonational movements and multinationalism. "Socialism," or bourgeois democracy, failed to solve these problems. Therefore, the state is facing challenges from above and below to its prerogatives: the intensification of globalization from above is requiring building supranational institutions. Multinationalism, particularly ethnonationalism, is challenging the existing structure of the state from below. "The transition from nationalism to multinationalism, and its associated multiculturalism," Anthony Richmond writes, "will not take place without a struggle between competing power elites."[53]

Oromo nationalists need to develop sophisticated political and cultural strategies to uproot Ethiopian settler colonialism by creating a revolutionary democratic government while at the same time promoting a revolutionary multicultural democracy. A revolutionary Oromo government that will reflect the Oromo democratic tradition can be an effective central political force by making sure that Oromos achieve their national liberation and forge a political unity that provides full freedom for those ethnonations that voluntarily participate in forming a revolutionary multicultural democracy. In this way the racialization/ethnicization of state power can be eliminated in the Horn of Africa. Oromos and Ethiopians have been in confrontation since the sixteenth century culturally, ideologically, and militarily. Oromos and Ethiopians have contradictory national projects. Ethiopian national projects have included selective assimilation; ethnocide or genocide; destruction of Oromo history, culture, institutions, and leadership; and using Oromo economic and labor resources. Oromo national projects have included maintaining Oromo territorial and cultural integrity; reviving Oromo democracy; developing Oromo culture, history, and language; establishing an Oromian national power; and at the same time fundamentally transforming Oromia. While envisioning all these projects, the Oromo movement must endorse the principle of multicultural democracy in order to make sure that the problem of racialization/ethnicization of state power will be eliminated. When the Oromo reform nationalists created the Macha-Tulama Self-Help Association in the early 1960s and the Ethiopian National Liberation Front in the early 1970s, they envisioned the program of reforming and democraticizing Ethiopia so that Oromos could be equal citizens with Ethiopians. Although these movements laid the foundation of Oromo nationalism, they failed to achieve their main political objectives because of the opposition from the *Habasha* elites and their international supporters. Despite these political failures, some Oromo intellectuals and leaders have continued the idea of reforming and democraticizing Ethiopia.

Because of Ethiopian colonial politics, *Habasha* political culture, and the determination of the global interstate system to continue supporting the Ethiopian minority at the expense of the Oromo majority and other colonized nations, Oromo reform nationalism has become dead-end politics. The Oromo reform nationalists have attempted to reform the Ethiopian empire based on the following four implicit assumptions: The first assumption is that Ethiopia can be transformed from a colonial empire to a country through the alliance of the colonizing and the colonized ethnonations. This assumption implies that some *Habashas* can change and accept Oromos and other colonial subjects as equal citizens and partners. The second assumption is that the *Habasha* elites can begin to recognize and accept the autonomous development of Oromo leadership, institutions, organizations, culture, and history. The third assumption is that if Oromos get access to Ethiopian state power through democracy, they can use their cultural and economic resources without being exploited and oppressed. The fourth assumption is that since Oromos are the numerical majority, they can take over Ethiopian state power through the democratic process. The failed revolutions of the early 1970s and the early 1990s demonstrate that the assumptions of the Oromo reform nationalists are fundamentally flawed.

Habashas and Oromos cannot coexist peacefully within a single state system since they have contradictory national projects. Since the last decades of the nineteenth century, Ethiopians and their international supporters have been determined to destroy or subordinate the Oromo nation and exploit its resources. The Amhara-Tigrayan elites have been destroying the independent Oromo leadership with the help of global imperialism. Ethiopia is not a unique empire. An empire cannot be transformed into a country, because there is a fundamental contradiction between the colonizing and colonized structures, as in the cases of the empires of the former USSR and Yugoslavia, which recently disintegrated. Ethiopians are not willing to make themselves equal with the colonized populations by transforming Ethiopia, changing their political culture, and accepting democracy. The racist *Habasha* political culture and authoritarian political values do not allow the *Habasha* elites to accept democracy as far as they are strong and powerful. When they lose power because of the challenge from the colonized groups and the collapsing of the Ethiopian empire, it will be too late to transform and democratize Ethiopia. The Ethiopian state has made room only for collaborators, and not for reformers, democrats, and revolutionaries. Therefore, Oromo freedom and development require the destruction of Ethiopian colonial institutions, including the Ethiopian state. Oromo nationalists need to realize that at the same time they struggle to remove Ethiopian settler colonialism from the soil of Oromia, it is politically and economically necessary to promote the principle of revolutionary democratic multiculturalism in the Horn of Africa in particular and Africa in general in order not to racialize/ethnicize state power like Ethiopians.

While the African American and Oromo movements struggle to dismantle racial/ethnonational hierarchy and colonialism, they need to design political and cultural strategies that attempt to establish a single standard for all humanity by challenging all forms of oppression within and outside of their respective communities and by allying with antiracist, anticolonial, antisexist, and anticlassist forces on local, regional, and global levels. The movement of the oppressed people should not justify another form of cruelty and inhumanity, and it must discredit all oppressive social relationships. "To testify to a history of oppression is necessary," Edward Said notes, "but it is not sufficient unless that history is redirected into intellectual process and unversalized to include all sufferers."[54] Elitist policies that are not based on critical social scientific understanding of oppressed people cannot play emancipatory roles. Since African American and Oromo studies emerged as projects of liberation, they need to produce and disseminate critical social scientific knowledge that can help to build society from the bottom up by establishing a single standard for all humanity, challenging all forms of oppressive ideologies and relationships, and promoting revolutionary multicultural democracy.

Both African American and Oromo studies need to promote both the idea of building a democracy of knowledge and the principle of revolutionary democratic multiculturalism. Exploring how the struggle for revolutionary democratic multiculturalism attempts to solve the question of oppressed people from the bottom up in the United States by linking questions of culture and identity to the structure of White power and privilege, Marable says that radical democratic multiculturalists "emphasize the parallels between the cultural experiences of America's minority groups with oppressed people throughout the world. Discussions of culture are always linked to the question of power, and the ways in which ideology and aesthetics are used to dominate or control oppressed people. The goal of revolutionary democratic multiculturalists is not the liberal inclusion of representative numbers of blacks, Latinos and others into the literary canon, media and cultural mainstream, but the radical democratic restructuring of the system of cultural and political power itself. It is to rethink the entire history of this country, redefining its heritage in order to claim its future. It is to redefine 'America' itself."[55] Revolutionary democratic multiculturalism recognizes that human cultural identities change with the dynamic interaction of large social structures and human agency in the globalized world system; it fights for genuine egalitarian democracy by challenging the hypocrisy of bourgeois democracy.

Revolutionary democratic multiculturalism goes beyond nationalism. Revolutionary and progressive elements of oppressed people and groups need to start to rethink how to organize civil society so that groups cannot be subordinated to dominant institutions, particularly political and religious institutions. As the discussion in chapter III indicates, Oromos had constructed an egalitarian type of institutional form prior to their colonization. Therefore, there is no reason why we cannot build a humane and egalitarian democracy on a larger scale. Oromo political philosophy rejected the idea of hierarchically organizing and exploiting people; it endorsed the principle of popular decision making through public debate, full knowledge, consensus, and active participation of Oromos and non-Oromos who were brought into contact with Oromos through conflict, geography or economic interest. Oromos recognized the significance of popular or egalitarian democracy and the necessity of the transfer of enriched cultural and political experiences from Oromo society to another and from another society to that of the Oromo through reciprocal cultural borrowing based on democracy, equality, and social justice.

As the Oromo movement can learn much from the African American movement, particularly from its struggle for radical democratic multiculturalism, the African American movement can learn from the experience of precolonial egalitarian Oromo democracy to challenge elitist democracy. African American studies and politics that glorify African monarchies or chiefs need to reconsider their positions, because these African elites and their biological or ideological descendants have been engaging in the destruction of Africa by participating in the slave trade and becoming collaborative classes or "global pimps" that have contributed to the underdevelopment of Africa. Even Afrocentric scholars who claim to place Africa at the center of their scholarship ignore various African democratic traditions and focus their studies on monarchies like most Euro-American Africanists. Those Africanists, including most African scholars, degrade African democratic traditions just as their Euro-American counterparts do. Describing how Ethiopianists degraded the Oromo democratic system known as *Gada* by considering Oromo society "stateless" prior to their colonization, Asmarom Legesse asserts that "since monarchy was in decline in most of Europe, and the transition to democracy became the epitome of Europe's highest political aspirations, admitting that some varieties of democracy were firmly planted in Africa in the 16th century when in fact they were not fully established in Britain, the United States and France until the 17th or 18th centuries and in some part of Europe as late as the middle of the 20th century would have made the ideological premise of the 'civilizing mission' somewhat implausible. The idea, further, that African democracies may have some constitutional features that are more advanced than their European counterpart was and still is considered quite heretical."[56]

Recognizing the existence of various forms of democracy before Africa was partitioned and colonized and challenging Euro-American - centric scholarship that rationalizes and justifies ethnonational stratification can help to develop a human-centric and original scholarship. Learning about Oromo society, with its complex laws, elaborate legislative tradition, and well-developed methods of dispute settlement, and about the Oromo nation struggle can present a new perspective for African and African American studies and politics. African Americans and Oromos can ally with each other on global level by exchanging political and cultural experiences and re-creating the ideology of pan-Africanism and global solidarity based on the principles of popular democracy and egalitarian world order.

Scholars have a responsibility to challenge current assumptions that function to keep racialized/ethnicized states in power. Misleading assumptions about indigenous or dominated peoples and their movements must be exposed. It is important that the world community be informed about the danger of allowing the existence of double standards for humanity based on the criterion of race/ethnicity. Most existing liberal and Marxist historiographies do not adequately explain the phenomenon of oppressed nationalism and fail to develop a comprehensive and critical theory of nationalism. Since the subjugated ethnonations mainly engage in cultural and political struggles as a means to dismantle hierarchical racial/ethnonational relations, there is urgency for understanding problems and struggles for human liberation. There cannot be durable world peace without eliminating the root causes of these conflicts and achieving the liberation of the repressed sectors of humanity. Currently, world peace is maintained by force. One thing we need to realize is that peace maintained in this way is temporary and not durable. We have important lessons to learn from Great Britain, which one time boasted that "the sun never sets on the British Empire," and from the Soviet Union, which aspired to control the whole world. As England lost its empire and its hegemony, so the Soviet Union, despite its massive nuclear weapons and its illusive "socialist" ideology, recently lost its satellite states. Today, the core of the former Soviet

Union, Russia, is engaged in a destructive war with Chechens, who are determined to liberate themselves from Russian colonial control.

Racial/ethnonational stratification is oppressive and destructive, and it must be dismantled and transformed. Scholars who are interested in world peace, social justice, and multicultural democracy need to allow members of the subjugated ethnonations to actively participate in their research, because the experiences of these peoples are more valuable than any number of learned speculations. Participatory research approaches can help scholars better understand the question of oppressed nationalism by supplementing historical, quantitative, and qualitative methods of enquiry and helping them to identify the weaknesses of their own concepts, theories, and assumptions by learning from the actual experiences of the indigenous peoples. Introducing participatory research approaches emerged as part of resistance to colonial or neocolonial research practices in peripheral parts of the world. These kinds of research methods are necessary for studies of oppressed nationalism and indigenous peoples so that they can tell their stories without distortion and misinterpretation.

The issues of ethnonational diversity and oppressed nationalism are becoming central for world peace, social justice, and democracy with the intensification of globalization and with the increasing challenge to the state, its structures, and its role in the modern world system. This is because the subjugated ethnonational groups have been systematically repressed, and they are beginning to understand the mechanisms of this repression and use similar mechanisms and to respond in a comparable fashion. Since racialized/ethnicized states oppose multicultural democracy and self-determination or autonomy, they may disintegrate like the former Soviet Union and Yugoslavia. Such states oppose multicultural democracy because it loosens their hold and limits their power and profits by reducing the margin of expropriation and the concentration of benefits. Unfortunately, contradictory political processes inevitably result in conflict and outright war. Therefore, the world community needs to be aware of these possibilities and be capable of mediating the processes through developing democratic and fair procedures and criteria by which to resolve global problems. This comparative study strongly contributes to these processes.

Notes

Chapter I

1. Because of the politics involved there is disagreement on the size of the Oromo population in the Ethiopian empire. In *The Journal of Oromo Studies,* vol. 4, nos. 1 and 2, Feyisa Demie notes that "Oromia [the Oromo country] had an estimated population of 13 million in 1970. The most recent census in 1984 gave a total population of 21 million. By the year 2004, Oromia's population is expected to reach 34 million. The forecast is that the total population can easily exceed 39 million by the year 2014" (p. 165). However, some scholars, government census, and *The World Almanac and Book of Facts* (1999, p.787) estimate the Oromo population at 40 percent of the Ethiopian population.
2. Benjamin Quarles, *The Negro in the Making of America* (New York: Macmillan, 1987), p. 34.
3. Ibid.
4. Ibid., p. 22.
5. Ibid., p. 7.
6. For discussion on maroon settlements, see Richard Price, ed., *Maroon Societies: Rebel Slave Communities in the Americas,* 2nd ed. (Baltimore: John Hopkins, 1979).
7. See Julian B. Roebuck and Komanduri S. Murty, *Historically Black Colleges and Universities: Their Place in American Higher Education* (Westport, Conn.: Praeger, 1993).
8. For details, see Martial de Slaviac, *Un People antique au pays de Menelik: Les Galla, Paris, 1901;* Bonnie K. Holcomb and Sisai Ibssa, *The Invention of Ethiopia: The Making of Dependent Colonial State in Northeast Africa* (Trenton, N.J.: The Red Sea Press, 1990); Asafa Jalata, *Oromia and Ethiopia: State Formation and Ethnonational Conflict, 1868–1992* (Boulder: Lynne Rienner Publishers, 1993).
9. Martial de Slavic, Ibid.
10. Oromos call their region or country Oromia. Oromia occupies three-fourths of the Ethiopian empire. Currently, it is officially considered one of the administrative regions of Ethiopia.
11. See The National Summit on Africa, *Draft National Policy Plan of Action for U.S.-Africa Relations in the 21st Century,* February 16–20, 2000.
12. Theda Skocpol, *Social Revolutions in the Modern World* (Cambridge: Cambridge University Press, 1994), p. 303.
13. Ibid., p. 333.
14. See Andre Gunder Frank, *World Accumulation, 1492–1789* (New York: Monthly Review Press, 1978); Karl Marx, *Capital,* vol. I, ed. F. Engels (New York: International Publishers, 1967); Walter Rodney, *How Europe Underdeveloped Africa* (Washington, D.C.: Howard University Press, 1972); Immanuel Wallerstein, *The Politics of the World-Economy: The States, the Movements, and Civilizations* (Cambridge: Cambridge University Press, 1984); Immanuel Wallerstein, *The Modern World-System III: The Second Era of Great Expansion of the Capitalist World-Economy, 1730–1840* (San Diego: Sage, 1988).

15. Karl Marx, *Capital,* vols. I and II, ed. by F. Engels (New York: International Publishers, 1967), p. 17.

16. See Walter Rodney, *How Europe Underdeveloped Africa.*

17. Karl Marx, op. cit., p. 763.

18. For example, see Edward Said, *Orientalism* (New York: Vintage Books, 1978); Robert J. C. Young, *Colonial Desire: Hybridity in Theory, Culture and Race* (New York: Routledge, 1995); Howard Winant, *Racial Conditions: Politics, Theory, Comparisons* (Minneapolis: University of Minnesota Press, 1994).

19. See Perry Anderson, *Lineage of the Absolutist State* (London: Verso, 1974).

20. Ibid., p. 1.

21. According to Kamenka, "Economic developments were transforming the domestic economy of the rural manor and the urban guild into a national economy. Feudal and inter-urban warfare were gradually supplanted by warfare of a large scale . . . monarchies were becoming symbols of national power and prestige, while upper and middle classes were becoming more enthusiastic exponents of national, as against local or cosmopolitan interests." Eugene Kamenka, "Political Nationalism—the Evolution of the Idea," in *Nationalism: The Nature of the Idea,* ed. E. Kamenka (Canberra: Australia National University Press), pp. 1–20.

22. John Breuilly, *Nationalism and State* (Chicago: University of Chicago Press, 1985), p. 54.

23. Thomas R. Shannon, *An Introduction to the World-System Perspective* (San Francisco: Westview Press, 1989), p. 51.

24. Ibid., p. 44.

25. See Louis Synder, *Varieties of Nationalism: A Comparative Study* (Hinsdale: The Dryden Press), p. 77.

26. Ibid.

27. Ibid., p. 80.

28. Gurutz J. Bereciartu, *Decline of the Nation-State,* trans. W. A. Douglass (Reno: University of Nevada Press, 1994), p. 11.

29. Louis Synder, *Varieties of Nationalism,* p. 10.

30. Derek Heater, *National Self-Determination: Woodrow Wilson and His Legacy* (London: St. Martin's Press, 1994), p. 4.

31. Giovanni Arrighi, Terence Hopkins, and I. Wallerstein, *Anti-Systemic Movements* (London: Verso, 1989), p. 30.

32. Leonard Tivey, "Introduction," in *The Nation-State,* ed. L. Tivey (New York: St. Martin's Press, 1981), p. 13. Tivey comments that the nation-state "created the idea of the 'citizen'—the individual who recognized the state as his legal home. It created the idea of a uniform system of law throughout the country . . . of legal equality, where all citizens have the same status before the law . . . of a state that exists to serve those citizens . . . of loyalty to a larger group than clan . . . of common languages and common education systems, and common legal systems within clearly defined state boundaries."

33. Benjamin Quarles, op. cit., p. 21.

34. Ibid.

35. Asafa Jalata, op. cit.; Bonnie Holcomb and Sisai Ibssa, op. cit.

36. See Karl Marx, *Capital,* p. 765.

37. Amharas and Tigrayans prefer to call one another *Habashas* to indicate that they are the mixture of the so-called Semitic group and Africans. According to Jalata (1993, p. 31), "The Arab elements immigrated to this part of Africa [currently called Eritrea and northern Ethiopia] probably in the first half of the first millennium B.C., and the descendants of the Arab immigrants who assimilated with the Africans on the coast" evolved as *Habashas.* The name Abyssinia emerged from the term *Habasha.* The *Habasha* warlords called their country and the regions they colonized Abyssinia, and they later changed it to Ethiopia. For most people the difference between the ancient mythical

Ethiopia and contemporary Ethiopia is not clear because the Abyssinian warlords and clergy facilitated this confusion to appropriate the history of the ancient mythical Ethiopia. According to Budge (1928, pp. 120–121), "The translator of the Bible into Greek identified Kush with Ethiopia . . . and they, like the classical writers . . . apparently knew nothing of Abyssinia. . . . The name Ethiopia was definitely given to Abyssinia by those who translated the Bible from Greek into . . . Geez, and the Hebrew word Kush is translated by . . . Ethiopia." In reality, as Budge continues, "The descriptions of Ethiopia given by Homer, Herodotus, Diodorus, strabo and Pliny make it quite clear that they indicated by this name the vast tracts of country [regions] in Asia and Africa that were inhabited by dark-skinned and black-faced peoples." The name Ethiopia derived from the Greek word, "Aithiops"; this name was given by ancient Greek scholars to indicate that Ethiopia was the region of the black peoples or "burned-faces" peoples. Historically speaking Abyssinia and Ethiopia are not one and the same; Abyssinia is part of the Ethiopia. Today Amharas and Tigrayans are credited for things that are associated with the ancient mythical Ethiopia that was associated with all black peoples. According to Melbaa, replacing the name Abyssinia by Ethiopia enabled *Habashas* to claim that "Ethiopia, as a country and under their rule, existed in Biblical times and . . . maintained its independence for over 3000 years. On the basis of this myth . . . they justified their colonization of the Oromo. . . . More than anything else it is this substitution of Ethiopia for Abyssinia that led the colonized peoples such as Oromo to reject the term Ethiopian when applied to them" (1988, p. 36). In this book, I use interchangeably the names *Habashas,* Abyssinians, and Ethiopians to refer to Amharas and Tigrayans. A. Wallis Budge, *A History of Ethiopia,* vols. 1 and 2 (London: Methuen, 1928); Gadaa Melbaa, *Oromia: An Introduction* (Khartoum, 1988).

38. See Harry Magdoff, *Imperialism: From the Colonial Age to the Present* (New York: Monthly Review Press, 1978); Albert Bergesen, "Cycles of Formal Colonial Rule," *Process of the World System,* ed. T. Hopkins and I. Wallerstein (Beverly Hills: Sage, 1980); Andre Gunder Frank, *World Accumulation, 1492–1789.*

39. Andre Gunder Frank, ibid.; A. G. Frank, "The Modern World System Revisited: Rereading Braudel and Wallerstein," in *Civilizations and World Systems,* ed. S. K. Sanderson (Palo Alto, Calif.: Altmaira Press, 1995).

40. See Kenan Malik, *The Meaning of Race* (New York: New York University Press, 1996). Malik asserts that "the meaning of 'race' cannot be confined to a simple definition or reduced to a single property or relationship. Rather, race rises out of complex contradictions within capitalist society and articulates those contradictions in complex ways" (p. 265).

41. Howard Winant, *Racial Conditions,* p. 24.

42. For detailed discussion of these issues, see Benjamin P. Bowser and Raymond G. Hunt, eds., *Impacts of Racism on White Americans,* 2nd edition, (Thousand Oaks, Calif.: Sage, 1996), pp. 1–23.

43. Etienne Balibar and Immanuel Wallerstein, *Race, Nation, Class: Ambiguous Identities* (New York: Verso, 1991).

44. Ibid., p. 6.

45. Explaining why it is difficult to define *race,* Malik mentions the following points: "Geneticists have shown that 85 per cent of all genetic variation is between individuals within the same local population. A further 8 per cent is between local populations or groups within what is considered to be a major race. Just 7 per cent of genetic variation is between major races." Malik, *The Meaning of Race,* p. 4.

46. Robert Staples, "White Racism, Black Crime, and American Justice: An Application of the Colonial Model to Explain Crime and Race," in *Sources: Notable Selections in Race and Ethnicity* (Guilford, Conn.: Dushkin/McGraw-Hill, 1998), pp. 280–281.

47. Ibid.

48. Cultural universalism is seen as an ideology that the dominant groups and classes in the modern world system use to look at the world mainly from their own cultural perspective and to control economic, cultural, and political resources of the dominated groups and classes. It assists in creating and socializing a global collaborative class by subordinating or destroying multicultures in the name of science, technology, progress, and civilization (see Wallerstein, op. cit.); Edward Said, *Orientalism;* Robert J. C. Young, *Colonial Desire: Hybridity in Theory, Culture and Race.*

49. Immanuel Wallerstein, *The Capitalist World-Economy* (New York: Cambridge University Press, 1979), p. 234.

50. See Basil Davidson, "On Revolutionary Nationalism: The Legacy of Cabral," *Race and Class,* vol. 27, no. 3, (Winter 1986), pp. 21–45; Joane Nagel, "Ethnic Nationalism: Politics, Ideology, and the World Order," *International Journal of Comparative Sociology* vol. 34, no. 1–2 (1993), pp. 103–112.

51. For details regarding the Oromo case, see Jalata, *Oromia and Ethiopia,* pp. 83–114, 177–202.

52. See William I. Robinson, "Global Capitalism and the Oromo Liberation Struggle: Theoretical Notes on U.S. Policy Towards the Ethiopian Empire," *The Journal of Oromo Studies,* vol. 4, no. 1–2, pp. 1–46; Tecola W. Hagos, *Democratization? Ethiopia (1991–1994): A Personal View* (Cambridge, Mass.: Khepera Publishers, 1995).

53. See William I. Robinson, *Promoting Polyarchy: Globalization, US Intervention and Hegemony* (Cambridge: Cambridge University Press, 1996); Asafa Jalata, "Oromo Nationalism in the New Global Context," *The Journal of Oromo Studies,* vol. 4, no. 1–2 (July 1997), pp. 83–114.

54. See Immanuel Wallerstein, *Historical Capitalism* (London: Verso, 1983); Robert A. Huttenback, *Racism and Empire: White Settlers and Colored Immigrants in the British Self-Governing Colonies 1830–1910* (Ithaca, N.Y.: Cornell University Press, 1976); David R. Roediger, *The Wages of Whiteness: Race and the Making of the American Working Class* (London: Verso, 1991).

55. Anthony Smith, *Nationalism in the Twentieth Century* (Oxford: Martin Robertson, 1979), p. 1.

56. Gurutz J. Bereciartu, *Decline of the National State,* p. 1.

57. Ibid., p. 127.

58. See David R. Roediger, op. cit.

59. See Asafa Jalata, "African American Nationalism, Development, and Afrocentricity: Implications for the Twenty-First Century," in *Molefi Kete Asante and Afrocentricity: In Praise and in Criticism,* ed. Dhyana Ziegler (Nashville, Tenn.: James C. Winston, 1995), pp. 153–174; S. D. McLemore, *Racial and Ethnic Relations in America* (Boston: Allyn and Bacon, 1991).

60. John L. Comaroff and Paul C. Stern, "New Perspectives on Nationalisms and War," in *Perspectives on Nationalism and War,* ed. by John L. Comaroff and Paul C. Stern (Amsterdam: Gordon and Breach Publishers, 1995), p. 1.

61. See Anthony Smith, *National Identity* (Reno: University of Nevada Press, 1991).

62. This is one of the themes of my article titled, "Oromo Nationalism in the New Global Context," *The Journal of Oromo Studies.* My book *Oromia and Ethiopia* also takes these themes.

63. John Breuilly, op. cit. p. 131.

64. See I. Wallerstein, *Historical Capitalism,* p. 102.

65. Gloria Marshall, "Racial Classifications: Popular and Scientific," in *The "Racial" Economy of Science: Toward a Democratic Future,* ed. by Sandra Harding (Bloomington: Indiana University Press, 1993), p. 125.

66. See Robert J. C. Young, *Colonial Desire.*

67. See Howard Winant, *Racial Conditions: Politics, Theory, Comparisons* (Minneapolis: University of Minnesota Press, 1994).

68. See Alice M. Brues, *People and Races* (Prospect Heights, Ill.: Waveland Press, 1977).

69. Howard Winant, op. cit., xiii.

70. Thomas W. Heaney, "If You Can't Beat 'Em, Join 'Em: The Professionalization of Participatory Research," in *Voice of Change: Participatory Research in the United States and Canada,* ed. Peter Park, Mary Brydon-Miller, Budd Hall, and Ted Jackson (Westport, Conn. Bergin and Garvey, 1993), pp. 41–42.

71. See for example, Robert J. C. Young, op. cit. p. 4.

72. Ibid.

73. Ibid., p. 64.

74. David T. Goldberg, "The Social Formation of Racist Discourse," in *Anatomy of Racism,* ed. by David Theo Goldberg (Minneapolis: University of Minnesota Press, 1990), p. 295.

75. Sribala Subramanian, "The Story in Our Genes: A Landmark Global Study Flattens the Bell Curve, Providing that Racial Differences Are Only Skin Deep," *Time,* January 16, 1995, pp. 54–55.

76. Robert J. C. Young, op. cit., p. 92.

77. David T. Goldberg, op. cit., p. 310.

78. See Robert J. C. Young, op. cit.; Edward Said, op. cit.; Edward Said, "The Politics of Knowledge," in *Race, Identity and Representation in Education,* ed. Cameron McCarthy and Warren Crichlow (New York: Routledge, 1993); Robert Ross, "Reflections on a Theme," *Racism and Colonialism: Essays on Ideology and Social Structure,* ed. R. Ross (The Hague: Martinus Nijhoff Routledge, 1982).

79. See the argument presented in Asafa Jalata, "The Struggle for Knowledge: The Case of Emergent Oromo Studies," *The African Studies Review,* 39, no. 2, (September 1996), pp. 95–123.

80. See David. Roediger, op. cit.; Robert A. Huttenback, op. cit.

81. This argument is developed in Asafa Jalata, "Sociocultural Origins of the Oromo National Movement in Ethiopia," *The Journal of Political and Military Sociology* 21 (Winter 1993), pp. 267–286; A. Jalata, "African American Nationalisms," op cit. See also Amilcar Cabral, *Return to the Source,* ed. Africa Information Service (New York: Monthly Review, 1973).

82. Quoted in Patrick Chabal, *Amilcar Cabral: Revolutionary Leadership and People's War* (Cambridge: Cambridge University Press, 1983), p. 185.

83. Gurutz J. Bereciartu, op. cit., p. 129.

84. Benedict Anderson, *Imagined Communities: Reflections on the Origin and Spread of Nationalism* 2nd ed. (London: Verso, 1994).

85. Charles McKelvey, *Beyond Ethnocentrism: A Reconstruction of Marx's Concepts of Science* (New York: Greenwood, 1991), p. 42.

86. Ibid., p. 175.

87. See James G. Kellas, *The Politics of Nationalism and Ethnicity* (New York: St. Martin's Press, 1991); Walker Connor, *Ethnonationalism: The Quest for Understanding,* (Princeton: Princeton University Press, 1994); Ashok Kaul, "Ethno-nationalism in India: Political, Historical and Sociological Discourse," in *"Race," Ethnicity and Nation,* ed. by P. Ratcliffe, (London: University College of London, 1994), pp. 151–162; L. Adele Jinadu, "The Dialectics of Theory and Research on Race and Ethnicity in Nigeria," in *"Race," Ethnicity and Nation,* pp. 163–178; Gurutz J. Bereciartu, op. cit.

88. L. Adele Jinadu, op. cit., p. 176.

89. See Ernest Gellner, *Nations and Nationalism* (Oxford: Basil Blackwell, 1983); Arthur N. Waldron, "Theories of Nationalism and Historical Explanation," in *World Politics: A Quarterly Journal of International Relations,* vol. 37, no. 3 (April 1985), pp. 416–433.

90. For understanding some weaknesses of Marxism on nationalism, see Ephraim Nimni, *Marxism and Nationalism: Theoretical Origins of a Political Crisis* (London: Pluto Press, 1991); Asafa Jalata, "Poverty, Powerlessness and the Imperial Interstate System in the Horn of Africa," in *Disaster and Development in the Horn of Africa*, ed. John Sorenson (New York: St. Martin's Press, 1995), pp. 31–48.

91. Charles McKelvey, *Beyond Ethocentrism*, p. 55.

92. John Markakis, "Material and Social Aspects of National Conflict in the Horn of Africa," *Civilizations*, vol. 33, no. 1 (1983), p. 276.

93. Hugh Tinker, *Race, Conflict and the International Order: From Empire to United Nations* (New York: St. Martin's Press, 1977), p. 13.

94. Benjamin Schwarz, "The Diversity Myth: America's Leading Export," *The Atlantic Monthly*, May 1995, p. 58.

95. Ashok Kaul, "Ethno-nationalism in India" p. 161.

96. Tom Narin, "The Modern Janus," *New Left Review*, November–December 1994, p. 3.

97. See Gurutz J. Bereciartu, op. cit.; Benedict Anderson, op. cit.

98. Edward A. Tiryakian, "Nationalism and Modernity: A Methodological Appraisal," *Perspective on Nationalism and War*, p. 215.

99. Crawford Young, *The Rising Tide of Cultural Pluralism: The Nation-State at Bay?* (Madison, Wis.: University of Wisconsin Press, 1993), pp. 39–40.

100. Benedict Anderson, *Imagined Communities: Reflections on the Origin and Spread of Nationalism* (London: Verso, 1991), p. 161.

101. Ibid., p. 3.

102. Edward Said, *Orientalism*, p. 327.

103. Gurtuz J. Bereciartu, op. cit., p. 128.

104. See Eric J. Hobsbawm, *Nations and Nationalism Since 1780: Programme, myth, and reality* (New York: Cambridge University Press, 1990).

105. See Benedict Anderson, *Imagined Communities*, 1991.

106. See Ernest Gellner, *Nations and Nationalism;* Eric J. Hobsbawm and Terence Ranger, eds., *The Inventions of Traditions* (Cambridge: Cambridge University Press, 1983).

107. Eric J. Hobsbawm, *Nations and Nationalism Since 1970*, p. 10.

108. Anthony Oberschall, "Theories of Social Conflict," *Annual Review of Sociology* 4 (1978), p. 298.

109. Joane Nagel, "American Indian Ethnic Renewal: Politics and the Resurgence of Identity," *American Sociological Review*, vol. 60, no. 6 (December 1995), p. 948.

110. John Breuilly, *Nationalism and State*, p. 35.

111. Benedict Anderson, *Imagined Communities*, 1994, p. 4.

112. See Anthony Oberschall, "Theories of Social Conflict"; Craig Jenkins, "Resource Mobilization Theory and the Study of Social Movements," in *Annual Review of Sociology*, 9 (1983), pp. 527–553.

113. Howard Winant, op. cit.

114. Charles McKelvey, op. cit., p. 30.

115. Ibid., p. 155.

116. D. J. Haraway, *Simians, Cyborgs and Women: The Reinvention of Nature* (New York: Routledge, 1991) p. 191.

117. According to Smith, a nation is not "a given existence, a 'primordial' and natural unit of human association outside of time," it is also not "a wholly modern phenomenon." Similarly, nationalism emerges from collective grievances and certain aspects of shared historical past. See Anthony Smith, *National Identity* (Reno: University of Nevada Press, 1991), p. 3.

118. Amlicar Cabral, *Unity and Struggle*, trans. by Michael Wolfers (New York: Monthly Review, 1979), p. 142.

119. See, for example, John Markakis, "Material and Social Aspects of National Conflict," p. 279.

120. See, for example, Walker Connor, *Ethnonationalism: The Quest for Understanding.*

121. Ibid., p. 4.

122. Anthony Smith, *The Ethnic Origins of Nations,* p. 3.

123. John Markakis, op. cit., p. 279.

124. See Amilcar Cabral, *Unity and Struggle;* Ronald H. Chilcote, *Amilcar Cabral's Revolutionary Theory and Practice* (Boulder: Lynne Rienner Publishers, 1991).

125. Anthony Smith, *Theories of Nationalism* (New York: Harper and Row, 1971) p. 22.

126. Ibid.; Anthony Smith, *The Ethnic Revival* (Cambridge: Cambridge University Press, 1981); *The Ethnic Origins of Nations; National Identity.*

127. John Breuilly, op. cit.

128. Ibid., pp. 1–2.

129. Ibid., p. 35.

130. Anthony Smith, *The Ethnic Origins of Nations,* p. 154.

131. Amilcar Cabral, op. cit., pp. 65–66. See also Amilcar Cabral, *Revolution in Guinea,* trans. by R. Handyside (New York: Monthly Review Press, 1969), p. 103.

132. Ernest Gellner, *Nations and Nationalism,* pp. 1–2.

133. Elie Kedourie, *Nationalism* (London: Hutchinson, 1960).

134. For instance, Nagel suggests, "Two international factors contribute to ethnic conflict and ethnic movements: ideology and competition. Ethnic movements find their legitimacy in the ideology of the global order; an ideology that embraces such conflicting principles as, self-determination, sovereignty, territorial integrity, representative government, and home rule. Ethnic movements find their material support in the marketplace of inter-national competition, and major regional powers support dissident ethnic groups as they compete for economic and geopolitical advantage in the global arena." Joane Nagel, op. cit. p. 103.

135. Amilcar Cabral, *Return to the Source,* p. 41.

136. Amilcar Cabral, *Unity and Struggle,* p. 143.

137. Amilcar Cabral, *Return to the Source,* p. 60.

138. Ibid., pp. 43–44, 68.

139. Gurutz J. Bereciartu, op. cit., p. 141.

140. See Arthur N. Waldron, "Theories of Nationalism"; Aviel Roshwald, "Untangling the Knotted Cord: Studies of Nationalism," *Journal of Interdisciplinary History,* vol. 24, no. 2 (Autumn 1993), pp.293–303.

141. Theda Skocpol, *Social Revolutions in the Modern World,* p. 336.

Chapter II

1. Martin Luther King, Jr., *Why We Can't Wait* (New York: Harper & Row, 1964), p. 80.

2. Malcolm X, *Malcolm X Speaks: Selected Speeches and Statements,* ed. George Breitman (New York: Pathfinder Press, 1976), p. 158.

3. I have made similar arguments on Black nationalism in my previous work. See Asafa Jalata, "Two Freedom Movements Compared: The Cases of the Oromo and African Americans," *The Oromo Commentary,* vol. 2, no. 1 (1992), pp.13–16; A. Jalata, "African American Nationalism, Development, and Afrocentricity: Implications for the Twenty-First Century," in *Molefi Kete Asante and Afrocentricity: In Praise and in Criticism,* ed. Dhyana Ziegler (Nashville: James C. Winston, 1995), pp. 153–174.

4. See Leon Litwack and August Meier, *Black Leaders of the Nineteenth Century* (Chicago: University of Illinois Press, 1988); W. J. Moses, ed., *The Gold Age of Black Nationalism, 1850–1925* (Hamden, Conn.: 1978); W. J. Moses, ed., *Classical Black Nationalism* (New

York: New York University Press, 1996); H. Brotz, ed., *African-American Social and Political Thought 1850–1920* (London: Transaction Publishers, 1992).

5. Howard Brotz, ibid.

6. See Harold Cruse, *The Crisis of the Negro Intellectual* (New York: William Morrow, 1967).

7. Anthony D. Smith, *Nationalism in the Twentieth Century* (Oxford: Martin Robertson, 1979), p. 4.

8. See for example, James Turner, "Black Nationalism: The Inevitable Response," *Black World* (January 1971), pp. 5–13; Earl Ofari, "The Emergence of Black National Consciousness in America," *Black World* (January 1971), pp. 75–86; Rodney Carlisle, "Black Nationalism: An Integral Tradition," *Black World* (January 1973), pp. 4–11; Ronald Walters, "A Unifying Ideology: African-American Nationalism," *Black World* (October 1973), pp. 9–26; Freddie C. Colston, "The Ideology of Black Power: An Assessment," *The Western Journal of Black Studies,* vol. 3, no. 4 (Winter 1979), pp. 233–243; Aldon Douglas Morris, *The Origins of the Civil Rights Movement: Black Communities Organizing for Change* (New York: Free Press, 1984); Gayle T. Tate, "Black Nationalism: An Angle of Vision," *The Western Journal of Black Studies,* vol. 12, no. 1 (1983), pp. 40–48.

9. See for example, Aldon D. Morris, ibid.; Manning Marable, *How Capitalism Underdeveloped Black America* (Boston: South End Press, 1983); James Geschwender, "An Introduction to the Black Revolt," in *The Black Revolt,* ed. J. Geschwender (Englewood Cliffs, N. J.: Prentice-Hall, 1971); Rhoda Lois Blumberg, *Civil Rights: The 1960 Freedom Struggle* (Boston: Twayne Publishers, 1991).

10. John Breuilly, Peter Alter, and E. J. Hobsbawm define nationalism as a form of politics or a political program. Anthony D. Smith defines it as a cultural or a social movement. See John Breuilly, *Nationalism and the State* (Chicago: The University of Chicago Press, 1987); E. J. Hobsbawm, "Ethnicity and Nationalism in Europe Today," *Anthropology,* vol. 8, no. 4 (1992); Anthony D. Smith, *National Identity* (Reno: The University of Nevada Press, 1991); Peter Alter, *Nationalism,* trans. Stuart Amckinnon-Evans (London: Edward Arnold, 1989).

11. See W. J. Moses, op. cit.

12. Blumberg states, "The aim of desegregation or integration . . . was not to foster intermarriage or social 'mixing' but to insure equal access to such basic rights as seats on buses, education, the vote, and fair trials when accused." Rhoda Lois Blumberg, op. cit., p. 2.

13. Anthony D. Smith, *The Ethnic Origins of Nations* (Oxford: Basil Blackwell, 1986), p. 157.

14. Walker Connor notes that "many diverse attitudes and goals are cloaked under the single rubric of black nationalism." Walker Connor, *Ethnonationalism* (Princeton: Princeton University Press, 1994), p. 49.

15. August Meier and Elliot Rudwick, "Introduction," in *Black Protest Thought in the Twentieth Century* ed. A. Meier, E. Rudwick, and Francis L. Broderick (New York: Macmillan, 1985).

16. Clovis E. Semmes, *Cultural Hegemony and African American Development* (Westport, Conn.: Praeger, 1992), p. 11.

17. Ibid.

18. Fishman states that African Americans "were denied [freedom and equality] by a rapacious colonial system of mercantile capitalism, which relied on the brutalities of the primitive accumulation of wealth backed up by ruthless armed action. This wealth played a strategic role in the amassing of capital for the rise of industrial capitalism." George Fishman, *The African American Struggle for Freedom and Equality* (New York: Garland, 1997), p. 3.

19. Sterling Stuckey, *Slave Culture: Nationalist Theory and the Foundations of Black America* (New York: Oxford University Press, 1987), p. 3.

20. See Sterling Stuckey, *Slave Culture;* Barbara Jeanne Fields, *Slavery and Freedom on the Middle Ground: Maryland during the Nineteenth Century* (New Haven: Yale University Press, 1985).

21. Quoted in Sterling Stuckey, ed. *The Ideological Origins of Black Nationalism* (Boston: Beacon Press, 1972), p. 8.

22. Immanuel Wallerstein, "The Construction of Peoplehood: Racism, Nationalism, Ethnicity," in *Race, Nation, Class: Ambiguous Identities,* ed. Etienne Balibar and I. Wallerstein (London: Verso, 1988), p. 85.

23. Ibid., pp. 3, 4.

24. Ibid., p. 78.

25. Sterling Stucker, op. cit., p. 24.

26. See, for example, Newbell Niles Puckett, *Folk Beliefs of the Southern Negro* (New York: Dover, 1969); W. E. B. Du Bois, *Black Folk, Then and Now* (New York: Holt, 1939); Carter G. Woodson, *The African Background Outlined* (New York: Negro Universities Press, 1968; reprint of 1936 edition); Peter H. Wood, *Black Majority: Negroes in Colonial South Carolina from 1670 through the Stono Rebellion* (New York: Knopf, 1974); Lorenzo Turner, *Africanisms in the Gullah Dialect* (New York: Arno Press, 1968; reprint of 1949 edition); Melville J. Herkovits, *The Myth of the Negro Past* (Boston: Beacon, 1958; originally published in 1941); Norman Whitten and John Szwed, eds. *Afro-American Anthropology: Contemporary Perspectives* (New York: Free Press, 1970); Sidney W. Mintz and Richard Price, *An Anthropological Approach to the Afro- American Past: A Caribbean Perspective* (Philadelphia: Institute for the Study of Human Issues, 1976); Lawrence W. Levine, *Black Culture and Black Consciousness: Afro- American Folk Thought from Slavery to Freedom* (New York: Oxford University Press, 1977); Winifred Vass, *The Bantu Speaking Heritage of the United States* (Los Angeles: UCLA, Center for Afro-American Studies, 1979); Robert Farris Thompson and Joseph Cornet, *The Four Moments of the Sun: Kongo Art in Two Worlds,* (Washington, D.C.: National Gallery of Art, 1981); R.F. Thompson, *Flash of the Spirit: African and Afro- American Art and Philosophy* (New York: Vintage Books, 1983); Roger D. Abrahams and John F. Szwed, eds. *After Africa* (New Haven, Conn.: Yale University Press, 1983); Charles Joyner, *Down by the Riverside: A South Carolina Slave Community* (Urbana: University of Illinois Press, 1984); Margaret Washington Creel, "*A Peculiar People*": *Slave Religion and Community-culture among the Gullas* (New York: New York University Press, 1988); Joseph E. Holloway, ed. *Africanisms in American Culture* (Bloomington: Indiana University Press, 1990).

27. See for example, Carter G. Woodson, op.cit.

28. See Beverly J. Robinson, "Africanisms and the Study of Folklore," in *Africanisms in American Culture,* ed. Joseph E. Holloway (Bloomington: Indiana University Press, 1990), pp. 211–224.

29. See for example, Lorenzo Turner, op. cit.; Winifred Vass, op. cit.; Molefi Kete Asante, "African Elements in African-American English," in *Africanisms in American Culture,* ed. Joseph Holloway, pp. 19–33.

30. Ibid.

31. See Norman Whitten and John Szwed, eds., op.cit.

32. Peter H. Wood, op. cit.

33. John Edward Philips, "The African Heritage of White America," in *Africanisms in American Culture,* pp. 225–239.

34. See Sterling Stuckey, ed. *The Ideological Origins of Black Nationalism,* p. 5.

35. Ibid.

36. Ibid., p. 48.

37. Quoted in Sterling Stuckey, "Through the Prism of Folklore: The Black ethos in Slavery," in *Massachusetts Review* 9 (Spring 1968), p. 427.

38. Joseph E. Holloway, op. cit., pp. xviii–xix.

39. Ibid., p. xix.

40. Ibid.

41. Ibid.

42. See Sterling Stuckey, ed., *The Ideological Origins of Black Nationalism,* pp. 198–200.

43. Joseph E. Holloway, op. cit., p. xx.

44. Sterling Stuckey, ed., op. cit., p. 198.

45. Clovis E. Semmes, op. cit., p. x.

46. Ibid., p. 2.

47. Ibid.

48. John W. Blassingame, *The Slave Community* (New York: Oxford University Press, 1979).

49. Cited in Clovis E. Semmes, op. cit., p. 28, from Harold Cruse, *Crisis of the Negro Intellectual* (New York: William Morrow, 1967).

50. See Franz Fanon, *Black Skin and White Mask* (New York: Grove Press, 1967).

51. Clovis E. Semmes, op. cit., p. 8.

52. Ibid., pp. 3–6.

53. Ibid., p. 6.

54. Ibid., p. 12.

55. For details, see Amilcar Cabral, *Return to the Source* (New York: Monthly Review Press, 1973).

56. Clovis E. Semmes, op. cit., p. 2.

57. Ibid., pp. xi, xiii.

58. Ibid., p. ix.

59. Sterling Stuckey, ed., *The Ideological Origins of Black Nationalism,* p. 6.

60. Ibid., pp. 13–14.

61. Ibid., p. 15.

62. Ibid., p. 12.

63. Clovis E. Semmes, op. cit., p. 15.

64. See George Washington William, *History of the Negro Race in America: From 1619 to 1880,* 2 vols. (New York: G. P. Putnam's Sons, 1883); reprint, (New York: Bergman Publishers, 1968); Robert Alexander Young, "The Ethiopian Manifesto (1829)," in *The Ideological Origins of Black Nationalism,* ed. Sterling Stuckey, (Boston: Beacon Press, 1972), pp. 30–38; David Walker, "Walker's Appeal (1830)," in *The Ideological Origins of Black Nationalism,* pp. 39–117.

65. Sterling Stuckey, ed. *The Ideological Origins of Black Nationalism,* p. 7.

66. See Immanuel Wallerstein, *The Capitalist World-Economy* (Cambridge: Cambridge University Press, 1980); Walter Rodney, *How Europe Underdeveloped Africa* (Washington, D.C.: Howard University Press, 1972); Nathan Irvin Huggins, *Black Odyssey* (New York: Vintage Books, 1977); Stanley M. Elkins, *Slavery,* 2nd edition (Chicago: The University of Chicago Press, 1968).

67. See Ira Berlin, *Slaves Without Masters: The Free Negro in Antebellum South* (New York: The New Press, 1974).

68. Ibid., p. xiv.

69. W. H. McClendon, "The Foundations of Black Culture," in *The Black Scholar,* vol. 14, nos. 3 and 4 (Summer 1983), pp. 18–20.

70. Clovis E. Semmes, op. cit., p. P. 2.

71. See George Fishman, "The Ideology of Black Power."

72. See Maulana Karenga, *Introduction to Black Studies* (Inglewood: Kawaida Publications, 1982); John H. Clarke, "African Cultural Continuity and Slave Revolts in the New World, Part One and Two" in *The Black Scholar,* vol. 8, no. 1 (September 1976), pp. 41–49, vol. 8, no. 2 (October–November, 1976), pp. 2–9.

73. John H. Clarke, op. cit., p. 41.

74. Freddie C. Colston, op. cit., p. 234.

75. See Herbert Aptheker, "Additional Data on American Maroons," *Journal of Negro History,* vol. 32 (October 1947), pp. 452–460; Herbert Aptheker, "Maroons within the Present Limits of the United States," *Maroon Societies: Rebel Slave Communities in the Americas,* 2nd ed., ed. Richard Price (Baltimore: John Hopkins Press, 1979); Bernard M. McComack, *Slavery on the Tennessee Frontier,* ed. C. Kelly and Dan E. Pomeroy (Nashville: Tennessee American Revolution Bicentennial Commission, 1977); Gerald W. Mullin, *Flight and Rebellion: Slave Resistance in the Eighteenth-Century Virginia* (New York: Oxford University Press, 1972).

76. See George Fishman, op. cit., p. 70.

77. St. Clair Drake, "The American Negro: Relation to Africa," American Negro Leadership Conference on Africa (Proceedings of the Conference), Washington, D.C., January 15–30, 1967.

78. See Leon Litwack, *North of Slavery* (Chicago: University of Chicago Press, 1961).

79. See David R. Roediger, *The Wages of Whiteness: Race and the Making of the American Working Class* (London: Verso, 1991).

80. See L. Litwack, op. cit.; W. J. Moses, op. cit.; Howard Brotz, op. cit.; L. Litwack and A. Meier, op. cit.

81. For further information, see Letitia Woods Brown, *Free Negroes in the District of Columbia, 1790–1846* (New York: Oxford University Press, 1972); Luther Porter Jackson, *Free Negro Labor and Property Holding in Virginia, 1830–1860* (New York: D. Appleton-Century, 1942); John H. Franklin, *The Free Negro in North Carolina, 1790- 1860* (Chapel Hill: University of North Carolina Press, 1943); Rhoda Golden Freeman, *The Free Negro in New York City in the Era before the Civil War* (New York: Garland, 1994); Graham Hodges, ed., *Studies in African American History and Culture* (New York: Garland, 1994); John Russell, *The Free Negro in Virginia* (New York: Negro University Press, 1969).

82. Rhoda Golden Freeman, ibid., p. 323.

83. John H. Bracey, August Meier, and Elliot Rudwick, *Black Nationalism* (New York: Bobbs-Merril, 1970).

84. Asafa Jalata, "Two Liberation Movements Compared." In colonial America, the difference between indentured White servants and African slaves was blurred since they worked side by side, and the work of the former and that of the latter was similar. The American Revolution brought White freedom and perpetuated Black slavery (except for a few Blacks who were emancipated). Poor Whites became freemen, full citizens and wage-earners. White workers were allowed to share public facilities, like schools and workplaces, with powerful Whites. They were allowed to be culturally and structurally assimilated into English culture despite their non-English national origin, and permitted to own property and to have political freedom. Then poor Whites gradually developed the ideology of Whiteness or racial superiority and gained psychological and material benefits by pushing down the weakest segment of American society, both freed and enslaved Blacks. White workers embraced the white supremacist ideology specifically after the American Revolution with the change in their position when they become wage workers. Roediger argues that "White labor does not just receive and resist racist ideas but embraces, adopts and, at times, murderously acts upon those ideas. The problem is not just that the white working class is at critical junctures manipulated into racism, but that it comes to think of itself and its interests as white." During slavery, African Americans were mainly controlled and dominated by the White plantation owners and after the abolition of slavery by White society and their institutions.

85. Richard F. America, *Paying the Social Debt: What White America Owes Black America* (Westport, Conn.: Praeger, 1993), p. xi.

86. Jack M. Bloom, *Class, Race, and the Civil Rights Movement* (Bloomington: Indiana University Press, 1987), p. 22.

87. Julian B. Roebuck and Komanduri S. Murty, *Historically Black Colleges and Universities: Their Place in American Higher Education* (Westport, Conn.: Praeger, 1993), p. 22.

88. E. Foner, *Reconstruction: America's Unfinished Revolution, 1863–1877* (New York: Harper & Row, 1988), p. 198.

89. Julian B. Roebuck and K. S. Murty, op. cit., pp. 22, 28.

90. See Frances Fox Piven and Richard Cloward, *Poor People's Moments* (New York: Pantheon, 1977); Jack M. Bloom, op. cit.

91. See Manning Marable, op. cit.; Julian B. Roebuck and K. S. Murty, op. cit.

92. See Manning Marable, *Race, Reform, and Rebellion: The Second Reconstruction in Black America, 1945–1990* 2nd ed.(Jackson: University Press of Mississippi, 1991.)

93. J. B. Roebuck and K. S. Murty, ibid., p. 23.

94. Ibid., pp. 24–25.

95. Ibid., p. 25.

96. Ibid., pp. 32–33.

97. Martin Luther King, Jr., op. cit., p. 23.

98. Those whose grandfathers voted would be allowed to vote. This was intended to allow all adult White males to vote and exclude Black men from voting since their grandfathers were slaves and never voted.

99. For details, see Alferdteen Harrison, ed., *Black Exodus: The Great Migration from the American South* (Jackson: University Press of Mississippi, 1991).

100. Nicholas Lemann, *The Promised Land: The Great Black Migration and How It Changed America* (New York: Vintage Books, 1992), p. 6.

101. Alferdteen Harrison, op. cit., p. viii.

102. Neil R. McMillen, "The Migration and Black Protest in Jim Crow Mississippi," in A. Harrison, *Black Exodus,* p. 86.

103. Nicholas Lemann, *The Promised Land,* p. 5.

104. Lennox Yearwood, "National Afro-American Organizations in Urban Communities," *Journal of Black Studies,* vol. 8, no. 4 (June 1978), pp. 432–34.

105. See for example, Winston James, *Holding Aloft Banner of Ethiopia* (New York: Verso, 1998).

106. See August Meier and Elliot Rudwick, "Introduction," *Black Protest Thought,* p. xix.

107. Kenneth B. Clark, *Dark Ghetto: Dilemmas of Social Power* (New York: Harper and Row, 1965), p. 11.

108. Nicholas Lemann, op. cit., p. 6.

109. Lennox Yearwood, op. cit., p. 424.

110. Anthony D. Smith, *National Identity,* p. 7.

111. Maulana Karenga, op. cit.

112. Nicholas Lemann, op. cit., p. 99.

113. James Turner, op. cit., p. 11.

114. See Clovis E. Semmes, op. cit.; S. Dale McLemore, *Racial and Ethnic Relations in America* (Boston: Allyn and Bacon, 1991), pp. 52–54.

115. Quoted in Earl Ofari, op. cit., p. 83.

116. Bernard M. Magubane, *The Ties That Bind: African-American Consciousness of Africa* (Trenton, N.J.: Africa World Press, 1989), p. 55.

117. John H. Bracey, August Meier, and Elliot Rudwick, *Black Nationalism,* p. 299.

118. See August Meier and Elliot Rudwick, "Introduction," *Black Protest Thought,* p. xix.

119. According to Alain Locke, "Up to the present one may adequately describe the Negro's 'inner objectives' as an attempt to repair a damaged group psychology and reshape a warped social perspective. Their realization has required a new mentality for the American Negro. And as it matures we begin to see its effects; at first, negative, iconoclastic, and then positive and constructive. In this new group psychology we note the lapse of sentimental appeal, then the development of a more positive self-respect and self-

reliance; the repudiation of social dependence, and then the gradual recovery from hyper-sensitiveness and 'touchy' nerves, the repudiation of the double standard of judgement with its special philanthropic allowances and then the sturdier desire for objective and scientific appraisal; and finally the rise from social disillusionment to race pride, from the sense of social debt to the responsibilities of social contribution . . . the belief in ultimate esteem and recognition." Alain Locke, "The New Negro: A 'Forced Attempt to Build . . . Americanism on Race Values," in *Black Nationalism in America,* ed. J. H. Bracey, A. Meier, and E. Rudwick, (New York: Bobbs-Merril, 1970), pp. 341–342.

120. Clovis E. Semmes, op. cit., p. 14.

121. H. R. Isaacs, *Idols of the Tribe: Group Identity and Political Change* (Cambridge: Harvard University Press, 1989), p. 69.

122. Manning Nash, *The Cauldron of Ethnicity* (Chicago: The University of Chicago Press, 1989).

123. Gayle T. Tate, "Black Nationalism," p. 45.

124. Amilcar Cabral, *Return to the Source,* pp. 42–43.

125. Gene Marine, *The Black Panthers* (New York: New American Library, 1986), p. 25.

126. Bernard M. Magubane, op. cit., p. 127.

127. Martin Luther King, Jr., op. cit., p. 33.

128. Nathan I. Huggins, *Harlem Renaissance* (New York: Oxford University Press, 1971.)

129. Bernard M. Magubane, op. cit., p. 109.

130. Amritjit Singh, W. S. Shiver and S. Browdin, eds., *The Harlem Renaissance: Revaluations,* (New York: Garland, 1989), p. xi.

131. Nathan I. Huggins, op. cit., p. 14.

132. Ibid.; Arna W. Bontemps, *The Harlem Renaissance Remembered* (New York: Dodd and Mead, 1972).

133. Anthony D. Smith, *National Identity,* p. 99.

134. Nathan I. Huggins, op. cit., p. 305–306.

135. See Vincent Jubilee, "Philadelphia's Literary Circle and the Harlem Renaissance," in *The Harlem Renaissance: Revaluations,* p. 35.

136. See August Meier and Elliot Rudwick, "Introduction," *Black Protest Thought,* p. xxvi.

137. Anthony Oberschall, *Social Conflict and Social Movements* (Englewood Cliffs, N.J.: Prentice-Hall, 1973).

138. See A. Meier, Elliot Rudwick, and Francis L. Broderick, eds., *Black Protest Thought,* p. 59.

139. Ibid., p. xxvi.

140. Ibid., p. 42.

141. Ibid., p. 32.

142. August Meier and Elliot M. Rudwick, *From Plantation to Ghetto* (New York: Hill and Wang, 1966), p. 186.

143. August Meier, Elliot Rudwick, and Francis L. Broderick, eds., op. cit., p. 3.

144. Ibid.

145. Ibid., p. 5.

146. Ibid., p. 7.

147. Ibid., p. 178.

148. Ibid., p. 182.

149. August Meier and Elliot Rudwick, "Introduction," op. cit., p. xxv.

150. Ibid.

151. August Meier and Elliot M. Rudwick, *From Plantation to Ghetto.*

152. Aldon D. Morris, op. cit.

153. Ibid.

154. Ibid.

155. Manning Marable, *Race, Reform, and Rebellion,* p. 39.

156. See Shirley N. Weber, "Black Nationalism and Garveyist Influences," *The Western Journal of Black Studies,* Winter 1979, pp. 263–266.

157. Ibid., p. 264.

158. B. M. Magubane, op. cit., p. 96.

159. See August Meier and E. Rudwick, "Introduction," op. cit., p. xxxii.

160. E. Franklin Frazier, "The Garvey Movement," *Making of Black America,* ed. August Meier and Elliot Rudwick (New York: Atheneum, 1969), p. 207.

161. James Farmer, *Lay Bare the Heart: An Autobiography of the Civil Rights Movement* (New York: Arbor House, 1985).

162. Ibid.

163. Aldon D. Morris, *The Origins of the Civil Rights Movement,* pp. 28–30.

164. Ibid.

165. Ibid., pp. 54–55.

166. Martin Luther King, Jr., *Strength to Love* (New York: Pocket Books, 1964), p. 14.

167. Ibid.; Martin Luther King, Jr., *Where Do We Go From Here: Chaos or Community?*(New York: Harper & Row, 1967), p. 96; *Stride Toward Freedom* (New York: Perennial Library, 1964), p. 185.

168. See Ira G. Zepp, Jr., *The Social Vision of Martin Luther King, Jr.* (New York: Carlson, 1989).

169. See Patricia Hill Collins, *Black Feminist Thought: Knowledge, Consciousness and Politics of Empowerment* (New York: Unwin Hyman, 1990).

170. August Meier and E. Rudwick, "Introduction," p. xx.

171. Ibid.

172. Martin Luther King, Jr., *Why We Can't Wait* (New York: A Mentor Book), p. 111.

173. Martin Luther King, Jr., "A Testament of Hope," *Playboy,* January 1969, p. 234.

174. Martin Luther King, Jr., *Negro History Bulletin,* May 1968, p. 15.

175. Quoted in Ira G. Zepp, Jr., op. cit., p. 213.

176. Martin Luther King, Jr., "The Rising Tide of Racial Consciousness," *The YWCA Magazine,* December 1960.

177. Jack M. Bloom, op. cit., p. 143.

178. Martin Luther King, Jr., *Why We Can't Wait,* p. 112.

179. Robert Allen, *Reluctant Reformers: Racism and Social Reform Movements in the United States* (Washington, D.C.: Howard University Press, 1983), p. 323.

180. Martin Luther King, Jr., "The Last Major Political Speeches of Martin Luther King and Eldridge Cleaver," *The Black Politician,* July 1969, p. 4.

181. See Ira G. Zepp, Jr., *The Social Vision of Martin Luther King, Jr.,* p. 54.

182. Martin Luther King, Jr., "A Testament of Hope," p. 231.

183. See Arnold Schuchter, *White Power and Black Freedom: Planning the Future of Urban America* (Boston: Beacon Press, 1968), p. 569.

184. Martin Luther King, Jr., "Honoring Dr. Du Bois," *Freedom Ways,* Spring 1968, pp. 110–111.

185. Manning Marable, *Race, Reform, and Rebellion,* p. 105.

186. Ibid., p. 113.

187. Eric C. Lincoln, *The Black Muslims in America* (Boston: Beacon Press, 1961), p. 98.

188. Ibid.; E. U. Essien-Udom, *Black Nationalism: A Search for an Identity in America* (Chicago: The University of Chicago Press, 1962).

189. Manning Marable, *Race, Reform, and Rebellion,* p. 92.

190. Robert Allen, op. cit., p. 322.

191. William W. Sales, Jr., *From Civil Rights to Black Liberation: Malcolm X and the Organization of Afro-American Unity* (Boston: South End Press, 1994), p. 42.

192. Manning Marable, *Race, Reform, and Rebellion,* p. 55.

193. Quoted in William W. Sales, *From Civil Rights to Black Liberation,* p. 80.

194. Malcolm X, "Ballot or Bullet," in *Malcolm X Speaks* (New York: Grove Press, 1966); Stokely Carmichael and Charles V. Hamilton, *Black Power: The Politics of Liberation in America* (New York: Vintage Books, 1967).

195. William W. Sales, *From Civil Rights to Black Liberation,* p. 21.

196. Quoted in George Breitman, ed. *Malcolm X Speaks* (New York: Grove Press, 1965), p. 172.

197. Jack M. Bloom, op. cit.

198. Ibid., p. 187.

199. "Preamble, Statement of the Basic Aims and Objectives of the OAAU," in George Breitman, *The Last Year of Malcolm X: The Evolution of a Revolutionary* (New York: Merit, 1967), pp. 105–106.

200. Ibid., p. 90.

201. Ibid., p. 43.

202. Ibid.

203. Ibid., p. 45.

204. Ibid., p. 73.

205. See Ishmael Reed, "Preface," in Eldridge Cleaver, *Soul on Ice* (New York: Bantam Doubleday Dell, 1968), p. xiii; M. S. Handler, "Introduction," *The Autobiography of Malcolm X,* with the assistance of Alex Haley (New York: Ballantine Books, 1965), p. xii.

206. Quoted in August Meier, Elliot Rudwick, and Francis L. Broderick, op. cit., p. 469.

207. See Emily Stoper, *The Student Nonviolent Coordinating Committee: The Growth of Radicalism in a Civil Rights Organization* (New York: Carlson, 1989); Clayborne Carson, *In Struggle: SNCC and the Black Awakening of the 1960s* (Cambridge: Harvard University Press, 1981).

208. Clayborne Carson, ibid., p. 215.

209. Emily Stoper, op. cit., p. 121.

210. Ibid.

211. Clayborne Carson, op. cit., p. 198.

212. See A. Meier, E. Rudwick, and F. L. Broderick, op. cit., p. 491.

213. Clayborne Carson, ibid., p. 509.

214. Gene Marine, *The Black Panthers,* p. 23.

215. Ibid., pp. 35–36.

216. G. Louis Heath, ed. *The Black Panthers Leaders Speak* (Metuchen, N.J.: The Scarecrow Press, 1976).

217. William W. Sales, Jr., op. cit., p. 99.

218. Manning Marable, *Race, Reform, and Rebellion,* p. 93.

219. Robert Allen, op. cit., p. 321.

220. See Roger Wilkins, "The Underside of Black Progress," in *Race and Ethnic Relations 91/92,* ed. John A. Kromkowski (Guilford: The Dushkin Publishing Group, 1991).

221. August Meier and E. M. Rudwick, op. cit., p. 252.

222. Alphonso Pinkney, *The Myth of Black Progress* (Cambridge: Cambridge University Press, 1984), p. 1.

223. J. D. Kasarda, "Caught in the Web of Change," in *Readings on Social problems,* W. Feigelman, ed. (Orlando.: Holt, Rinehart and Winston, 1990), p. 223.

224. Roger Wilkins, "The Underside of Black Progress," p.127.

Chapter III

1. Quoted in Mohammed, "The Macha-Tulama Association 1963–1967 and the Development of Oromo Nationalism," in *Oromo Nationalism and the Ethiopian Discourse: The Search for Freedom and Democracy,* edited by A. Jalata (Lawrenceville, N.J.: The Red Sea Press, 1998), p. 278.

2. Baro Tumsa was the Oromo nationalist who played a central role in establishing the OLF after the Macha Tulama Self-Help Association was banned by the Haile Selassie government in 1963 and its top leaders were killed or imprisoned. The author was present at a secret meeting held at Leenco Lata's home in Finfinee in the summer of 1974, when Baro talked to the audience. I was impressed by his speech and still remember the paragraph I quoted at the beginning of this chapter. There were several Oromo university students from different parts of Oromia at this meeting. As a result of this meeting, with other Oromo students like Sanbato Lubo, who gave his life for the Oromo cause, we established a youth association known as *Lalisa Nedjo*. This youth organization, in coordination with *Burqitu Boji* and *Biqilitu Mendi,* tried to coordinate some political activities in Western Oromia.

3. See Benedict Anderson, *Imagined Communities: Reflections on the Origin and Spread of Nationalism,* 2nd ed. (London: Verso, 1991).

4. Edward A. Tiryakian, "Nationalism and Modernity: A Methodological Appraisal," in *Perspectives on Nationalism and War,* ed. John L. Comaroff and Paul C. Stern (Amsterdam: Gordon and Breach Publishers, 1995), p. 218.

5. Amilcar Cabral, *Return to the Source* (New York: Monthly Review Press, 1973); Gurtuz J. Bereciartu, *Decline of the Nation-State,* trans. W. A. Douglas (Reno: University of Nevada Press, 1994).

6. See Gurtuz J. Bereciartu, ibid., p. 129.

7. See John Breuilly, *Nationalism and the State* (Chicago: The University of Chicago Press, 1985).

8. For further understanding of the concept of ethnocracy, see Ali Mazrui, *Soldiers and Kinsmen in Uganda: The Making of a Military Ethnocracy* (Beverly Hills: Sage Publications, 1975).

9. For details, see Bonnie K. Holcomb and Sisai Ibssa, *The Invention of Ethiopia: The Making of a Dependent Colonial State in Northeast Africa* (Trenton, N.J.: The Red Sea Press, 1990); Asafa Jalata, *Oromia and Ethiopia: State Formation and Ethnonational Conflict, 1868–1992* (Boulder: Lynne Rienner Publishers, 1993).

10. The colonized Oromos were reduced to the status of semislaves and were divided among Ethiopian colonial settlers and their collaborators to produce commodities for local consumption and the international market. The Oromo *gabbar* did not have control over land he farmed, product he produced, his life or children.

11. See Bonnie K. Holcomb and Sisai Ibssa, ibid.; A. Jalata, *Oromia and Ethiopia.*

12. Bonnie K. Holcomb and Sisai Ibssa, ibid., p. 387.

13. William I. Robinson, "Global Capitalism and the Oromo Liberation Struggle: Theoretical Notes on U.S. Policy Towards the Ethiopian Empire," *The Journal of Oromo Studies,* vol. 4, nos. 1 and 2 (July 1997), p. 10.

14. For details, see A. Jalata, "The Modern World-Economy, Ethiopian Settler Colonialism and the Oromos," *Horn of Africa,* vol. 13, nos. 3 and 4, vol.9, nos. 1 and 2, (1991), pp. 59–80; Evelyn Waugh, *Waugh in Abyssinia* (London: Longmans, 1936).

15. For details, see P. P. Garretson, *A History of Addis Ababa from its Foundation in 1886 to 1919,* Ph. D. Dissertation, University of London, 1974; Richard Pankhurst, *Economic History of Ethiopia 1800–1935* (Addis Ababa, 1968).

16. See Richard Pankhurst, *Economic History of Ethiopia.*

17. For details see A. Jalata, *Oromia and Ethiopia,* pp. 83–114.

18. See William I. Robinson, "Global Capitalism and the Oromo Liberation Struggle," pp. 1–46; Bonnie K. Holcomb, "The Tale of Two Democracies: The Encounter Between U.S.-Sponsored Ethiopian 'Democracy' and Indigenous Oromo Democratic Forms," *The Journal of Oromo Studies,* vol. 4, nos. 1 and 2 (July 1997), pp. 47–82.

19. For details see A. Jalata, "Oromo Nationalism in the New Global Context," *The Journal of Oromo Studies,* vol. 4, nos. 1 and 2 (July 1997), pp. 83–114; A. Jalata, "US-Sponsored

Ethiopian 'Democracy' and State Terrorism," in *Crisis and Terror in the Horn of Africa*, ed. Pat Lauderdale, A. Zegeye, and A. Oliverio, (Vermont: Darthmouth Publishing, 2000).

20. For detailed discussion of the colonization of Oromos, see Bonnie K. Holcomb and Sisai Ibssa, op. cit.

21. See Virginia Luling, *Government and Social Control Among Some Peoples of the Horn of Africa* (M.A. thesis, University of London, 1965); Asafa Jalata, *Oromia and Ethiopia* p. 3.

22. Although almost all Ethiopians oppose the Oromo struggle, they have accepted the name Oromia as a geographical and political fact since 1991 as the result of the Oromo national struggle.

23. For discussion on the significance of space and culture in Oromo society, see Odd Eirik Arnesen, "The Becoming of Place: A Tulama-Oromo Region in Northern Shoa," in *Being and Becoming Oromo: Historical and Anthropological Enquiries*, ed. P. T. W. Baxter, Jan Hultin, and Alessandro Triulzi (Uppsala: Nordiska Afrikainstitutet, 1996), pp. 210–238.

24. See for example Aleqa G. Mariam, *YeEthiopia Hizb Tarik* (Addis Ababa, 1948 Ethiopian Calendar); Taddesse Tamrat, *Church and State in Ethiopia* (Oxford: Clarendon, 1972).

25. See for example, Darrel Bates, *The Abyssinian Difficulty: The Emperor Theodorus and the Magdala Campaign, 1867–68* (Oxford: Oxford University Press, 1979), p. 7.

26. See for example, Edward Ullendorff, *The Ethiopians* (London: Oxford University Press, 1960), p. 76.

27. Ibid., pp. 43–68.

28. See Mohammed Hassen, *The Oromo of Ethiopia: A History 1570–1860* (Cambridge: Cambridge University Press, 1990), pp. 4–6; Interview with Blatta Deressa Amante, Dec. 15, 1962, Bishoftu, Oromia; interviewed by Baissa Lemmu; Asmarom Legesse, *Oromo Democracy: An Indigenous African Political System* (Lawrenceville, NJ: The Red Sea Press, 2000).

29. For detailed discussion, see Asafa Jalata, "The Struggle for Knowledge: The Case of Emergent Oromo Studies," *The African Studies Review*, vol. 39, no. 2 (September 1996), pp. 95–123.

30. See for example, Amilcar Cabral, *Unity and Struggle* (New York: Monthly Review Press, 1979), p. 140.

31. See for example, Aneesa Kassam, "The Oromo Theory of Social Development," in *Between the State and Civil Society in Africa: Perspective on Development*, ed. T. Mkandawire and E. E. Osagahae (Dakar: Codesria, in press); Gemetchu Megerssa, *Knowledge, Identity and Colonizing Structure: The Case of the Oromo in East and Northeast Africa* (Ph. D. Dissertation, University of London: School of Oriental and African Studies, 1993.)32. Baissa Lemmu, "The Political Culture of Gada: Building Blocks of Oromo Power," paper presented at the Oromo Studies Association Conference, Toronto, July 31–August 1, 1993, p. 3.

33. B. K. Holcomb, op. cit., 1997, p. 4.

34. Benedict Anderson, op. cit., 1991, p. 4.

35. Lambert Bartels, *Oromo Religion: Myths and Rites of the Western Oromo of Ethiopia—An Attempt to Understand* (Berlin: Dietrich Reimer Verlag, 1990), p. 16.

36. P. T. W. Baxter, "Ethnic Boundaries and Development: Speculations on the Oromo Case," in *Inventions and Boundaries: Historical and Anthropological Approaches to the Study of Ethnicity and Nationalism*, ed. Preben Kaarsholm and Jan Hultin (Roskilde, Denmark: Roskilde University, 1994), p. 248.

37. Since the Oromo kinship system is not yet adequately studied, the information we have on this subject is fragmentary and incomplete. However, here it is important to have some information about the system to better understand Oromo social institutions that have been built on this system. See Asmarom Legesse, *Gada: Three Approaches to the Study of African Society* (New York: The Free Press, 1973); K. E. Knutsson, *Authority and Change: A Study of the Kallu Institution among the Macha of Galla of Ethiopia*

(Gotenborg: Ethnografiska Museet, 1967), pp. 37–42; Hilarie A. Kelly, *From Gada to Islam: The Moral Authority of Gender Relations among the Pastoral Orma of Kenya* (Ph.D. dissertation, University of California, Los Angeles, 1992), pp. 40–63; Von Eike Haberland, *Galla Sud-Athiopens* (Stuttgart: Verlag W. Kohlhammer, 1963); Paul Baxter, "The Problem of the Oromo or the Problem for the Oromo?," *Nationalism and Self-Determination in the Horn of Africa,* ed. I. M. Lewis, (London: Ithaca, 1983); Asafa Jalata, *Oromia and Ethiopia: State Formation and Ethnonational Conflict, 1868–1992)* (Boulder: Lynne Rienner Publishers, 1993); Gemetchu Megerssa Ruda, *Knowledge, Identity and the Colonizing Structure: The Case of the Oromo in East and Northeast Africa* (Ph.D. Thesis, University of London School of Oriental and African Studies, 1993).

38. Lamber Bartels, *Oromo Religion,* p. 205. Bartels explains that the Macha Oromo members of a lineage group believe that they are related to one another by blood: "In contrast to the clan, the lineage (*balballa-door*) is in practice considered by people as of homogenous descent. 'All people of the same lineage are of one blood,' they say. Outwardly this results, among other things, in the obligation of blood-vengeance, when somebody of their lineage has been killed by a member of another lineage. Inwardly it results in the prohibition against 'shedding one's own blood.' This can be done in two ways, either by manslaughter or by sexual intercourse. Lineage members . . . may not marry one another and any sexual intercourse between them is regarded as incest. . . . In other words: all people of the same lineage are seen to be brothers and sisters to one another."

39. Von Eike Haberland, *Galla Sub-Athiopiens,* p. 775.

40. Gemetchu Megerssa Ruda, op. cit., p. 31. He also identifies another conceptual category that divides Oromos into Borana and Gabarro "based on the notions of primogeniture and ultimogeniture, or the idea of the elder or first born sons (*angafas*) and that of the other or youger sons (*qutisu*)." Oromo political leaders were elected from the Borana group and religious leaders emerge from the Gabarro group.

41. See for further discussion, Asmarom Legesse, *Oromo Democracy,* pp. 133–193.

42. P. T. W. Baxter, "The Creation and Constitution of Oromo Nationality," in *Ethnicity & Conflict in the Horn of Africa,* ed. Katsuyoshi Fukui and John Markakis, (Athens: Ohio University Press, 1994), p. 174; U. Braukamper, "The Sanctuary of Shaykh Husayn and the Oromo-Somali Connections in Bale (Ethiopia)," *Frankfurter Afrikanistische blatter,* 1, 1989, p. 428.

43. See Gemetchu Megerssa, op. cit., p. 27. Baxter explains that "the adoption of adults, and often all their dependants, used to be a common practice, which thereby incorporated them and their descendants into the family, and hence into the lineage, clan. . . . These practices, though almost certainly widespread and frequent, took place despite the firm ideological contention that descent and inheritance were both rigidly patrilineal. Oromo social theory, like most others, was often very flexible in practice." P. T. W. Baxter, "The Creation and Constitution of Oromo Nationality," p. 174.

44. Hector Blackhurst, "Adopting an Ambiguous position: Oromo Relationships with Strangers," in *Being and Becoming Oromo: Historical and Anthropological Enquiries,* eds. P. T. W. Baxter, Jan Hultin, and Alesandro Triulzi (Uppsala: Nordiska Afrikainstitutet, 1996), p. 243.

45. Ibid., pp. 243–244.

46. According to Blackhurst, "Oromo political structure as it existed before [the sixteenth century] expansion began was flexibly centralised in that major office holders were located at fixed points but power was sufficiently diffused throughout the system to enable local-level decision making to continue without constant reference back to the centre. However, the whole system was renewed spiritually and structurally by the meetings at the *chaffe* where legal matters were discussed and the law laid down or reiterated." Ibid., pp. 243–244.

47. The first three sets belong to Borana, and the second two sets are branches of Barentu. The descendants of these moieties occupy specific areas in Oromia today: The Raya and Assabo branches occupy northern Oromia (i.e., include some part of Tigray, the whole of Wallo, and some part of northern Shawa). The regions of Macha and Tulama include most of the present regions of Shawa, Wallaga, Ilu Abba Bor, and some part of present Kaffa. The branches of Sabbo and Gona occupy some part of the present Sidamo, part of Gammu-Gofa, and Borana, Gabra, and Guji lands, and some part of Kenya. The descendants of Siko and Mando occupy the Arssi and Bale lands, and part of the Rift Valley. Finally, the branches of Itu and Humbana live in most of Haraghe and some part of Wallo in the north. Nevertheless, there have not been demarcated boundaries among these parts of Oromia. Asmarom Legesse (1973, pp. 39–40) explores the kinship system of Borana Oromo of southern Oromia and identifies Sabbo and Gona as the dual organization of a system of moieties with almost equal number; marriage or sexual intimacy is exogamous. He notes that members of these two moieties are not geographically separated, but rather intermingled. According to Legesse (p. 41), these two moieties "stand in opposition to each other. Borana make a conscious effort to try to represent both moieties in forming a council for any purpose, even in the deliberation of intra-moiety problems. The source of social justice in Borana is the perpetual balance in the power delegated to the two primary divisions at all levels of the social system."

48. Baxter comments on the Oromo kinship as follows: "The presence of similarly named and widely dispersed descent groups has . . . eased and encouraged individual and group movements. There is a solid body of ethnography which supports these contentions, so two simple examples must suffice here for illustration. First, Arssi . . . is the overall name taken by the several million-strong Oromo group whose territories extend from the Rift Valley to the Bale-Ogaden boundary. Among the Boran, the Arssi are one of the clans of the Gona exogamous moiety. Among the neighbouring Gabbra they are a subclan of the Alganna phratry. They are also a Guji subclan. Second, Karaiyu is the name of the largest clan of the Sabho [Sabbo] moiety of the Boran. It is also the name of . . . [the clan] living along the Awash, and of Guji subclan. Guji is also the name of a Boran clan. The recurrence of a name across a wide range of putative descent groups of varied depths and spans is as much a feature of the Oromo as it is of the interlacustrine Bantu." Baxter, "The Creation and Constitution of Oromo Nationality," p. 177.

49. See Gemetchu Megerssa, op. cit., pp. 20–23.

50. Ibid.

51. Ibid.

52. Aneesa Kassam, "The Oromo Theory of Social Development."

53. Ibid., p. 93.

54. Ibid.

55. Gemetchu, p. 14.

56. Ibid., p. 95.

57. Ibid., pp. 94–95.

58. Asafa Jalata, "The Cultural Roots of Oromo Nationalism," in *Oromo Nationalism and the Ethiopian Discourse: The Search for Freedom and Democracy,* ed. A. Jalata, (Lawrenceville N.J., The Red Sea Press, 1998), p. 34.

59. John Hinnant, "The Guji: Gada as a Ritual System," in *Age, Generation and Time: Some Features of East African Age Organizations,* ed. P. T. W. Baxter and U. Almagor, (New York: St. Martin's Press, 1978), p. 210.

60. See Addisu Tolesa, "Documentation and Interpretation of Oromo Cultural Traditions," *Proceedings of the Conference on the Oromo Nation,* Toronto, Canada, August 4–5, 1990, pp. 41–42.

61. Aneesa Kassam, "The Oromo Theory of Social Development."

62. Ibid.

63. Ibid.

64. P. T. W. Baxter, "Oromo Blessings and Greetings," in *The Creative Communion: African Folk Models of Fertility and the Regeneration of Life,* ed. A. Jacobson-Widding and W. Van Beek (Uppsala: Acta Universitatis Upsalienis, 1990), p. 238.

65. Practically, there were mixed results on the application of this theory to other societies. It is true that when Oromos expanded their territories between 1522 and 1618 and established Oromia's present boundaries, increased their numbers by also expanding their cultural boundaries through the process known as *mogasa* or *gudifacha* (adoption to the Oromo clan). Despite the fact that the conquered and adopted groups at the beginning had limited cultural and political rights, as Asmarom Legesse (1989 pp. 12–13) notes, "Conquest, in the history of the Oromo has never given rise to sharp stratification between the conquerors and the conquered. The latter were given all the rights and responsibilities of citizenship." Therefore, today it is impossible to differentiate the Oromo who expanded and the Oromo who were assimilated. Although there is historical evidence that preclass Oromo society used Oromo democracy to integrate conquered peoples through adoption to clans, marriage and structural assimilation, there are scholars who, without periodizing Oromo history, emphasize the existence of ethnic stratification during the *gada* administration in Oromo society. Based on the *Habasaha* royal chronicles, scholars such as Abba Barey, Merid Wolde Aregay, and Alessandro Triulzi focus on ethnic stratification in precolonial Oromia. There is no doubt that the disintegration of the *gada* system in the early nineteenth century and the processes of class and state formation led to ethnic stratification in Western and central Oromia. Although we recognize the need for further study, it is wrong to universalize Oromo history without periodization. The egalitarian nature of the *gada* system did not allow the emergence of ethnic stratification despite its limitations, until classes emerged in Oromo society. See Asafa Jalata, *Oromia and Ethiopia,* p. 16; Mohammed Hassen, "The Historian Abba Bahrey and the Importance of His 'History of the Galla,'" *Horn of Africa,* vol. 13, nos. 3 and 4, and vol. 8, nos. 1 and 2, 1991, p. 93; Asmarom Legesse, "Oromo Democracy," paper presented at Oromo Studies Conference, August 12–13, 1989, Toronto, Canada; Abba Bahrey, "History of the Galla," in *Some Records of Ethiopia, 1593–1646,* ed. C. Beckingham and G. W. B. Huntington, (London: Hakluyt Society, 1954), pp. 111–139; Merid Wolde Aregay, *Southern Ethiopia and the Christian Kingdom, 1508–1708: With Special Reference to the Galla Migrations and their Consequences,* Ph.D. Thesis, University of London, 1971), p. 417; Mohammed Hassen, op. cit.; Alessandro Triulzi, "United and Divided: Boorana and Gabro among the Macha Oromo in Western Ethiopia," in *Being and Becoming Oromo,* pp. 251–264.

66. See Asmarom Legesse, *Gada: Three Approaches to the Study of African Society.*

67. See Abba Bahrey, "History of the Galla," pp. 111–139. See also Baissa Lemmu, *The Democratic Political System of the Galla [Oromo] of Ethiopia and the Possibility of its Use in Nation-Building* (M.A. thesis, George Washington University, 1971); B. Lemmu, "The Political Culture of *Gada:* Building Blocks of Oromo Power."

68. Bonnie K. Holcomb, "Akka Gadaatti: The Unfolding of Oromo Nationalism—Keynote Remarks," *Proceedings of the 1991 Conference on Oromia,* University of Toronto, Canada, August, 3–4, pp. 1–10.

69. Asmarom Legesse, "Oromo Democracy," p. 2.

70. Baissa Lemmu, "The Political Culture of Gada."

71. See Yilma Deressa, *Yee Ethiopia Tarik* (Addis Ababa, 1959 Ethiopian Calendar); Baissa Lemmu, *The Democratic Political System;* Dinsa Lepisa, *The Gada System of Government and Sera Cafee Oromo* (LL.B. thesis, Addis Ababa University, 1975); Sisai Ibssa, "Implications of Party and Set for Oromo Political Survival," paper Presented at the 35th Annual Meeting of the African Studies Association, Seatle, Washington, November 20–23, 1992.

72. See Dinsa Lepisa, ibid., p. 58.

73. A. Jalata, *Oromia and Ethiopia,* p. 19.

74. Mohammed Hassen, *The Oromo of Ethiopia: A History 1570–1860* (Cambridge: Cambridge University Press, 1990), p. 9.

75. John Hinnant describes that this system "divides the stages of life, from childhood to old age, into a serious of formal steps, each marked by a transition ceremony defined in terms of both what is permitted and what is forbidden. The aspect of *gada* which throws the concept of age grading into confusion is that of recruitment. A strict age-grade system assumes that an individual's social passage through life is in tune with his biological development. An individual enters the system at a specific age and passes through transition rites at intervals appropriate to the passage from childhood through full adulthood to senility. However, recruitment into the *gada* system is not based upon biological age, but upon the recruitment that an individual remain exactly five stages below his father's level. Recruitment is thus based on the maintenance of one socially defined generation between father and son." John Hinnant, "The Guji: *Gada* as a Ritual System," in *Age, Generation and Time: Some Features of East African Age Organisations,* ed. P. T. W. Baxter and Uri Almagor (London: c. Hurst & Company, 1978), pp. 213–214.

76. Asmarom Legesse, *Gada,* p. 8.

77. Ibid., p. 81.

78. See John Hinnant, "The Guji," pp. 207–243; P. T. W. Baxter, "Boran Age-sets and Generation-sets: *Gada,* a Puzzle or a Maze?," *Age, Generation and Time,* ibid., pp. 151–182; Hector Blackhurst, "Continuity and Change in the Shoa *Gada* System," in *Age, Generation and Time,* pp. 245–267; W. Torry, "Gabra Age Organisation and Ecology," in *Age, Generation and Time,* pp. 183–206.

79. Asmarom Legesse, op. cit. pp. 50–51.

80. H. A. Kelly, op. cit., p. 166.

81. K. E. Knutsson, op. cit. pp. 66–67.

82. *Ibid.,* p. 148.

83. Mohammed Hassen, "The Historian Abba Bahrey," p. 79.

84. See K. E. Knutsson, op. cit.; Tedecha Gololcha, *The Politico-Legal System of the Guji Oromo* (LL.B. thesis: Addis Ababa University, 1988).

85. K. E. Knutsson, op. cit. p. 148.

86. Ibid.

87. Ibid., pp. 133–135.

88. Ibid., p. 142.

89. J. Van de Loo, *Guji Oromo Culture in Southern Ethiopia,* (Berlin: Dietrich Reimer Verlag, 1991), p. 25.

90. J. Hinnant, op. cit.; P. T. W. Baxter, "Boran Age-sets and Generation-sets: Gada a Puzzle or a Maze?" *Age, Generation and Time,* pp. 151–182; Marxo Bassi, "Gada as an Integrative Factor of Political Organization," in *A River of Blessing: Essays in Honor of Paul Baxter,* ed. David Brokensha (Syracuse: Maxwell School of Citizenship and Public Affairs of Syracuse University, 1994), pp. 15–30.

91. Dan F. Bauer and J. Hinnant, "Normal and Revolutionary Divination: A Kuhnian Approach to African Traditional Thought," in *Exploration in African Systems of Thought,* ed. Ivan Karp and C. S. Bird (Washington, D.C.: Smithsonian Institutional Press, 1980).

92. See Asmarom Legesse, *Gada,* p. 12.

93. P. T. W. Baxter, "Oromo Blessings and Greetings," p. 239.

94. Asmarom Legesse, *Gada,* pp. 43–44.

95. Gemetch Megerssa, op. cit. p. 278.

96. Lambert Bartels, *Oromo Religion,* p. 42.

97. P. T. W. Baxter, "Oromo Blessings and Greetings," p. 247.

98. Ibid., p. 361.

99. Ibid., p. 15.
100. Asmarom Leggesse, Gada, p. 93.
101. See Gollo Huqqaa, *The 37th Gumii Gaayo Assembly* (Addis Ababa: The Norwegian Church Aid, 1998)
102. Asmarom Legesse, *Gada*, p. 220.
103. Ibid. pp. 224–225.
104. Baissa Lemmu, "The Political Culture of Gada."
105. Qabbanee Waqayyo, "Women's Influence in Oromo Society During the Period of *Gada* Rule," *Waldhaansso: Journal of the Union Oromo in North America*, vol. 26, no. 2 (August 1991), p. 8.
106. Hilarie Kelly, *From Gada to Islam*.
107. Qabbanee Waqayyo, "Women's Influence," p. 9.
108. Asmarom Legesse, *Gada*, pp. 19–20.
109. Kuwee Kumsa, "The *Siqqee* Institution of Oromo Women," in *The Journal of Oromo Studies*, vol. 4, nos. 1 and 2 (July 1991), p. 119.
110. Ibid., pp. 115–145.
111. Ibid., pp. 129–130.
112.. Ibid., p. 126.
113. Ibid., p. 127.
114. Hilarie Kelly, *From Gada to Islam*, p. 187.
115. See Asafa Jalata, *Oromia and Ethiopia*.
116. See Joseph Van de Loo, *Guji Oromo Culture in Southern Ethiopia*, p. 25.
117. Bonnie K. Holcomb, "The Tale of Two Democracies," p. 56.
118. See Bonnie K. Holcomb, "Ideological Bases for Oromo Empowerment," paper presented at the Oromo Studies Association Conference, The University of Toronto, Canada, July 31-August 1, 1993. Holcomb (p. 3) quotes one farmer from eastern Oromia: "When the OLF showed up saying to us the same things that our fore fathers had told us, we accepted them."
119. Bonnie K. Holcomb, "The Tale of Two Democracies," p. 71.
120. See videocassette on Naqamte, n.d.; two videocassettes on "Ayyaana Oddaa Bultum," Habroo, Oromiya, Hidar 3, 1984 (Ethiopian Calendar); Videocassettee "Aaadanno Annolee," Arssi, n.d.; videocassette "Jibatfi Macha," Ambo, n.d.; videocassette on Finfine, Yekatiti 29, 1984; videocassette on Dadar, n.d.
121. See all these videocassettes, ibid.
122. See Asafa Jalata, *Oromia and Ethiopia*, pp. 177–197.
123. See for instance, Asafa Jalata, "The Struggle for Knowledge: The Case of Emergent Oromo Studies," *The African Studies Review*, vol. 39, no. 2 (September 1996), pp. 95–123.
124. For further information, see Bonnie K. Holcomb, "Oromo in the World Community," *The Journal of Oromo Studies*, vol. 6, no. 1 and 2 (July 1999), pp. 1–48.
125. Ibid., p. 17.
126. Ibid., pp. 20–21.
127. See Asafa Jalata, "The Cultural Roots of Oromo Nationalism," pp.27–49. Some modernist scholars, such as John Sorenson, characterize Oromo nationalism as essentialist, romanticist and chauvinist because it attempts to restore some Oromo democratic heritages. By negatively characterizing this nationalism, Sorenson and others try to delegitimize the Oromo struggle for self-determination and democracy. For Sorenson, since the Oromo cultural heritages are backward, the idea of restoring them is essentialist and racist; however, he justifies the Tigrayan ethnocratic regime by rationalizing that it attempts "to construct a new form of civic nationalism." Sorenson, who advocates democratic capitalism and civic nationalism, fails to understand the oppression and exploitation of the Oromo people under Tigrayan colonial domination. He seems to argue that since Oromos necessarily struggle to

create an independent state, they are against democracy and civic nationalism. He argues that since Oromo nationalism is ethnonationalism it racializes cultural traditions and moral values and is used to differentiate Oromos from others. Since his assumptions fail to address how cultural repression is associated with economic exploitation and human rights violations, Sorenson sees that the Oromo struggle is needed to create a racial boundary between Oromos and different Ethiopian ethnonational groups. These kinds of arguments are promoted to exonerate Tigrayan ethnocracy that is engaged in exploitation and oppresion of Oromos. By blaming the victim, Sorenson considers the Oromo national movement led by the Oromo Liberation Front (OLF) as a racialized movement and the Tigrayan People's Liberation Front (TPLF) and its surrogate organization, the Ethiopian People's Revolutionary Democratic Front (EPRDF) as a democratic and civic movement. The relationship between the OLF and the TPLF/EPRDF will be explored in the context of the Oromo national movement.

128. See for example, Alessandro Triulzi, "Social Protest and Rebellion in Some Gabbar Songs from Qellam, Wallaga," in *Proceedings of the Fifth International Conference of Ethiopian Studies,* ed. J. Tubiana, 1980; Mohammed Hassen "The Oromo Nation under Amhara Colonial Administration," School of Oriental and African Studies, 1981; Zewde Gabre-Slassie, *Yohannes IV of Ethiopia: A Political Biography* (Oxford: Clarendon Press, 1975); A. Jalata, *Oromia and Ethiopia,* pp. 151–152.

129. A. Jalata, *Oromia and Ethiopia;* Abbas Haji, "Arsi Oromo Political and Military Resistance Against the Shoan Colonial Conquest," *The Journal of Oromo Studies,* vol. 2, nos. 1 and 2 (Winter 1995 and Summer 1995), pp. 1–21.

130. Abbas Haji, ibid., p. 11.

131. J. S. Trimingham, *Islam in Ethiopia* (New York: Barnes and Noble, 1965).

132. A. Jalata, "Sociocultural Origins of the Oromo National Movement in Ethiopia," *Journal of Political and Military Sociology,* vol. 21 (Winter 1993), p. 272.

133. See A. Jalata, *Oromia and Ethiopia,* pp. 152; A. Triulzi, op. cit. p. 177–181.

134. See Gebru Tareke, *Rural Protest in Ethiopia, 1941–1970: A Study of Three Rebellions,* Ph.D. dissertation, Syracuse University, 1977, pp. 167–149; James McCann, "The Political Economy of Rural Rebellion in Ethiopia: Northern Resistance to Imperial Expansion, 1928–1935," *The International Journal of African Historical Studies,* vol. 18, no. 4 (1985), pp. 601–623.

135. Paul Baxter, "The Problem of the Oromo," *Nationalism and Self-Determination in the Horn of Africa,* ed. I. M. Lewis (London: Ithaca, 1983), p. 139.

136. See G1-pro–1dn, Western Galla, British Archival Document, 1936; Patrick Gilkes, *The Dying Lion: Feudalism and Modernization in Ethiopia* (New York: St. Martin's Press, 1975), p. 211.

137. Cited in H. Marcus, *Ethiopia, Great Britain and the United States, 1941–1974: The Politics of Empire* (Los Angeles: University of California Press, 1983), p. 23.

138. For example, Ethiopians say that "Galla na sagara iya daree yigamal"; "ye Galla chewa ye gomen choma yelem." (Literally, the first one means that as you recognize the bad smell of the toilet with time, you recognize the dirtiness and evilness of the Galla when you know them closely; the second one means as you cannot find fat in cabbage, you cannot find a civilized Galla).

139. According to Bulcha, "The life of assimilated Oromos was often peripheral. In spite of their total submission to 'pressures for their cultural suicide' and to the dominance of the Amhara over non-Amhara peoples in aspects of life', they were seldom treated as equals by the Amhara. The Amharization of the Oromo and other groups was attempted 'without integrating them as equals or allowing them to share power in any meaningful way.' As the 'Amhara mask' they wore was often too transparent, assimilated Oromos rarely reached decision-making positions within the Ethiopian bureaucracy.

Despite the hard efforts they were making to sound like a native speaker, and the change of their personal names to Amharic ones, their pronunciation of some of the Amharic words often exposed their ethnic origins. Hence, they usually were confined to middle and lower rungs of the bureaucracy, and were expected to act like zombies carrying out orders from their Amhara superiors." Mekuria Bulcha, "The Language Policies of Ethiopian Regimes and the History of Written Afaan Oromoo: 1844–1994," *The Journal of Oromo Studies*, vol. 1, no. 2 (Winter 1994), p. 104.

140. Cultural racism is the conviction that dominant and superior cultural patterns and practices must be reflected in political economy, literature, music, art, and other cultural values at the cost of that of the subordinated ethnonations. For details, see Benjamin P. Bowser and Raymond G. Hunt, eds. *Impact of Racism on White Americans,* (Thousand Oaks: Sage Publications, 1996), pp. 2–3.

141. See Mekuria Bulcha, "The Politics of Linguistic Homogenization in Ethiopia and the Conflict over the Status of Afaan Oromoo," *African Affairs,* 1997, pp. 325–352.

142. Mekuria Bulcha, "The Language Policies of Ethiopian Regimes," p. 91.

143. Ibid., p. 92.

144. Ibid., p. 93.

145. See, for details, Aren Gustave, *Evangelical Pioneers in Ethiopia: Origins of the Evangelical Church Mekane Yesus* (Stockholm: Uppsala University, 1978).

146. For details, see Mekuria Bulcha, op. cit., pp. 93–101.

147. See, for details, R. J. Hayward and Mohammed Hassen, "The Oromo Orthography of Shaykh Bakri Sapalo," *Bulletin of the School of Oriental and African Studies,* 44 (1981); Mohammed Hassen, "The Matcha-Tulama Association 1963–1967 and the Development of Oromo Nationalism."

148. Mohammed Hassen, "Matcha-Tulama Association."

149. Ibid.

150. Cited in Peter Alter, *Nationalism,* trans. Stuart McKinnon-Evans (London: Edward Arnold, 1989), p. 79.

151. See A. Jalata, *Oromia and Ethiopia.*

152. Margery Perham, *The Government of Ethiopia,* 2nd ed. (London: Longmans, 1968), pp. 380 and 377, respectively.

153. Ibid.

154. S. D. McLemore discusses how the English-speaking settlers in the United States gradually reduced cultural and political barriers among all European settlers through structural assimilation. See S. D. McLemore, *Racial and Ethnic Relations in America* (Boston: Allyn and Bacon, 1991).

155. A. Jalata, "Oromo Nationalism in the New Global Context," *The Journal of Oromo Studies,* vol. 4, nos. 1 and 2 (July 1997), p. 84.

156. A. Jalata, "Ethiopia and Ethnic Politics: The Case of Oromo Nationalism," *Dialectical Anthropology,* vol. 18 (1993), p. 381.

157. Mekuria Bulcha, "Beyond the Oromo-Ethiopian Conflict," *The Journal of Oromo Studies,* vol. 1, no. 1 (1993), p. 1.

158. See for example A. Jalata, *Oromia and Ethiopia,* pp. 83–114.

159. Herbert S. Lewis, "The Development of Oromo Political Consciousness from 1958 to 1994," in *Being and Becoming Oromo* (Uppsala: Nordiska Afrikainstitute, 1996), p. 38.

160. See for example, A. Jalata, "Ethiopia and Ethnic Politics," pp. 381–402; Mekuria Bulcha, "The Survival and Reconstruction of Oromo National identity," in *Being and Becoming Oromo,* pp. 48–66; Mohammed Hassen, "The Development of Oromo Nationalism," in *Being and Becoming Oromo,* pp. 67–80; Gemetchu Megerssa, "Oromumma: Tradition, Consciousness and Identity," in *Being and Becoming Oromo,* pp. 92–102.

161. Interview with Lubee Biru on August 5, 1988, Riverdale, Maryland.

162. In its revised Constitution of 1955 by Article 45, and by Article 14, Number 505 of the Civil Code, the Haile Selassie government allowed the people to be organized in a self-help association.
163. Paul Baxter, "The Problem of the Oromo," p. 139.
164. Mohammed Hassen, "The Oromo Nation under Amhara Colonial Administration," Bulletin of the School of Oriental and African Studies, 44 (1981), p. 36.
165. Olana Zoga, *Gazatena Gezot,* p. 29.
166. Peter Alter, *Nationalism,* p. 79.
167. A. Jalata, *Oromia and Ethiopia,* p. 156.
168. Interview with Lubee Biru on August 5, 1988, Riverdale, Maryland.
169. A. P. Wood, "Rural Development and National Integration in Ethiopia," *Review of African Political Economy,* vol. 26 (1983), p. 516.
170. Mohammed Hassen, "The Matcha-Tulama Association"; A. Jalata, *Oromia and Ethiopia,* pp. 158–160.
171. Quoted in A. Jalata, *Oromia and Ethiopia,* p. 157.
172. P. T. W. Baxter, "Ethiopia's Unacknowledged Problem: The Oromo," *African Affairs,* vol. 77, no. 308 (1978), p. 288.
173. Quoted in A. Jalata, *Oromia and Ethiopia,* p. 157 and quoted in Mohammed Hassen, "The Matcha-Tulama Association."
174. Ibid.; Olana Zoga, op. cit., p. 297.
175. "The Oromo: Voice against Tyranny," reprinted in *Horn of Africa,* vol. 3, no. 3 (1980), p. 23.
176. Ibid.
177. C. Wondji, "Toward a Responsible African Historiography," in *African Historiographies: What History for Which Africa?,* ed. B. Jewsiewicki and D. Newbury (Beverley Hills: Sag Publications, 1986), p. 269.
178. Interview with Galasa Dilbo, OLF General Secretary, OLF office, Washington, D.C., August 27, 1993; interview with Dima Noggo, member of the central Committee of the OLF, Nairobi, Kenya, July 12, 1993; interview with Deressa Kitte, OLF member, June 8, 1993. The author is also familiar with these conditions, since he was a student at this university and participated in some of these activities between 1972 and 1978.
179. Interviews with Galasa Dilbo, Dima Noggo, and Deressa Kitte.
180. Amilcar Cabral, *Return to the Source* (New York: Monthly Review, 1973), pp. 39–40.
181. See A. Jalata, "The Emergence of Oromo Nationalism and Ethiopian Reaction," *Social Justice,* vol. 22, no. 3 (1995), pp. 165–189.
182. Oromo Liberation Front, "Democratic Resolution of the Oromo National Liberation Struggle and other Conflicts in the Ethiopian Empire," April 18, 1990.
183. Oromo Liberation Front, "OLF Statement About the TPLF-Sponsored OPDO," July 5, 1990, p. 3.
184. Gadaa Melbaa, *Oromia,* 2nd ed. (Khartoum, 1988), p. 135.
185. Ibid., p. 136.
186. Ibid., p. 137.
187. Ernest Gellner, *Nations and Nationalism* (Oxford: Basil Blackwell, 1983), p. 84.
188. Gadaa Melbaa, *Oromia,* p. 133.
189. Mohammed Hassen, "The Development of Oromo Nationalism," p. 68.
190. Almerigo Griz, "Ethiopia Fights a War of Confusion," *Jane's Defense Weekly,* vol. 7, no. 16, 1987.
191. Gadaa Melbaa, *Oromia,* pp. 138–139.
192. Almerigo Griz, "Ethiopia Fights."
193. Paul Baxter, "The Problem of the Oromo," p. 146.
194. For more information, see Mikhail Gorbachev, *Perestroika: New Thinking for Our Country and the World* (New York: Harper & Row, 1987).

195. A. Jalata, *Oromia and Ethiopia,* p. 179.

196. For details, Gebru Tareke, *Ethiopia: Power and Protest* (New York: Cambridge University Press, 1991), p. 224.

197. Ibid., p. 220.

198. A. Jalata, op. cit., p. 181.

199. See Kahsay Berhe, "The National Movement of Tigray: Myths and Realities," unpublished manuscript, February 1991.

200. AFP (Agency France Press), "Ethiopia–Politics," Nairobi, June 24, 1992.

201. See A. Jalata, *Oromia and Ethiopia,* p. 180; *Urjii,* "Yehulatu Hagaroch Alemagibbat Milikit Yihun?: YeSha'ibiiya Tor Sarawit Itiopian Lakiko Iyewata Nawu," 4th year, no. 38, December 2, 1997, pp. 1 and 6.

202. Lisa Beyer, "Ethiopia: Rebels Take Charge," *Time,* June 10, 1991.

230. "Ethiopia: Sea Access Granted," *Africa Research Bulletin,* July 1991.

204. Getachew Ghebre, "Ethiopia: Honeymoon Over," *New Africa,* December 1991, p. 19.

205. See Ibssa Gutama, "Ethiopia: Transtion to Ethnic Dictatorship," paper presented at Fortieth Annual Meeting of African Studies Association, November 13–16, 1997, Columbus, Ohio.

206. Amilcar Cabral, *Revolution in Guinea: An African People's Struggle* (London: Monthly Review Press, 1969), p. 103.

207. Galasa Dilbo's Speech at Emory University, Atlanta, November 1, 1993; OLF Central Committee, "Statement of the Secretary General on the State of the Oromo People's Struggle," March 1, 1993.

208. Ibid.

209. See videocassette at Naqamte, n.d.; two videocassettes, "Ayyaana Odda Bultum," Habroo, Oromia, Hidar, 3, 1984, Ethiopian Calendar; videocassette, "Aaadanno Annole," Arssi, n.d.; videocassette, "Jabatfi Macha," Ambo, n.d.; videocassette at Finfinne, Yekatit 29, 1984 (E.C.); videocassette at Dadar, n.d; videocassette at Gara Mulata, 7–9–1991.

210. Michael A. Hiltzik, "Ethnic Pride Gets a Test in Africa," *Los Angeles Times,* February 11, 1992.

211. Ben Barber, "Coming Back to Life: Will Oromos' Cultural Revival Split Ethiopia?" *Culture-Crossroads,* 1994, pp. 1–5.

212. Ibid., p. 3.

213. See videocassettes in note 210.

214. See Abera Tefera, "Interview with Abbiyuu Galata, *Qunnamtii Oromia,* Spring 1992.

215. See Robert M. Press, "In New Ethiopia, Main Tribe Takes Peaceful Route to Reclaim Rights," *Christian Science Monitor,* July 15, 1991.

216. See Andrew Lycett, "Federalism Flourishes," *New Africa,* May 1992.

217. See resolutions of Oromo organizations and associations; these resolutions include, "To the President of the Transitional Government of Ethiopia, Addis Ababa," signed by 18 elders of the Arssi and Bale Oromos, Nov. 16, 1991; "Resolutions of Representatives of Oromos drawn from Eleven Regions—Professional Associations and Mass Organizations," Oromo Assembly at Odaa Bultum, Haraghe, Dec. 4, 1991; "Yee Ethiopia Yee Shigigir Tawakayoch," Baa Walaga Yee Sidist Awuraja Hizib Twakayoch, Hidar 1, 1994 E.C.; "To the Council of Representatives of the Transitional Government of Ethiopia, Addis Ababa," the representatives of the Oromo nation from all over Oromia and Oromos working in Fifinne, Feb. 1992; "The Transitional Government of Ethiopia, Addis Ababa," The Coordinating Committee for Peace in Eastern Oromia, Dadar, March 21, 1992; "Resolutions on the Current Situation in Ethiopia," representatives of Union Oromos in North America," n.d.; "Report on the Emergency Conference of Oromo Scholars and Professionals on the Current

Situation in Oromia," Convened by the Oromo Studies Association, March 13–15, 1992, Washington, D.C.

218. For example, see *Qunnamtii Oromia,* Summer/Fall 1992, pp. 2–3.

219. Interview with Abdiisa Baay'isaa; he was imprisoned in the Didhesa Camp for one year; Interview with Bakalcha Hussein, who was imprisoned at the Bilate Camp for nine months, Summer 1993, Nairobi, Kenya.

220. For example, see Sue Pollock, "Ethiopia-Human Tragedy in the Making: Democracy or Dictatorship?"; Sue Pollock, "Politics and Conflict: Participation and Self-Determination," in *Ethiopia: Conquest and the Quest for Freedom and Democracy,* ed. Seyoum Y. Hameso, T. Trueman, and T.E. Erena (London: TSC Publications, 1997), pp. 81–110; Trevor Trueman, "Democracy or Dictatorship," in *Ethiopia: Conquest and the Quest for Freedom and Democracy,* pp. 141–150.

221. For details, see A. Jalata, "U.S.-Sponsored Ethiopian 'Democracy' and State Terrorism."

222. *Impact International,* "Cleansing 'Islamic fundamentalism' from the Horn," March 1997, p. 1.

223. Ibid.; *Africa Confidential,* vol. 38, no. 21. (October 1997).

224. *Africa Confidential.*

225. "Ethiopia: Federal Sham," *The Economist,* August, 16, 1997, p. 51.

226. Theodore M. Vestal, "Deficits of Democracy in the Transitional Government of Ethiopia Since 1991," 1994, p. 7.

227. John Sorenson, "Learning to be Oromo," p. 441.

228. John Young, "The Tigray and Eritrean Peoples Liberation Fronts: A History of Tensions and Pragmatism," *The Journal of Modern African Studies,* vol. 34, no. 1 (1996), pp. 105–120; John Young, "Development and Change in Post-Revolutionary Tigray," *The Journal of Modern African Studies,* vol. 35, no. 1 (1997), pp. 81–99.

229. Sandra Fullerton Joireman, "Opposition Politics and Ethnicity in Ethiopia: We Will Go Down Together," *The Journal of Modern African Studies,* vol. 35, no. 3 (1997), p. 388.

230. Ibid., pp. 394–395.

231. Annamarie Oliverio, "The State of Injustice: The Politics of Terrorism and the Production of Order," *International Journal of Comparative Sociology,* vol. 38, nos. 1–2 (June 1997), pp. 48–63.

232. Annamarie Oliverio, *The State of Terror* (New York: SUNY Press, 1997).

233. A. Oliverio, "The State of Injustice," p. 52.

234. *Oromia Support Group,* "Urgent Action—November 1997," p. 1.

235. *Oromia Support Group,* "Urgent Action—November 1997," pp. 1–2.

236. See Sue Pollock; Trevor Trueman, op. cit.; Amnesty International; Human Rights Watch/Africa, 1997; Survival International, "Ethiopia: Human rights hypocrisy must end now," press release, July 14, 1995; Bruna Fossati, Lydia Namarra, and Peter Niggli, *The New Rulers of Ethiopia and the Persecution of the Oromo* (Frankfurt, 1996).

237. *U.S. Department of State on Human Rights,* 1997, p. 1.

238. Bruna Fossati, Lydia Namarra, and Peter Niggli, op. cit.

239. Umar Fatanssa, quoted in *The New Rulers of Ethiopia,* p. 43.

240. *Oromia Support Group,* "Press Release -May/June 1997," p. 18.

241. *U.S. Department of State on Human Rights,* 1997, p. 4.

242. "Ethiopia: Federal Sham," p. 4.

Chapter IV

1. This chapter was presented at the Forty-first Annual Meeting of the African Studies Association, October 29–November 1, 1998, Chicago, Illinois. I would like to thank Bonnie K. Holcomb, Chip Hastings, Wanda Rushing, Bill Robinson, and Lemmu

Baissa for providing comments on earlier drafts of this paper. This chapter is published in *The Journal of Oromo Studies,* vol. 4, nos.1 and 2 (July 1999), pp. 49–89.

2. See Leenco Lata, "Peculiar Challenges to Oromo Nationalism," in *Oromo Nationalism and the Ethiopian Discourse: The Search for Freedom and Democracy,* ed. Asafa Jalata, (Lawrenceville: The Red Sea Press, 1998), pp. 125–152; A. Jalata, "The Struggle for Knowledge: The Case of Emergent Oromo Studies," *The African Studies Review,* vol. 39, no. 2 (September, 1996), pp. 95–123; John Sorenson, "Ethiopian Discourse and Oromo Nationalism," in *Oromo Nationalism and the Ethiopian Discourse,* pp. 223–252; "Ethiopia: Federal Sham," *The Economist,* August 16, 1997, p. 36.

3. V. Y. Mudimbe, *The Invention of Africa: Gnosis, Philosophy, and the Order of Knowledge* (Bloomington: Indiana University Press, 1988), p. 16.

4. See, for example, William I. Robinson, "Global Capitalism and the Oromo Liberation Struggle: Theoretical Notes on U.S. Policy Towards the Ethiopian Empire," *The Journal of Oromo Studies,* vol. 4, nos. 1 and 2 (July 1997), pp. 1–46; Bonnie K. Holcomb, "The Tale of Two Democracies: The Encounter Between U.S.-Sponsored Ethiopian 'Democracy' and Indigenous Oromo Democratic Forms," *The Journal of Oromo Studies,* vol. 4, nos. 1 and 2 (July 1997), pp. 47–82; Sisai Ibssa, "The Ideological Foundations of Current U.S. Foreign Policy: the 'Promotion of Democracy' and its Impact on the Oromo National Movement," *The Journal of Oromo Studies,* vol. 5, nos. 1 and 2 (July 1998), pp. 1–34.

5. See Asafa Jalata, "U.S.-Sponsored Ethiopian 'Democracy' and State Terrorism," in *Crisis and Terror in the Horn of Africa,* ed. Pietro Toggia, Pat Lauderdale, and Abebe Zegeye (Dartmouth, Burlington: Ashgate, 2000).

6. Douglas Hellinger, "U.S. Assistance to Africa: No Room for Democracy," *TransAfrica Forum,* vol. 9, no. 2 (Summer 1992), p. 80.

7. For the connection between racism in U.S. domestic and foreign policies, see Gerald Horne, "Race for the Globe: U.S. Foreign Policy and racial Interests," *Impacts of Racism on White Americans,* pp. 88–112.

8. See Asafa Jalata, *Oromia and Ethiopia: State Formation and Ethnonational Conflict, 1868-1992* (Boulder: Lynne Rienner Publishers, 1993), pp. 88–99. This book argues that the Haile Selassie regime was corrupt and oppressive.

9. See Asafa Jalata, ibid.; Bonnie K. Holcomb and Sisai Ibssa, *The Invention of Ethiopia* (Trenton: N.J.: The Red Sea Press, 1990).

10. The policy of the Soviet Union was also racist toward the Oromo people. It supported the Ethiopian colonizing structure and suppressed the Oromo struggle for self-determination and democracy almost for two decades.

11. See Asafa Jalata, *Oromia and Ethiopia,* pp. 178–181.

12. Agency France Press notes that the United States "backed the Tigre People's Liberation Front (TPLF) for several years in their struggle against Lieutenant-Colonel Mengistu's regime and it was on American advice that the TPLF became the EPRDF, though former Tigrean guerrillas are still dominant in the government." AFP (Agency France Press), "Ethiopia-Politics," Nairobi, June 24, 1992.

13. As the leader of TPLF/EPRDF, "Meles had strong CIA support even when he was known for his Marxist belief (s). . . . 'He dropped it in exchange for US support and military power.'" *The Oromia Support Group,* September 1994, p. 6.

14. Paul Henze, *Rebels and Separatists in Ethiopia: Regional Resistance to a Marxist Regime,* (Prepared for the office of the Under Secretary of Defense for Policy), (Santa Monica: The Rand Corporation, 1985), p. 74.

15. Ibid., p. 65.

16. Ibid., p. 74.

17. Ibid.

18. Ibid., p. 65.

19. For details, see Leenco Lata, "The Making and Unmaking of Ethiopia's Transitional Charter," in *Oromo Nationalism and the Ethiopian Discourse,* ed. Asafa Jalata, pp. 51–77.

20. See William I. Robinson, op. cit.; Bonnie K. Holcomb, op. cit.

21. George E. Moose, "Testimony of Assistant Secretary of State Before the House Subcommittee on Ethiopia," July 27, 1994.

22. For example, see Susan Rice, "Statement before the Subcommittees on Africa and on International Operations and Human Rights of the House International Relations Committee," Washington, D.C., July 29, 1998.

23. Secretary of State Madeleine K. Albright, "Departure Remarks Ababa, Ethiopia, December 10, 1997, as released by the Office of the U.S. Department of State, http://secretary.state.gov/www/statements/971210.html., p. 1.

24. Michael Sealy, "Creating a Partnership: The United States and the Black World," *TransAfrica Forum,* vol. 9, no. 4, Special Issue (1993) p. 38.

25. See Asafa Jalata, "U.S.-Sponsored Ethiopian 'Democracy' and State Terrorism"; William Robinson, op. cit. Bonnie K. Holcomb, op. cit.

26. Interview with Muhammed Abbas in Knoxville, on May 25 and 27, 1998; see also A. Jalata, "U.S.-Sponsored Ethiopian 'Democracy' and State Terrorism"; see also Ibssa Gutama, "Ethiopia: The Transition to Ethnic Dictatorship under the Guise of Democracy," Paper delivered at Fortieth Annual Meeting of the African Studies Association, Columbus, Ohio, November. 13–16, 1997.

27. Interview with Muhammed Abbas; A. Jalata, "U.S.-Sponsored Ethiopian 'Democracy.'"

28. According to Fanon, "In the colonies it is the policeman and the soldier who are the official instituted go-betweens, the spokesman of the settler and his rule of oppression. . . . By their immediate presence and their frequent and direct action, they maintain contact with the native and advise him by means of rifle-butts and napalm not to budge. It is obvious here that the agents of government speak the language of pure force." Frantz Fanon, *The Wretched of the Earth* (New York: Grove Press, 1966), p. 31.

29. See A. Jalata, *Oromia and Ethiopia,* pp. 178–186.

30. See Ibssa Gutama, "The Transition to Ethnic Dictatorship."

31. Theodore M. Vestal, "Deficit of Democracy in the Transitional Government of Ethiopia since 1991," Oklahoma State University, 1994, p. 19

32. Interview with Muhammed Abbas.

33. Interview with Gadisa Bula in Knoxville on May 22, 1998.

34. History shows that in all colonized populations, there have been marginalized individuals who participated in the projects of their colonizers. For further discussion, see Clovis E. Semmes, *Cultural Hegemony and African American Development* (Westport, Conn.: Praeger, 1992), p. 6; Luana Ross, *Inventing the Savage: The Social Construction of Native American Criminality* (Austin: University Press of Texas Press, 1998).

35. Luana Ross, ibid., pp. 11–12.

36. *Maxanne* is an Oromo concept that explains the attachment of something to something else since it cannot exist by itself; here this concept indicates that the OPDO is an organization that is attached to the Tigrayan-led EPRDF. Hence, it does not have an independent life and it serves mainly the interests of the enemies of Oromos.

37. Frantz Fanon, op. cit.

38. *Oromia Support Group,* "Urgent Action-November 1997," p. 1.

39. For example, see Bonnie K. Holcomb, op. cit.; Asafa Jalata, "The Cultural Roots of Oromo Nationalism," in *Oromo Nationalism and the Ethiopian Discourse,* pp. 27–49.

40. See Immanuel Wallerstein, *The Capitalist World-Economy* (Cambridge: Cambridge University Press, 1980); Walter Rodney, *How Europe Underdeveloped Africa* (Washington, D. C.: Howard University Press, 1972); Nathan Irvin Huggins, *Black Odyssey* (New York: Vintage Books, 1977); Stanley M. Elkins, *Slavery* (Chicago: The University of Chicago Press, 1968).

41. See David R. Roediger, *The Wages of Whiteness: Race and the Making of the American Working Class* (London: Verso, 1991).

42. Ibid.

43. Ibid.

44. Bobby Wright and William G. Tierney, "American Indians in Higher Education: A History of Cultural Conflict," B. Wright and W. G. Tierney, eds. In *Sources: Notable Selections in Race and Ethnicity* (Guilford, Conn.: Dushkin/McGraw-Hill), p. 199.

45. Quoted in Michael Hunt, *Ideology and U.S. Foreign Policy* (New Haven: Yale University Press, 1987), p. 55.

46. Luana Ross, op. cit., p. 266.

47. See Asafa Jalata, "African American Nationalism, Development, and Afrocentricity: Implications for the Twenty-First Century," in *Molefi Kete Asante and Afrocentricity: In Praise and in Criticism,* ed. Dhyana Ziegler, (Nashville: Winston-Derek, 1995)

48. Fishman states that African Americans "were denied [freedom] by a rapacious colonial system of mercantile capitalism, which relied on the brutalities of the primitive accumulation of wealth backed up by ruthless armed action. This wealth played a strategic role in the amassing of capital for the rise of industrial capitalism." George Fishman, *The African American Struggle for Freedom and Equality* (New York: Garland, 1997), p. 3.

49. Michael Hunt, *Ideology and U.S. Foreign Policy,* pp. 52–52.

50. Robert Staples, op. cit.

51. Ibid., p. 161.

52. Michael Hunt, ibid., p. 52.

53. The African American peoplehood was mainly formed from the melting pot of various African ethnonational groups, such as Yorubas, Akans, Ibos, Angolas, and others who experienced a common horror of slavery in the United States. The name *Negro* was used by the Portuguese slavers in the fifteenth century. Monges asserts that Gomes Eaannes Azurara, in the *Chronicle of the Discovery and Conquest of Guinea* (1453), initially used this the name. Azurara mentions how one Portuguese "passed the land of the Moors and arrived in the land of blacks, that is called Guinea. But when the *negroes* saw that those in the ship were men, they [attempted to flee] . . . but because our men had a better opportunity than before, they captured them, and these were the first to be taken by Christians in their own land" (Monges, 1997, p. 34). Explaining the negative image attached to this name by those who invented and used the name, Asante (1990, p. 132) argues, "There is no ethnic group in Africa that calls itself negro or its language negro. The term is preeminently a creation of the European mind to refer to any African group or people who correspond to a certain negative image of culture. The term is meaningless in reality but has become a useful word for those who would serve a political purpose by the term." Mariam Ma'at-Ka-Re Monges, *Kush: The Jewel of Nubia* (Trenton, N.J.: Africa World Press, 1990).

54. Berkholfer contends that "Native Americans were and are real, but the *Indian* was a White invention." Robert F. Berkholfer, *The White Man's Indian: Images of the American Indian from Columbus to the Present* (New York: Random House, 1978), p. 3.

55. See Asafa Jalata, "The Struggle for Knowledge"; Leenco Lata, "Peculiar Challenge to Oromo Nationalism."

56. John Sorenson, *Imagining Ethiopia* (New Brunswick, N.J.: Rutgers University Press, 1993), p. 60.

57. See for example, Edward Ullendorf, *The Ethiopians* (London: Oxford University Press, 1965), p. 4.

58. See Donald Donham, "Old Abyssinia and the New Ethiopian Empire: Themes in Social History," in *The Southern Marches of Ethiopia,* ed. Donald Donham and Wendy James (Cambridge: Cambridge University Press, 1986), p. 13; John H. Spencer, *Ethiopia at Bay* (Algonac: Mich.: Reference Publications, 1984), pp. 123–124.

59. Alberto Sbacchi, *Legacy of Bitterness: Ethiopia and Fascist Italy, 1935–1941* (Lawrenceville, N.J.: The Red Sea Press, 1997), p. 25.

60. John Sorenson, op. cit., p. 29.

61. Ibid.

62. Quoted in ibid., p. 29; quoted in Harold G. Marcus, "Racist Discourse about Ethiopia and Ethiopians before and after the Battle of Adwa," *Adwa Conference,* AAU, March 1996, p. 5.

63. See Harold G. Marcus, ibid.

64. Racist Euro-American scholars who believe in racial distinctions use these kinds of racist phrases to show the significance of Whitenness and denigrate Blackness in human civilizations. For further discussion, see Mariam Ma'at-Ka-Re Monges, *Kush: The Jewel of Nubia,* pp. 23–29; Harold G. Marcus, "Racist Discourse," op. cit., p. 7.

65. Cited in Harold G. Marcus, "Racist Discourse," op. cit., p. 6.

66. Cedric J. Robinson, "The African Diaspora and the Italo- Ethiopian Crisis," *Race and Class* 2 (1985), p. 53.

67. P. T. W. Baxter, "The Creation and Constitution of Oromo Nationality," in *Ethnicity and Conflict in the Horn of Africa,* ed. Katsuyoshi Fukui and John Markakis (Athens: Ohio University Press, 1994), p. 172.

68. Cultural racism can be defined as the conscious or subconscious conviction of the politically dominant population group that imposes its cultural patterns and practices through its social institutions in an attempt to destroy or suppress the cultural patterns and practices of the colonized and dominated population. For detailed discussion, see Benjamin P. Bowser and Raymond G. Hunt, ed. *Impacts of Racism on White Americans.*

69. For example see, Mariam Ma'at-Ka-Re Monges, op. cit.; Molefi K. Asante, op. cit.; Martin Bernal, *Black Athena: The Afroasiatic Roots of Classical Civilization, vol. I. The Fabrication of Ancient Greece, 1785–1985* (New Brunswick, N.J.: Rutgers University Press, 1987).

70. P. T. W. Baxter, op. cit., p. 172.

71. John Sorenson, "Ethiopian Discourse and Oromo Nationalism," in *Oromo Nationalism and the Ethiopian Discourse,* ed. Asafa Jalata, pp. 233–234.

72. *Habasha* elites several times attempted to use the African diaspora for their economic and political interests by capitalizing on the emotion they had for the name Ethiopia. See for example, William R. Scott, *The Sons of Sheba's Race: African-Americans and the Italo-Ethiopian War, 1935–1941* (Bloomington: Indiana University Press, 1993); Joseph Harris, "Race and Misperceptions in the Origins of United States-Ethiopian Relations," *TransAfrica Forum,* vol. 3, no. 2 (Winter 1986), pp. 9–23.

73. William R. Scott, ibid., p. 26.

74. Edward Ullendorff, *The Ethiopians,* pp. 76 and 73 respectively.

75. See for example, John Sorenson, "Ethiopian Discourse"; Jordan Gebre-Medhin, *Peasants and Nationalism in Eritrea* (Trenton, N.J.: The Red Sea Press, 1989).

76. John Sorenson, ibid., p. 234.

77. See W. C. Harris, *The Highlands of Ethiopia* (Philadelphia: T. B. Peterson, 1844), vol. 3, pp. 72–73; M. de Almeida, "History of Ethiopia," in *Some Records of Ethiopia 1593-1646,* trans. and ed. C. F. Beckingham and G. W. B Huntingford (London: Hakluyt Society, 1954), pp. 111–139.

78. See Abba Bahrey, "History of the Galla," in *Some Records of Ethiopia,* ibid.; James Bruce, *Travels in Abyssinia and Nubia 1768–1773* (Edinburgh: Adam and Charles Black, 1973), p. 86; Edward Ullendorf, *The Ethiopians,* p. 76; Harold G. Marcus, *A History of Ethiopia* (Berkeley: University of California Press, 1994), p. 4.

79. See L. Fargo, *Abyssinia on the Eve* (London: Putnam, 1935), p. 45; C. F. Rey, *The Real Abyssinia* (New York: Negro Universities Press, 1969), p. 47.

80. See Harold G. Marcus, op. cit., p. xii; Edward Ullendorf, op. cit.; Christopher Clapham, *Haile Selassie's Government* (New York: Praeger, 1969), p. 81; Patrick Gilkes, *The Dying Lion: Feudalism and Modernization in Ethiopia* (London: St. Martin's Press, 1975), pp. 204 and 206.

81. See for example, Margery Perham, *The Government of Ethiopia,* 2nd ed. (London: Faber & Faber, 1969), p. 377; Christopher Clapham, *Haile Selassie's Government,* p. 81; C. Clapham, "Ethnicity and the National Question in Ethiopia," in *Conflict and Peace in the Horn of Africa,* ed. Peter Woodward and M. Forsyth Brookfield (Dartmouth: Vermont, 1994); Donald Levine, *Greater Ethiopia* (Chicago: University of Chicago Press, 1994); Gebru Tareke, *Ethiopia: Power and Protest* (New York: Cambridge University Press, 1991).

82. For further discussion, see Donald Donham and W. James, eds., *The Southern Marches of Imperial Ethiopia* (Cambridge: Cambridge University Press, 1986).

83. Alberto Sbacchi, *Legacy of Bitterness,* p. 22.

84. William R. Scott, *The Sons of Sheba's Race,* p. xv.

85. John Sorenson, "Ethiopian Discourse," p. 232.

86. Quoted in Leenco Lata, "Peculiar Challenge to Oromo Nationalism," p. 143.

87. Quoted in Teshale Tibebu, *The Making of Modern Ethiopia 1896–1974* (Lawrenceville, N.J.: The Red Sea Press, 1995), p. 44.

88. In all racist societies, these prejudices and stereotypes have been reproduced and disseminated to perpetuate racism. For further understanding of the roles of these institutions, see Adalberto Aguirre, Jr. and David V. Baker, eds. *Sources: Notable Selections in Race and Ethnicity,* 2nd ed. (Guilford, Connecticut: Dushkin/McGraw-Hill, 1998), pp. 189–310.

89. Richard Delgado, "Words That Wound," in *Sources,* p. 346.

90. See Leenco Lata, "Peculiar Challenge to Oromo Nationalism," pp. 139–144.

91. See for example, Teklu Gerbee, "The Geda Militarism and Oromo Expansion," *Ethiopian Review,* October 1993, p. 50.

92. Leenco Lata, op. cit., p. 135.

93. A. Jalata, "U.S.-Sponsored Ethiopian 'Democracy' and State Terrorism."

94. Leenco Lata, op. cit.

95. Quoted in Harold G. Marcus, "Racist Discourse," p. 7.

96. Bonnie K. Holcomb and Sisai Ibssa, *The Invention of Ethiopia* (Trenton, N.J.: The Red Sea Press, 1990), p. 1.

97. Quoted in ibid., p. 8.

98. Quoted in ibid., p. 141.

99. Ibid., pp. 176.

100. Quoted in ibid.

101. Ibid., pp. 171–279; Asafa Jalata, *Oromia and Ethiopia.*

102. Bonnie K. Holcomb and Sisai Ibssa, ibid., p. 111.

103. Ibid., p. 143.

104. For detailed discussion, see ibid., pp. 143–144; A. Jalata, op. cit.; Gemetchu Megerssa, "The Oromo and the Ethiopian State Ideology in a Historical Perspective," *Papers of the 8th International Conference of Ethiopian Studies, Kyoto,* December 12–17, 1997, vol. II, pp. 479–485.

105. Donald Levine, op. cit., p. 16.

106. Bonnie K Holcomb and Sisai Ibssa, op. cit., p. 176.

107. Evelyn Waugh, *Waugh in Abyssinia* (Harmondsworth, Middlesex; Penguin Books, 1985), p. 16.

108. *U.S. State Department: Country Report on Human Rights,* 1993, 1994, 1995, and 1997.

109. Stevens Trucker, "Ethiopia's Democratic Transition Moves Forward Amid Challenges," *African Voices: A Newsletter on Democracy and Governance in Africa,* Winter/Spring, 1997, p. 1.

110. Terrence Lyons, "Closing the Transition: The May 1995 Elections in Ethiopia," *The Journal of Modern African Studies,* vol. 34, no.1, (1996), p. 142.

111. Ibid.

112. A. Jalata, "U.S.-Sponsored Ethiopian 'Democracy.'"

113. Madeleine K. Albright, op. cit.

114. Secretary of State Madeleine K. Albright, "Remarks at the Entoto Civic Education Club, Entoto Secondary School," December 9, 1997, Addis Ababa, Ethiopia, http://secretary.state.gov/www/statements/971209a.html., p.3.

115. See *Human Rights Watch/Africa 1997;* Amnesty International, *Ethiopia: Accountability Past and Present–Human rights in transition, 1995, 1996, and 1997; New African,* "Ethiopia, Around Africa: Persecution of Oromos Continues," June 1998, pp. 1–3; "Terror Against Oromos," *oct97-ed.htm at www.mdx.ac.uk,* pp. 1–3.

116. "Ethiopia: Federal Sham," *The Economist,* August 16, 1997, p. 36.

117. Susan E. Rice, "A New Partnership for the 21st Century," *ASA News,* vol. 31, no. 1 (January/March 1998), p. 7–9.

118. A. Jalata, op. cit.

119. Susan E. Rice, op. cit.

120. Secretary of State Madeleine K. Albright, "Address on U.S. Policy Toward Africa," George Mason University, Fairfax, Virginia, March 19, 1998, *http://secretary.state.gov/www/* statements/980319.html., p. 3.

121. "Clinton Pledges Help for Democracy in Africa," *African Voices* (Summer/Fall 1998), p. 6.

122. Quoted in Michael H. Hunt, op. cit., pp. 56–57.

123. Quoted in Michael H. Hunt, op. cit., p. 53.

124. Marc Baas, "Minutes of Briefing to American community in Addis Ababa," November 14, 1991.

125. Michael H. Hunt.

126. See *Hizbawi Adera,* an EPRDF political pamphlet, Tahisas–Yekatit, 1989 Ethiopian Calendar, (1997).

127. *Oromia Support Group,* "Oromo Refugees Threatened with Refoulement: Summary Press Release," no. 24, August–September 1998, pp. 1–3.

128. Ibid.

129. *Human Rights Watch/World Report 1999: Ethiopia: The Role of the International Community, http://www.hrw.org/hrw/worldreport99/africa/ethiopia3. html,* p. 3.

130. See A. Jalata, "The Struggle for Knowledge," pp. 95–123.

Chapter V

1. A. Jalata, "The Impact of a Racist U.S. Foreign Policy on the Oromo National Struggle," *The Journal of Oromo Studies,* vol. 6, nos. 1 and 2, (1999), pp. 49–89; A. Jalata, "Oromo Nationalism in the New Global Context," *The Journal of Oromo Studies,* vol. 4, nos. 1 and 2 (1997), pp. 83–114; A. Jalata, ed., *Oromo Nationalism and the Ethiopian Discourse: The Search for Freedom and Democracy* (Lawrenceville, N.J.: The Red Sea Press, 1998).

2. J. H. Clarke, "African Cultural Continuity and Slave Revolts in the New World, Part One and Part Two," *The Black Scholar,* vol. 8, no. 1 (September 1976), pp. 41–49, and vol. 8, no. 2 (October-November), pp. 2–9, p. 41.

3. F. C. Colston, "The Ideology of Black Power: An Assessment," *The Western Journal of Black Studies,* vol. 3, no. 4 (1976), pp. 233–243.

4. H. Aptheker, "Additional Data on American Maroons," *Journal of Negro History*, vol. 32 (1974), pp. 452–460; H. Aptheker, "Maroons within the Present Limits of the United States," in *Maroon Societies: Rebel Slave Communities in the Americas*, ed. Richard Price, 2nd ed. (Baltimore: John Hopkins, 1979).

5. St. C. Drake, "The American Negro: Relation to Africa," *American Negro Leadership Conference on Africa* (Washington, D.C., January 1967), pp. 15–30.

6. Asante notes that "[a]s products of African amalgamation (Hausa, Asante, Yoruba, Ewe, Ibo, Wolof, Mandingo, Congo, and a hundred other ethnic groups) and the American crucible we have become a new people unknown prior to the 15th century, our perspectives, attitudes, and experiences are peculiarly fitted to change the frame of reference for African people." M. K. Asante, *Afrocentricity* (Trenton, N.J.: The Africa World Press, 1989), p. 59.

7. E. B. Bethel, *The Roots of African-American Identity: Memory and History in Antebellum Free Communities* (New York: St. Martin's Press, 1999).

8. W. J. Moses, *Classical Black Nationalism* (New York: New York University Press, 1996), p. 1.

9. D. McAdam, J. D. McCarthy, and M. N. Zald, "Social Movements," in *Handbook of Sociology*, ed. Neil J. Smelser (Newbury Park: Sage, 1998), p. 697.

10. D. McAdam, "The Political Process Model," in *Social Movements: Perspectives and Issues*, eds. Steven M. Buechler and F. Kurt Clykes, Jr. (Mountain View, Calif.: Mayfield Publishing, 1997), p. 178.

11. E. B. Bethel, *Roots of African-American Identity*, p. 96.

12. Ibid., p. 172.

13. Quoted in ibid., p. 78.

14. Ibid.

15. Ibid., pp. 83–84.

16. Ibid., pp. 92–93.

17. Ibid., p. 168.

18. Ibid.

19. Ibid., p. 194.

20. Ibid., p. 25.

21. Ibid., p. 19.

22. Ibid., p. 22.

23. M. L. Dillon, *The Abolitionists: The Growth of Dissenting Minority* (DeKalb: Northern Illinois University Press, 1974), p. xiii.

24. C. Chase-Dunn, "The Development of Core Capitalism in the Antebellum United States: Tariff Politics and Class Struggle in an Upwardly Mobile Semiperiphery," in *Studies of the Modern World-System*, ed. A. Bergesen (Tucson: University of Arizona Press, 1980), pp. 189–230.

25. Ibid., p. 221.

26. Ibid.

27. Ibid., pp. 222–223.

28. Ibid., p. 223.

29. M. L. Dillion, *The Abolitionists: The Growth of Dissenting Minority* (DeKalb: Northern Illinois University Press, 1974), p. 254.

30. Ibid., pp. 254–255.

31. Ibid., p. 256; C. Chase-Dunn, op. cit., p. 222.

32. J. C. Jenkins and M. Eckert, "Channeling Black Insurgency: Elite Patronage and Professional Social Movement Organizations in the Development of the Black Movement," *The American Sociological Review*, 51 (1986), pp. 812–815.

33. D. McAdam, J. D. McCarthy, and M. N. Zald, op. cit., p. 711.

34. Ibid., p. 709.

35. Ibid., p. 703.

36. A. Jalata, "Oromo Nationalism in the New Global Context."
37. A. Jalata, *Oromia and Ethiopia,* pp. 152–153.
38. A. Jalata, ibid., p. 153.
39. M. Hassen, "The Macha-Tulama Association 1963–1967 and the Development of Oromo Nationalism," in A. Jalata, ed., *Oromo Nationalism and the Ethiopian Discourse* (Lawrenceville, N.J.: The Red Sea Press, 1998), p. 194.
40. Ibid., p. 193.
41. Ibid., p. 189.
42. See A. Jalata, *Oromia and Ethiopia.*
43. Anthony D. Smith, "Nationalism, Ethnic Separatism and Intelligentsia," in *National Separatism,* ed. C. H. Williams (Vancouver: University of British Columbia Press, 1982), p. 31.
44. See A. Jalata, ed., *Oromo Nationalism and the Ethiopian Discourse.*
45. O. Zoga, *Gezatena Gezot and Macha-Tulama Association* (Addis Ababa, unknown publisher, 1993), pp. 75–77.
46. M. Hassen, op. cit., p. 183.
47. Quoted in op. cit., pp. 205–206.
48. O. Zoga, op. cit., pp. 118–133.
49. C. Greetz, "Primordial and Civic Ties," in *Nationalism,* eds. J. Hutchinson and A. D. Smith (Oxford: Oxford University Press, 1994), p. 30.
50. A. P. Wood, "Rural Development and National Integration in Ethiopia," *Review of African Political Economy,* 26 (1983), p. 516.
51. P. Gilkes, *The Dying Lion: Feudalism and Modernization in Ethiopia* (New York: St. Martin's Press, 1975), pp. 217–218.
52. M. Hassen, op. cit., p. 196.
53. B. K. Holcomb and Sisai Ibssa, *The Invention of Ethiopia: The Making of a Dependent Colonial State in Northeast Africa* (Trenton, N.J.: The Red Sea Press, 1990), p. 299.
54. A. Jalata, "Sheik Hussein Suura and the Oromo National Struggle," *The Oromo Commentary,* vol. 4, no. 1 (1994), pp. 5–7.
55. See *The Political Program of the Oromo Liberation Front,* Finfinne, 1976; OLF, "Statement on the Current State of the Oromo People's Struggle and the Situation in the Horn of Africa," June 1996.
56. See Sue Pollock, "Politics and Conflict: Participation and Self-Determination," in *Ethiopia: Conquest and the Quest for Freedom and Democracy,* eds. Seyoum Y. Hameso, T. Trueman and T. E. Erena (London: TSC Publications, 1997), pp. 81–110; T. Trueman, "Democracy or Dictatorship?," in *Ethiopia: Conquest and the Quest,* pp. 11- 150.
57. See *Reuters Business Briefing,* July 5, 1994; *Reuters,* May 15, 1995.
58. Ibid.; J. Gibbs, "Conceptualization of Terrorism," *The American Sociological Review,* 54 (June 1989), pp. 329–340.
59. See A. Oliverio, "The State of Injustice: The Politics of Terrorism and the Production of Order," *International Journal of Comparative Sociology,* vol. 38, nos. 1 and 2 (June 1997), pp. 48–63.
60. *The Oromia Support Group,* November 1997, p. 1.
61. See *Seifa Nabalbal,* no. 94, Nov. 8, 1996; *Urjii* 1994, 1995, 1996 and 1997 series; *Amnesty International,* 1995 and 1996; *Oromia Support Group,* 1996 and 1997 series.
62. See *Oromia Support Group,* 1997.
63. A. Jalata, "Oromo Nationalism in the New Global Context."
64. See *Amnesty International,* 1995; *Human Rights Watch/Africa,* 1997; *Survival International,* 1995; *Oromia Support Group,*1997 series.
65. See B. Fossati, L. Namarra, and Peter Niggli, *The New Rulers of Ethiopia and the Persecution of the Oromo: Reports from the Oromo Refugees in Djibouti,* Dokumentation, Evangelischer Pressedienst Frankfurt am Main, 1996.

66. See *U.S. Department of State, 1993.*
67. B. Fossati, et al., op. cit.
68. See *Hizbawi Adera,* Tahisas to Yekatit, 1989 E.C. This paper of the Tigrayan ruling roup only circulates among its members; accidentally the copy of this paper was obtained by Oromos.
69. T. Dibaba, "Humanity Forsaken: The Case of the Oromo Relief Association (ORA) in the Horn of Africa," paper presented to the Oromo Studies Association Annual Meeting at the University of Minnesota, 1997, p. 7.
70. Ibid.
71. See *Oromia Support Group,* August/September 1996.
72. B. Fossati, et al., op. cit., p. 3.
73. T. Dibaba, op. cit.
74. B. Fossati, et al., op. cit.
75. Quoted in Fossati, Namarra, and Niggli, p.10.
76. Ibid., p. 44.
77. Ibid., p. 36.
78. Quoted in Richard A. Couto, "Narrative, Free Space, Political Leadership in Social Movements," in *The Journal of Politics,* vol. 55, no. 1 (February 1993), p. 59.
79. See for details, Asafa Jalata, *Oromia and Ethiopia,* pp. 62–73.
80. Bonnie K. Holcomb, "Oromo in the World Community," *The Journal of Oromo Studies,* vol. 6, nos. 1 and 2 (July 1999), p. 5.
81. Amilcar Cabral, *Return to the Source* (New York: Monthly Review Press, 1973), p. 61.
82. Elizabeth Rauh Bethel, *The Roots of African-American Identity: Memory and History in Antebellum Free Communities* (New York: St. Martin's Press, 1999), p. 78.
83. Ibid., pp. 54–55.
84. Richard A. Couto, "Narrative, Free Space, Political Leadership in Social Movement," p. 60.
85. Lawrence W. Levine, *Black Culture and Black Consciousness* (New York: Oxford University Press, 1978), p. xi.
86. Ibid.
87. Addisu Tolesa, *Geerarsa Folksongs as the Oromo National Literature* (Lewiston, New York: The Edwin Mellen Press, 1990).
88. Quoted in Anthony D. Smith, *The Ethnic Revival* (New York: Cambridge University Press, 1981), p. viii.
89. Quoted in Harold R. Isaacs, *Idols of the Tribe: Group Identity and Political Change* (Cambridge, Mass.: Harvard University Press, 1975), p. 115.
90. Elizabeth Rauh Bethel, *The Roots of African-American Identity,* p. 26.
91. Ibid., p. 27.
92. Anthony D. Smith, *National Identity* (Reno, Las Vegas: University of Nevada Press, 1991), p. 71.
93. Asafa Jalata, "The Cultural Roots of Oromo Nationalism," in *Oromo Nationalism and the Ethiopian Discourse,* pp. 27–49.
94. Ben Barber, "Coming Back to Life: Will the Oromos' Cultural Revival Split Ethiopia?" *Culture-Crossroads,* 1994, p. 1.
95. A. Jalata, *Oromia and Ethiopia.*
96. C. H. Enloe, "Ethnicity, the State, and the International Order," *in The Primordial Challenge: Ethnicity in the Contemporary World,* ed. J. F. Stack, Jr. (New York: Greenwood Press, 1986), p. 39.
97. See A. Jalata, "The Struggle For Knowledge: The Case of Emergent Oromo Studies," *The African Studies Review,* 39 (September 1996), pp. 95–123; L. Lata, "Peculiar Challenges to Oromo Nationalism," *Oromo Nationalism and the Ethiopian Discourse,* pp. 125–152.

98. D. McAdam, J. D. McCarthy, and M. N. Zald, op. cit., p. 716.

99. A. Jalata, "The Impact of a Racist U.S. Foreign Policy on the Oromo National Struggle."

100. D. McAdam, et al., op. cit., p. 709.

101. See D. Baasa, "Oromo Students in the Higher Education System: An Outline," in *Oromo of Fifinne University, 1993–1994 Graduates,* Finfinne (Addis Ababa), no name of publisher, 1994, p. 30.

102. B. K. Holcomb and Sisai Ibssa, *The Invention of Ethiopia,* p. 135.

103. A. Jalata, *Oromia and Ethiopia,* pp. 67–68; K. Schmitt, "Machuba—An Oromo Slave-Girl Who Won the Heart of a German Prince," *The Oromo Commentary,* vol. 4, no. 2 (1994), pp. 32–34; M. Bulcha, "Religion, the Slave Trade and the Creation of the Ethiopian Empire," *The Oromo Commentary,* vol. 7, no. 2 (1997), pp. 19–33.

104. A. Jalata, *Oromia and Ethiopia,* p. 67.

105. R. Pankhurst, *Economic History of Ethiopia 1800–1935* (Addis Ababa, 1968), p. 75; H. Marcus, *The Life and Times of Menelik II, Ethiopia, 1844–1913* (Oxford: Clarendon, 1975), p. 73.

106. M. Hassen, "The Growth of Written Oromo Literature," *Proceedings of the International Conference on Resource Mobilization for the Liberation of Oromia,* University of Toronto, Ontario, Canada, July 31-August 1, 1993, p. 77.

107. A. Jalata, *Oromia and Ethiopia,* pp. 99–100.

108. D. McAdam, "The Political Process Model," p. 178.

109. D. McAdam, J. D. McCarthy, and M. N. Zald, pp. 49–66.

110. J. D. McCarthy, "Pro-Life and Pro-Choice Mobilization."

111. Ibid., p. 711.

112. J. C. Jenkins and M. Eckert, "Channeling Black Insurgency," pp. 815–816.

113. M. Hassen, "The Macha-Tulama Association," pp. 203–204.

114. W. A. Shack, "Book Review of *The Oromo of Ethiopia: A History 1570–1860,*" *American Ethnologist,* vol. 21, no. 3 (1994), pp. 642–643.

115. See A. Jalata, *Oromia and Ethiopia,* pp. 253–292.

116. J. C. Jenkins and M. Eckert, "Channeling Black Insurgency," pp. 816–817.

117. See Lois Benjamin, *The Black Elite: Facing the Color Line in the Twilight of the Twentieth Century* (Chicago: Nelson-Hall, 1991).

118. Ibid.

119. M. Marable, *Beyond Black and White: Transforming African-American Politics* (London: Verso, 1995), p. 89.

120. Ibid., p. 130.

121. D. McAdam, "The Political Process Model," p. 177.

122. S. M. Buechler, "Beyond Resource Mobilization: Emerging Trends in Social Movement Theory," *The Sociological Quarterly,* vol. 34, no. 2 (1993), p. 228.

123. Ibid.

124. Ibid.

125. Ibid., p. 229.

Chapter VI

1. Anthony Giddens, *New Rules of Sociological Method,* 2nd ed. (Oxford: Polity Press, 1993), pp. 168–169.

2. I. Wallerstein, "Social Science and the Quest for a Just Society," *The American Journal of Sociology,* vol. 102, no. 5 (1997), pp. 1255.

3. Quoted in M. Marable, *Beyond Black and White: Transforming African-American Politics* (London: Verso, 1995), pp. 81–82.

4. See for example, S. M. Lyman, "The Race Question and Liberalism: Casuistries in American Constitutional Law," *The International Journal of Politics, Culture, and Society,* vol. 5, no. 2 (1991), p. 233.

5. Ibid.

6. Gunnar Myrdal, *An American Dilemma* (New York: Harper & Row, 1944), p. 1016.

7. See W. R. Edwards, "Mediated Inequality: The Role of Governmental, Business, and Scientific Elites in Public Education," Ph.D. dissertation, University of Tennessee at Knoxville, 1998, pp. 97–98.

8. M. L. Dudziak, "Desegregation as a Cold War Imperative," *The Stanford Law Review,* 41 (1988), p. 111.

9. W. R. Edwards, op. cit., p. 100.

10. M. L. Dudziak, op. cit., p. 62.

11. G. Horne, *Black and Red: W.E.B. Du Bois and the Afro-American Response to the Cold War, 1944–1963* (New York: State University of New York Press, 1986), p. 227.

12. W. R. Edwards, op. cit., p. 101.

13. Ibid., p. 108.

14. According to Winant, "The overt *domination* of the Jim Crow era thus gave way to the racial *hegemony* of the post-civil rights period, as the state both adopted and demonstrated the limits of the movement." Howard Winant, *Racial Conditions: Politics, Theory, Comparisons* (Minneapolis: The University of Minnesota Press, 1994), p. 126.

15. M. Marable, op. cit., p. 21.

16. Ibid., p. 87.

18. Ibid., p. 81.

19. D. Schwartzman, *Black Unemployment: Part of Unskilled Unemployment* (Westport, Conn.: Greenwood Press, 1997), p. 2.

20. See the Sentencing Project, *New Justice Department Figures Mark a Quarter Century of Prison Building,* www.sproject.com. 1998; see also Andrew Austin, "The Era of Reaction: Class, Racial Caste, and the Structure of Crime and Punishment in the Post WWII Era," unpublished manuscript, the University of Tennessee, Department of Sociology, August 13, 1999.

21. N. Chomsky, *Year 501: The Conquest Continues* (Boston: South End Press, 1993), p. 275.

22. R. J. Herinstein and C. Murray, *The Bell Curve: Intelligence and Class Structure in American Life* (New York: The Free Press, 1994).

23. R. Allen, *Reluctant Reformers: Racism and Social Reform Movements in the United States* (Washington, D.C.: Howard University Press, 1983), p. 327.

24. See C. Murray, *Losing Ground: American Social Policy, 1950–1980* (New York: Basic Books, 1984); T. Sowell, *Civil Rights: Rhetoric or Reality?* (New York: William Morrow, 1984); S. Steele, *The Content of Our Character: A New Vision of Race in America* (New York: Harper Collins, 1990); J. G. Conti and B. Stetson, *Challenging the Civil Rights Establishment: Profiles of a New Black Vanguard* (Westport, Conn.: Praeger, 1993).

25. T. Sowell, *Civil Rights.*

26. S. Steele, *Content of Our Character,* p. 66.

27. Ibid.

28. M. K. Asante, *Afrocentricity* (Trenton, N.J.: The African World Press, 1989), p. 91.

29. Ibid.

30. M. Marable, op. cit., p. 108.

31. Ibid., p. 101.

32. Ibid., p. 102.

33. Ibid., p. 116.

34. I. Wallerstein, *Historical Capitalism* (London: Verso, 1983), p. 83.

35. Ngugi Wa Thiong'o, *Moving the Centre: The Struggle for Cultural Freedoms* (London: James Currey, 1993), p. 9.

36. D. J. Haraway, *Simians, Cyborgs, and Women: The Reinvention of Nature* (New York: Routledge, 1991), p. 187.

37. Ibid., p. 198.

38. United Nations, Human Development Report for 1999, www.undp.org/hdro/indicators.html.

39. See Sentayehu Dejenie, "The Role of NGOs in Health in Ethiopia," (unpublished paper), International Health Department, Tulane University of school of Public Health and Tropical Medicine, 1998.

40. See World Health Organization, *Ethiopia: Epidemiological Fact Sheet on HIV/AIDS and Sexually Transmitted Diseases,* 1998.

41. Planning and Project Department, Ministry of Health, Ethiopia, *Health and Health Related Indicators,* 1995.

42. The Oromo heroines and heroes who were assassinated by the Tigrayan racist regime include Mohamed Aman, Dr. Temesgen (major in rank), Lama Warqee, Dagaga Baissa, Ebssa Adunya (artist), Kasahun Habte, Yoseph Ayele Batii, Hunduma Kaba, Balcha Tola, Musxafa Idiris, Wako Tola, Terefe Qumbi, Gudisa Anissa, Shamsi Shambo, Zara Shek Bakiri, Sofiya Mohammed, Jara Uddessa, Roba Hanale, Bulti Gurmessa, Alamu Kiisii, Mammee Qasim, Kadir Adam, Hassan Rashid, Surur Ismael, Zahari Ali, Chala Bekele, Tesfaye Nega, Yegazu Edea, Kumala Mirkana, Tesfaye Hundessa, Habib Kadir Gobana, Lamessa Boru, Mohammed Xayib, Jirenya Ayana, and Badhadha Dilgassa.

43. Interview with Mohammed Abbas, May 25, 1998, Knoxville, Tennessee.

44. Ibid.

45. Ibid.

46. Bonnie K. Holcomb, "The Tale of Two Democracies: The Encounter Between U.S.-Sponsored Ethiopian 'Democracy' and Indigenous Oromo Democratic Forms," *The Journal of Oromo Studies,* vol. 4, nos. 1 and 2 (July 1997), pp. 72–73.

47. See for example, Guluma Gemeda, "Political Domination and Exploitation of the Mineral Resources of Oromia: From Menelik to Meles," *The Journal of Oromo Studies,* vol. 5, nos. 1 and 2 (July 1998), pp. 133–154; Gobena Huluka, "Environmental Impacts of Gold Mining in Oromia," *The Journal of Oromo Studies,* vol. 6, 1 and 2 (July 1999), pp. 159–172.

48. Gobena Huluka, ibid., p. 161.

49. Edward Said, "The Politics of Knowledge," in *Race, Identity and Representation in Education,* ed. Cameron McCarthy and Warren Crichlow (New York: Routledge, 1993), p. 310.

50. Frantz Fanon, *The Wretched of the Earth, 2nd ed.* (New York: Grove Press, Inc., 1968), pp. 148–149.

51. Edward Said, "The Politics of Knowledge," pp. 310–311.

52. Asmarom Legesse, *Oromo Democracy: An Indigenous African Political System* (Lawrenceville, N.J.: The Red Sea Press, 2000), after the contents, from his own book written in 1973.

53. Anthony H. Richmond, "Ethnic Nationalism and Post-industrialism," in *Nationalism,* ed. John Hutchinson and Anthony D. Smith (New York: Oxford University Press, 1994), p. 297.

54. Edward Said, op. cit., p. 313.

55. Manning Marable, op. cit., pp. 123–124.

56. Asmarom Legesse, op. cit., p. 30.

References

Abrahams, Roger D. and Szwed, John F. (eds.). 1983. *After Africa*. New Haven, CT: Yale University Press.

AFP (Agency France Press). 1992. "Ethiopia—Politics," Nairobi, June 24.

Africa Confidential. 1997. Vol. 21, no. 21, Oct.

African Voices. 1998. "Clinton Pledges Help for Democracy in Africa," Summer/Fall.

Africa Research Bulletin. 1991. "Ethiopia: Sea Access Granted," July.

Aguirre, Adalberto Jr. and Baker, David B., (eds.). 1998. *Sources: Notable Selections in Race and Ethnicity*. Second Edition. Guilford, CT: Dushkin/ McGraw-Hill.

Albright, Madeleine K. 1997. "Departure Remarks" (as released by the Office of the Spokesman, U.S. Department of State) from Addis Ababa, Ethiopia, Dec. 10. http://secretary.state.gov/www/statements/971210html.

———. 1997. "Remarks at the Entoto Civic Education Club, Entoto Secondary School," from Addis Ababa, Africa. Dec. 9: 3. http://secretary.state.gov/www/statements/971209a.html.

———. 1998. "Address on U.S. Policy Toward Africa," from George Mason University at Fairfax, VA, March 19: 3. http://secretary.state.gov/www/statements/980319.html.

Allen, Robert. 1983. *Reluctant Reformers: Racism and Social Reform Movements in the United States*. Washington, D.C.: Howard University Press.

Almeida, M. de. 1954. "History of Ethiopia," in *Some Records of Ethiopia 1593–1646*. Translated and edited by C. F. Beckingham, G. W. B Huntingford. London: Hakluyt Society, 111–139.

Alter, Peter. 1989. *Nationalism*. Translated by Stuart Amckinnon-Evans. London: Edward Arnold.

America, Richard F. 1993. *Paying the Social Debt: What White America Owes Black America*. Westport, CT: Praeger.

Amnesty International. "Ethiopia: Accountability Past and Present—Human Rights in Transition," 1995, 1996, and 1997 Series.

Anderson, Benedict. 1991. *Imagined Communities: Reflections on the Origin and Spread of Nationalism*. London: Verso.

———. 1994. *Imagined Communities: Reflections of the Origin and Spread of Nationalism*. 2nd ed. London: Verso.

Anderson, Perry. 1974. *Lineage of the Absolutist State*. London: Verso.

Aptheker, Herbert. 1974. "Additional Data on American Maroons," *Journal of Negro History,* October, 32: 452–460.

———. 1979. "Maroons within the Present Limits of the United States," in *Maroon Societies: Rebel Slave Communities in the Americas*. Second edition. Edited by Richard Price. Baltimore: John Hopkins Press.

Aregay, Merid W. 1971. "Southern Ethiopia and the Christian Kingdom, 1508–1708, with Special Reference to the Galla Migrations and Their Consequences." Ph. D. thesis, University of London.

Arnesen, Odd E. 1996. "The Becoming of Place: A Tulama-Oromo Region in Northern Shoa," in *Being and Becoming Oromo: Historical and Anthropological Enquiries*. Edited by P. T. W. Baxter, Jan Hultin, and Alessandro Triulzi. Uppsala: Nordiska Afrikainstitutet, 210–238.

Arrighi, Giovanni, and Hopkins, Terence, and Wallerstein, I. 1989. *Anti-Systemic Movements.* London: Verso.

Asante, Molefi Kete. 1989. *Afrocentricity.* Trenton, NJ: The Africa World Press.

———. 1990. *Kemet, Afrocentricity and Knowledge.* Trenton, NJ: The Africa World Press.

———. "African Elements in African-American English," in *Africanisms in American Culture.* Edited by Joseph E. Holloway. Bloomington: Indiana University Press, 19–33.

Baas, Marc. 1991. "Minutes of briefing to American community in Addis Ababa." (Unpublished).

Baasa, D. 1994. "Oromo Students in the Higher Education System: An Outline," in *Oromo of Fifinne [Addis Ababa] University, 1993–1994 Graduates.* (Magazine). Finfinne (Addis Ababa).

Bahrey, Abba. 1954. "History of the Galla," in *Some Records of Ethiopia 1593–1646.* Translated and edited by C. F. Beckingham and C. W. B. Huntingford. London: Hakluyt Society, 111–139.

Balibar, Etienne and Wallerstein, Immanuel. 1991. *Race, Nation, Class: Ambiguous Identities.* New York: Verso.

Bassi, Marco. 1994. "Gada as an Integrative Factor of Political Organization," in *A River of Blessing: Essays in Honor of Paul Baxter.* Edited by David Brokensha. Syracuse: Maxwell School of Citizenship and Public Affairs of Syracuse University, pp. 15–30.

Barber, Ben. 1994. "Coming Back to Life: Will the Oromos' Cultural Revival Split Ethiopia?" *Culture-Crossroads.* (Magazine), 1–5.

Bartels, Lambert. 1990. *Oromo Religion: Myths and Rites of the Western Oromo of Ethiopia—An Attempt to Understand.* Berlin: Dietrich Reimer Verlag.

Bates, Darrel. 1979. *The Abyssinian Difficulty: The Emperor Theodorus and the Magdala Campaign, 1867–68.* Oxford: Oxford University Press.

Bauer, Dan F. and Hinnant, J. 1980. "Normal and Revolutionary Divination: A Kuhnian Approach to African Traditional Thought," in *Exploration in African Systems of Thought.* Edited by Ivan Karp and C. S. Bird. Washington, D.C.: Smithsonian Institutional Press, 213–236.

Baxter, P. T. W. 1978. "Boran Age-sets and Generation-sets: *Gada,* a Puzzle or a Maze?" in *Age, Generation and Time: Some Features of East African Age Organisations.* Edited by Uri Almagor and Paul Baxter. London: Hurst & Company, 151–182.

———. 1978. "Ethiopia's Unacknowledged Problem: The Oromo," *African Affairs,* 77/ 308: 283–296.

———. 1983. "The Problem of the Oromo or the Problem for the Oromo?" in *Nationalism and Self-Determination in the Horn of Africa.* Edited by I. M. Lewis. London: Ithaca, 129–149.

———. 1990. "Oromo Blessings and Greetings," in *The Creative Communion: African Folk Models of Fertility and the Regeneration of Life.* Edited by A. Jacobson-Widding and W. Van Beek. Uppsala: Acta Universitatis Upsalienis, 235–250.

———. 1994 "Ethnic Boundaries and Development: Speculations of the Oromo Case," *Inventions and Boundaries: Historical and Anthropological Approaches to the Study of Ethnicity and Nationalism.* Edited by Preben Kaarsholm and Jan Hultin. Roskilde, Denmark: Roskilde University, 248–260.

———. 1994 "The Creation and Constitution of Oromo Nationality," *Ethnicity and Conflict in the Horn of Africa.* Edited by Katsuyoshi Fukui and John Markakis. Athens: Ohio University Press, 166–185.

Benjamin, Lois. 1991. *The Black Elite: Facing the Color Line in the Twilight of the Twentieth Century.* Chicago: Nelson-Hall Publishers.

Bereciartu, Gurutz J. 1994. *Decline of the Nation-State.* Translated by W. A. Douglas. Reno, Las Vegas: The University of Nevada Press.

Bergesen, Albert. 1980. "Cycles of Formal Colonial Rule," in *Process of the World System.* Edited by T. Hopkins and I. Wallerstein. Beverly Hills: Sage Publications, 119–126.

Berhe, Kahsay. 1991. The National Movement of Tigray: Myths and Realities. Unpublished manuscript.

Berkholfer, Robert F. 1978. *The White Man's Indian: Images of the American Indian from Columbus to the Present*. New York: Random House.

Berlin, Ira. 1974. *Slaves without Masters: The Free Negro in Antebellum South*. New York: The New Press.

Bernal, Martin. 1987. *Black Athena: The Afroasiatic Roots of Classical Civilization, vol. I. The Fabrication of Ancient Greece, 1785–1985*. New Brunswick, NJ: Rutgers University Press.

Bethel, Elizabeth R. 1999. *The Roots of African-American Identity: Memory and History in Antebellum Free Communities*. New York: St. Martin's Press.

Beyer, Lisa. 1991. "Ethiopia: Rebels Take Charge," *Time*, June 10, 26–28.

Blackhurst, Hector. 1978. "Continuity and Change in the Shoa *Gada* System," in *Age, Generation and Time: Some Features of East African Age Organizations*. Edited by P. T. W. Baxter and Uri Almagor. London: Hurst & Company, 245–267.

———. 1996. "Adopting an Ambiguous Position: Oromo Relationships with Strangers," in *Being and Becoming Oromo: Historical and Anthropological Enquiries*. Edited by Paul Baxter, Jan Hultin, and Alessandro Triulzi. Uppsala: Nordiska Afrikainstituet, 239–250.

Blassingame, John W. 1979. *The Slave Community*. New York: Oxford University Press.

Bloom, Jack M. 1987. *Class, Race, and the Civil Rights Movement*. Bloomington: Indiana University Press.

Blumberg, Rhoda L. 1991. *Civil Rights: The 1960 Freedom Struggle*. Revised edition. Boston: Twayne Publishers.

Bontemps, Arna W. 1972. *The Harlem Renaissance Remembered*. New York: Dodd and Mead.

Bowser, Benjamin P. and Hunt, Raymond G. (eds.). 1996. *Impacts of Racism on White Americans*. Second edition. Thousand Oaks: Sage Publications.

Bracey, John H., Meir, August, and Rudwick, Elliot. 1970. *Black Nationalism*. New York: The Bobbs-Merril Company.

Braukamper, Ulrich. 1980. "Oromo Country of Origin: A Consideration of Hypothesis," in *Proceedings of the Second International Ethiopian Studies*. This paper was edited and published in 1986 in G. Goldenberg and B. Podolsky. *Ethiopian Studies*: Proceedings of the sixth international conference 1980, Rutterdam: A. A. Balkema, 255–40.

———. 1989. "The Sanctuary of Shayky Husayn and the Oromo-Somali Connections in Bale (Ethiopia)," *Frankfurter Afrikanisticsche Blatter*, 1.

Breitman, George (ed.). 1965. *Malcolm X Speaks*. New York: Grove Press.

———. 1967. "Preamble, Statement of the Basic Aims and Objectives of the OAAU," in *The Last Year of Malcolm X: The Evolution of a Revolutionary*. New York: Merit, 105–106.

Breuilly, John. 1985. *Nationalism and the State*. Chicago: University of Chicago Press.

Brotz, H. (ed.). 1992. *African-American Social and Political Thought 1850–1920*. London: Transaction Publishers.

Brown, Letitia W. 1972. *Free Negroes in the District of Columbia, 1790–1846*. New York: Oxford University Press.

Bruce, James. 1973. *Travels in Abyssinia and Nubia 1768–1773*. Edinburgh: Adam and Charles Black.

Brues, Alice M. 1977. *People and Races*. Prospect Heights, IL: Waveland Press.

Budge, Wallis A. 1928. *A History of Ethiopia*. London: Methuen.

Buechler, S. M. 1993. "Beyond Resource Mobilization? Emerging Trends in Social Movement Theory," *The Sociological Quarterly*, 34/2: 217–235.

Bulcha, M. 1993. "Beyond the Oromo-Ethiopian Conflict," *The Journal of Oromo Studies*, 1/ 1: 1–16.

———. 1996. "The Survival and Reconstruction of Oromo National Identity," *Being and Becoming Oromo*. Edited by Paul Baxter, Jan Hultin, and Alessandro Triullzi. Uppsala: Nordiska Afrikainstitutet, 48–66.

———. 1997. "The Politics of Linguistic Homogenization in Ethiopia and the Conflict Over the Status of Afaan Oromoo," *African Affairs*, 325–352.

————. 1997. "Religion, the Slave Trade and the Creation of the Ethiopian Empire," *The Oromo Commentary,* 7/ 2: 19–33.

Cabral, Amilcar. 1969. *Revolution in Guinea: An African People's Struggle.* Translated by R. Handyside. New York: Monthly Review Press.

————. 1973. *Return to the Source.* Edited by Africa Information Service. New York: Monthly Review Press.

————. 1979. *Unity and Struggle.* New York: Monthly Review Press.

Carlisle, Rodney. 1973. "Black Nationalism: An Integral Tradition," *Black World,* January, 4–11.

Carmichael, Stokely, and Hamilton, Charles V. 1967. *Black Power: The Politics of Liberation in America.* New York: Vintage Books.

Carson, Clayborne. 1981. *In Struggle: SNCC and the Black Awakening of the 1960s.* Cambridge: Harvard University Press.

Chabal, Patrick. 1983. *Amilcar Cabral: Revolutionary Leadership and People's War.* Cambridge: Cambridge University Press.

Chase-Dunn, C. 1980. "The Development of Core Capitalism in the Antebellum United States: Tariff Politics and Class Struggle in an Upwardly Mobile Semiperiphery," in *Studies of the Modern World-System.* Edited by A. Bergesen. Tucson, AZ: University of Arizona Press, 189–230.

Chilcote, Ronald H. 1991. *Amilcar Cabral's Revolutionary Theory and Practice.* Boulder: Lynne Rienner.

Chomsky, N. 1993. *Year 501: The Conquest Continues.* Boston: South End Press.

Clapham, Christopher. 1969. *Haile Selassie's Government.* New York: Praeger.

————. 1994. "Ethnicity and the National Question in Ethiopia," in *Conflict and Peace in the Horn of Africa.* Edited by Peter Woodward and M. Forsyth Brookfield. Brookfield, Vermont: Dartmouth Publishing Company, 27–40.

Clark, Kenneth B. 1965. *Dark Ghetto: Dilemmas of Social Power.* New York: Harper & Row.

Clarke, John H. 1976. "African Cultural Continuity and Slave Revolts in the New World, Part One," *The Black Scholar,* September, 8/1: 41–49.

————. 1976. "African Cultural Continuity and Slave Revolts in the New World, Part Two," *The Black Scholar,* October November, 8/2: 2–9.

Collins, Patricia H. 1990. *Black Feminist Thought: Knowledge, Consciousness and Politics of Empowerment.* New York: Unwin Hyman.

Colston, Freddie C. 1979. "The Ideology of Black Power: An Assessment," *The Western Journal of Black Studies,* Winter, 3/ 4: 233–243.

Comaroff, John L., and Stern, Paul C. (ed.). 1995. "New Perspectives on Nationalism and War," *Perspectives on Nationalism and War.* Edited by John L. Comaroff and Paul C. Stern. Amsterdam: Gordon and Breach Publishers, 1–13.

Connor, Walker. 1994. *Ethnonationalism: The Quest for Understanding.* Princeton: Princeton University Press.

Conti, J. G., and Stetson, B. 1993. *Challenging the Civil Rights Establishment: Profiles of a New Black Vanguard.* Westport, CT: Praeger.

Couto, Richard A. 1993. "Narrative, Free Space, Political Leadership in Social Movements," *The Journal of Politics,* February, 55/1: 59–60.

Creel, Margaret W. 1988. *A Peculiar People: Slave Religion and Community-culture among the Gullas.* New York: New York University Press.

Cruse, Harold. 1967. *Crisis of the Negro Intellectual.* New York: William Morrow.

Davidson, Basil. 1986. "On Revolutionary Nationalism: The Legacy of Cabral," *Race and Class,* Winter 27/ 3: 21–45.

Dejenie, Sentayehu. 1998. "The Role of NGOs in Health in Ethiopia," International Health Department, Tulane University School of Public Health and Tropical Medicine. Unpublished paper.

Delgado, Richard. 1998. "Words that Wound," in *Sources: Notable Selections in Race and Ethnicity.* Edited by Adalberto Aguirre, Jr. and David V. Baker. Second edition. Guilford, CT.: Dushkin/McGraw-Hill, 345–351.

Demie, Feyisa. 1997. "Population Growth and Sustainable Development: The Case of Oromia," *The Journal of Oromo Studies,* 4/1–2: 153–178.

Deressa, Yilma. 1959 (Ethiopian Calendar). *Yee Ethiopia Tarik Baasra Sidisteenga Kifla Zaman.* Addis Ababa. No publisher name.

De Vos, George, and Rommanucci-Ross, Lola. 1972. *Ethnic Identity: Cultural Continuities and Change.* Chicago: The University of Chicago Press.

Dibaba, T. 1997. "Humanity Forsaken: The Case of the Oromo Relief Association (ORA) in the Horn of Africa," paper presented at the Oromo Studies Association Annual Meeting, the University of Minnesota, Minneapolis, July 28–30.

Dillion, M. L. 1974. *The Abolitionists: The Growth of a Dissenting Minority.* De Kalb: Northern Illinois University Press.

Donham, Donald. 1986. "Old Abyssinia and the New Ethiopian Empire: Themes in Social History," in *The Southern Marches of Ethiopia.* Edited by Donald Donham and Wendy James. Cambridge: Cambridge University Press, 1–48.

Donham, Donald, and James, W. (eds.). 1986. *The Southern Marches of Imperial Ethiopia.* Cambridge: Cambridge University.

Drake, St. Clair. 1967. "The American Negro: Relation to Africa," paper presented at *The American Negro Leadership Conference on Africa in Washington, D.C.,* January: 15–30.

Du Bois, W. E. B. 1939. *Black Folk, Then and Now.* New York: Holt.

Dudziak, M. L. 1988. "Desegregation as a Cold War Imperative," *The Stanford Law Review,* 41:61–120.

The Economist. 1997. "Ethiopia: Federal Sham," Aug. 16, 36.

Edwards, W. R. 1998. "Mediated Inequality: The Role of Governmental, Business, and Scientific Elites in Public Education." Ph. D. dissertation, University of Tennessee at Knoxville.

Elkins, Stanley M. 1968. *Slavery.* Chicago: The University of Chicago Press.

Enloe, C. H. 1986. "Ethnicity, the State, and the International Order," *The Primordial Challenge: Ethnicity in the Contemporary World.* Edited by J. F. Stack, Jr. New York: Greenwood Press.

Essien-Udom, E. U. 1962. *Black Nationalism: A Search for an Identity in America.* Chicago: The University of Chicago Press.

Fanon, Franz. 1966. *The Wretched of the Earth.* New York: Grove Press.

———. 1967. *Black Skin and White Mask.* New York: Grove Press.

Fargo, L. 1935. *Abyssinia on the Eve.* London: Putnam.

Farmer, James. 1985. *Lay Bare the Heart: An Autobiography of the Civil Rights Movement.* New York: Arbor House.

Fields, Barbara J. 1985. *Slavery and Freedom on the Middle Ground: Maryland during the Nineteenth Century.* New Haven: Yale University Press.

Fishman, George. 1997. *The African American Struggle for Freedom and Equality.* New York: Garland.

Foner, E. 1988. *Reconstruction: America's Unfinished Revolution, 1863–1877.* New York: Harper & Row.

Fossati, B., Namarra, L., and Niggli, Peter. 1996. *The New Rulers of Ethiopia and the Persecution of the Oromo: Reports from the Oromo Refugees in Djibouti.* Dokumentation. Frankfurt am Main: Evangelischer Pressedienst.

Frank, Andre G. 1978. *World Accumulation 1492–1789.* New York: Monthly Review Press.

———. 1995. "The Modern World System Revisited; Rereading Braudel and Wallerstein," *Civilizations and World Systems.* Edited by S. K. Anderson. Palo Alto, CA: Altmaria Press, 163–194.

Franklin, John H. 1943. *The Free Negro in North Carolina, 1790–1860.* Chapel Hill: The University of North Carolina Press.

Frazier, Franklin E. 1969. "The Garvey Movement," *The Making of Black America*. Vol. 1. Edited by August Meier and Elliot Rudwick. New York: Atheneum, 204–208.

Freeman, Rhoda G. 1994. *The Free Negro in New York City in the Era before the Civil War*. New York: Garland Publishing.

Gabre-Slassie, Zewde. 1975. *Yohannes IV of Ethiopia: A Political Biography*. Oxford: Clarendon Press.

Garretson, P. P. 1974. "A History of Addis Ababa from Its Foundation in 1886 to 1919." Ph. D. dissertation, the University of London.

Gebre-Medhin, Jordan. 1989. *Peasants and Nationalism in Eritrea*. Trenton, NJ: The Red Sea Press.

Gellner, Ernest. 1983. *Nations and Nationalism*. Oxford: Basil Blackwell.

Gemeda, Guluma. 1998. "Political Domination and Exploitation of the Mineral Resources of Oromia: From Menelik to Meles," *The Journal of Oromo Studies*, July, 5/1 and 2: 133–154.

Gerbee, Teklu. 1993. "The Geda Militarism and Oromo Expansion," *Ethiopian Review*. October: 50.

Geschwender, James (ed.). 1971. "An Introduction to the Black Revolt," *The Black Revolt*, Englewood Cliffs, NJ: Prentice-Hall.

Ghebre, Getachew. 1991. "Ethiopia: Honeymoon Over," in *New Africa*, Dec.: 19.

Gibbs, J. 1989. "Conceptualization of Terrorism," *The American Sociological Review*, 54/ June: 329–340.

Giddens, Anthony. 1993. *New Rules of Sociological Method*. Second edition. Oxford: Polity Press.

Gilkes, P. 1975. *The Dying Lion: Feudalism and Modernization in Ethiopia*. New York: St. Martin's Press.

Goldberg, David T. 1990. "The Social Formation of Racist Discourse," in *Anatomy of Racism*. Edited by David T. Goldberg. Minneapolis: The University of Minnesota Press.

Gololcha, Tedecha. 1988. "The Politico-Legal System of the Guji Oromo." L.L.B. thesis. Addis Ababa University.

Goodwin, Jeff, and Skocpol, Theda. 1994. "Explaining Revolutions in the Contemporary Third World," in *Social Revolutions in the Modern World*. Written by Theda Skocpol. Cambridge: Cambridge University Press, 259–278.

Gorbachev, Mikhail. 1987. *Perestroika: New Thinking for Our Country and the World*. New York: Harper & Row.

Greetz, C. 1994. "Primordial and Civic Ties," *Nationalism*. Edited by J. Hutchinson and A. D. Smith. Oxford: Oxford University Press, 29–34.

Griz, Almerigo. 1987. "Ethiopia Fights a War of Confusion," *Jane's Defense Weekly*, 7/ 16.

Gustave, Aren. 1978. *Evangelical Pioneers in Ethiopia: Origins of the Evangelical Church Mekane Yesus*. Stockholm: Uppsala University.

Gutama, Ibssa. 1997. "Ethiopia: Transition to Ethnic Dictatorship," paper presented at the *Fortieth Annual Meeting of the African Studies Association* in Columbus, Ohio, Nov. 13–16.

Haberland, Eike Von. 1963. *Galla Sud-Athiopiens*. Stuttgart: Verlag W. Kohlhammer.

Hagos, Tecola W. 1995. *Democratization? Ethiopia (1991–1994): A Personal View*. Cambridge, MA: Khepera Publishers.

Haji, Abbas. 1995. "Arsi Oromo Political and Military Resistance Against the Shoan Colonial Conquest," *The Journal of Oromo Studies*, Winter and Summer 2/1–2: 1–21.

Handler, M. S. 1965. "Introduction," *The Autobiography of Malcolm X, with the assistance of Alex Haley*. New York: Ballantine Books.

Haraway, D. J. 1991. *Simians, Cyborgs, and Women: The Reinvention of Nature*. New York: Routledge.

Harris, Joseph. 1986. "Race and Misperceptions in the Origins of United States-Ethiopian Relations," *TransAfrica Forum*, Winter, 3/ 2:9–23.

Harris, W. C. 1844. *The Highlands of Ethiopia*. Volume 3. Philadelphia: T. B. Peterson.

Harrison, Alfredteen (ed.). 1991. *Black Exodus: The Great Migration from the American South*. Jackson: University Press of Mississippi.

Hassen, Mohammed. 1981. "The Oromo Nation under Amhara Colonial Administration," *School of Oriental and African Studies*. June.

————. 1990. *The Oromo of Ethiopia: A History 1570–1860.* Cambridge: Cambridge University Press.

————. 1991. "The Historian Abba Bahrey and the Importance of His 'History of the Galla,'" *The Horn of Africa,* 13/3–4 and 14/ 1–2.

————. 1993. "The Growth of Written Oromo Literature," *The Proceedings of the International Conference on Resource Mobilization for the Liberation of Oromia* at the University of Toronto, Ontario, Canada, July 31-August 1.

————. 1996. "The Development of Oromo Nationalism," *Being and Becoming Oromo.* Uppsala: Nordiska Afrikainstitutet, 67–80

————. 1998. "The Macha-Tulama Association 1963–1967 and the Development of Oromo Nationalism," in *Oromo Nationalism and the Ethiopian Discourse.* Edited by A. Jalata. Lawrenceville, NJ: The Red Sea Press, 183–221.

Hayward, R. J. and Hassen, Mohamed. 1981. "The Oromo Orthography of Shaykh Bakri Sapalo," *Bulletin of the School of Oriental African Studies,* 44: 550–566.

Heaney, Thomas W. 1993. "If You Can't Beat 'Em, Join 'Em: The Professionalization of Participatory Research," *Voice of Change: Participatory Research in the United States and Canada.* Edited by Peter Park, Mary Brydon-Miller, Budd Hall, and Ted Jackson. Westport, CT: Bergin and Garvey.

Heater, Derek. 1994. *National Self-Determination: Woodrow Wilson and His Legacy.* London: St. Martin's Press.

Heath, Louis G. 1976. *The Black Panthers Leaders Speak.* Metuchen, NJ: The Scarecrow Press.

Hellinger, Douglas. 1992. "U.S. Assistance to Africa: No Room for Democracy," *TransAfrica Forum,* 9/2, 78–82.

Henze, Paul. 1985. *Rebels and Separatists in Ethiopia: Regional Resistance to a Marxist Regime.* Santa Monica, CA: The Rand Corporation.

Herkovits, Melville J. 1958. *The Myth of the Negro Past.* Boston: Beacon.

Herrnstein, R. J., and Murray, C. 1994. *The Bell Curve: Intelligence and Class Structure in American Life.* New York: The Free Press.

Hizbawi Adera. 1989. "Ethiopian Calendar," *Tahisas to Yekatit,* an underground TPLF/EPRDF paper.

Hiltzik, Michael A. 1992. "Ethnic Pride Gets a Test in Africa," *Los Angeles Times,* Feb. 11.

Hinnant, John. 1978. "The Guji: *Gada* as a Ritual System," *Age, Generation, and Time: Some Features of East African Age Organizations.* Edited by P. T. W. Baxter and U. Almagor. New York: St. Martin's Press, 207–243.

Hobsbawm, Eric J. 1990. *Nations and Nationalism Since 1780: Programme, Myth, and Reality.* New York: Cambridge University Press.

————. 1992. "Ethnicity and Nationalism in Europe Today," *Anthropology,* 8/4.

Hobsbawm, Eric J., and Ranger, Terence (eds.). 1983. *The Invention of Traditions.* Cambridge: Cambridge University Press.

Hodges, Graham (ed.). 1994. *Studies in African American History and Culture.* New York: Garland Publishing.

Holcomb, Bonnie K., and Ibssa, Sisai. 1990. *The Invention of Ethiopia: The Making of a Dependent Colonial State in Northeast Africa.* Trenton, NJ: The Red Sea Press.

Holcomb, Bonnie K. 1991. "Akka Gadaatti: The Unfolding of Oromo Nationalism—Keynote Remarks," in *The Proceedings of the 1991 Conference on Oromia,* the University of Toronto, August 3–4.

————. 1993. "Ideological Bases for Oromo Empowerment," paper presented at the *Oromo Studies Association Conference,* The University of Toronto, July 31-August 1.

————. 1997. "The Tale of Two Democracies: The Encounter Between U.S.-Sponsored Ethiopian 'Democracy' and Indigenous Oromo Democratic Forms," *The Journal of Oromo Studies,* July, 4/ 1–2: 47–82.

————. 1999. "Oromo in the World Community," *The Journal of Oromo Studies,* 6:1 and 2: 1–48.

Holloway, Joseph E.,(ed.). 1990. *Africanisms in American Culture*. Bloomington: Indiana University Press.

Horne, Gerald. 1996. "Race for the Globe: U.S. Foreign Policy and Racial Interests," *Impacts of Racism on White Americans,* 88–112.

———. 1986. *Black and Red: W. E. B. Du Bois and the Afro-American Response to the Cold War, 1944–1963*. New York: State University of New York Press.

Huggins, Nathan I. 1971. *Harlem Renaissance*. New York: Oxford University Press.

———. 1977. *Black Odyssey*. New York: Vintage Books.

Huluka, Gobena. 1999. "Environment Impacts of Gold Mining in Oromia," *The Journal of Oromo Studies,* July, 6/ 1 and 2: 159–172.

Human Rights Watch/World Report. 1999. "Ethiopia: The Role of the International Community," http://www.hrw.org/hrw/worldreport99/africa/ethiopia3.html. : 3.

Hunt, Michael. 1987. *Ideology and U.S. Foreign Policy*. New Haven: Yale University Press.

Huqqaa, Gollo. 1998. *The 37th Gumii Gaayo Assembly*. Addis Ababa: The Norwegian Church Aid.

Huttenback, Robert A. 1976. *Racism and Empire: White Settlers and Colored Immigrants in the British Self-Governing Colonies 1830–1910*. Ithaca, NY: Cornell University Press.

Ibssa, Sisai. 1992. "Implications of Party and Set for Oromo Political Survival," paper presented at the *35th Annual Meeting of the African Studies Association,* Seattle, Washington, Nov. 20–23.

———. 1998. "The Ideological Foundations of Current U.S. Foreign Policy: The 'Promotion of Democracy' and Its Impact on the Oromo National Movement," *The Journal of Oromo Studies,* 5/ 1–2: 1–34.

Impact International. 1997. "Cleansing 'Islamic Fundamentalism' from the Horn," March 1.

Isaacs, Harold R. 1989. *Idols of the Tribe: Group Identity and Political Change*. Cambridge, MA: Harvard University Press.

Jackson, Luther P. 1942. *Free Negro Labor and Property Holding in Virginia, 1830–1860*. New York: D. Appleton-Century Company.

Jalata, Asafa. 1991. "The Modern World-Economy, Ethiopian Settler Colonialism and the Oromos," *Horn of Africa,* 8/ 4–3 and 9/ 1–2: 59–80.

———. 1992. "Two Freedom Movements Compared: The Cases of the Oromo and African Americans," *The Oromo Commentary,* 2/ 1: 13–16.

———. 1993. *Oromia and Ethiopia: State Formation and Ethnonational Conflict, 1868–1992*. Boulder, Co: Lynne Rienner Publishers.

———. 1993. "Ethiopia and Ethnic Politics: The Case of Oromo Nationalism," *Dialectical Anthropology,* 18: 381.

———. 1993. "Sociocultural Origins of the Oromo National Movement in Ethiopia," *The Journal of Political and Military Sociology,* Winter, 21: 267–86.

———. 1994. "Sheik Hussein Suura and the Oromo National Struggle," *The Oromo Commentary,* 4/ 1: 5–7.

———. 1995. "African American Nationalism, Development, and Afrocentricity: Implications for the Twenty-First Century," in *Molefi Kete Asante and Afrocentricity: In Praise and in Criticism.* Edited by Dhyana Ziegler. Nashville, TN: James C. Winston Publishing, 153–174.

———. 1995. "The Emergence of Oromo Nationalism and Ethiopian Reaction," in *Social Justice,* 22/ 3: 165–189.

———. 1995. "Poverty, Powerlessness and the Imperial Interstate System in the Horn of Africa," in *Disaster and Development in the Horn of Africa.* Edited by John Sorenson. New York: St. Martin's Press, 31–48.

———. 1996. "The Struggle for Knowledge: The Case of Emergent Oromo Studies," *The African Studies Reviews,* Sept. 39/ 2.: 95–123.

———. 1997. "Oromo Nationalism in the New Global Context," *The Journal of Oromo Studies,* July, 4/ 1–2: 83–114.

———. 1998. "The Cultural Roots of Oromo Nationalism," *Oromo Nationalism and the Ethiopian Discourse: The Search for Freedom and Democracy.* Edited by Asafa Jalata. Lawrenceville, NJ: The Red Sea Press, 27–49.

———. 2000. "U.S.-Sponsored Ethiopian 'Democracy' and State Terrorism," in *Crisis and Terror in the Horn of Africa.* Edited by Pat Lauderdale, A. Zegeye, and A. Oliverio. Burlington: Ashgate/Darthmouth, 64–89.

James, Winston. 1998. *Holding Aloft the Banner of Ethiopia.* New York: Verso.

Janis, I. 1972. *Victims of Groupthink.* Boston: Houghton Mifflin.

Jenkins, Craig. 1983. "Resource Mobilization Theory and the Study of Social Movements," *Annual Review of Sociology,* 9: 527–553.

Jenkins, J. C., and Eckert, M. 1986. "Channeling Black Insurgency: Elite Patronage and Professional Social Movement Organizations in the Development of the Black Movement," *The American Sociological Review,* 51: 812–815.

Jinadu, L. Adele. 1994. "The Dialects of Theory and Research on Race and Ethnicity in Nigeria," in *"Race," Ethnicity and Nation.* Edited by P. Ratcliffe. London: University College of London, 163–178.

Joireman, Sandra F. 1997. "Opposition Politics and Ethnicity in Ethiopia: We Will Go Down Together," *The Journal of Comparative Sociology,* 38/3.

Joyner, Charles. 1984. *Down by the Riverside: A South Carolina Slave Community.* Urbana: University of Illinois Press.

Jubilee, Vincent. 1989. "Philadelphia's Literary Circle and the Harlem Renaissance," in *The Harlem Renaissance: Revaluations.* Edited by Amritjit Singh, William S. Shiver, and Stanley Brodwin. New York: Garland Publishing, 35–47.

Kamenka, Eugene. 1973. "Political Nationalism-the Evolution of Idea," *Nationalism: The Nature of Idea.* Edited by E. Kamenka. Canberra: Australia National University Press, 1–20.

Karenga, Maulana. 1982. *Introduction to Black Studies.* Inglewood: Kawaida Publications.

Kasarda, J. D. 1990. "Caught in the Web of Change," in *Readings on Social Problems: Probing the Extent, Causes, and Remedies of America's Social Problems.* Edited by W. Feigelman. Orlando, FL.: Holt, Rinehart, 223.

Kassam, Aneesa. in press. "The Oromo Theory of Social Development," in *Between the State and Civil Society in Africa: Perspectives on Development.* Edited by T. Mkandawire and E. E. Osagahae. Dakar: Codesria.

Kaul, Ashok. 1994. "Ethno-nationalism in India: Political, Historical, and Sociological Discourse," in *"Race," Ethnicity and Nation.* Edited by P. Ratcliffe. London: University College of London, 151–162.

Kellas, James G. 1991. *The Politics of Nationalism and Ethnicity.* New York: St. Martin's Press.

Kelly, Hilarie A. 1992. "From Gada to Islam: The Moral Authority of Gender Relations among the Pastoral Orma of Kenya." Ph. D. dissertation, University of California at Los Angeles.

King, Martin Luther, Jr. 1960. "The Rising Tide of Racial Consciousness," *The YWCA Magazine,* December.

———. 1964. *Strength to Love.* New York: Pocket Books.

———. 1964. *Stride Toward Freedom.* New York: Perennial Library.

———. 1964. *Why We Can't Wait.* New York: Harper & Row.

———. 1967. *Where Do We Go From Here: Chaos or Community?* New York: Harper & Row.

———. 1968. "Honoring Dr. DuBois." *Freedom Ways,* Spring: 110–111.

———. 1968. *Negro History Bulletin.* May.

———. 1969. "A Testament of Hope," *Playboy.*

———. 1969. "The Last Major Political speeches of Martin Luther King and Eldridge Cleaver," *The Black Politician,* July: 4.

Knutsson, K. E. 1967. *Authority and Change: A Study of the Kallu Institution among the Macha of Galla of Ethiopia.* Gotenborg: Ethnografiska Museet or Elanders Boktryckeru Aktibolag.

Kumsa, Kuwee. 1991. "The *Siqqee* Institution of Oromo Women," *The Journal of Oromo Studies,* July, 4/1–2, 115–152.

Lata, L. 1998. "The Making and Unmaking of Ethiopia's Transitional Charter," in *Oromo Nationalism and the Ethiopian Discourse.* Edited by A. Jalata. Lawrenceville, NJ: The Red Sea Press, 125–152.

———. 1998."Peculiar Challenges to Oromo Nationalism," in *Oromo Nationalism and the Ethiopian Discourse.* Edited by Asafa Jalata. Lawrenceville, NJ: The Red Sea Press, 51–77.

Legesse, Asmarom. 1973. *Gada: Three Approaches to the Study of African Society.* New York: The Free Press.

———. 1989. "Oromo Democracy," paper presented at the Oromo Studies Conference, Toronto, August 12–13.

———. 2000. *Oromo Democracy: An Indigenous African Political System.* Lawrenceville: The Red Sea Press.

Lemann, Nicholas. 1992. *The Promised Land: The Great Black Migration and How It Changed America.* New York: Vintage Books.

Lemmu, Baissa. 1971. "The Democratic Political System of the Galla [Oromo] of Ethiopia and the Possibility of Its Use in Nation-Building." M.A. thesis, George Washington University.

———. 1993. "The Political Culture of Gada: Building Blocks of Oromo Power," paper presented at *The Oromo Studies Association Conference,* Toronto, July 31-August 1.

Lepisa, Dinsa. 1975. "The Gada System of Government and Sera Cafee Oromo." L. L. B. thesis, Addis Ababa University.

Levine, Donald. 1994. *Greater Ethiopia.* Chicago: University of Chicago Press.

Levine, Lawrence W. 1977. *Black Culture and Black Consciousness: Afro-American Folk Thought from Slavery to Freedom.* New York: Oxford University Press.

Lewis, Herbert S. 1996. "The Development of Oromo Political Consciousness from 1958–1994," in *Being and Becoming Oromo.* Uppsala: Nordiska Afrikainstitute, 38.

Lincoln, Eric C. 1961. *The Black Muslims in America.* Boston: Beacon Press.

Litwack, Leon and Meier, August. 1988. *Black Leaders of the Nineteenth Century.* Chicago: University of Illinois.

Litwack, Leon. 1961. *North of Slavery.* Chicago: University of Chicago Press.

Locke, Alain. 1970. "The New Negro: A Forced Attempt to Build Americanism on Race Values," *Black Nationalism in America.* Edited by J. H. Bracey, A. Meier, and E. Rudwick. New York: The Bobbs-Merril Company, 341–342.

Loo, Joseph Van de. 1991. *Guji Oromo Culture in Southern Ethiopia: Religious Capabilities in Rituals and Songs.* Berlin: Dietrich Reimer Verlag.

Luling, Virgina. 1965. "Government and Social Control among Some Peoples of the Horn of Africa." M.A. thesis, University of London.

Lycett, Andrew. 1992. "Federalism Flourishes," *New Africa,* May.

Lyman, S. M. 1991. "The Race Question and Liberalism: Casuistries in American Constitutional Law," *The International Journal of Politics, Culture, and Society,* 5/ 2: 183–247.

Lyons, Terrence. 1996. "Closing the Transition: The May 1995 Elections in Ethiopia," *The Journal of Modern African Studies,* 34/ 1: 142.

Magdoff, Harry. 1978. *Imperialism: From the Colonial Age to the Present.* New York: Monthly Review Press.

Magubane, Bernard M. 1989. *The Ties That Bind: African-American Consciousness of Africa.* Trenton, NJ: The African World Press.

Malcolm X. 1976. *Malcolm X Speaks: Selected Speeches and Statements.* Edited with prefatory notes by George Breitman. New York: Pathfinder Press.

———. 1966. "Ballot or Bullet," in *Malcolm X Speaks.* Edited by George Breitman. New York: Grove Press.

Malik, Kenan. 1996. *The Meaning of Race.* New York: New York University Press.

Marable, Manning. 1983. *How Capitalism Underdeveloped Black America.* Boston: South End Press.

————. 1991. *Race, Reform, and Rebellion: The Second Reconstruction in Black America 1945–1990.* Second edition. Jackson: University Press of Mississippi.

————. 1995. *Beyond Black and White: Transforming African-American Politics.* London: Verso.

Marcus, H. 1975. *The Life and Times of Menelik II, Ethiopia, 1844–1913.* Oxford: Clarendon.

————. 1983. *Ethiopia, Great Britian and the United States, 1941–1974: The Politics of Empire.* Los Angeles: The University of California Press.

————. 1994. *A History of Ethiopia.* Berkeley: University of California Press.

————. 1996. "Racist Discourse About Ethiopia and Ethiopians Before and After the Battle of Adwa," paper presented at *The Adwa Conference.* AAU: March, 5.

Mariam, Aleqa G. 1948. *YeEthiopia Hizb Tarik.* Addis Ababa.

Marine, Gene. 1986. *The Black Panthers.* New York: New American Library.

Markakis, John. 1983. "Material and Social Aspects of National Conflict in the Horn of Africa," *Civilizations,* 33/ 1.

Marshall, Gloria. 1993. "Racial Classifications: Popular and Scientific," in *The "Racial" Economy of Science: Toward a Democratic Future.* Edited by Sandra Harding. Bloomington: Indiana University Press, 125.

Marx, Karl. 1967. *Capital.* Edited by F. Engels. New York: International Publishers.

Mazrui, Ali. 1975. *Soldiers and Kinsmen in Uganda: The Making of a Military Ethnocracy.* Beverly Hills, CA: Sage Publications.

McAdam, D. 1997. "The Political Process Model," in *Social Movements: Perspectives and Issues.* Edited by Steven M. Buechler and Kurt Clykes, Jr. Mountain View, CA: Mayfield Publishing, 172–192.

McAdam, D., and McCarthy, J. D., and Zald, M. N. 1998. "Social Movements," in *Handbook of Sociology.* Edited by Neil J. Smelser. Newbury Park, CA: Sage, 695–737.

McClendon, W. H. 1983. "The Foundations of Black Culture," *The Black Scholar,* Summer, 14/ 3, 4: 18–20.

McCann, James. 1985. "The Political Economy of Rural Rebellion in Ethiopia: Northern Resistance to Imperial Expansion, 1928–1935," *The International Journal of African Historical Studies,* 18/ 4: 601–623.

McCarthy, J. D. 1987. "Pro-life and Pro-choice Mobilization: Infrastructure Deficits and New Technologies," in *Social Movements in an Organizational Society.* Edited by Mayer N. Zald and John D. McCarthy. New Brunswick, NJ: Transaction Books, 49–66.

McComack, Bernard M. 1977. *Slavery on the Tennessee Frontier.* Edited by C. Kelly and Dan E. Pomeroy. Nashville: Tennessee American Revolution Bicentennial Commission.

McKelvey, Charles. 1991. *Beyond Ethnocentrism: A Reconstruction of Marx's Concepts of Science.* New York: Greenwood.

McLemore, S. D. 1991. *Racial and Ethnic Relations in America.* Boston: Allyn and Bacon.

McMillen, Neil R. 1991. "The Migration and Black Protest in Jim Crow Mississippi," in *Black Exodus: The Great Migration from the American South.* Edited by Alferdteen Harrison. Jackson: University Press of Mississippi.

Megerssa, Gemetchu. 1993. "Knowledge, Identity and Colonizing Structure: The Case of the Oromo in East and Northeast Africa." Ph. D. dissertation, University of London: School of Oriental and African Studies.

————. 1996. "Oromumma: Tradition, Consciousness and Identity," in *Being and Becoming Oromo.* Uppsala: Nordiska Afrikainstitute, 92–102.

————. 1997. "The Oromo and the Ethiopian State Ideology in a Historical Perspective," in *Papers of the 8th International Conference of Ethiopian Studies at Kyoto,* 2/ Dec. 12–17, 479–485.

Meier, August, and Rudwick, Elliot. 1985. "Introduction," in *Black Protest Thought in the Twentieth Century.* Edited by A. Meier, E. Rudwick, and Francis L. Broderick. New York: Macmillian.

Meier, August. 1966. *From Plantation to Ghetto.* New York: Hill and Wang.

Melbaa, Gadaa. 1988. *Oromia: An Introduction.* Khartoum.

Mintz, Sidney W., and Price, Richard. 1976. *An Anthropological Approach to the Afro-American Past: A Caribbean Perspective*. Philadelphia: Institute for the Study of Human Issues.

Monges, Mariam M. 1997. *Kush: The Jewel of Nubia*. Trenton, NJ: The Africa World Press.

Moose, George E. 1994. "Testimony of Assistant Secretary of State Before the House Subcommittee on Ethiopia," Washington, D.C., July 27.

Morris, Aldon D. 1984. *The Origins of the Civil Rights Movement: Black Communities Organizing for Change*. New York: Free Press.

Moses, W. J. (ed.). 1978. *The Golden Age of Black Nationalism, 1850–1925*. Hamden, CT.

———. (ed.). 1996. *Classical Black Nationalism*. New York: New York University Press.

Mudimbe, V.Y. 1988. *The Invention of Africa: Gnosis, Philosophy, and the Order of Knowledge*. Bloomington: Indiana University Press.

Mullin, Gerald W. 1972. *Flight and Rebellion: Slave Resistance in the Eighteenth-Century Virginia*. New York: Oxford University Press.

Murray, C. 1984. *Losing Ground: American Social Policy, 1950–1980*. New York: Basic Books.

Myrdal, Gunnar. 1944. *An American Dilemma*. New York: Harper & Row.

Nagel, Joane. 1993. "Ethnic Nationalism: Politics, Ideology, and the World Order," in *International Journal of Comparative Sociology*, 34/ 1–2: 103–112.

———. 1995. "American Indian Ethnic Renewal: Politics and the Resurgence of Identity," *American Sociological Review*, December, 60, 947–965.

Narin, Tom. 1994. "The Modern Janus," *New Left Review*, 94, Nov.-Dec.: 3, 3–29.

Nash, Manning. 1989. *The Cauldron of Ethnicity*. Chicago: The University of Chicago Press.

"New Justice Department Figures Mark a Quarter Century of Prison Building." 1999. *Sentencing Project @ www.sproject.com*.

New African. 1998. "Ethiopia, Around Africa: Persecution of Oromos Continues," June: 1–3.

Nimni, Ephraim. 1991. *Marxism and Nationalism: Theoretical Origins of a Political Crisis*. London: Pluto Press.

Oberschall, Anthony. 1973. *Social Conflict and Social Movements*. Englewood Cliffs, NJ: Prentice-Hall.

———. 1978. "Theories of Social Conflict," *Annual Review of Sociology*, 4:291–315.

Ofari, Earl. 1971. "The Emergence of Black National Consciousness in America," *Black World*, January, 75–86.

Oliverio, A. 1997. "The State of Injustice: The Politics of Terrorism and the Production of Order," *International Journal of Comparative Sociology*, 38/ 1–2, June: 48–63.

———. 1997. *The State of Terror*. New York: The SUNY Press.

"The Oromos: Voice Against Tyranny," reprinted in *Horn of Africa*, 3/ 3. 1980, 81–110.

OLF. 1974. *The Political Program of the Oromo Liberation Front*, Finfine, Oromia. (Amended in 1976).

———. 1990. "Democratic Resolution on the Oromo National Liberation Struggle and other Conflicts in the Ethiopian Empire," April 18.

———. 1990. "OLF Statement about the TPLF-Sponsored OPDO," July 5.

———. 1996. "Statement on the Current State of the Oromo People's Struggle and the Situation in the Horn of Africa."

The Oromia Support Group. 1997. Nov.: 1. (Also 1996 series).

Pankhurst, R. 1968. *Economic History of Ethiopia 1800–1935*. Addis Ababa.

Perham, Margery. 1968. *The Government of Ethiopia*. Second edition. London: Longmans.

Philips, John E. 1990. "The African Heritage of White America," in *Africanisms in American Culture*. Edited by Joseph E. Holloway. Bloomington: Indiana University Press, 225–239.

Pinkney, Alphonso. 1984. *The Myth of Black Progress*. Cambridge: Cambridge University Press.

Piven, Frances F., and Cloward, Richard. 1977. *Poor People's Movements*. New York: Pantheon.

Pollock, Sue. 1997. "Politics and Conflict: Participation and Self-Determination," in *Ethiopia: Conquest and the Quest for Freedom and Democracy*. Edited by Seyoum Y. Hameso, T. Trueman, and T. E. Erena. London: TSC Publications, 81–110.

Planning and Project Department, Ministry of Health, Ethiopia, Health and Health Related Indicators. 1995.

Press, Robert M. 1991. "In New Ethiopia, Main Tribe Takes Peaceful Route to Reclaim Rights," *The Christian Science Monitor,* July 15.

Puckett, Newbell N. 1969. *Folk Beliefs of the Southern Negro.* New York: Dover.

Quarles, Benjamin. 1987. *The Negro in the Making of America.* New York: Macmillian.

Reed, Ishmael. 1968. "Preface," in *Soul on Ice,* xiii.

Rey, C. F. 1969. *The Real Abyssinia.* New York: Negro Universities Press.

Rice, Susan. 1998. "Statement Before the Subcommittees on Africa and on International operations and Human Rights of the House International Relations Committee," Washington, D.C.: July 29.

———. 1998. "A New Partnership for the 21st Century," *ASA News,* 31/ 1, Jan/ March: 7–9.

Richmond, Anthony H. 1994. "Ethnic Nationalism and Post-Industrialism," in *Nationalism.* Edited by John Hutchinson and Anthony D. Smith. New York: Oxford University Press.

Robinson, Beverly J. 1990. "Africanisms and the Study of Folklore," in *Africanisms in American Culture.* Edited by Joseph E. Holloway. Bloomington: Indiana University Press, 211–224.

Robinson, Cedric J. 1985. "The African Diaspora and the Italo-Ethiopian Crisis," in *Race and Class,* 2, 51–65.

Robinson, William I. 1996. *Promoting Polyarchy: Globalization, U.S. Intervention and Hegemony.* Cambridge: Cambridge University Press.

———. 1997. "Global Capitalism and the Oromo Liberation Struggle: Theoretical Notes on U.S. Policy Towards the Ethiopian Empire," *The Journal of Oromo Studies,* 4/ 1–2: 1–46.

Rodney, Walter. 1972. *How Europe Underdeveloped Africa.* Washington, D.C.: Howard University Press.

Roebuck, Julian B., and Murty, Komanduri S. 1993. *Historically Black Colleges and Universities: Their Place in American Higher Education.* Westport, CT: Praeger.

Roediger, David R. 1991. *The Wages of Whiteness: Race and the Making of the American Working Class.* London: Verso.

Roshwald, Aviel. 1993. "Untangling the Knotted Cord: Studies of Nationalism," *Journal of Interdisciplinary History,* Fall, 24/ 2: 293–303.

Ross, Luana. 1998. *Inventing the Savage: The Social Construction of Native American Criminality.* Austin: The University Press of Texas.

Ross, Robert (ed.). 1982. "Reflections on a Theme," in *Racism and Colonialism: Essays on Ideology and Social Structure.* The Hague: Martinus Nijhoff Routledge.

Reuters. 1994. "Reuters Business Briefing," July 5.

Reuters. 1995. May 15.

Russell, John. 1969. *The Free Negro in Virginia.* New York: Negro University Press.

Said, Edward. 1978. *Orientalism.* New York: Vintage Books.

———. 1993. "The Politics of Knowledge," in *Race, Identity and Representation in Education.* Edited by Cameron McCarthy and Warren Crichlow. New York: Routledge, 306–314.

Sales, William W., Jr. 1994. *From Civil Rights to Black Liberation: Malcolm X and the Organization of Afro-American Unity.* Boston: South End Press.

Salvice, Marial de. 1901. *Un People Antique au Pays de Menelik: les Galla, grande nation africaine.* Paris: Oudin.

Sbacchi, Alberto. 1997. *Legacy of Bitterness: Ethiopia and Fascist Italy, 1935–1941.* Lawrenceville, NJ: The Red Sea Press.

Schmitt, K. 1994. "Machuba—An Oromo Slave-Girl Who Won the Heart of a German Prince," *The Oromo Commentary,* 2/ 2: 32–34.

Schuchter, Arnold. 1968. *White Power and Black Freedom: Planning the Future of Urban America.* Boston: Beacon Press.

Schwartzman, D. 1997. *Black Unemployment: Part of Unskilled Unemployment.* Westport, CT: Greenwood Press.

Schwarz, Benjamin. 1995. "The Diversity Myth: America's Leading Export," *The Atlantic Monthly,* May, 57–67.

Scott, William R. 1993. *The Sons of Sheba's Race: African-Americans and the Italo-Ethiopian War, 1935–1941.* Bloomington: Indiana University Press.

Sealy, Michael. 1993. "Creating a partnership: The United States and the Black World," *TransAfrica Forum,* 9/ 4 (special issue): 38.

Seifa Nabalbal. 1996. Nov. 8. (An independent Oromo newspaper).

Semmes, Clovis E. 1992. *Cultural Hegemony and African American Development.* Westport, CT: Praeger.

Shack, W. A. 1994. "Book Review on the Oromo of Ethiopia: A History 1570–1860," *American Ethnologist,* 21/ 3: 642–43.

Shannon, Thomas R. 1989. *An Introduction to the World-System Perspective.* San Francisco: Westview Press.

Singh, Amritjit, Shriver, W.S., and Browdin, S. 1989. (eds.). *The Harlem Renaissance: Revaluations.* New York: Garland Publishing.

Smith, Anthony D. 1971. *Theories of Nationalism.* New York: Harper & Row.

———. 1979. *Nationalism in the Twentieth Century.* Oxford: Martin Robertson.

———. 1981. *The Ethnic Revival.* New York: Cambridge University Press.

———. 1982. "Nationalism, Ethnic Separatism and Intelligentsia," in *National Separatism.* Edited by C. H. Williams. Vancouver: University of British Columbia Press, 17–41.

———. 1986. *The Ethnic Origins of Nations.* Oxford: Basil Blackwell.

———. 1991. *National Identity.* Reno, Las Vegas: The University of Nevada Press.

Snyder, Louis L. 1976. *Varieties of Nationalism: A Comparative Study.* Hinsdale: The Dryden Press.

Sorenson, John. 1993. *Imagining Ethiopia.* New Brunswick, NJ: Rutgers University Press.

———. 1998. "Ethiopian Discourse and Oromo Nationalism," in *Oromo Nationalism and the Ethiopian Discourse,* 223–252.

———. 1996. "Learning to be Oromo: Nationalist Discourse in the Diaspora," *Social Identities,* 2/ 3: 439–467.

Sowell, T. 1984. *Civil Rights: Rhetoric or Reality?* New York: William Morrow and Company.

Spencer, John H. 1984. *Ethiopia at Bay.* Algonac, MI: Reference Publications.

Staples, Robert. 1998. "White Racism, Black Crime, and American Justice: An Application of the Colonial Model to Explain Crime and Race," in *Sources: Notable Selections in Race and Ethnicity.* Guilford, CT.: Dushkin/ McGraw-Hill, 280–281.

Steele, S. 1990. *The Content of Our Character: A New Vision of Race in America.* New York: Harper Collins.

Stoper, Emily. 1989. *The Student Nonviolent Coordinating Committee: The Growth of Radicalism in a Civil Rights Organization.* New York: Carlson Publishing.

———. 1968. "Through the Prism of Folklore: The Black Ethos in Slavery," *Massachusetts Review,* Spring, 9.

Stuckey, Sterling, ed. 1972. *The Ideological Origins of Black Nationalism.* Boston: Beacon Press.

Subramanian, Sribala. 1995. "The Story in Our Genes: A Landmark Global Study Flattens the Bell Curve, Providing that Racial Differences are Only Skin Deep," *Time,* January, 16: 54–55.

Survival International. 1995. "Ethiopia: Human Rights Hypocrisy Must End Now," July 14.

Ta'a, Teseam. 1980. "The Oromo of Wollega: A Historical Survey to 1910." M.A. thesis, Addis Ababa University.

Tamrat, Taddesse. 1972. *Church and State in Ethiopia.* Oxford: Clarendon.

Tareke, Gebru. 1977. "Rural Protest in Ethiopia, 1941–1970: A Study of Three Rebellions." Ph. D. dissertation, Syracuse University.

———. 1991. *Ethiopia: Power and Protest.* New York: Cambridge University Press.

Tate, Gayle T. 1983. "Black Nationalism: An Angle of Vision," *The Western Journal of Black Studies,* 12/ 1: 40–48.

"Terror Against Oromos." 1997. *Ed.htm @ www.mdx.ac.uk* : 1–3.

Thiong'o, Ngugi Wa. 1993. *Moving the Centre: The Struggle for Cultural Freedoms.* London: James Currey.

Thompson, Robert F. 1983. *Flash of the Spirit: African and Afro-American Art and Philosophy.* New York: Vintage Books.

Thompson, Robert F., and Cornet, Joseph. 1981. *The Four Moments of the Sun: Kongo Art in Two Worlds.* Washington, D.C.: National Gallery of Art.

Tibebu, Teshale. 1995. *The Making of Modern Ethiopia 1896–1974.* Lawrenceville, NJ: The Red Sea Press.

Tinker, Hugh. 1977. *Race, Conflict and the International Order: From Empire to United Nations.* New York: St. Martin's Press.

Tiryakian, Edward A. 1995. "Nationalism and Modernity: A Methodological Appraisal," in *Perspectives on Nationalism and War.* Edited by John L. Comaroff and Paul C. Stern. Amsterdam: Gordon and Breach, 205–235.

Tivey, Leonard (ed.). 1981. *The Nation-State.* New York: St. Martin's Press.

Tolesa, Addisu. 1990. "Documentation and Interpretation of Oromo Cultural Traditions," in *Proceedings of the Conference on the Oromo Nation,* Toronto, August 4–5, 41–42.

———. 1999. *Geerarsa Folksongs as the Oromo National Literature: A Study of Ethnography, Folklore, and Folklife in the Context of the Ethiopian Colonization of Oromia.* Lewiston, New York: The Edwin Mellen Press.

Torry, W. 1978. "Gabra Age Organization and Ecology," in *Age, Generation and Time: Some Features of East African Age Organizations.* Edited by P. T. W. Baxter and Uri Almagor. London: Hurst & Company, 183–206.

Trimingham, J. S. 1965. *Islam in Ethiopia.* New York: Barnes and Noble.

Triulzi, Alessandro. 1980. "Social Protest and Rebellion in Some Gabbar Songs from Qellam, Wallaga," in *Proceedings of the Fifth International Conference of Ethiopian Studies,* edited by J. Tubiana.

———. 1996. "United and Divided: Boorana and Gabro among the Macha Oromo in Western Ethiopia," in *Being and Becoming Oromo: Historical and Anthropological Enquiries.* Edited by P. T. W. Baxter, Jan Hultin, and Alessandro Triulzi. Uppsala: Nordiska Afrikainstitutet, 251–264.

Trucker, Stevens. 1997. "Ethiopia's Democratic Transition Moves Forward Amid Challenges," *African Voices: A Newsletter on Democracy and Governance in Africa,* Winter/Spring.

Trueman, T. 1997. "Democracy or Dictatorship?" in *Ethiopia: Conquest and the Quest for Freedom and Democracy.* Edited by Seyoum Y. Hameso, T. Trueman, and T.E. Erena. London: TSC Publications, 11–150.

Turner, James. 1971. "Black Nationalism: The Inevitable Response," *Black World,* January, 5–13.

Turner, Lorenzo. 1968. *Africanisms in the Gullah Dialect.* New York: Arno Press.

U.S. Department of State on Human Rights: 1993, 1994, 1995, 1997.

Ullendorff, Edward. [1960] 1965. *The Ethiopians.* London: Oxford University Press.

United Nations. *Human Development Report.* 1999. *www.undp.org/hdro/indicators.html.*

Uriji. 1994–1997 series. (This an independent Oromo newspaper was banned and its journalists have been imprisoned.)

Van de Loo, Joseph. 1991. *Guji Oromo Culture in Southern Ethiopia: Religious Capabilities in Rituals and Songs.* Berlin: Berietrich Reimer Verlag.

Vass, Winifred. 1979. *The Bantu Speaking Heritage of the United States.* Los Angeles: The University of California at Los Angeles, Center for Afro-American Studies.

Vestal, Theodore M. 1994. "Deficits of Democracy in the Transitional Government of Ethiopia Since 1991," The Oklahoma State University, unpublished paper.

Waldron, Arthur N. 1985. "Theories of Nationalism and Historical Explanation," *World Politics: A Quarterly Journal of International Relations,* April, 37/ 3: 416–433.

Walker, David. 1972. "Walker's Appeal (1830)," in *The Ideological Origins of Black Nationalism.* Edited by Sterling Stuckey. Boston: Beacon Press, 39–117.

Wallerstein, Immanuel. 1980. *The Capitalist World-Economy*. Cambridge: Cambridge University Press.

———. 1983. *Historical Capitalism*. London: Verso

———. 1984. *The Politics of the World Economy: The States, the Movements and Civilizations*. Cambridge: Cambridge University Press.

———. 1997. "Social Science and the Quest for a Just Society," *The American Journal of Sociology*, 102/5, 1241–1257.

———. 1988. "The Construction of Peoplehood: Racism, Nationalism, Ethnicity," in *Race, Nation, Class: Ambiguous Identities*. Edited by Etienne Balibar and I. Wallerstein. London: Verso, 71.

———. 1988. *The Modern World System III: The Second Era of Great Expansion of the Capitalist World-Economy, 1730–1840*. San Diego: Sage.

Walters, Ronald. 1973. "A Unifying Ideology: African-American Nationalism," *Black World*, October, 9–26.

Waqayyo, Qabbanee. 1991. "Women's Influence in Oromo Society During the Period of *Gada* Rule," *Waldhaansso: Journal of the Union Oromo in North America*, 3–14.

Waugh, Evelyn. 1936. *Waugh in Abyssinia*. Harmondsworth, Middlesex: Penguin Books.

Weber, Shirley N. 1979. "Black Nationalism and Garveyist Influences," *The Western Journal of Black Studies*, Winter, 263–266.

Whitten, Norman, and Szwed, John (eds.). 1970. *Afro-American Anthropology: Contemporary Perspectives*. New York: Free Press.

William, George W. [1883] 1968. *History of the Negro Race in America: From 1619 to 1880*. Reprint, New York: Bergman.

Wilkins, Roger. 1991. "The Underside of Black Progress," in *Race and Ethnic Relations 91/92*. Edited by John A. Kromkowski. Guilford: The Dushkin Publishing Group.

Winant, Howard. 1994. *Racial Conditions: Politics, Theory, Comparisons*. Minneapolis: University of Minnesota Press.

Wondji, C. 1986. "Toward a Responsible African Historiography," in *African Historiographies: What History for Which Africa?* Edited by B. Jewsiewicki and D. Newbury. Beverly Hills: Sage Publications.

Wood, A. P. 1983. "Rural Development and National Integration in Ethiopia," *Review of African Political Economy*, 82(329), 509–539.

Wood, Peter H. 1974. *Black Majority: Negroes in Colonial South Carolina from 1670 through the Stono Rebellion*. New York: Knopf.

Woodson, Carter G. 1968. *The African Background Outlined*. New York: Negro Universities Press.

The World Almanac and Book of Facts. 1999. Mahwah, NJ: The World Almanac Books.

World Health Organization. 1998. *Ethiopia: Epidemiological Fact Sheet on HIV/ AIDS and Sexually Transmitted Diseases from World Health Organization*.

Wright, Bobby, and Tierney, William G. 1998. "American Indians in Higher Education: A History of Cultural Conflict," in *Sources: Notable Selections in Race and Ethnicity*. Edited by Adalberto Aguirre, Jr. and David V. Baker. Guilford, CT: Dushkin/McGraw-Hill, 198–206.

Yearwood, Lennox. 1978. "National Afro-American Organizations in Urban Communities," *Journal of Black Studies*, June, 8/ 4: 432–34.

Young, Crawford. 1993. *The Rising Tide of Cultural Pluralism: The Nation-State at Bay?* Madison, WI: The University of Wisconsin Press.

Young, John. 1996. "The Tigray and Eritrean Peoples Liberation Fronts: A History of Tensions and Pragmatism," *The Journal of Modern African Studies*, 34/ 1: 105–120.

———. 1997. "Development and Change in Post-Revolutionary Tigray," *The Journal of Modern African Studies*, 35/ 1: 81–99.

Young, Robert A. 1972. "The Ethiopian Manifesto (1829)," in *The Ideological Origins of Black Nationalism*. Edited by Sterling Stuckey. Boston: Beacon Press, 30–38.

Young, Robert J. C. 1995. *Colonial Desire: Hybridity in Theory, Culture and Race.* New York: Routledge.

Zepp, Ira G., Jr. 1989. *The Social Vision of Martin Luther King, Jr.* New York: Carlson Publishing.

Ziegler, Dhyana (ed.). *Molefi Kete Asante and Afrocentricity: In Praise and in Criticism.* Nashville, Winston-Derek Publishers.

Zoga, O. 1993. *Gezatena Gezot and Macha-Tulama Association.* Addis Ababa, publisher unknown.

Index

ASAFA JALATA is Associate
Professor of Sociology and African
and African American Studies at the
University of Tennessee, Knoxville.
He is the author of *Oromia and
Ethiopia: State Formation and
Ethnonational Conflict, 1868-1992*
(1993) and editor of *Oromo
Nationalism and the Ethiopian
Discourse: The Search for Freedom
and Democracy* (1998). He has pub-
lished in a wide variety of journals,
and was president of the Oromo
Studies Association from 1993-1995
and editor of the *Journal of Oromo
Studies* from 1996 to 2000.